Women in different global contexts

Women in different global contexts

Culture – Gender – Violence

edited by

Jolanta Maćkowicz
Ewa Pająk-Ważna

impuls

Cracow 2015

Reviews:
Prof. Pella Calogiannakis
Prof. Elżbieta Górnikowska-Zwolak

Proofread:
Agnieszka Boniatowska
Michał Chmiel

Desktop publisher:
Katarzyna Kerschner

Cover design:
Ewa Beniak-Haremska

The first edition of this publication was financed by
Pedagogical University of Cracow

ISBN 978-83-7850-931-8

Oficyna Wydawnicza 'Impuls'
30-619 Kraków, ul. Turniejowa 59/5
phone/fax: (12) 422 41 80, 422 59 47, 506 624 220
www.impulsoficyna.com.pl, e-mail: impuls@impulsoficyna.com.pl
Edition II, Revised and Updated, Kraków 2015

Contents

2
Women in public and domestic spheres

3
Women and violence
Legal, social and cultural contexts

Introduction

According to a 50-year-old Chinese saying 'women hold up half the sky'. Today women make up more than half of the world's population. References to the Chinese saying can be found, for example, in the publication by Nicholas Kristof and his wife Sheryl WuDunn entitled *Half the sky: Turning oppression into opportunity for women worldwide* (2009), who declared the global struggle for women's equality 'the paramount moral challenge' of our era. It is obvious that although the issues of gender equality have been addressed in many documents (including international law documents), girls and women all over the world still suffer from violence, discrimination and limited access to education. Their situation varies depending on world regions, but it seems that there is no country that could be a model example of absolute and actual equality of women and men. Agnieszka Gromkowska-Melosik (2011, p. 11) writes that in contemporary society, analysis of the situation of women should focus on equality rather than inequality as it is the equality that is shaping women's everyday life, their social experience and identity more and more often. However, issues raised in this work concern various geographical regions and contexts, thus the notion of heterogenity of female sub-population, for example living conditions, as well as the social and cultural capital of women, is becoming more noticeable.

Therefore, we would like to present our readers with a work that addresses the issue of recognition and resolution of problems of women all over the world, regardless of their race, nationality, culture or geographical region. The issues discussed in the work concern cultural aspects, various activities of women, roles of women in various cultures, both today and in the past. Issues related to social and cultural masculinity and femininity models constitute a part of the recent heated social discourse in Poland concerning the gender problem.

This paper groups the above mentioned issues in three sections entitled: *Women in various cultures – change of roles over time and space* (section 1), *Women in public and domestic spheres* (section 2) and *Women and violence. Legal, social and cultural contexts* (section 3). Each section contains ten articles.

The first part deals with the issue of women in various cultures, focusing the reader's attention on changing roles of women over time and space. In Western societies, women seem to enjoy increasing equality, which could be an optimistic conclusion drawn from the analysis of the beginning of the 21st century

(Gromkowska-Melosik 2011, p. 11). How can we evaluate the dynamics of changes of women's roles, transformations in contemporary world and various cultures? Readers can try to answer this question after reading the articles by Elżbieta Dubas, Sylwia Skuza, Nadia Lutsan, Małgorzata Matlak, Kazimierz Mazurek, Margret Winzer, as well as Bashkim Rrahmani and Majlinda Belegu. Two articles – one by Katarzyna Pabis-Cisowska and one by Elżbieta Mach are devoted to roles of women from ethnic minorities. The first part also contains discussions on broadening the perspective on the view of the role of women in various cultures, focused on the results of research carried out among teachers (Ewa Pająk-Ważna) and the theory formulated by Simon Kuznets (article by Onur Tutulmaz and Peter Victor).

The second part is devoted to the issue of women in public and domestic spheres. Cultural models that regulate relations between women and men, as well as visions of roles to be played by women in public and private life affect e.g. individual life choices and structure of relations in various interpersonal contexts. Texts by: Katarzyna Dormus, Dominika U. Popielec, Agnieszka Świątek and Paweł Łubiński concern mainly civil and political activity of women, as well as changes in those areas taking into consideration historic contexts. There are also texts focusing on the issue of social activity of the specific sub-population of women, i.e. teachers (text by Justyna Miko-Giedyk), students (article by Adrian Biela and Ewa Sierankiewicz-Miernik), as well as female members of one of local communities, whose consumer behavior is the subject of analyses by three authors (Grzegorz Libor, Dorota Nowalska-Kapuścik and Monika Szpoczek-Sało).

While presenting the issues discussed in this section of the paper, it is worth to quote A. Giddens (Giddens 2001, p. 294), who wrote that 'by freeing themselves from home and family setting, women encountered a closed social environment'. In this way, contemporary women gained the opportunity to create new identities, although the conditions for pursuing specific life models are still unspecified and uncertain. Two authors of the texts in section two raised the issue of identity, referring to individual identity (Joanna Łukasik) and regional identity (Halina Rusek). Various faces of women are presented in the article by Monika Sulik, who used biographic approach to discuss the research, didactic and autobiographical perspective.

The third part of this paper presents women in situation of violence in legal, social and cultural context. Violence against women is a serious social issue in European countries and, in many parts of the world, a part of local culture and traditions. According to the report published by the European Union Agency for Fundamental Rights (FRA 2014), one third of European women were affected by violence and

> [...] the scale of the problem shows that violence against women is not something incidental, but rather a social issue. Therefore, politicians, representatives of civil society and workers of institutions for victims must reconsider the solutions used today so that every form of violence against woman can be prevented, regardless of the place; see: pl.globalvoicesonline.org (Accessed: 14.07.2014).

This section of the work reflects on various aspects of women experiencing violence (mainly as victims), but the readers also have the opportunity to read the text about female perpetrators of violence. Issues raised by authors concern the process of raising awareness of rights in victims of violence, show both the statistical image of the problem and a case study. Problems discussed by the authors (Zofia Szarota, Fernando Barragán Medero, Katarzyna Gajek, Małgorzata Halicka, Anna Szafranek, Jolanta Maćkowicz, Dorota Kamińska-Jones, Muhammad Mumtaz and Muhammad Shahbaz Arif, Malwina Misiąg, Antonio Llorens de la Cruz and Justyna Kusztal) are present in various corners of the world: India, Pakistan, Spanish Tenerife and Poland.

The editors of this volume would like to thank all the Authors, who contributed to this work. We would also like to thank the supervisors: professor Elżbieta Górnikowska-Zwolak from The Cardinal August Hlond University of Education in Myslowice and professor Pella Calogiannakis from the University of Crete in Rethymnon for their valuable comments and suggestions, which helped us make necessary corrections and give this work its final form.

Editors,
Jolanta Maćkowicz and *Ewa Pająk-Ważna*
Kraków, October 2015

1
Women in various cultures – change of roles over time and space

Elżbieta Dubas[1]
University of Łódź, Poland

Contemporary woman – reflections at the beginning of the century (the voice in the discussion)

Introduction

Pertinent questions raised in the discussion on the modern woman in the context of the subject formulated above touch upon woman's identity and her role in the modern society and culture: Who is the woman of today? Who could she be? Who should she be? Could we extract a 'core', which would encapsulate the essence of being a modern woman? To what extent should the modern woman constitute a subject for scientific research? Another vital question is whether answers to these questions are important for modern societies. Life goes on incessantly bringing novel and difficult challenges – what kind of a woman do 'our times' need? The reflections below pertain mostly to modern Polish women, although they also take into account the vast variety of 'worlds' in which modern women function as citizens of the world at the beginning of the 21st century[2]. These considerations constitute an invitation for reflection and discussion about modern womanhood.

---

1 Department of Andragogy and Social Gerontology.
2 In this context one might refer to the current research results on the Polish modern woman included in the thesis edited by Anna Witkowska-Paleń and Justyna Maciaszek (2010), while the aspects of comparative studies on women in a cultural context may be found in an elaboration edited by Aneta Chybicka and Maria Kaźmierczak (2006).

1. Female identity in the context of gender

The 'search' for the identity of the modern woman may be commenced with the primary and natural indicator of her role as a woman, i.e. the biological gender[3]. How does it determine the way she functions in society and culture?

Becoming independent from the biological clock. While following the tendencies of modern highly developed societies, one may note that the social clock ticks slower than the biological clock. An example here may be late motherhood, taken up by women after their careers have stabilised and they have achieved a satisfactory material status. Another phenomenon, although still a rare one, is ignoring the biological clock and procreating even during menopause, which is made possible by modern highly developed fertility technologies. Lastly, a phenomenon which gives rise to particular concern, women limit or even rule out procreation from their life plans; modern women in highly developed countries are reluctant to get pregnant or they give birth to fewer children, often only one. One may think then that the modern woman leads her life increasingly 'outside' the biological gender and the natural indicator of gender is pushed to the 'margins' of her life roles. The consequences of this situation are the low birth rate and many social and demographic problems connected with it, including economic and cultural problems, destabilising the functioning of societies or even threatening their continuity. One should especially highlight, rarely mentioned yet frightening in its significance, the decline of motherly functions, which gives rise to a question: Could we have a world without the figure of a Mother, without this special human relationship marked by a deep unconditional emotional bond? Can one imagine normal development of a human being without a Mother (as well as grandmothers, aunts, sisters etc.)? The procreative function (giving birth to offspring) is also interconnected with other important social and cultural functions which a woman might not get the chance to perform and which are vital for the continuity of society and culture. These functions are: teaching how to cope in difficult situations and existential crises, shaping the sphere of intimacy (the mother-child intimacy constitutes 'training' of intimacy in the deepest sense, impossible to achieve in other relations), and communication of tradition and values. All of the above, if it is effective, happens in family, in everyday life, in the feeling of safety and love.

Genders becoming alike. Procreative functions are the thing that makes women and men rudimentally different, and their dismissal, makes to some extent both genders seem alike. The assimilation refers to many dimensions of life and to the functioning of individuals: to tasks performed in society, to the way people express thoughts and emotions, but also directly to the external appearance,

---

3 A multi-aspect analysis of human biological and cultural gender is presented in the handbook by Claire M. Renzetti and Daniel J. Curran (2005), with an introduction by Agnieszka Gromkowska-Melosik and Zbyszko Melosik.

including clothes, hair, make up etc. Based on the observation of this phenomenon, one should reflect whether this assimilation of genders reinforces the development of individuals and societies. One should note that the differences between men and women are mutually supplementary in the fullness of humanity, and the variety resulting form gender differences are 'potent' natural stimulators of development.

Self-fulfilment tendencies. Undoubtedly, the identity of the modern woman is strongly determined by her right for self-determination. The important achievements of civilisational development, scientific and social thought in the area of universal human rights gave women the option of living in accordance with their needs. The triumph of individualisation in 1990s resulted in subjectivity. A woman is able to manage her own development and strive for self-fulfilment, follow her interests. You can see women everywhere releasing their development potentials, which very often have laid hidden or even undiscovered and through that they change the face of societies and cultures. One has to bear in mind, however, that a woman's individual good often stands in opposition to the good of the society, and her individual development creates a threat to the life of the community. It is also worth highlighting that the pernicious phenomenon of solitude – a destructive and unnatural state, caused by alienation from the communal life and retraction from the community, is on the increase.

2. Multidimensional *versus* one-dimensional aspects of the modern woman's life

A woman's life is and always has been strongly determined by the development of social and cultural processes as well as civilisational offers and challenges. They determine the facets of women's functioning, and the complicity of these processes enriches, and at the same time complicates this functioning. Traditional societies offered a natural one-dimensional path of life, strongly connected with procreation and concentrated around the 'hearth and home'. While 'open' societies provide women with the possibility of living in modern multidimensionality, i.e. combining many roles, often contradictory to each other, e.g. the role of a mother and a professional, realisation of an individualised program of life as a mosaic of roles. Post-modern culture has proposed a kind of secondary one-dimensionality to women, through pointing to the option of life-fulfilment in accordance with the male model, concentrated on professional career while sacrificing motherhood and elevating the importance of self-fulfilment.

Life choices, and even more frequently – life necessities of many modern women are often clearly located between the conflicting multidimensionality and the secondary one-dimensionality. This gives rise to many threats to the creation and development of family life, to emotional stability of individuals, their feeling of safety, to building deep relationships, not only within a family.

3. Woman's place in culture and society

A woman in social relations. Without doubt, a woman's place in the modern society is expressed in her relations with others, including her relations with the other sex. Women's relations with men are very varied and undergo transformations: from subjugation through equality, to domination or even hegemony. Finding equilibrium in these relations is a condition of harmonious co-existence and development of both individuals and societies. Dialogue and direct contact are the best means to achieve it. They build the fullest relation with the Other as a Fellow Human Being[4], a relation marked by human kindness, willingness to approach, to get to know, learn from each other and support one another.

The female factor. The traditional understanding of femininity, involving emotionality, charm, gentleness, motherhood (Dubas 2001, p. 49), is slowly deteriorating. Modern femininity is strongly modified by 'male' style of functioning, which comprises self-assurance, authoritarian attitude, decisiveness, aggression, power, rivalry, life in the outside world. One may state that the current social and cultural experience of womanhood is 'undergoing change', strongly conditioned by culture and the so called 'contemporary times'. Modern womanhood is determined by:

a) the still present traditional cultural and religious models,
b) currently proposed ideologies, influence of politics and economy, science and mass media,
c) strong factor of change, commonly present in modern social life,
d) critical global events involving history, economics, religion, etc.
e) in Poland's case – current strong impact of political transformation,
f) the possibility of making personal choices.

Therefore, modern times propose numerous images of womanhood as general proposals for paths of life, while revealing many individual ways of implementing life roles by modern women. At the same time, it also reflects many individualised identities of modern women[5]. It also bears noting that difficult living conditions, e.g. in the context of global events or personal crises, which destroy the foundations of safety and development for one's nearest and dearest, extract the 'core' of womanhood – its universal characteristics such as resourcefulness, self-sacrifice, generosity.

---

4 Three types of relations with the Other: the Other as the Enemy, the Other as a Stranger, the Other as a Fellow Human Being (Dubas, 2011a, p. 5–6). The thesis is mainly based on Ryszard Kapuściński's (2006) reflections.
5 Interesting research, showing the various identities of women in the context of their biographical narrations, is presented in a thesis by Agnieszka Majewska-Kafarowska (2010).

4. Between tradition and modernity/late modernity

When observing the life of a modern woman, one can't help thinking that she is suspended between the traditional model of femininity and the modern and postmodern influences, which modify this model. The modern woman is burdened or even over-burdened with too many goals, tasks and duties, challenges and claims. She seems to be lost in the mosaic of lifestyle choices. Tempted by post-modernity, which propagates extreme subjectivity, individualisation and isolated interpretations of important social idea such as freedom and equality. Increasingly more self-sufficient and independent, but also more and more lonely and alienated. Very often well educated, but not necessarily more aware, self-aware or wise.

And what kind of a woman is needed in modern times? The easiest answer, which comes forward in the context sketched out above, points to the ability to draw on tradition and bravely face the future. It would seem then that modern times need a woman, who is:

a) a partner – for Others, capable of creating relations of dialogue and direct contact;

b) 'a companion on a path' – e.g. in a situation of an increase in care needs of children who take long to become independent or the longevity of older parents and grandparents;

c) emotionally warm – in the times of postmodern superficiality, institutionalised and formalised relations, 'emotional hunger', lack of deep intimacy, facing the 'pandemic' of alienation;

d) a creator of community – in situations of atrophy of family ties, lack of 'hearth and home', devaluation of pro-social values;

e) wise – coping in such difficult and changing life situations, capable of finding meaning in life and of communicating it to others, counteracting existential disorientation.

In this context the role of older women seems to be invaluable, as they communicate traditions and values, introduce the young to culture. Older women act as mentors and often lend effective support by sharing their experience by active participation in confessional conversations.

5. A woman in a biographical context

Numerous currently conducted biographical studies[6] present women of various ages starting from the oldest, born at the end of the 19th century and the beginning

---

6 Especially pertinent here is the research conducted by Olga Czerniawska (2011), Monika Sulik (2011) and Elżbieta Dubas (2011b), which takes into account the context of women functioning in difficult life situations including global events, e.g. World War II.

of the 20th century, through to modern women born at the end of the 20th century. The analysis of these biographies reveals several important characteristics of their existence and of femininity in general. They are the following:

a) Resourcefulness – especially visible in difficult situations, including global conflicts, World War II in particular, but also the poverty and the destitution of the interwar period, the difficult times of reconstruction of Poland after the war, the economic crises of 1980s, the consequences of political transformation after 1989. Being able to cope with the difficulties of everyday reality, ingenuity in day-to-day existence are qualities which helped them and others survive.

b) Care for one's nearest and dearest – mainly children, involving self-sacrifice for the family, generosity, 'struggle' for securing their basic needs, taking responsibility for their life, providing upbringing and education. In case of younger women raising children today – care for providing them with the best possible conditions of existence and high standards of education.

c) Reconciling various roles – after World War II, as a result of women's emancipation movement, but also in connection with the needs of the reconstructing state, women were given – apart from their traditional family roles – also professional roles. Fulfilling both of those roles, which were often contradictory, constituted a considerable burden. Despite fulfilling professional roles, often forced by a lack of economic resources, a woman nevertheless devoted herself to the family caring for its development and endurance. Undoubtedly, this situation, although not connected with warfare, is proof of feminine heroism.

d) Self-fulfilment tendencies – especially visible in women from the 1980s and 1990s onwards. They signify striving for self-fulfilment, for the feeling of satisfaction in life, meeting one's own needs, including education and development of professional carriers. On the other hand, however, they also come to light in conquering difficult personal trauma, borderline situations, connected e.g. with one's own sickness [7] or the sickness or disability of others. Modern women find fulfilment in roles ascribed to them by society, in roles they take up of their own accord and in situations, which they encounter in life – brought by fate.

When attempting to generalise these observations, one may state that women in their roles and functions 'evolved' form the model of a woman who sacrifices herself for others – meeting social expectations, to a woman who decides about her development; one may state then that women 'evolved' from adaptive-social functions to personal development functions.

---

7 E.g. breast cancer (Mazurek 2013).

6. Women and education

Without doubt, the thing which 'determined' and modified a woman's place in society and culture is education.

Formal education and schooling, as an intensive historical process common after World War II in Poland, has been very distinctively used by women. They currently are the better educated group as compared to men. This also pertains to the inhabitants of the countryside, where education is placed since 1990s beyond gender and beyond profession (Zasada 2013). An important effect of education is the emancipation of women, which is symptomatic of the increase of awareness and self-awareness, which in turn stands behind a higher level of independent decisions in all areas of their life.

Non-formal education is a domain in which women participate more and more commonly. Courses, post-graduate studies, trainings, seminars, etc. are used for the purpose of professional training. Although they are more and more often undertaken for the sake of implementation of women's own developmental needs.

Women's participation in life-long learning is also increasingly more pronounced. They use not only books and magazines, which are traditional means of self-development, but also, more and more often, mass media and modern IT technologies. The Internet and the computer became important sources of education for women, including also the older generation. Lifelong learning is also used for 'diverting interest' and changing lifestyles, e.g. in old age. It may, in a more pronounced way than formal and informal education, go beyond professional life and combine with leisure, as a time devoted to self-realisation.

Numerous contemporary studies of educational paths[8] reveal hindrances in achieving education by women, as well as their struggle to realise their interests. They picture individualised educational experiences set against life stories strongly influenced by external factors, e.g. historical or social. The question arising here is what education a modern woman needs? And a follow up question: what kind of a woman is needed by a modern society?

Conclusion

In responding to those questions one has to consider the incredibly complex context of 'being a woman' in contemporary times. Being a woman today is full of dilemmas, as are our times and our world. A woman herself, one might say, is a complex manifestation of humanity expressing many aspects in her existence. She is difficult to recognize and define, also as a subject of research.

---

8 Important examples of life-stories and education paths: Dubas, Czerniawska (2002), Wesołowska (2002), Skibińska (2006), Wnuk-Olenicz (2012), Zasada (2013).

What kind of a woman is needed by modernity? In the context of important threats brought by modernity it would seem that at the moment we need a woman who knows how to make appropriate choices: to support the development of culture and civilisation, to support the society in which she lives and to support herself. When referring to vital deficiencies of modern life, it is important to highlight a woman's role as a keeper of culture and tradition, a supporter of the development of her family as a community, and as the 'first teacher' of every human being.

Therefore, what kind of education does a modern woman need to meet these requirements? She needs education directed at wisdom. The concept of 'wisdom' needs to be revisited, set as an important goal (Szmidt 2002) and value of education. Education in wisdom is a task of educational institutions (although not only them), starting from childhood and ending on old age. Education in wisdom means being raised in striving for self-awareness, awareness of Others and the world. It equips people to cope with difficult existential challenges, teaching the ability to make conscious decisions in fast changing situations, conditioning to find sense and chose life values.

Education in wisdom is not only a female need, but a human need. It should also refer to men. It should include mutual relations, the value of learning from each other's differences, the skill of enriching oneself with Otherness, 'accompanying each other' on life's paths.

In 1980s Jerzy Semków wrote that female values may save our world from a civilisational 'collapse' (Semków 1984, p. 67). Are those values still important for women, for the society? What system of reinforcement and education should be provided for a woman for her to be able to realise her womanhood? 'Our' times clearly show that these questions still remain pertinent.

Katarzyna Pabis-Cisowska
Pedagogical University of Cracow, Poland

Jewish women's charitable activity in the nineteenth and early twentieth century illustrated with an example of selected organizations operating in Cracow

The issues of Jewish charity constitute a very important part of Jewish tradition. Charity activity of Jewish women also stems from the Jewish heritage and the nature of Judaism. However, due to social and political change as well as civilization breakthrough, a systematic and organized activity of the Jewish community, including women, aiming to improve the situation of the poor and needy, can be noted in the Polish lands as late as in the nineteenth century.

In traditional Judaism women were perceived differently from men, as different from them but equal to them. Women's responsibilities were and still are different from the men's ones, but they are not less important; some of them are regarded even as somehow more important (see: http://www.jewfaq.org/women.htm#Mitzvot, accessed: 30.05.2014).

What is worth mentioning is the fact that the perception of woman in the Jewish culture is also determined by the perception of God in Judaism, who is not presented in the biblical tradition neither as a man, nor as a woman, and the use of the masculine when writing the Name of God is caused by the lack of neuter gender in Hebrew. Equality between men and women starts, therefore, in this tradition on the highest possible level (see: http://www.jewfaq.org/women.htm#Mitzvot, accessed: 30.05.2014). This statement is complemented with the words of the Book of Genesis:

> Male and female he created them, and he blessed them and named them 'Humankind' when they were created (Kameraz-Kos, 2000, p. 109 and Genesis 5:2, retrieved from http://www.scripture4all.org/OnlineInterlinear/OTpdf/gen5.pdf, accessed: 30.05.2014).

The role of women in Jewish tradition until the nineteenth century was per-petuated by the rules of Jewish life resulting from the Torah and the Talmud. By that time, the ideals of woman had been described e.g. in the Pentateuch (Sarah, Rebecca, Rachel, Leah or Miriam, Deborah and Queen Esther, etc.). Rabbinic lit-erature highlights the feminine qualities and merits as well as the husband's duties towards his wife. So does the Talmudic tractate Yevamoth, which contains the following excerpt:

> R. Tanhum stated in the name of R. Hanilai: Any man who has no wife lives without joy, without blessing, and without goodness. 'Without joy', for it is written. And thou shalt rejoice, thou and thy house. 'Without blessing', for it is written, To cause a blessing to rest on thy house. 'Without goodness', for it is written, It is not good that the man should be alone (Yevamoth 62b, http://halakhah.com/pdf/nashim/Yevamoth. pdf, accessed: 30.05.2014).

The same tractate says:

> Our Rabbis taught: Concerning a man who loves his wife as himself, who honours her more than himself, who guides his sons and daughters in the right path and ar-ranges for them to be married near the period of their puberty, Scripture says, And thou shalt know that thy tent is in peace (Yevamoth 62b, http://halakhah.com/pdf/nashim/ Yevamoth.pdf, accessed: 30.05.2014).

On the other hand, however, the woman was to be a complement of the man. Another excerpt from the Pentateuch, the Book of Genesis, is an illustration of this statement:

> And the rib that the LORD God had taken from the man he made into a woman and brought her to the man (Genesis 2:22) Then the man said, 'This at last is bone of my bones and flesh of my flesh; this one shall be called Woman, for out of Man this one was taken (Genesis 2:23, http://www.scripture4all.org/OnlineInterlinear/OTpdf/gen2. pdf, accessed: 30.05.2014),

in which the origin of the Hebrew word 'woman' can be traced back: *isha* (אשה), as may be deduced on the basis of its structure and core, is derived from the word 'man': *ish* (איש).

Therefore, the woman was supposed to be helpful to the man in the fulfilment of the divine and life responsibilities. She was to be the guardian of the hearth and home, and as it is clear from the following passages of the Pentateuch, was to become a wife and mother, responsible for appropriate education of children – daughters until their marriage, and sons until entrusting them to the fatherly care. The woman in Jewish tradition is obliged to observe the commandments just like a man. However, because of the feminine qualities and characteristics, according to the Talmudic rulings and opinions of the Jewish authorities, such as Maimo-nides, women cannot be burdened with male responsibilities, even for biological reasons – the woman, therefore, is not obliged e.g. to saying the morning prayer, because at the same time she is required to devote her attention to children (see: http://www.jewishvirtuallibrary.org/jsource/Judaism/woman_commandments. html, accessed: 30.05.2014). However, sometimes the woman had to take on the maintenance of her family and thus the husband in case of his learning or studying Torah, and support him if necessary, also financially (Freeze 2002, p. 35).

The nineteenth century in Polish lands, and therefore also in Cracow, was a time of changes related to the Enlightenment Jewish movement known as the *Haskalah*, which emerged in the eighteenth century in the German lands. In addition to the changes in the perception of the Jewish group by non-Jewish societies, this movement has led to the change in the perception of their 'Jewishness' by the Jews themselves. An eighteenth-century German thinker and philosopher, Moses Mendelssohn, was the initiator of the Jewish transformations at that time, also in the Polish lands. His vision of an enlightened perspective on Judaism evolved, bringing emancipation to broadly defined inclusion of Jews in the all-European culture (Tyloch 1987, p. 256). As Artur Eisenbach writes in his book about Jewish emancipation, *Haskalah* was a movement that

> [...] promoted the need to break the Jews out of medieval torpor, traditional patterns of life; in a word, to overcome isolationism. It propagated the idea of autoemancipation through improving the level of education, reforming customs, abandoning old costumes, secularization of life, rebirth of Jewish culture and the ideas of productiveness and restratification of the population (Eisenbach 1988, pp. 47–48).

As it is known, reforming Judaism through Mendelssohn's actions was not the only way leading to changes in Judaism, which occurred in a great number since the eighteenth century throughout Europe. However, the successors of Mendelssohn, his followers

> [...] were concerned mainly with a revision of the life and customs of their coreligionists. As people bridging two worlds, they were engaged in the reform of education, introducing changes to the liturgy of worship [...] and modifying the Jewish ritual (Untermann 2002, p. 81).

Despite emancipatory transformation, a large part of Judaism followers stuck to its traditional version. For many of them, the role and place of women in Jewish life was and still is less significant, and the differences between the sexes were seen in the rituals that accompany the birth and life of boys and girls (Untermann 2002, p. 135), as indicated in the excerpts from the Talmud, e.g.:

> A daughter was born to R. Simeon the son of Rabbi, and he felt disappointed. His father said to him: Increase has come to the world. Bar Kappara said to him: Your father has given you an empty consolation. The world cannot do without either males or females. Yet happy is he whose children are males, and alas for him whose

children are females. The world cannot do without either a spice-seller or a tanner. Yet happy is he whose occupation is that of a spice-seller, and alas for him whose occupation is that of a tanner (Baba Bathra 16b, http://halakhah.com/pdf/nezikin/Baba_Bathra.pdf, accessed: 30.05.2014).

The nineteenth century brought development and formation of numerous charity organizations among Polish Jews. Charity work was of great importance, also because of the changes caused by emancipation. Enlightened Jews worked actively in many organizations, not only the Jewish ones:

> In addition to activity in the social institutions mentioned before, they were also involved in Polish and Jewish philanthropic societies and religious corporations. They were among the donors who gave different social associations a significant support for their philanthropic activity (Eisenbach 1988, p. 284).

Many women found fulfilment in such activity as well. In this way, the traditional role of woman and her importance in social life was transformed during the *haskalah* changes. The activity of charity organizations in Cracow and Podgórze[1], where Jewish women worked, may serve as an example of that.

The idea of Jewish charity stems directly from the Jewish tradition, and thus the Torah – the Pentateuch of Moses and the Talmud – Jewish wise men's comments to the text of Jewish law, the Torah. The Talmud is full of texts directly or indirectly related to the issue of charity. The idea of charity activity was associated for centuries with the idea of mutual assistance, which was widely known and promoted among the Jews, including the female portion of the Jewish population of Cracow. Among all the good deeds, a special part was played by *tzedakah*[2] and all of its manifestations[3].

Talmudic excerpts referring to *tzedakah* are very numerous. It is worth quoting some of them, such as the Berachoth tractate, which speaks of *tzedakah* as of 'mercy':

> R. Johanan said to him: I grant you Torah and acts of charity, for it is written: By mercy and truth iniquity is expiated. 'Mercy' is acts of charity, for it is said: He that followeth after righteousness and mercy findeth life, prosperity and honour (Berachoth, http://halakhah.com/pdf/zeraim/Berachoth.pdf, accessed: 30.05.2014).

---

1 The Jewish communities of Cracow and Podgórze did not merge until 14 July 1936 (cf. Zbroja 2004, p. 58).

2 From Hebrew: צדקה – charity, donation, alms, justice, mercy, fair action, charitable activity.

3 Charity is defined in the Jewish tradition in many ways. Other very important terms, along with *tzedakah*, are also *chesed*, from Hebrew: חסד – 'grace, benevolence, goodness, mercy', and *Gemilut Hasadim*, from Hebrew:, גמילות חסדים – 'showing mercy, deeds of kindness' i.e. doing good, love, compensation, doing good to others through divine goodness.

Another excerpt from the Talmud is as follows:

> The Holy One, blessed be He, says: If a man occupies himself with the study of the Torah and with works of charity and prays with the congregation, I account it to him as if he had redeemed Me and My children from among the nations of the world (Berachoth, http://halakhah.com/pdf/zeraim/Berachoth.pdf, accessed: 30.05.2014).

Charity is therefore one of four ways to affect the destiny of a man – saving his life:

> R. Isaac further said: Four things cancel the doom of a man, namely, charity, supplication, change of name and change of conduct. Charity, as it is written, And charity delivereth from death (Berachoth, http://halakhah.com/pdf/moed/Rosh_HaShanah.pdf, accessed: 30.05.2014).

The importance of *tzedakah* and charitable activities has been recorded in the statute of the Jewish religious community of Podgórze (State Archive in Kraków, Kr 7942 [...] of Podgórze). We learn from there that this type of activity was one of the key issues on which the functioning of community was concentrated in the nineteenth century. As the text of the statute infers, the community sovereignty took care of some foundations subordinate to the Jewish community. A very specific type of charity, that is, care of the sick constituted a recorded and unchanging duty of *kahal* (Cała, Węgrzynek, Zalewska 2000, p. 72). In the community of Podgórze, it was manifested by running a hospital, an orphanage and a nursing home. The nineteenth century brought changes in the activities of already specialized organizations run in the community, such as *Chevra Kadisha*, that is funeral fraternity or *beit lehem*[4] – house of bread, a company supplying the poor with food, especially during the holidays (Cała, Węgrzynek, Zalewska 2000, p. 72).

Similar assumptions of social service to the community in the form of good deeds, were also included in the Statute of Jewish religious community of Cracow:

> The purpose of Jewish community is to strive to meet the religious needs of its members within the limits of state laws and to maintain and promote its religious, scientific and merciful institutions (paragraph 2) (State Archive in Kraków, Kr 7942 [...] of Kraków).

One of the four sections of the religious council, in addition to the religious section, the section for research and educational issues and the section for taxes in *kahal* of Cracow, was a section for charitable issues. The affiliation of members of the religious community to relevant sections was regulated with the provision in the Statute:

> Each member of the religious community, with the exception of the President, must be a member of at least one section. The choice of individual members of the

---

4 From Hebrew: בית לחם – 'house of bread'.

section is made as through a mutual agreement, and should especially take into account the vocation and inclination (paragraph 16) (State Archive in Kraków, Kr 7942 [...] of Kraków, p. 5).

According to another paragraph of the Statute,

The supervision of synagogues and the houses of worship, which are owned by the religious community, as well as of the scientific and charity institutions of the community (paragraph 17) (State Archive in Kraków, Kr 7942 [...] of Kraków, p. 6)

comes under community administration. Besides that the municipality had to take on charity activity, in rights and obligations of members of the Jewish community, at the first place, there was also a relevant record of the possibilities of using help from the charity organized by the community. Chapter VII, paragraph 36 states:

Members of the Jewish religious community are given the following rights:
a) The right to use, within the existing standards and the provisions of the statute – both for oneself, and for one's wives, widows and children of all clerical, ritual, scientific as well as other charitable institutions owned by the religious community (State Archive in Kraków, Kr 7942 [...] of Kraków, p. 11).

Looking at the charity activities in the community of Cracow in the nineteenth century, it can be seen that those related to the care of the sick and needy were considered the most relevant. What is more, this type of activity was often one of the purposes of private benefactors' activity. One of the institutions operating under the auspices of the community but established thanks to a private initiative was a refuge for Jewish children. It was founded in Cracow in 1846. It was run within the committee by the wives of Orthodoxes from Kazimierz, headed until the end of 1860s. by Maria Schreiber, the rabbi's wife and assisted by six other women from the committee. Unfortunately, there are no exact information about the shelter. It is known that in 1868 the public opinion learned about the problems of the shelter as a result of the interest from the Jewish Committee, which interfered in the activities of the ladies' committee, wanting to verify the sanitary conditions in the shelter, which did not meet the standards set by the municipal authorities. Due to the situation of the community at that time, the ladies did not want the members of progressive groups to interfere in their activities, since it caused harm to children living in the orphanage. In 1871 the orphanage was home for forty orphans aged 3 to 13. The orphanage building, donated to the association by the community, was managed by Cerka Goldgart. However, due to poor technical condition of the building, the city decided to support the association and offered a plot at Dietla Street 64 for the construction of a new building. The association was also supported by private donors; for this reason it gained legacies and plots, which were fit for sale. Despite that, the cost of the construction of a new orphanage was too high for the association. The community decided to provide support for the ladies, but only on the condition that the content of the statutes was verified 'in order to

guarantee legally constant control of the orphanage and finances of the association'
(Żbikowski 1994, pp. 235, 236). Another subsidy was given to the association by the
Cracow City Council in 1875, and one year later the representation of community
agreed to sell the community's plot and invest the financial means obtained in this
way in the construction of an orphanage building. In spite of that,

> The deadlock lasted until mid-eighties. Only in 1885 the association adopted
> a new acceptable statute. It included a clause saying that the children would attend pub-
> lic school in Kazimierz and learn the craft up to the age of 15. Some conflicts probably
> continued, because in 1894 the tax section of community representation categorically
> refused to support the association, justifying the decision on the grounds of the lack of
> control over its activity (Żbikowski 1994, pp. 236, 237).

The issue of financing the association kept returning and in 1898 the president
of the community, Leon Horowitz, suggested the acquisition of the association by
the community due to the continuous need for financing its operations. Despite
this, the following year the association was granted a funding in the amount of
300 zloty. At that time also the attempt to take over the association by another
group of Jewish women was made,

> [...] representing much more moderate, if not progressive, religious and social views.
> However, as Reichenberg wrote, ladies of the orthodox views 'were not caught napping'
> [...] and everything remained as it was before' (Żbikowski 1994, pp. 236, 237).

Subsequent years and the activity of vice-president of the community, Rafał
Landau, produced positive changes. A. Żbikowski reports that

> The community dealt directly with the Jewish orphans only in some extraordinary
> circumstances, such as in 1873 during the cholera epidemic (Żbikowski 1994, p. 237).

Another example of women's charity organisation cooperating with *kahala* at
that time was Women's Association for the Support of Jewish Widows of Cracow
(Krakowskie Stowarzyszenie Kobiet dla Wsparcia Wdów Wyznania Izraelickiego).
The association was established by a decision of k.k. Governorship, with a rescript
on October 2, 1874 (Żbikowski 1994, p. 238). Its aim was to support widows of
the Jewish community of Cracow, and the association funds came mainly from
monthly premiums and gifts 'donated for the Association'. In order to become members of the association, in addition to have been accepted as members, women had
to commit themselves to bring a systematic monthly premium to the cash. The sum
fixed as the minimum amount was 15 crowns. The essence of this institution's activity was paying support for the widows in need. The rules of functioning of the
association are comprehensively regulated in paragraph 2 of its statute. The funds
received by the organisation were to be distributed once a month among the poor-
est widows belonging to the Jewish Community of Cracow. According to the statute, the association was directed by the Board consisting of eight members. The

association was headed by the chairwoman, her deputy, cashier, secretary, almoner and three additional women having substitute roles. Elections to the department were organised every three years. A separate body was established that had to deal with the most important issue, i.e. funds. It was a three-woman committee elected at the general meeting, which reported their work to the general assembly. The board of the association included: Barbara Heumann, Amalia Oettinger, Johanna Schönborn, Ludwika Mendelsburg and Teofilia Propper. Tracking the content of the annual report of the activities of the association for the 1874, one can see that on December 31, 1873 (State Archive in Kraków, Kr 7942 [...] Jewish Widows, p. 1), there was 55 złr[5] 97 ct. in the association's account. Monthly premiums in 1874 amounted to 423 złr 50 ct., gifts – 419 złr. and 60 ct. Lottery tickets yielded 162 złr. and 92 ct. The association was co-funded with the interest from the foundation. In addition to the premiums and legacies, the association was supported with single payments, such as 100 crowns donated by Ludwik and Izrael Rapaport, the children of Rozalia Rapaport, née Wechsler, to honour her memory (Archives of the Jewish Historical Institute Cracow Association, letter No 1085/09).

Financial matters and struggling with problems often made it difficult to undertake charitable activities – that was the case of Jewish women too. The main source of income for charities operating in the nineteenth century in the community were private donations. Charitable activity of both communities and its associations cooperating with the *kahala* in the second half of the nineteenth century, did not satisfied all needs of the Jewish part of the population. The best example of charitable projects and a complement to the commandments of *tzedakah*, was the activity of private funders, which was becoming more and more popular then. Women's contribution to the charitable activity of Jews from Cracow was Teresa Abelles' great fund created in the second half of the nineteenth century. The money collected there was to be allocated in two ways not by the Jewish community, but since 1867 by the Cracow City Council. The first part of the fund was intended to support a variety of Jewish societies, for which the share capital in bonds accounted in 1873 for 908 zl 86 ct. The second part 'in bonds was 1765 zl, in the savings account – 7 zl 42 ct.', the interest of which was to be spent annually by the board of the city council for Association of Jewish Women for Educating Poor Jewish Orphans in Cracow (Stowarzyszenie pań izraelickich dla wychowywania ubogich sierot izraelickich w Krakowie) on 'the support of orphaned boys of Jewish religion' ('Szematyzm [...] na rok 1873', p. 632).

The above mentioned association existed in the second half of the nineteenth century in Cracow as one of the few charity organisations 'that aimed at supplying, supporting and educating orphans and other people in need of special assistance'

---

5   Złr – Austro-Hungarian gulden or forint (in Polish: *złoty reński*); the currency of Austro-Hungarian Empire until 1892; from 1858 to 1892, an Austro-Hungarian gulden was equal to 100 *grajcars* – kreutzers (cents).

and was funded thanks to private bequests. The Cracow Association of Jewish Women for Educating Poor Jewish Orphans (Stowarzyszenie pań izraelickich dla wychowywania ubogich sierot izraelickich w Krakowie) was founded in 1874:

> The share capital is a house worth 15 000 zł, built for the money from contributions and legacies received from Ignacy Paprocki and Teresa Abeles, as well as securities worth 3 520 zl and the mortgage debt of 500 zl. The income from the capital and the house is used to supply 36 Jewish boys (orphans) ('Szematyzm [...] na rok 1879', p. 586).

In 1875 the share capital amounted to 947 zl 99 ct. in bonds ('Szematyzm [...] na rok 1875', p. 676). In 1875 the interests on the amount of the share capital in bonds of 1762 zl 42 ct. was allocated for the support of orphan boys. In the savings account there were 7 zl 42 ct ('Szematyzm [...] na rok 1875', p. 676). In 1879 the share capital in bonds amounted to 523 zl ('Szematyzm [...] na rok 1879', p. 638). In the annals of 1897 and 1898 there was a record saying: 'Income from equity and the house used to supply 36 boys and 26 girls (Jewish orphans)' ('Szematyzm [...] na rok 1897', p. 697 and 1898, p. 801). Marjem Schreiber was the president of the Association in 1879 and 1881, Deiche Goldgard was the secretary and Ettel Bertram was the cashier. In 1892 Deiche Goldgard took the role of administrator while Fajgel Ester Cypres became the secretary ('Szematyzm [...] na rok 1892', p. 699). In 1898 Fajgel Ester Cypres was the head of the association, Dwojra Fränkel was the vice-president, Ettel Bertram still held the position of cashier, Cipora Horowitz was the inspector and Rachel Blankstein was the secretary ('Szematyzm [...] na rok 1898', p. 801). In 1899 and 1900 there was a vacancy on the position of president, and the remaining roles did not change ('Szematyzm [...] na rok 1899', p. 801 and 1900, p. 801). In 1881, 1882 and 1892, the assets of the Association amounted to 15 000 zl coming from contributions and legacies of I. Paprocki and T. Abeles. Securities in the amount of 3520 zl remained unchanged as well as the mortgage debt of 500 zl and the number of orphaned children looked after by the Association.

As seen in the example of the analysed cases, charitable activity of Jewish women in the nineteenth-century Cracow was multifaceted. Women did not only run institutions and associations, often occupying managerial positions, but also fought for the right to take decisions by themselves, not only against their female rivals, but also against men occupying positions in *kahal* authorities that cooperated with those institutions, and even against men holding positions in the city council. They supported institutions with their daily physical and mental work, organised the way in which institutions worked, being at the same time initiators and donors of foundations and funds, thanks to which various other institutions and organizations, not just those listed in this article, could work towards the improvement of the situation of Jews in need in the nineteenth-century Cracow.

Sylwia Skuza
Nicolaus Copernicus University in Toruń

The social and legal status of women in Italy between the 19th and 21st centuries

This issue mainly concerns women's rights to have the active and passive right to vote, to have the opportunity to perform a public function, to work, to receive a fair salary, to obtain an education and to have the right of physical integrity and autonomy. The struggle to achieve the above mentioned rights for Italian women seems to be one of the most difficult in Europe.

The status of women before Italian Unification

Before Italian Unification women's efforts were concentrated on attempts to obtain the right to vote at general elections. Women were aware of the fact that only the achievement of the right to vote could make them equal with men on a social level. However, in those days, a woman's place was in the home: she was an 'Angel of the Hearth and Home'; she was supposed to fulfil the social roles of wife, mother and daughter. Hundreds of Italian proverbs (Skuza 2010) that can be quoted indicate the woman's role in Italian society, e.g.:

Gli uomini fanno la roba e le donne la conservano – Men produce, women preserve.

Moglie e sardine vanno chiuse in scatoline – Wives and sardines should be closed in their boxes.

Tre volte la donna deve uscir di casa in tutta la sua vita: Quando va a battesimo, quando va a marito, e quando va a sepoltura – Throughout the term of a woman's life she should leave home only three times: when she is christened, when she gets married and when she is buried.

Talking about the status of women in Italy before Unification, I should mention the personality of Anna Maria Mozzoni (1837–1920), suffragette and author of the book *La donna e i rapporti sociali* (*Woman and social relations*), who believed that a woman should protest against the contemporary situation and should insist on the necessary reforms for either giving the simple woman the opportunity to be elected, or through the right to elect another in the general election. The book, followed by petitions addressed to the Italian Parliament by Mozzoni regarding open discussions in Parliament on this issue, first resumed and then suspended throughout the years 1877–1883; however, it did not in any way question the electoral rights of women. In 1890 Mrs. Mozzoni again made efforts to further push for a project of constituency for women, but again it was a failed attempt mainly due to a lack of support for the initiative by Italian deputies. In 1906 Mozzoni sent another petition asking them to support the initiative of many well-known Italian women (including Maria Montessori, who signed the document), but the application did not gain any support in Parliament. Despite the failure we should appreciate the contribution and the influence of Anna Maria Mozzoni as a leading suffragette in Italy at the end of the nineteenth century.

Before the unification of Italy, i.e. 1861, women living on the Apennine Peninsula, however, enjoyed certain rights at the polling stations where they were confined, but there were only opportunities for participation in elections at a local level. And so, in Lombardy, under Austrian domination, women could take part in the local elections (in the presence of a male guardian), or even have the same rights. In Tuscany and the Veneto region, women participated in local elections, but did not have the right to be elected (Graziani, Corti 1996, p. 25–38).

The rights and duties of women in Italy from 1861 (the Unification of Italy) until the end of the 19th century

Along with the Unification of Italy, all local women's rights, as was just mentioned, disappeared – there was a total withdrawal of women from political affairs, and a return to the house and to cultivating family traditions. The commonly used formula for the newly created State in decrees or resolutions in the united legal Italy referred exclusively to men: 'the State citizens' (*i cittadini dello Stato*). It could be said that the Kingdom of Italy ignored the female section of the citizens and that was why, in the year of unification, women from the Lombardy region called themselves 'women citizens' (*le cittadine dello Stato*) and submitted a petition to the Italian Parliament demanding the right to vote in the elections for both sexes. The years 1861–1890 saw continuous attempts to implement reforms that would give women suffrage by ministers such as Giovanni Lanza, Giovanni Nikotera and Benedetto Cairoli, who were in favour of an extension of electoral rights for women, but their proposals and projects met with little support, and there was never a serious debate in Parliament.

The education of girls and women in Italy, as in the whole of Europe, depended on the social status and if this was high-family – families either having contracted a well-educated governess or having sent the young lady to private schools, where the emphasis was not on general knowledge but to prepare girls for being a wife and mother. At the end of the 19th century, first steps were taken with regard to women's education in order to increase the number of girl students, as well as to broaden the opportunities in a particular profession.

Official access to higher education for women – colleges and universities – took place only in 1874. However, women were first granted admission to college by the university authorities. Twenty-six years later, in 1900, 250 Italian women were studying at universities, and 187 girls in colleges; this number, however, clearly increased every year. Before the outbreak of World War I, about 100,000 girls were being taught in secondary schools (colleges and vocational colleges). It happened, however, especially in the first years of the admission of women to study at universities, that getting an education did not guarantee access to professions. This is shown by the history of Lidia Poët – who, in 1881 became the first Italian woman to receive a master's degree in law, after that she completed two years of mandatory practices, however, the Council's lawyers and prosecutors refused her admission to its ranks. Being a woman excluded her from the profession of lawyer or prosecutor, and on this basis the Court of Appeal of Turin rejected the appeal of Poët[1]. It wasn't until 1920 that Lidia Poët as a 64 year-old woman was enlisted in the record of the members of the Council of Lawyers and officially recognized as a lawyer.

Women's rights in Fascist Italy

The outbreak of World War I pushed women's efforts to promote gender equality into the background. However, at the end of the war, the Italian State, trying to some extent to honour the women's contribution to the war years, proposed on 9 March 1919 to adopt the so called Sacchi Act, which was to eliminate the domination of the man in the family and, as it was assumed, to grant women their voting rights. It was very close, but the same year's events, known as *Impresa di Fiume*, blocked the Senate's work, whereas all regulations waiting to be voted on in Parliament – expired. The bill on women's rights, following a stabilisation of the political situation, was never returned to.

---

1 *Il titolo e l'esercizio di avvocato non è ammissibile, per l'unico ma essenziale motivo che il titolo e l'esercizio di avvocato non possono essere assunti a tenore di legge dalle donne'*; see: Lidia Poët (n.d.), http://www.fidapa.com/index.php?option=com_content&view=article&id=387:lidiapoet&catid=904:distretto-nord-ovest&Itemid=46 (Accessed: 13.12.2013).

In 1922 power in Italy fell into the hands of Benito Mussolini (1883–1945). In 1923 the *duce* participated in a suffragists congress and promised to grant Italian women their voting rights provided that no exceptional circumstances arose. As history would show, Mussolini made many promises to the Italian nation, including women, but keeping them was a different matter. Italian Fascism stressed the role of the family and the Fascists pursued the policy of 'moral hygiene'. According to Mussolini, women's role was to be limited to that of mothers, whereas men were to be warriors. Mussolini claimed that war was for men and maternity was for women (*La guerra sta all'uomo come la maternità alla donna*). The government financially supported not only large families, but it also looked after single mothers and even pregnant teenagers whose family or partner refused to care for them.

The Fascist government was keen to lower the number of working women as they were primarily expected to bear children. Prior to 1930, an educational reform of minister Giovanni Gentili (1875–1944) excluded women as teachers of Italian, classical literature, history and philosophy in secondary schools. Only men were deemed as being able to teach these subjects. In turn, in 1938, a law was passed stipulating that women could comprise a maximum of 10% of all employees in both public and private institutions.

The Fascists founded numerous women's organisations focusing on the role of the mother and housewife: in 1933, under a demographic campaign, a Mother and Child's Day (*Giornata della madre e del fanciullo*) was created and as a part of celebrations, the *duce* met with mothers of the largest families presenting them with financial awards; in 1934 the Union of Country Housewives (*le Massaie Rurali*) was established which aimed at cultivating the values of family, sacrifice and maternity (Palla 2006).

In 1930, a new Legal Code (the so-called *Codice Rocco* from the surname of its chief originator, minister Alfredo Rocco) was adopted, it included very important amendments in respect to women's issues. Abortion, recognised as a crime against the state, was prohibited, as was the use of contraceptives. Two new regulations were introduced, which, as would be seen later on, not only totally subjugated women to men but, it may be said, also enslaved them in a complete and humiliating manner. I have in mind the law stipulating the 'shotgun marriage' or 'marriage in recovery' (*il matrimonio riparatore*) and a law (Article 587 of the Criminal Code) normalising the punishment for honour killing (*il delitto d'onore*).

The shotgun marriage referred to Biblical commands and stipulated that if a virgin was raped by a man, then he, in order to avoid legal sanctions related to the punishment for rape, could express the will to pay the family a given amount for the disgrace and marry the victim. As it was assumed, the shotgun marriage was aimed at safeguarding a woman as it was obvious that a disgraced woman would never find a husband and it was her – not the rapist – who was doomed to mockery and slander (according to the mentality of the day, a good woman could not have been raped). Thus, the marriage to the rapist seemed the only good solution. For the victim there was practically no other way out but to marry the perpetrator.

Obviously, it often happened that young people, whose parents were against their marriage, simulated abduction of the girl against her will and spent the night together. Then, families on both sides were forced to accept their union as a shotgun marriage. Thus, the law was frequently used for mutual benefit. However, it should not be forgotten that the majority of shotgun marriages was related to actual harm caused to a woman. The shotgun marriage was in force from 1930; after World War II it was still applied, predominantly in southern Italy: Sicily, Campania, Apulia and Calabria.

Not until 1966 was there a woman who said 'no' to the shotgun marriage and the tradition surrounding it. Franca Viola, a Sicilian, refused to marry her abductor and rapist, as a result of which the man and his helper were judged and sentenced to prison (initially for 11 years, later the sentence was reduced to 2 years). The decision of brave young Sicilian (the decision not to marry the rapist provoked the burning of her father's house and demolishing the vineyard belonging to the family as a punishment for not abiding by the law and tradition) resulted in a number of interpellations in Parliament and a broad social discussion on the position of women in democratic Italy. The case of Franca Viola paved the way for similar decisions to be made by other young victims. The shotgun marriage was not repealed until 5 September 1981 (Arcidiacono 2012, p. 29).

Another law which Italian women 'owed' to the Mussolini government and which, as was the case with the shotgun marriage, wasn't repealed until 1981, was the honour killing. The honour killing, a term known and still used to define the treatment of women in Muslim countries, justified a man – husband, father or brother for killing a woman – wife, daughter or sister, if she, in his opinion, had brought dishonour upon their family. Until 1981, the law allowed to minimise the punishment (reduction by at least 1/3 of the punishment) for the murder if it was justified by man's emotions related to the 'loss of honour' or a stain on the family's good name. Currently, the Italian Criminal Code, Article 587, stipulates that: *Any person who causes the death of a spouse, daughter or sister, in the moment when he discovers a prohibited physical relationship of that person, and being in a state of distress induced by the sustained dishonour brought upon him or his family, is subject to imprisonment from three to seven years*[2].

The two above mentioned laws left a deep imprint on social life of Italy, particularly in the South (Arcidiacono 2012, p. 24–28).

---

2 *Chiunque cagiona la morte del coniuge, della figlia o della sorella, nell'atto in cui ne scopre la illegittima relazione carnale e nello stato d'ira determinato dall'offesa recata all'onor suo o della famiglia, è punito con la reclusione da tre a sette anni.* (Codice Penale, art. 587); see: http://www.unaqualunque.it/a/2737/il-gioco-del-potere-delitto-d%27onore.aspx (Accessed: 13.12.2013).

The situation in Fascist Italy, during World War II, and the fact that men at war had to be replaced by women, caused awareness of their value and their independence grew. In 1940 Mussolini called on women to deputise for men in public administration, in factories and the services sector. In 1943 'Groups for the defence of women and for the assistance to freedom fighters' (*Gruppi di Difesa della Donna e per l'Assistenza ai Volontari della Libertà*) were established – organisations composed of women, regardless of their political views, who helped families in need and offered support to partisan groups. It is worth mentioning that many women not only assisted the partisans in terms of logistics but they were also a part of the partisan groups, fighting side by side with men. In 1944 the Fascists introduced a propaganda image of a woman soldier (*donna soldato*) fighting in defence of the threatened homeland.

The legal and social situation of Italian women after World War II

The end of the war was a moment when women in Italy from housewives, mothers, guardians of hearth and home, without any right to work outside their houses, became labourers, workers in different public and private sectors, soldiers fighting shoulder to shoulder with men. Paradoxically then, World War II accelerated the changes in their social status, gave them greater freedom and independence, which consequently led to the granting to women (who were at least 25 years old) the right to vote in general elections (the initiative of ministers Palmiro Togliatti and Alcide De Gasperi). This law was passed on 10 March 1946, while the new constitution (1945) spoke of the equality between women and men. However, Italian women had to wait another 25 years for the right to stand in elections, not only to vote. Nevertheless, there were instances of women occupying high positions during that period, e.g. Angela Cingolani was nominated undersecretary in the Ministry of Industry and Trade in 1951 and she was the first woman in the Italian government after the war.

The end of the war and granting voting rights were the start of wining by women the rights and privileges reserved before only to men. The legal and social situation of women in Italy was still very difficult. As I already mentioned, until 1981 the so-called marriage in recovery was official and murders of female family members could be justified by the case of honour killing and the punishment for such an act could be minimised. The end of the war was also the time when men were returning from the army to their former workplaces which had been occupied by women for several years. That obviously led to a conflict of interest, because women wanted to continue working. Despite that men took over their jobs, gradually pushing women down in the social hierarchy and confining them within the four walls of their homes.

In 1959 Gabriella Parca wrote a book entitled *Italian women confess* (*Le italiane si confessano*), which triggered a scandal in the country. For the first time women of different social status and at different age spoke about their relations with the opposite sex, the extortions, violence and prohibitions, as well as numerous prejudices that imposed upon women what they should and should not do. Cesare Zavattini, a film director and scriptwriter, and a leading figure of the Italian neorealism, wrote in the preface of the book: '*Italy is still a huge harem; our society consists of what is left unsaid, not of what is being said*' (*L'Italia è ancora un grande harem, la nostra è ancora società fatta di quello che si tace e non di ciò che si dice*; Parca 1973, p. 11). In 1958, a new law (*la legge Merlin*) which abolished earning money by the state from prostitution was passed; simultaneously, the same law abolished limitation of civil rights for women engaged in prostitution. In 1959, police forces consisting of women (*Corpo di polizia femminile*) were established; they specialised in dealing with crimes committed against women and children. Women were given the opportunity to begin a career in a diplomatic corps for the first time in 1961.

Italians were given the right to divorce in 1970. It was a huge step forward, especially in terms of the situation of women; before, in case of a permissible separation, only the man retained all the privileges and parental rights, or the right to decide about the common property of the family. The right to divorce led to a situation when in 1975 the Italian government passed another law on the legal equality between spouses and the possibility to share the common property which had been managed only by the man after the date of marriage.

The year 1970 was also the year when the Women's Liberation Movement (*Movimento di Liberazione della Donna* or MLD) was born, which – as opposed to other similar movements established in the whole of Europe – allowed men to be its members. The most important issues in the operations of MLD included the struggle to make people, including at schools, aware of contraception; the Movement also wanted to distribute contraceptives free-of-charge, reduce the ban on abortion and work out a more liberal abortion law. The organisation demanded elimination of school curricula which differed depending on gender, i.e. domestic education and technical education (*educazione domestica e tecnica*), as well as strived to establish day care centres that would enable young mothers to go to work.

The fact that the Vatican was always located in the very heart of Italy affected to a large extent the delay in the creation of laws associated with the right to divorce or abortion. Italian pro-abortion organisations fought a very hard battle with their opponents in the 1970s. In 1974 the supporters of the abolition of the ban on abortion were not able to collect 500,000 votes; however, a year later more than 800,000 Italians signed a petition in favour of an abortion referendum. The Italian government, without organising the said referendum, changed the law in 1977 and approved the act that allowed abortion.

The Italian society changed throughout the entire 20th century, and the rights discriminating against women changed as well. The last archaic bastions, i.e. the rights concerning marriage in recovery and honour killing, were eliminated as late as in 1981. However, it was only in 1996 when the law was changed (*la legge 66*, the law established also in 1930 as part of the aforementioned *Codice Rocco*) and specified that a rape was not 'a crime against morality' (*delitto contro la moralità*) but a crime against personal freedom (*reato contro la libertà personale*), which substantially altered the approach to rape and its penalisation.

Italian women in the 21st century

At the beginning of the 21st century, in a special act (*legge 380of 20/10/1999*) Italy – being the last country within the structures of NATO to do so – allowed women to serve in the military. One may say that with the entry into the 21st century the rights and obligations of women inhabiting the Italian Peninsula were made equal with men, and the Italian women can now proudly call themselves citizens of the Country for which their great grandmothers, grandmothers and mothers fought for decades. Therefore, in legal terms, women have won everything they could gain.

However, what causes anxiety and uneasiness is the social situation and certain mental influences connected with stereotypes and prejudices which cannot be changed so easily as acts of law. There are two exceptionally dangerous social phenomena; the first one is *donnicidio* or *femminicidio*, which may be translated as 'famicide'. This phenomenon refers to the murders of women committed not because of a need to steal something or for sexual reasons, but murders committed by fiancées, partners, husbands or even relatives of the women (Spinelli 2008). The honour killing law, which existed for a long time in Italy, must not be omitted at this point. In my opinion, famicide is the outcome of this law, hence Italy – like no other country in the European Union – struggles with excessive violence in relation to women, which often leads to their death.

Let me present some statistical data to back my opinion: in 2006 Italian police recorded 181 murders of women, out of which 101 were classified as *femminicidio*, i.e. a murder committed by a partner or husband; in 2010, out of 151 murders of women, 127 were cases of famicide. In 2011 a woman was murdered by a theoretically close person every third day, while in 2012 statistics show that *femminicidio* took place in Italy every other day. Attorney Maria Teresa Manente spoke about the escalation of this dangerous phenomenon during an interrogation by the Human Rights Commission in the Italian senate. Presently, some 70% of homicides in Italy are committed against women[3]. This situation keeps causing a wave of protests in

---

3 Il fatto quotidiano; see: http://www.ilfattoquotidiano.it/2012/10/19/femminicidio-cento-vittime-nel-2012-donna-uccisa-ogni-due-giorni/ (Accessed: 07.12.2013).

Italy, they take the form of marches with thousands of participants who want to emphasise the problem of continuous escalation of the *femminicidio* phenomenon.

The second women-associated social phenomenon is the attitude of men towards women and the acceptance of objectification at the cost of fame and money by some of them. Italian television RAI has caused a lot of harm to the image of women; a serious and elegant host wearing a smart suit accompanied by a female co-host with excessive make-up and showing off her breast and other parts of the body in an exaggerated way can be found in every program produced by this station. Additionally, a group of half-naked and young girls (in Italy referred to as *veline*), whose intelligence is often the subject of jokes by the male host, serve as the background for such a pair. The message is clear: a woman does not have to say anything, she has to look good and show her body – that is what counts.

In the European patriarchal culture a woman always had to be obedient to a man. At this point, I need to refer to the specific climate of southern Italy, where only several dozen years ago the father chose the husband for his daughter. Even in such an important matter the girl had to accept the decision of the family and was handed over submissively by her father to her new husband. The fact that male domination in the south of Italy is still a problem is confirmed by the unexpected success of a novel entitled *Volevo i pantaloni* (*Good Girls Don't Wear Trousers*), written in 1989 by Lara Cardella, a nineteen-year-old Sicilian. The novel – with distinct autobiographical accents – tells the story of a Sicilian girl from a small town who was not allowed to wear trousers because, according to her parents, they were reserved only to the world of men and prostitutes. When her parents found out that their daughter fell in love and was seeing a boy, first they locked her inside the house (the mother was wearing black as a sign of mourning after the daughter who disgraced the entire family), and then placed her in the house of a relative. The unexpected success of the novel, which was translated into a dozen or so languages, as well as a film created on the basis of the book, focused the attention of many people on southern Italy and the difficult situation of many young girls coming from southern regions of the country. In 2009, at the twentieth anniversary of publishing the novel, L. Cardella gave an interview in which she bitterly admitted: 'Twenty years have passed and the same male mentality is still omnipresent in Sicily. Girls have no idea what freedom means'[4].

To sum up: Italian women in the 21st century enjoy full civil rights; however new problems have emerged, resulting mainly from the mentality and prejudices associated with gender and with assigning certain features and patterns of behaviour to either men or women. The problems of women are inseparably linked with the role of men and their ability or inability to find a place in a dynamically changing society, where stereotypical gender-based roles start to fade away.

---

4 Interviste madyur; see: http://intervistemadyur.blogspot.com/2009/08/intervista-con-lara-car-della-ventanni.html (Accessed: 14.12.2013).

Elżbieta Mach
Pedagogical University of Cracow, Poland

The role of a woman in Romani environment – in the past and now

> *Every person is free and a Romani woman can also do*
> *everything on their own: wear trousers, a mini, but should she?*
> Krystyna Markowska – Perełka

We are living in a world full of stereotypes. In a given culture they portray the belief concerning features, attributes of some social groups. They are created both on the basis of directly made observations as well as by means of information passed from generation to generation (Szarota, Łaszyn 2013, p. 34). Stereotypes and anti-gypsyism are evident when we focus on considering the role of a Romani woman played in the Romani society.

No reliable knowledge concerning this society in connection with information found in the media, which often prove to be wrong, present a highly deformed image of a Romani woman.

The society treats a Romani woman with disrespect and their own group perceives them as a worse person. Are there any grounds for that? In order to define her position we should have a closer look at the culture of this ethnic group. At the same time, it should be borne in mind that the Romanis are not a cultural, custom or language monolith. In spite of many similarities observed between given groups, huge differences may be noted (Jakimik, Gierliński 2009, p. 5). Problems concerning the division of gypsy groups as well as ordering knowledge about them is quite complex, and the information obtained does not provide unambiguous answers. None from the so far existing suggestions to order or classify is free from mistakes or simplifications (Mirga, Mróz 1994, p. 103).

In Poland the Romanis also do not constitute a cultural monolith. Every Romani group within Poland has its own nature and differences in some aspects may be considerable. Five groups may be distinguished in Poland: Polska Roma, Karpacka Roma, Lowari, Kełderysze and Sinti. With such group diversity, it is hard to unambiguously answer the question what a Romani woman is like. Her image will depend on what group she belongs to and what her moral and ethical code of the formation is.

The Romani language has a full range of words describing a woman: woman, a human – *manuśni*, a Romani woman – *Romni and chaj, rakli, rani*. Additionally, there are terms defining her place in the family or social situation. There terms include: *ciułani* – a housewife, *romanduni* – a married woman, *daj* – a mother, *mami* – a grandmother, *kirwi* – a godmother.

Nowadays the word Gypsy has been replaced with the word Romani (*a person, a husband*). However, when describing a woman, there is no language correctness in introducing the term 'Romka' meaning nothing to the Romanis. In order to preserve not only language correctness, but also respect, the authors of *Kobieta w środowisku romskim* – E.A. Jakimik and K.P. Gierliński – suggest to adopt the form Romani (Jakimik, Gierliński 2009, p. 25).

A belief exists, according to which a woman in the Romani environment performs a secondary role, the role of a servant. Nowadays, the group of women breaking these patterns and standards of behaviour of their ethnic groups grows bigger. They pursue happiness at the same time not opposing their group's rules. The contemporary generation of Romani women has grown in a reality different than their grandmothers'. Much has changed throughout this period in the way of life, which has changed from migratory to sedentary. This kind of situation introduced a totally different type of contacts with the surrounding environment, forced particular patterns of behaviour, for instance learning a language necessary to function in a society. Many young Romanis are bi-cultural now and have assimilated with the Polish culture to great extent, while the previous generations are closed in their own culture. However, it cannot be described as a gap between the cultures, since more progressive Romanis are aware of their place in the cultural group (Wronko 2013, p. 2). Attention should still be paid to the fact that the young generation starts having beliefs their mothers or grandmothers could not even think of. It is present in a certain group of women, who break out of the adopted canon. Change in their attitudes and values is of specific nature. Their emancipation does not consists in levelling the position of a man and a woman, but in making rigid principles not fitting into the contemporary reality more flexible (Isztok 2006, p. 1).

A Romani woman, regardless of age, is strongly attached to her family A family is the most important for all the Romanis. It is the carrier of tradition, culture and language. It constitutes a barrier for assimilation, prevents loss of identity. A Romani woman, just as in the case of women in a non-Romani society, is a full member of her group. Men are occupied only with managerial positions in the group or family, the purpose of which is, e.g. sustaining the bonds between generations, women are occupied with activities related to the household and maintaining the family's existence. Young Romani girls are prepared to perform this role since childhood. The closest family becomes the teacher – women from mother, grandmother, aunt to older sisters or cousins. An important role in their upbringing is also played by respect for the older ones, customs and honesty. A woman having all these features has a specific place in the society and she is granted the title *patyw*. The title is ennobling for a woman granting her a specific place in the group. It often happens that during publicly held debates, the opinion of a Romani woman is more important than ones of her less respected husband (Jakimik, Gierliński 2009, p. 11).

A marriage based deeply on the Romani tradition is a monogamous relationship. It is unthinkable, according to the custom, to consider sexual initiation before marriage as well as abortion is prohibited (Bartosz 2004, p. 175). In the majority of cases a family is patrilocal and patriarchal. It means that the married couple lives with the husband's family or close and the woman is subordinate to the man. In practice, the position of a woman, despite many similarities, in various tribes differs significantly. In many older cultures, the family is passed from the mother – a woman is the carrier of good or bad fame of the family. Romani women – in spite of the existing myths – are not submissive. They are backed up by customs.

The Romani culture is based on a set of rules defined as Gypsiness: *romanipen* (Polska Roma) or *romanin* (Lowary, Kełderysze). This notion includes fixed elements of a culture, i.e. tradition, customs, beliefs, rituals as well as standard ways of proceeding. *Romanipen* is a set of rules to assess individuals. These rules constitute the basis for problem-solving (Godlewska-Goska, Kopańska 2011, p. 215).

Romanipen is a powerful tool in a Romani's hands. It may result in tainting bad conduct of a Romani man. Tainting is performed by public condemnation by the society as well as temporary or permanent exclusion from the Romani society.

The most serious cases of tainting include:
a) *Dźuvlitko Mageripen* (it is female tainting concerning the intimate sphere of life related to sex and all deviations in sexual relations);
b) *Podbitko Mageripen* (skirt tainting consisting in hitting a man with a woman's skirt on purpose);
c) *Erachitko Mageripen* (it is a boot tainting after hitting a man with a woman's shoe on purpose);
d) *Maminko* or *Mamiakro Mageripen* (tainting concerning the increased tainted impurity of a woman while in labour, afterwards and during menstruation).

The average age of marrying Romani women has now exceeded the threshold of 16, which has no impact on the fact that there are girls aged 14–15 being married. It is closely related to the education of the Romani environment (Wronko 2013, p. 2.).

The manner of marrying and the ceremony itself (on the example of the Romska Roma group) remains almost unchanged. Marriage may be arranged and feelings are of secondary importance. It is also a practice to kidnap the bride-to-be with her connivance as well as buying her (Ficowski 1985, p. 309).

Currently it is possible to notice changes in the attitude of women towards marriage. They do not want to be treated like objects, they feel the urge to present their own opinions and choose their spouse. In vast majority, however, Romani women act passively and accept the long-time tradition (Isztok 2006, p. 1.).

The most common reason for young Romani women to stop their education is pregnancy. Therefore, an important issue in teaching young Romani girls is awareness, since abortion in the Romani environment is forbidden and contraception almost not used. It is a taboo topic not discussed at home (Wronko 2013, p. 2).

When introducing teaching programmes addressed at the Romanis, Polish authorities took much from Czech and Slovak models. Then, people from Romani environments were introduced to schools – Romani assistants. At first schools were sceptical when it comes to the suggestion. However, it turned out that in spite of appropriate education, Romani assistants were a bridge between the school and the household environment of Romani children. Wherever Romanis performing the function of assistants were present, the average scale of children's grades increased and barriers between culturally diversified peers are easily overcome (Wronko 2013, p. 2).

At present, part of young Romani women enter universities.

Table 1. Statistics drawn up by the Polish Roma Union concerning higher education between 2004 and 2013 (among 16 thousand people declaring being members of the Romani ethnic group in Poland)

Studying in 2012–2013		
Women	Men	Total
40	18	58
Graduates with Bachelor degree in 2004–2012		
Women	Men	Total
25	12	37
Graduates with Master's degree in 2004–2012		
Women	Men	Total
41	10	51
Resigned from studying in 2004–2013		
Women	Men	Total
2	5	7
Completed studies without defending the degree in 2004–2012		
Women	Men	Total
20	16	36[1]

Source: GUS – Central Statistical Office of Poland, *The results of National General Census in 2011* (www.stat.gov.pl/cps/rde/xbcr/gus/lu_nps2011_wyniki_nsp201122032012.pdf, accessed: 17.09.2013).

Taking into consideration the whole Romani society, despite early motherhood and other culturally-shaped duties, a Romani woman is far better educated then

1 See more: http://www.romowie.com/index.php?newlang=polish (Accessed: 17.09.2013).

men in her society. A change is observed in Romani families, different approach towards education of women. Previously it was unthinkable for a woman to go to school, while nowadays she has the support of her parents despite reluctance on the side of conservative Romani environments.

Many Romani women, owing to their art or professional activities, are permanently present in the Romani history. They include such personalities as: Bronisława Was – Papusia – a poet, Alfreda Markowska – Noncia – decorated by the President of Poland with the Knight's Cross for saving lives of war orphans, Krystyna Markowska – Perełka – a woman of great learning, an artist of the band 'Perła i Bracia', Rita Hayworth (Margarita Carmen Cansino) – an actress, daughter to a Spanish Romani, Esma Redzepova – a singer, an ambassador of Macedonian culture, Carmen Amaya – the greatest flamenco dancer, Tracy Koci – an Australian activist working for the benefit of Romani children, Eva Hovath – hosts her own programme on Hungarian TV, Anna Polakova – an editor-in-chief or the Romani section of the Czach Radio, Losie Doughty – a writer and script writer working for the British BBC radio, Katarzyna Pollock – a painter and sculptor showing the evil of the Holocaust, Lynbov sisters and Natalia Pankove from Russia – successful in science: chemistry and biology, Juana Martin Manzano (Spain) – a fashion designer[2] and Joanna Talewicz-Kwiatkowska – the first Romani woman in Poland to defend a Ph.D. dissertation at the Institute of Ethnology and Cultural Anthropology of the Jagiellonian University.

The previously known image of a gypsy woman is changing now. Emancipation is being observed among Romani women – they are emphasising their freedom of art, mental independence and political involvement. They are doing their best to benefit from the possibilities of the modern world.

Romani women are more and more often abandoning tradition in order to get away from poverty and illiteracy. They are derogating from moral and ethical principles present in their environment and taking up the occupation of a doctor or a lawyer. The decision to go against the tide is hard for them and often incomprehensible for the older generation. However, economic activity among the Romanis is gradually increasing, since they are starting to appreciate the possibility of undertaking a permanent job.

The planes where men and women function should not be mixed. Traditionally, a woman's activity is ascribed to biological and economic areas. The first one involves childbearing and upbringing, while the latter earning money, getting and preparing food as well as keeping the house clean. The role of a man involves cultural and social plane consisting in, e.g. leading a group, a family (Mirga, Mróz 1994, pp. 128–129).

In the period of the Romanis' migration, mainly women were responsible for getting means necessary for living. Their ways of earning money was described,

---

2 See: http://www.cygańskawyspa.pl/cms/aktualności/romsko-kobieta (Accessed: 17.09.2013).

for instance, by Jerzy Ficowski in his book *Pod berłem króla pikowego* (Godlewska-
-Goska, Kopańska 2011, p. 257).

Change in economic conditions and previously change in the way of life from
migratory to sedentary results in changing the division of duties in a Romani family.
At present it is possible that both the spouses work, sometimes one of them. Some
live only thanks to social benefits or alimony along with some small trading. Women
used to be forced to work, now it depends on how affluent the family is (Godlewska-
-Goska, Kopańska 2011, p. 258).

Economic conditions in Poland resulted in the fact that the role of a Romani
woman consisting in getting means for life is no longer so essential. At present,
there is no one duties distribution model. However, regardless of whether a woman
works or not, she still has some constant duties. It applies predominantly to bringing children up and maintaining the house as well as keeping the household members' clothes clean, preparing and serving meals. When performing all her works,
a Romani woman should be guided by the principles of *romanipen*.

Training young girls to perform the duties of a woman starts since early childhood. The time when the girls start helping with household chores, depends mostly
on the mother. In some families 13-year-old girls are able to cook the dinner and clean
the house. Girls also help in taking care over younger siblings. Romani men usually
do not help women in the household. This results from the fact that among the
Romani there is a strong division into the duties of a man and a woman (Godlewska-
-Goska, Kopańska 2011, p. 265). An exception may be a forced situation, e.g. child-
birth, since a woman is then tainted and cannot perform household chores or prepare meals. The decision to help her depends solely on the man's will.

Looking through the prism of the Romani tradition, the basis of which is the
dominant position of a man, we can notice young girls who stop learning very early
to get married and have children. Being old may only level them with men and
give the right to express opinion in disputes and debates. The Romanis think that
an older woman needs rest and that they should pay her off for her effort to bring
children up and take care of the family. Among older women there are outstanding
ones, whose superiority is commonly acknowledged, but usually it is the man who
is considered wiser. An older woman may benefit from the so far unavailable privileges, but as Romani women say, it is better to resign from them. To sum up, old
age is a period in the Romani woman's life when she can enjoy the greatest respect
among her children, grandchildren and the whole Romani society.

Much has changed since the time when the Romanis migrated. Conditions
of their lives have changed. They were forced to stop migrating and lead sedentary
lives, where own flat increased the degree of intimacy. At their own homes, not observed by close ones or friends, the Romanis may ignore some rules. However, they
stick to them tightly in the presence of the older generation. Romani professions or
professional activity have also changed. The model of a family and division of duties
have also changed to some extent. The Romanis have access to the media, schooling

which allows them to observe new behaviour patterns to help in modifying and adjusting the *romanipen* rules to real life conditions.

In the Romani culture, despite changes, the relations between sexes, social roles, manner of functioning in the society, work or education are defined by the Romani rules (*romanipen*). Breaking the non-written rules may lead to exclusion from the society. Despite this fact, Romani women start being actively involved in social and political life, representing their society in national, European institutions or during non-governmental organisations meetings. They actively participate in programmes for helping the Romanis and prove to be very effective. They noticed the chance to live a different life. They are developing and pursuing their needs and ambitions. They did not reject their roots in this process. They are women who are aware of their origin and who function in two worlds and regardless of their individual approach towards customs, they commonly agree that the most important thing for their social group to survive is acting in accordance with tradition. And nowadays, as was the case in the past, passing tradition is largely the responsibility of a woman.

Nadia Lutsan
Precarpathian National University by V. Stefanyk Ivano-Frankivsk, Ukraine

The role of women in Ukrainian society

Introduction

The position and role of women in society is a timeless question. Historically, women have had significantly fewer opportunities than men to exhibit their abilities. The reason for this has always been the attitude of society towards women. A woman can pursue for herself as a person only motherhood or being simply a member of a family; therefore professional growth and socio-political activity were seen as of secondary importance. This attitude towards women is a violation of their rights (Kulachek 2001, p. 29).

The renewal and reform of modern Ukrainian society, and the improvement of the standard of living in Ukraine towards a European level, are inextricably linked to the reconstruction of individual, familial, and state gender relationships as fundamental principles of the democratization and humanization of any society.

In Ukrainian culture women have always been the guardians of the heart and soul of the family. The Ukrainian land has generated thousands of effective, strong-willed, charming, and talented women who have influenced the country's history and culture. They had different origins, social statuses, and personal fates, yet still they contributed their strength to their native land and people, and were the real protectors of Ukraine. The concept of 'Protector' is indeed historically evident with Ukrainian women. Combined with the eternal domination of the patriarchy, in the absence of any awareness of a deeper knowledge of the history of Ukraine and, more importantly, the history and characteristics of the women's movement, the concept of 'Protector' narrows the role of women to housekeepers. It is no coincidence that the future of women in politics and other areas of Ukrainian society is expressed so pessimistically.

In the annals of national history, the great names of Ukrainian women glow brightly, contributors to the education of the population and to the betterment of our world: Princess Olga; the Queen of France, Anna Yaroslavna; the Queen of Norway, Elizabeth Yaroslavna; Evpraksiya Vsevolodivna, the Queen of Germany;

Yevtymiya and Euphrosyne; and the Hungarian queen, Anne Mstyslavivna, wife of King Danylo Galician. One must not forget about the good work done by Halshka Gulevichivna and Elizabeth Miloradovich, important women whose role in society was major. We must not overlook the grand achievements of Christina Alchevska and Sofia Rusova, outstanding pedagogues who, in difficult times in our history, attempted to create the image of Ukrainian man who must be connected to their national roots. Writers like Anna Periwinkle, Kobrynska, Lubov Yanovska, Juliana Kravchenko, Olga Kobylyanskaya, the mother and daughter Kosach, known in the world of literature by the names Pchilka and Lesya Ukrainian... – in any literature in the world these are well known and not forgotten, remembered as astute, creative individuals.

It is worth returning to one of those famous women already mentioned, Princess Olga, who in her 50's and 60's sat on the Kyiv throne as regent for her son. For twenty years she ruled the state peacefully and quietly, representing its uniqueness as 'the wisest of all men'. She should also be remembered for her high level of culture and advanced morality The state government obeyed a woman who, in a day known for the rule of physical force in Europe, honored wisdom and spiritual beauty. After the reforms of the state, acknowledging and building the international prestige of Kiev Rus, Princess Olga was holding, according to M. Grushevskyi, in her strong and agile hand a state system she would not let run loose and fall apart. She preserved and multiplied the culture, traditions, and way of life of the Ukrainian people as a community and formed social relationships that celebrated high moral principles; in short, she gave much to the sense Ukrainian national consciousness.

Outstanding glory was brought to Ukraine by Nastya Lisovska (Roxolana). From a position of slavery as a concubine, she become the beloved wife of Suleiman the Magnificent, one of the most powerful sultans the Ottoman Empire had ever seen. Astute and beautiful, she had enormous musical talent, was fluent in many languages, and she played a significant role in the political life of the Ottoman Empire. Through her influence over the Sultan, the Turkish and Tartar invasions in Ukraine significantly diminished. The name of this woman as a symbol of self-sacrifice for the sake of the liberty and happiness of her native land and people has rightly entered the history books of Ukraine.

The problem of gender's equality

Special attention is given to the role and position of women in modern society as one of the eternal questions of our life. They are particularly relevant to the present discussion. These problems occur mostly during a transformational period, when civil society has already been built. We must not forget that almost all historical periods of Ukraine were greatly influenced by women. They did not occupy high positions, yet still Ukrainian women were able to influence government policy, the economy, and the economic development of the country. Often as mothers they were the guardians of the family and if necessary the defenders of their native land.

Without allowing women access to the highest positions in society, even well-developed countries cannot be considered refined and rich. The status of women as a component in a particular socio-political structure of the country affects the economy, culture, governance, and rule of law. This is connected to the foundation of changes in all sectors of public consciousness and to the orientation of values. For the majority of able-bodied women adaptation to market changes is too difficult. Women are objectively a less competitive group on the labor market. This has its reflection in wages, employment, businesses, specialization, and career growth. The expectation for women to somehow combine all of their public functions related to their professional work with their responsibilities to the family sometimes causes them to abandon the former in favor of the latter. As a result society pays for the consequences because women remain unfulfilled in their spiritual and intellectual potential. The government has opportunities for highly educated women to take on leadership functions and leadership activity, yet still these remain low ([Reznik] Резнік 2001).

The greatest problem of gender equality in Ukrainian society is that society is not aware there even exists a problem. And no one seeks to create a civilized modern political and legal system of equality between women and men.

The overall 'pyramid' of employment of women is formed today on the principle that the higher the social status, the smaller the representation by women.

Among civil servants women represent 68%, but in leadership positions at a decision-making level there is just one. Today, there are no women in the government in the management for the Administration of the President of Ukraine, as heads of regional (local) administrations. In the current arrangement of The Supreme Senate, women constitute 5% of the total number of Deputies compared to the global average of – 10%; in Sweden –this is 46% and in the UK – this is a fifth of the parliament.

The negative impact of patriarchal rule has had an impact on three levels: individual, interpersonal, and social.

At the individual level among women the patriarchal influence runs contrary to their own aspirations and desires, and affects women's mental and physical health, and their general satisfaction with life, work, and family.

At the level of the interpersonal inequality of women in the family and their subordination to men, this leads to the fact that married women are significantly more likely to suffer from physical and mental illness than single woman are.

At the social level, gender stereotypes established in the past delay the effective integration of women in the areas of production, science, and the economic and political management of society.

Running contrary to these three there is the growth in the women's community. There is a process of the creation of mass women's organizations and women's associations. The reasons for these movements are diverse because the range of interests and activities is very wide, from simple clubs to organizations seeking to influence the political stage. Most women's organizations agree to the idea of Ukrainian statehood. The responsibility for the outcome of these women's organizations, families, Ukraine as a whole is growing. The cooperation on these issues with women's organizations and parliament and other state institutions is expanding. Women's organizations or their affiliates are present in almost every Ukrainian city, and their number is growing. This is leading to an increase in the professional, social, and personal status of Ukrainian women. Self-reflection is an important obligation within women's organizations, to see their place in Ukrainian society and to make an objective assessment of any problems that are hindered by this movement.

The problems with the women's movement in Ukraine

One of the most serious problems that the women's movement is facing in general is to overcome the bias of Ukrainian society on the typical stereotypes by which the social role of women is limited to taking care of the male population and the family. The second problem is the lack of resources for women's movements. The real and complex socio-economic situation in Ukraine causes woman to deny herself her many opportunities and desires to engage in social activity. The third important issue with the women's movement is society's reluctance to accept the women's movement as an important and significant factor in the development of society. The fourth problem is the lack of society's awareness of the women's movement in Ukraine.

An analysis of the results of sociological research shows that women's organizations in Ukraine are very popular among the population and their potential in addressing women's issues are not fully realized. This prevents and limits the access of women to governmental and administrative structures, leading to a poor dissemination of feminist values. In the women's organizations the traditional view of women has long dominated. The fifth issue with the women's movement is related to gender content and the formation of gender issues in public relations. The recognition of gender studies as a field of research, the development of fundamental research papers, ensuring gender training courses in schools and higher education institutions that would provide a scientific basis for the women's movement as a social phenomenon, are all still required. Eventually this may lead to the creation of a new culture and the development of gender democracy. The sixth issue that hinders the consolidation of the efforts of women's organizations concerns the loss of women's autonomy. On the other hand, there is the lack of activity on the consolidation of ordinary states of motion. Among other reasons this is caused by a lack of organizational experience, a lack of the necessary management skills, and ethical issues. Cultural relationships need to stretch ambitious interests; personal responsibilities for the women's movement that often rises at meetings (Ivchenko 2007, p. 25–28).

The problem is to overcome the stereotypes of the traditional patriarchal society and this is mainly in the field of social psychology. The solution is a task not only designated to the state but also to society if it really wants to be civilized. Education is required for both women and men to establish the principles of gender democracy in the country. Special programs are required to help the public understanding of this aspect in the future. Certain benefits are required that would encourage women to reach a higher level in the social hierarchy.

The issue of the working conditions of women, material level, life, leisure, legal protection, participation in government, health, and motherhood, cannot and should not be the concern of a representative of the 'fair sex'. They define the level of the state, culture, nation, and therefore require the right evaluation, attitude, and decision. Because of the active involvement of women in all stages of life, the improved status of women will contribute to the success of the democratic transformations in Ukraine. The implementation of policy for the advancement of women and the introduction of a mechanism for its implementation would create equal opportunities for women and men and will result in prosperity for Ukraine.

The socio-cultural environment generates and modifies these models. In recent years, three images of women can be seen: first – an image of female beauty, the second – the image of women as housewives, 'guardians', mothers, and the third – a businesswoman.

The more widespread image of a man in this patriarchal society is that of a breadwinner; this difference in stereotypes has led to the difference in average wages earned by men and women. For a long time the wages of women in the national average did not exceed 70% of men's salaries. The most significant manifestation of this inequality is in those sectors of the economy that employ mostly women: health, retail, and education.

During the years 1995–2012 there was a series of activities aimed at building a national mechanism for the advancement of women, including:

1995 – Establishment of the Committee on Women, Mothers and Children under the President of Ukraine;

1999 – Foundation of the National Women's Council, which aims at the unification of women's organizations in the country;

1999 – Decree of the President of Ukraine establishing Mother's Day – a holiday honoring mothers, thanking her for her work, parenting (this festival was introduced in the late nineteenth century and was banned in the 1920s and 30s, and has now been revived);

1995–2012 – a number of conferences, seminars, and 'round table discussions', devoted to gender issues ([Pasova] Пасова 2009).

Thus, the positive changes are associated with changes in the social roles of women from raising their status in a global collaboration, increasing the number of women working in senior positions in ministries, state committees and in other central executive bodies. However, there is a definite pattern: the higher executive body, the lower the percentage of women managers in the unit (_Ukrayina. Five years after Beijing_ 2001, p. 111).

In contemporary Ukraine women are practically absent among the members of the executive and legislative bodies at the highest level. The representation of women in state legislatures is only a few percent.

However, most women are present on the lowest political administrative levels. Working in such conditions is most difficult because it requires direct contact with voters, solving specific problems in life, usually with minimal ability and resources. Unfortunately, the active participation of women in the lower levels of government and self-government is not a causal relationship and it is involved through the participation of higher authorities and access to decision-making at the state level ([Kis] Кісь 2000).

However, among civil employers, as heads of the first (highest) category women constitute less than 10%. In The Supreme Senate of Ukraine only 9.4% of people's deputies for Ukraine were female.

Women make up more than half of the students of higher educational institutions, and almost half of those who are studying in graduate schools. According to the statistics, higher or secondary special education in Ukraine has significantly fewer male workers than female workers. However, the proportion of women with higher education in leadership positions at all levels is less than 20%.

Generally, education as a professional activity is where women make up the overwhelming majority – 74% of the total number of employees. The number of female teachers prevails in preschool education (a completely female area), public schools, and in higher education. However, in schools and universities among leadership positions the majority are men, as well as in the administration of education. Yes, all the rectors of state higher educational institutions of III–IV accreditation are male. Among the heads of departments of education women represent 7.4%, and among the leadership of the Ministry of Education and Science of Ukraine they number – 23.5% ([Tsokur] Цокур, [Ivanova] Іванова 2014).

In the business sector, there are significantly fewer women entrepreneurs than men. Their access to financial and material resources is limited due to unequal starting conditions. 47% of respondents believe that income level for managers depends on gender. This is true. This is confirmed by 14% of respondents faced with a situation where as managers, women were paid less than men. Remuneration of senior executives is limited to 8012 for women thus far. While at the same salary as men this can reach 25 000. It is likely that there is an opportunity for women to take jobs in small businesses but this requires the improvement of what is imperfect legislation, as well as legal and social differences.

Conclusion

Thus, the main task by the state for women at this time is to raise their social status; to promote their personality by creating equal opportunities for the realization of their interests and abilities in any area of public life. It would be a prerequisite for the success of the process of nation-creation, because women do not just give life, they can make it worthwhile, not only for themselves. A woman with her wisdom and desire for harmony balances the world against uncontrollable aggression and bellicose ambitions. Ukraine took the first step as a civilized institution to address the issue of gender equality: to the Parliament there was presented a draft law 'On Ensuring Equal Opportunities for Women and Men'. This is 'the first step' in awareness and its legislative expression.

Małgorzata Matlak
Jagiellonian University, Poland

The powerful woman... at home
The portrait of Italian women in the private sphere based on the observation of everyday life

Introduction

The main fields of feminist research and sociology of the family's studies seem to be strongly associated with the public and private spheres and the visibility of women in them. The phenomenon of the 'glass ceiling', the difficulties with the presence of women in the public sphere, their underestimation and their unpaid work in the household have been discussed in many different studies around the world. It is worth underlining that relatively few researchers undertake analyses of the private sphere from the angle of emotional domination of certain women over men. It is especially visible in Italy – the society well known as the kingdom of 'Mammoni' and men with the Peter Pan syndrome; these two psychological syndromes are particularly severe during economic crises. They provide an interesting base for the analysis of the relationship between mothers and their adult sons and the analysis of the distribution of power in intimate relationships. This article marks the beginning of this type of research.

The text below presents case studies which show certain regularities and which have been selected in the course of conversations and observations made in Rome from February to July 2013. The author refrained from drawing too far-reaching conclusions – they would not be allowed given a small sample of the research (25 people).

Methodology of research

The main goal of this study was to verify the thesis that women in Italy compensate for their lack of participation in the public sphere through the acquisition of domestic power. In the process of verifying this assumption a covert observation method has been used – partly involved. As it is widely known, the observational method gives the researcher the opportunity to be in the environment of the research, enter into interactions with the observed subjects and obtain from them the information which will serve to explore the research hypothesis (Chomczyński 2006, pp. 69–71). In the present study it was used in a special way: firstly, the external observation focused on relationships between sons and their mother and romantic relationships between men and women; secondly, everyday conversations were conducted with them without disclosing the objective of the research to them. The aim to the study was revealed to the subjects only after the research had been completed, which posed a high risk of losing confidence of the subjects. In order to ensure the anonymity of the people participating in the study their names have been changes for the purposes of this paper.

The selection of the research sample was random; these were the people with whom I lived, studied at university or whom I met during social gatherings - native Italians. 25 people have been observed in various configurations – for the purposes of this article only five selected cases have been described due to the limited volume of this paper and the desire to present the most illustrative examples of the relationship between men and women. Below a brief description of each individual is offered.

Federico is a 27-year-old architecture student, he lives in an apartment with three other people – the owners of the property are formally his parents, so he does not pay the fees associated with its maintenance. He has a 'student' lifestyle, often goes out with friends. He does not work, which he justifies by his time-consuming studies. The analysis has been focused on his relationships with his mother – Felicia and his girlfriend – Laura.

Laura, Federico's girlfriend, is a 21-year-old medicine student and lives with her parents. She spends almost every evening in the house of her boyfriend and they go out together with their common friends. She does not work. The analysis has been focused on her relationship with her boyfriend – Federico.

Roberto is a 28-year-old medicine student, he lives in an apartment with three other people. He works at the hospital. In his free time he plays in a music band. He sees his girlfriend Gloria every day. The analysis has been focused on his relationship with his girlfriend.

Maria is a 23-year-old economics student, she lives in her own apartment with one person (the property donated by her parents). She does not work. She rarely goes out in the evenings. She does not have a boyfriend. The analysis has been focused on her relationship with her mother – Cristina.

Vincenzo is a 30-year-old employee of the corporation, he lives alone in a rented apartment. In his free time he does sport, he goes out with his friends several times a week. He is also an active participant of an online community providing free accommodation for travelers from all over the world. The analysis has been focused on his relationship with his mother – Eleonora.

Italy – the country of unhappy women?

In the context of the thesis that the lack of power in the public sphere is compensated by taking control in the private sphere, it is worth presenting the results of a survey on the happiness of Italian women. The study conducted by Discovery Networks was comparative, with women from nine European countries – the United Kingdom, Sweden, Russia, Poland, the Netherlands, Germany, Denmark and Italy – taking part in it. In almost all areas analyzed in terms of happiness Italians reached the lowest rates of satisfaction. It is worth noticing that only 22% of Italian women described themselves as happy – in case of other countries this indicator oscillated between 30–45%. In addition, more than a half of Italian women declared that they felt unfulfilled and did not feel satisfied with their achievements. More than three fourths of the respondents indicated that they felt unhappy due to the fact that they could not realize their professional aspirations. 65% of the respondents reported that in Italy women in the role of leaders were a rarity. It should be mentioned that in Italy there is a strong belief that a woman cannot earn more than a man – it was underlined by more than 50% of the respondents. It is worth noting that for 83% of Italian women the domestic sphere is more important than the public one. One may therefore assume that for certain reasons the family context should have a dominant role in the analysis of the situation of women in Italy (L'Italia: un Paese di Donne Infelici..., 2012).

Peter Pan, 'Mammoni' and the deviations of motherhood

In order to analyse relationships between women and men, it is appropriate to refer to the two syndromes known from the sociological and psychological literature – the '*Mammoni*' and Peter Pan syndromes as this reference may be considered in the context of relationships between men and women. This is demonstrated by some of the cited cases. However, before they are further discussed, both syndromes should be defined.

The '*Mammoni*' syndrome (also known as '*bamboccioni*'), particularly visible in Italian society, is associated with a strong dependence of the young generation of Italians, particularly men, on their mothers – they stay longer with their families, they find romantic partners later in life, which is linked with their economic and emotional dependence on their parents, especially mothers (Gonzalez Silva 2012). This infantilisation of men may stem from economic issues, which are linked with the country's economic problems, and their inability to become independent from their parents. However, on the other hand it may result from their mentality and strong bonds, even power relations with their mothers. It seems that this phenomenon should be analyzed precisely in the context of the distribution of emotional power in the family and the emotional attitudes of mothers to their adult children (especially sons).

The 'Peter Pan Syndrome' is associated with the psychological reluctance to grow up and assume responsibility – an additional dimension of this phenomenon is a particular form of narcissism, called social narcissism. It involves a total focus on oneself. As Massimo Barberi demonstrates, it may also have a biological basis – an attempt to overcome difficulties by seeking profits from somebody else (Barberi 2011, pp. 27–29). On the one hand, this syndrome may also be considered in the context of a narcissistic attempt to solve problems (mainly economic); on the other hand, it may be the result of a strong attachment to a mother who wishes to keep her adult child to herself, not allowing them to to achieve full independence.

This may be associated with deviations of motherhood which have been described by Aleksandra Maciarz (2004), among other researchers. They include excessive emotional concentration on the child which manifests itself in possessiveness, submissiveness or perfectionism; this may also be an emotional distance towards the child, hostility or excessive concentration of the mother on herself.

I will briefly discuss these deviations, beginning with the excessive emotional focus on the child. If it manifests itself in possessiveness, mothers try to be inseparable from their children and to make their children completely dependent on them, regardless of the children's age. On the other hand, they are also eager to solve problems for their children and isolate them from their environment in order to eliminate possible unpleasant events. Possessive mother usually concentrate all their lives on the tasks resulting from their maternal role, subordinating all other forms of existence to this role. The mothers' dedication requires a reciprocity from their children – it limits their contacts with their friends and stifles their emotional relationships with other people, thus significantly reducing the children's autonomy. The pattern is different in case of submissive mothers as they do not have any expectations from their children and cannot make them fulfil their obligations. Such mothers seek to fulfil wishes of their children and are uncritical of them. In consequence, sons and daughters of submissive mothers manipulate their mothers according to their whims and currents needs. As for perfectionist mothers, they impose on their children expectations which are inadequate to the children's abilities. Such mothers set many goals for their children and fully control their achievement. This deprives the children of the possibility to decide for themselves and imposes on them the necessity to strive for the idealized image of themselves that has been created by their mother (Maciarz 2004, pp. 47–48).

Another form of deviation of motherhood linked to the excessive emotional involvement is the mother's excessive focus on herself. It is manifested by excessively rigorous approach to the child and egoism. The mother focused on herself relates all forms of behaviour of her child exclusively to her own experiences and convictions, which leads to imposing her opinions on her child, the lack of empathy towards them and a complete subordination of the child to his mother (Maciarz

2004, pp. 49–51). The relation of power based on the unquestioned authority of the mother is clear in this case.

Another form of it deviation of motherhood is the attitude of emotional detachment from the child, which is manifested by emotional coldness and the lack of adequate childcare. It may sometimes lead to negligence associated with parental responsibilities. Similar is the case with the attitude of hostility towards the child. Apart from hostility towards the child, this attitude is also reinforced by the aggression of the mother towards her child (Maciarz 2004, pp. 49, 51–52). However, these forms of deviation are only enumerated for the purpose of information – they have not been observed in the analysed relationships.

Case studies: relations between mothers and their adult children

Let me begin the analytical part of the research by examining several cases of relationships between mothers and their adult children. Below are presented three cases chosen due to the diversity of the respondents' situations.

The first subject of the analysis, 27-years-old Federico, does not live with his parents but lives in their flat (he occupies one room and rents the remaining three rooms to students or people who work). Federico's relationship with his mother is based on trust but also on his mother's complete devotion to his son. She calls him several times a day, they talk about everyday issues. She visits her son at least once a week, bringing shopping for several days which sometimes includes homemade food, clothes and cosmetics. Federico also visits his parents once every two or three weeks, always returning home with stockpiles of food and small gifts. Based on the observation, it can be stated that although the young man feels and tries to present himself this way, he is still strongly influenced by his mother. Felicia does not interfere in his life, she however wishes to be constantly kept up to date with everything that her son does during a day. She works as a teacher, while Federico is still a student, he leads a 'student' lifestyle associated with going to a variety of social events, seeing his girlfriend every day and preparing romantic dinners for her – all paid by his parents. Felicia seems to want to make Federico completely dependent on her, she wants to help him with everything, removes all difficulties for him and takes control of all his decisions, including those relating to daily activities such as shopping. The characteristic features of the two above mentioned syndromes are visible in this case – firstly, Federico displays a slight degree of the Peter Pan syndrome as despite an ostensible adulthood he still leads a life typical of a teenager. Secondly, one can observe the manifestation of the deviation of motherhood associated with the excessive emotional involvement of the mother towards her son and her attitude of submissiveness towards him. It appears therefore that on the one hand Felicia's son has control over her, but on the other hand, under the pretense of submission it is Felicia who has full control over her adult child's seemingly independent life.

The situation is different in the relationship between Maria and her mother, Cristina. The girl is a 23 year-old student of economics at university in Rome, she however comes from another city in Italy. Like Federico, Maria lives in the apartment belonging to her parents and lets a spare room to a student. Maria does not have many friends, she seldom and casually speaks even with her flat mate, discussing only matters related to her rent or cleaning the shared space in the flat. The only person with whom Maria often and willingly talks is her mother Cristina. The women talk on the phone over a dozen times a day and every two days they talk on Skype. The parents visit their daughter once a month. During those visits Maria and Cristina sleep together in one bed (despite the fact that in the flat there are spare beds for guests) and they spend together every moment, not separating from the moment Cristina arrives and leaves Maria's flat. Maria's father, who arrives with his wife, is usually devoted to family responsibilities, such as repairing broken equipment. He does not spend too much time with Maria and Cristina. The mother and daughter enjoy each other's company alone. Their relationship reveals the signs of the possessive mother's over-concentration on the child. The mother and her daughter are not able to live independently. Maria has not made any decision without consulting it with her mother who, being unemployed, devotes all her attention to her daughter. This causes the social isolation of both women.

The relationship between Vincenzo and his mother Eleonora follows yet another pattern. Vincenzo is a 30-year-old employee of an international software company, he lives alone in an apartment in Rome and offers the possibility of accommodation (for up to three days) in his apartment free of charge. He talks with his mother every day. He however does not reveal to her that his accommodation activity, neither does he talk with her about his intimate relationships. Theoretically, Eleonora does not interfere too much in her son's life; however, due to contacts with her Vincenzo is forced to create his identity in an infantilized way. As it can be inferred from observations of Vincenzo and conversations with him, his mother is so important to him that he does not want to upset her by telling her he has a life partner that could take the place of his mother as the most important woman in his life.

Case studies: intimate relationships

The dominance of women over men is also noticeable in intimate relationships, which is illustrated by the two selected cases below.

The first analysed relationship was that of 21-year-old Laura and 27-year-old Federico. Although Laura lives with her parents, she often calls her mother, also during her visits in Federico's flat. Despite her submissive attitude towards her mother,

Laura completely dominates her boyfriend. From the observations and interviews it can be inferred that Federico is responsible for preparing meals, arranging plans for the evening, providing accommodation for Laura's friends after all-night clubbing and paying for Laura and her girlfriends in public places. Federico considers this situation natural and sees his girlfriend as a shy and conciliatory person. The couple quarrels almost every date because Laura claims that Federico does not meet her expectations, whereas he always apologizes and takes the blame regardless of the fact who is right. In this case Federico's dependence on his partners can be seen, Laura dominates nearly in all spheres of their relationship and uses a subtle form of manipulating Federico so that her power remains imperceptible and their relationship is perceived as an equal partnership.

Another example of hidden power in the relationship is a couple of Roberto and Gloria. Roberto is a 28-year-old medicine student, Gloria is a 27-year-old architect. Roberto seems to be the one who has power in their relationship – while with his friends he tries to show his position, coming across as a strong and independent man; however, when he is in a smaller group of friends it turns ot that he consults many daily decisions with his girlfriend. It is also him who is usually responsible for organizing plans for the evenings, and faced with an argument or conflict, he is always the person who takes the blame. Therefore, it seems that Roberto and Gloria's relationship is based on manipulation which is manifested by the apparent power of the man and the real power of the woman.

Summary

In conclusion, it should be emphasized that the described case studies represent only a small sample, and the study is anecdotal. However, the survey data allow us to make a presumption that women in Italy, being unhappy because of their inability to achieve their aspirations in the public sphere, seek to assume a wide range of power in their private life - in intimate and parental relationships. As the selected case studies indicate there are relationships between mothers and their children in which Italian women in various ways become excessively emotionally involved in lives of their children, being either possessive or submissive towards them. Attempts to manipulate their partners and subordinate them are also noticeable in Italian women's intimate relationships. All this may provide important information about Italian women's behaviour in the private sphere of their lives. It however seems necessary to conduct additional, larger-scale observation-based research or the research based on the biographical method in order to corroborate and generalize the observed patterns.

Kazimierz Mazurek, Margret Winzer
University of Lethbridge, Canada

Immigration, changing demographics, and women: Challenges to social roles, rights, and status

Introduction

Women's liberation movements have diverse forms and it is important not to generalize. But it is fair to say, without being overly simplistic, that in all its variations, feminism has at least two fundamental values and objectives. One is the principal of equality; the other is respect. In this focus on equality and respect, women's movements complement many other contemporary social justice movements – the struggles to reduce racism, religious intolerance, social class inequalities, unequal educational opportunities, workplace discrimination, marginalization of special needs populations, prejudices based on gender-identity and lifestyle, and so on.

Equality and respect: the two seem to go hand in hand; where one is found, the other seems also to be present. But, what happens in situations where these two ideals come into conflict? Are there circumstances in which an 'either-or' choice must be made? – choosing to work toward equality; or choosing instead to respect the values, beliefs, and lifestyles of women even if they contradict and offend our ideas of equality? Our paper asks these questions in the context of a social phenomenon that is sweeping Europe and so-called 'New World' countries like Canada, the United States, and Australia. A rapidly accelerating and fundamental social change is in progress as governments increasing rely on immigration to avoid the economic and social crises aging populations pose. In Canada today, immigration accounts for 73.4% of population growth (Quarterly demographic... 2013). At the international level, 'in almost all OECD countries, migration is the main source of population growth' (*International perspective...* 2013). The result is a demographic revolution that is rapidly and radically transforming the cultural, religious, linguistic, ethnic, and racial compositions of Canada (*Immigration and ethnocultural...* 2013) and other western industrialized democracies.

We think this topic is of particular relevance and significance for Poland. True, Poland today is the least multicultural society in Europe: only 0.1% of people were born abroad, and it is one of the most homogenous countries – ethnically, linguistically, religiously, and culturally – in the world. But that will change as Poland turns to increased immigration to address intense economic pressures (Henley 2012, n.p.).

The issues our paper raises are: How will Poles, and Polish women in particular, respond as their society becomes increasingly diverse? Will women embrace their new sisters – those women and girls coming from sometimes very different cultural backgrounds and holding fundamentally different value systems, religious beliefs, views on child rearing, definitions of social roles, approaches to schooling, and so on? Will the women in a multicultural Poland – all women; the new immigrants and those whose Polish ancestry can be traced back for centuries – be able to come to a consensus on the meanings and actions that define respect and equality? Will they work together in mutual respect and in common cause to advance equality for all Polish women; or will they divide into factions based on differences such as color, religion, ethnicity, culture, and social class?

In Canada, the United States, Australia, England, and other Western democracies with diverse populations and high rates of immigration, multiculturalism has proven to be a challenge. Rapidly increasing social diversity has resulting in a great deal of soul-searching for the leaders of women's movements, feminists, academics, and public opinion leaders. We believe that these debates will soon come to Poland. We also believe that public schools are able to contribute a great deal to positively address the challenges girls in a multicultural society face. We stand before you only to share the experiences of our country, to raise some social issues, to communicate progressive solutions public schools can offer.

The scope of the topic is huge, and we cannot hope to be comprehensive in our brief article. We begin by purposely raising very disturbing and controversial issues. We do this consciously in order to illuminate clearly the depth and intensity of the debates and dilemmas that can arise in a multicultural society and that Canada has experience with. We will raise issues in three areas – health, civil and criminal law, and child-rearing practices – before speaking to how public schools in Canada are facilitating the creation of a harmonious multicultural country.

Health

We begin with an illustration that is both outrageous and frustratingly difficult to resolve. In Canada, one major debate centers on the intersection of culture, gender, and women's health. This takes many forms. One dimension is unequal access to preventive health services.

For example, there is evidence linking cultural beliefs to the fact that certain immigrant women are less likely to participate in cancer screening programs, such as mammograms or Pap smears (Vissandjee 2001, p. 4).

We also know that some cultures attach a stigma to many women's health issues –reproductive health and mental health in particular – that prevent women and girls belonging to those groups from seeking conventional medical treatments (Hansson *et al.* 2009). It is also true that women from some minority cultures often do not seek medical assistance because they find the medical system alienating and unwelcoming (Scheppers *et al.* 2006).

On the other hand, Canada's medical system is being used by some cultural groups for purposes for which it was never intended – specifically, gender identification of a fetus. If the fetus is female, it is aborted. Brought to national attention by an editorial in 'The Canadian Medical Association Journal', the result was a great public debate in Canadian society on how some cultures value boys over girls and whether or not parents should be told the gender of their unborn child when ultrasound examinations are performed (Kale 2012; 'National Post' 2012; *Selective abortions prompt call for ultrasound rules* 2012).

However, perhaps most disturbing are some covert practices engaged in by women and girls in some cultures. The one that has attracted the most attention and debate in Canada is the highly secretive and completely illegal practice of so-called female circumcision. Even in Canada, we find some support for the practice in some populations. Indeed, girls have been taken out of the country to have the procedure performed and accusations of 'physicians' from abroad coming to Canada to perform the procedure have been raised.

What is the appropriate response to all this? On the one hand we, like the overwhelming majority of Canadians, are outraged about female circumcision in particular. On the other hand, it is imperative to recognize that such behaviors are intimately connected to the customs and the cultural and religious beliefs of some groups (Vissandjee *et al.* 2003). To change the behaviors is to undermine the very basis of the identity and self-concept of the individuals within that group. It is therefore difficult to claim that we are respecting an individual and her culture, while at the same time insisting not only that she must change her attitudes and behaviors, but that her entire cultural group must abandon its deeply held values and beliefs. Of course, the simple answer is to claim that, in the name of equality, we must liberate these women and girls from their erroneous beliefs because they are brainwashed victims of religious and cultural indoctrination, and/or victims of chauvinistic oppressors. They therefore need to be 'saved' and 'enlightened' – even though they themselves may not feel that they are in need of either salvation or enlightenment.

However, that answer is both unsatisfying for the speaker and unconvincing for the listener. The debate is not new; it is international; and it is a continuing dilemma. It even crosses gender lines. In Canada, there is an ongoing debate about whether male circumcision can be equated with female genital mutilation. In the past, the Canadian Pediatric Society opposed the routine circumcision of new-borns. However, that is about to change. The President of the Society acknowledges that 'there are very strong opinions on both sides of this issue', and a new policy that is 'respectful of personal preferences, religious issues and many other things' will soon be released (Kirkey 2013, n.p.).

The above raises a basic question that multicultural societies give rise to, and which feminists and women's groups struggle with: On what basis do we decide which cultural values and practices – including the ones we personally find undesir-able, even repulsive – should be respected, and which ones should be condemned as assaults on the dignity and equality of women? The same logic applies, and the same dilemmas permeate, our next illustrations of multicultural dilemmas Cana-dian society faces.

Legal contexts

In terms of civil law, matters are equally confused and complex. For example, from the perspective of equality, it seems clear to many Canadians that women are disadvantaged in terms of the laws on marriage and divorce. It is argued that this is particularly so in the context of some specific religious groups. However, because the Canadian Constitution explicitly protects religious freedom, an interesting debate has arisen: What happens when women's rights, religious choice, cultural traditions, and state legislation intersect and conflicts arise?

Just one illustration of this is the challenge to Canada's laws against polygamy. Some religions and cultures allow polygamous marriage. It is on the basis of re-ligious freedom that one Christian sect in Canada challenged Canada's ban on polygamy. The legal challenge was not successful, but the ruling did explicitly ac-knowledge that 'the law violates the religious freedom of [the group], but the harm against women and children outweighs that concern' ('National Post' 2011, n.p.). On the other hand, some legal scholars have reached opposite conclusions: A

> [...] study commissioned by the federal government recommends that Canada legalize polygamy and change legislation to help women and children living in plural relation-ships (*Legal experts recommend Canada legalize polygamy* 2006, n.p.).

As more and more immigrants come to Canada from countries and cultures that allow polygamy and practice religions that sanction polygamy, the issue of polygamy as an expression of religious freedom will continue to percolate.

Similarly, in some religious groups 'Councils' mediate matrimonial disputes and, in the case of a divorce, set the terms and conditions. The divorce settlement is then presented to the state courts for approval. But some influential women's groups object to both the procedures of these so-called Councils and the substance of the settlements. The argument is that women are disadvantaged in both, and the process and the Councils themselves should be abolished (*Faith based-arbitration* n.d.) The heated public debate resulted in an announcement that the government of Canada's largest province 'would be banning all faith-based arbitration' (McMahon 2005, n.p.). Christians, Jews, and Muslims are all affected.

Crime and criminal laws in a multicultural society is another contentious arena. It is well established that contextual variables should be taken into account when criminals are sentenced. This has led to a very interesting legal argument in Canadian law – the so-called 'cultural defense' (Fournier 2002–2003; Renteln 2005). Put simply, the argument is this: In some cultures some crimes are less serious offences than they are under Canadian law; this should be taken into account, and a relatively lesser punishment should be given. A huge public outcry resulted when this defense was successfully employed in two sexual assault trials. Does the 'cultural defense' constitute a valid form of 'respect' for another culture? Is there 'equality' for women and girls who are the victims of such crimes?

Obviously, how to accommodate cultural variables into a criminal justice system to make it fair to all groups and individuals is a difficult question in a multicultural society. It is a question that logically leads to many issues that are important for educators: child-rearing practices is just one.

Child-rearing practices

Interestingly, the cultural defense has been employed in cases where parents have been charged with using excessive corporal punishment to discipline their children (Renteln 2010). Obviously, the issue touches educators directly as teachers are often the public officials who first notice and report suspicions of child abuse. But what may be perceived as abuse in one cultural group may not be regarded as such in another culture (Futterman 2003). The difficulty of drawing a clear and objective distinction between what may be considered mere differences in child-drearing practices within different cultures and actual child abuse is a real dilemma for teachers in multicultural societies. The problem becomes even more acute when sexual abuse is suspected – and here girls are disproportionally affected (Ahn, Gilbert 1992).

Child-rearing practices and role definitions of course go hand in hand. Correlations between family backgrounds and values, and children's self-perceptions and ambitions, are well recognized. That is where the responsibilities of education institutions enter the debate. Schoolgirls from some cultures are at a great disadvantage when the culture of the school clashes with the culture of their homes.

Schooling

In multicultural countries, there are many groups that intuitively recognize how Eurocentric the gender agenda of public schools is. Alienation and marginalization are minute to minute experiences for schoolgirls from some cultures – from the role models portrayed in the schoolbooks they read, to educators' definition of success in terms of academic achievement and future careers, to the social expectations of classmates, and so on. Thus many girls are caught between two worlds – home and school – where the definitions of what it means to be 'successful', 'moral', even 'normal', are at odds.

Obviously, this can be a source of profound cognitive dissonance. Yet, educators are very reluctant to acknowledge that they may be disrespecting the cultures of some of their students and assaulting the values of the children in their care. Multicultural societies are constellations of different world-views. If public schools do not reflect that spectrum, then they are no longer truly 'public' schools; they are institutions that reflect the perspective of only dominant groups and marginalize students from other groups. Again women are disproportionally disadvantaged here: their childhood schooling experiences exasperate and reinforce inequalities.

Unfortunately, the response of ministries of education is to explain unequal educational outcomes between groups – whether in the form of dropout rates, academic achievement, parent satisfaction ratings, school absenteeism, and so on – as problems to be solved with interventions such as smaller class sizes, tutorial help for students, more professional development for teachers, and so on. Multicultural societies, however, do not require better 'delivery mechanisms' – for lack of a better term – for monolithic social institutions. The institutions themselves must be change to reflect the citizens they serve.

Again, this is not easy. And, we are certainly not suggesting that the process and content of schooling in Canada is not permeated with many biases. But Canadian public schools are working hard to ameliorate cultural biases, and they have succeeded to a significant degree. As an example, I will use the province of Alberta which occupies an area twice the size of Poland (661,848 km^2) and has a population of just 4 million. When we speak of 'public' schools in Alberta – understood as schools that are fully funded by the government through public money – we are actually referring to three school jurisdictions in my province that are – one system is non-denominational; another is Roman Catholic, and the third is Francophone. And, within both the non-denominational and Roman Catholic systems – which together enroll 92% of the total student population – there is an incredible degree of diversity in schools and school programs (Alberta Teachers' Association 2008) to meet the diversity of cultural groups in Alberta.

There are about one million Poles in Canada, and Poles – numbering 170,000 – are the 7th largest ethnic group in Alberta (Romanowski n.d.; http://www.polonia. cc). The remarkably vibrant Polish community in Alberta has Polish bilingual and bicultural programs available for its children in the public school systems. That is, students take ½ of their courses in Polish and ½ in English. But, the really important part is that the mission of these schools goes beyond simply maintaining the Polish language. All aspects of education – the curriculum, school activities, community involvement, and so on – in these schools are infused with Polish culture, and the teachers themselves are not merely proficient in the Polish language but are from the Polish community.

There are also Arabic, American Sign Language, Chinese (Mandarin), German, Hebrew, Spanish, Ukrainian and Aboriginal language bilingual and bicultural programs. Other public schools reflecting the multicultural character of my province are Aboriginal heritage schools, Islamic schools, Jewish schools, and schools associated with specific Christian sects.

There is also support for teachers. Multicultural education courses and training in multicultural teaching practices are available in university. Once new teachers graduate, they have support in the form of specialist groups for multicultural education, multicultural education consultants are available, multicultural school counseling and multicultural resource centers can be accessed, and schools have active and established channels of communication and cooperation with cultural groups in their jurisdictions.

The above initiatives are just one concrete illustration of how educators can give real strength and meaning to the concepts of respect and equality. It is possible, in a multicultural society, to have an education system that embodies and embraces cultural diversity. Within an inclusive school system, surely girls will be one of the chief beneficiaries.

What the end result of multicultural education will be generations from now is something that cannot be predicted with absolute certainty. But, if multicultural schooling is offered in multicultural societies, that certainly creates a space and sets a context for a dialogue on inclusion. Perhaps the best empirical data for that is to be found in the cultural attitudes of Canadians. A summative overview of public opinion research reveals that the majority of Canadians: support multiculturalism; view immigration and immigrant favorably; are tolerant of different cultures, languages and religions; believe in minority rights; think that cultural diversity is one of the best things about Canada; feel that multiculturalism strengthens and enriches Canadian identity; think that cultural diversity enhances tolerance; and feel that increasing diversity would be desirable (Soroka, Roberton 2010). Certainly, these values consititute encouraging data for the argument that 'multiculturalism works'.

On the other hand, it must emphasized that this embracing of multiculturalism does not mean that Canadians accept that all cultural expressions and values must be unconditionally accepted and respected. The research shows that 'Canadians are supportive of diversity with some reservations.' While Canadians do not advocate full assimilation of diverse cultures, they do insist on integration and believe that Canadians of every cultural shade and hue must find common consensus on important social values.

> Overall, there is broad support for multiculturalism and immigration, [but this] is accompanied by majority support for a certain degree of integration (Soroka, Roberton 2010, pp. 5, 41).

Clearly, as Canadians search for a common core of values and beliefs while at the same time respecting, nurturing, and encouraging diversity, they expect their public schools to take a leadership role. As immigration continues to increase across the European continent, Polish public schools will face the same challenges.

Concluding comments

The above should be interpreted to mean that we think the issues we raised are easily resolved, or that the ability of schools to solve the complex problems social diversity gives rise to is assured. Neither does our embracing of multiculturalism blind us to the unique challenges individual women and women's collective movements face (Ludgate 2009) as Canada's population becomes increasingly diverse. None-the-less, while we remain alert to the dilemmas and debates increasing social diversity gives rise to, we are also proud of the progress toward multicultural harmony Canada has made. And, as educators, we are proud that Canada's multicultural society is well reflected and well supported our schools.

Ewa Pająk-Ważna
Pedagogical University of Cracow, Poland

Gender in the classroom:
Polish teachers' opinions[1]

Introduction

In Poland the educational offer of Polish universities included gender studies in the 1990s, although nowadays it seems that contemporary universities and colleges in Poland still treat such issues marginally. Questions concerning gender usually appear in the educational curriculum as optional subjects.

Poland belongs to the group of states where gender stereotypes deeply affect public and individual life (Graff 2001, p. 8). Moreover, education in contemporary Polish schools also promotes a patriarchal model of family and men's and women's roles and contributes to the consolidation of gender-based divisions (Kuklińska 2012, p. 98).

> Views interpreting differences between genders in terms of inequality spread easily and influence socialisation processes which reinforce old inequalities and create new ones. Polish textbooks for primary schools contain an easily discernible message about the intellectual superiority of boys (Szacka 2011, p. 22).

Instead of eliminating gender-based stereotypes, textbooks reinforce them. According to A. Dzierzgowska and E. Rutkowska,

---

[1] This article is based on the results of the studies carried out as part of an international project coordinated by the team from the Faculty of Education, Department of Primary Teachers Education/Centre of the Study of History of Education and Teaching Profession at the University of Crete (Greece) in 2012–2013. The article refers only to certain aspects of the results such as gender and school hierarchy, gender and teachers' opinions on school subjects, gender and teachers' contact with parents. The full text entitled *Teachers and gender – a case of Poland* has been developed by a team conducting research in Poland (Dr. Ewa Pająk-Ważna, Dr. Iwona Ocetkiewicz) and published in: K.G. Karras, P. Calogiannakis, C.C. Wolhuter, N. Andreadakis (eds.), *Gender and Teachers. An international Study*, Studies & Publishing, Cyprus 2014, ISBN: 978-9963-2093-6-1, pp. 181–236.

Polish schools are national, conservative, unifying, with the only acknowledgment of existing difference reflected in the acknowledgment of the differences between genders: ultimately, schools socialise young people to assume traditional gender roles (Dzierzgowska, Rutkowska 2008, p.5).

The present text shows the results of a study conducted in 2012/13 among professionally active teachers in Poland (177 respondents) working in nursery and primary schools. All questionnaires were distributed in November 2012 in 9 kindergartens, 27 primary schools and 12 schools which form different educational institutions. The schools were located in southern Poland, both in large urban centres and in rural areas.

The characteristics of the study population

Among the respondents (N = 177), 89.8% were women and 10.2% men. The average age of all surveyed teachers was 39.35. Data on marital status of the respondents indicated that most of them were married (76.6% of the respondents), whereas slightly more than 20% of the respondents were unmarried (22.3%). The average length of service as a teacher among the respondents was 15.5 years. Only 3.4% of the questionnaires was completed by school principals (96.6% of the respondents were teachers who did not work as the heads of the schools).

The statements of the respondents indicate that principal positions in the schools they teach were covered mostly by women, not men – as many as 74% of the teachers surveyed indicated that a woman was the principal of the school in which they work. The average number of men employed as teachers in the schools in which this study was conducted amounts to 5.92 while the number of women – 28.55.

Most teachers did not participate in any forms of training connected with the topic of gender (81.5%).

Gender and the school hierarchy – analyses of the study results[2] (Poland)

The question for whom the profession of a teacher/being a teacher is more appropriate was answered by the respondents in various ways. Most, as many as 82.5% of those surveyed believe that teaching is a profession appropriate for both men and women. Almost 16% (15.8%) marked the answer that women are suitable to work as a teacher/to teach more than men. 0.6% of the respondents claimed that teaching

---

2 In the description of the results and in many cases of variables the mean but also the standard deviation are presented as measures of central tendency and dispersion of answers of teachers' sample. The previously mentioned measures were used in all questions (variables) that are

should be exclusively reserved to women. None of the people surveyed believed that exclusively men are suitable to teach.

The questionnaire included a question about teachers' preferences as to the sex of students in the classes they teach. The majority, as many as 89.2% of the respondents prefer to teach in mixed-sex classes. Classes comprising exclusively girls are preferred by 6.8% of the respondents. Classes comprising exclusively boys would be selected by fewer teachers, only 4.0% of the teachers surveyed.

As many as 66.5% of the teachers surveyed do not have precise preferences as to what sex the head of the school should be – their direct superior at work (see: Table 1).

A man in such a position would be preferred by 17.0% of the respondents, while a woman – by 11.4%. According to 2.8% of the people surveyed, a man exclusively and a man only is capable of holding a management function well, while in the opinion of 2.3%, a woman exclusively should hold this function.

Table 1. Would you prefer the head of your school to be a man or a woman?

Would you prefer the head of your school to be a man or a woman?	%
A man exclusively and a man only	2.8
A man more than a woman	17.0
Either	66.5
A woman more than a man	11.4
A woman exclusively and a woman only	2.3
Total	100.0
No answer	0.6
Mean	2.93
St. deviation	0.70

Source: own research.

---

formulated in a five degree scale. The coding of data has been done in the following way: 1 = 'Men exclusively' or 'A man exclusively and a man only' or 'Fathers exclusively and fathers only' or 'Boys exclusively and boys only' or 'Boys exclusively' or 'Very interested' or 'Continuously' or 'Always' or 'Very much'. 2 = 'Men more than women' or 'A man more than a woman' or 'Fathers more than mothers' or 'Boys more girls' or 'Quite interested' or 'Quite' or 'Frequently'. 3 = 'Equally men and women' or 'Either' or 'Equally fathers and mothers' or 'Equally boys and girls' or 'Fairly interested' or 'Fairly' or 'Sometimes'. 4 = 'Women more than men' or 'A woman more than a man' or 'Mothers more than fathers' or 'Girls more than boys' or 'A little interested' or 'A little' or 'Rarely'. 5 = 'Women exclusively' or 'A woman exclusively and a woman only' or 'Mothers exclusively and mothers only' or 'Girls exclusively and girls only' or 'Girls exclusively' or 'Not at all interested ' or 'Not at all'. Thus, mean = 2,2 it means that the teachers of sample on average considered 'Men more than women' or 'A man more than a woman' or 'Fathers more than mothers' or 'Boys more than girls' or 'Quite interested' or 'Quite' or 'Frequently'.

The reasons for which a woman exclusively and a woman only is more desirable in the position of the head of school than a man are more varied. According to 66.7% of the respondents, women deal better with social relations, are more committed (58.3%) and more emotionally involved in their work (54.2%). They dedicate more time to their work(37.5%), using their good communication skills (41.7%). Following their ambitions (41.7%), they indeed compete (95.8%), but contrary to men they are considered more responsible (41.7%).

The questionnaire included a question about preferences when selecting a partner for co-operation on an educational programme. The respondents largely declared that the sex of the collaborator does not matter to them (70.5%). A woman more than a man was the choice of 19.3% of the respondents, while a man more than a woman – of 6.3%. Work with a woman exclusively and a woman only was preferred by 2.8% of the respondents, while a man exclusively and a man only – by just 1.1% of the teachers surveyed.

Gender and teachers' contact with parents – analyses of the study results (Poland, N = 177)

When analysing the data, it can be noticed that a significant proportion of the respondents (82.9%) think that mothers are more likely than fathers to contact teachers. None of the teachers chose the cafeteria 'fathers more than mothers' and 'fathers exclusively and fathers only' for this question. On the other hand, 2.9% of the teachers responded that there were 'mothers exclusively or mothers only' who contacted them in matters of their children (see: Table 2).

Table 2. Do the mothers or the fathers of your pupils contact you more?

Do the mothers or the fathers of your pupils contact you more?	%
Fathers exclusively and fathers only	0.0
Fathers more than mothers	0.0
Equally fathers and mothers	14.3
Mothers more than fathers	82.9
Mothers exclusively and mothers only	2.9
Total	100.0
No answer	1.1
Mean	3.89
St. deviation	0.40

Source: own research.

For the majority of the respondents (58.5%) the sex of the parents with regard to discussions about the child's problems is not significant. Other respondents more often prefer to talk about such problems with mothers than fathers (29% of the responses), 2.8% of the teachers declared they would rather discuss these issues with mothers exclusively (see: Table 3).

Table 3. With which of the two parents do you feel more comfortable discussing pupil's problems?

With which of the two parents do you feel more comfortable discussing pupil problems?	%
Fathers exclusively and fathers only	0.6
Fathers more than mothers	9.1
Equally fathers and mothers	58.5
Mothers more than fathers	29.0
Mothers exclusively and mothers only	2.8
Total	100.0
No answer	0.6
Mean	3.24
St. deviation	0.68

Source: own research.

The teachers pointed to the following causes of this situation: mothers know their children better than fathers (62.5% of the respondents marked 'yes', 37.5% – 'no') or the fact that they more frequently contact their mothers ('Because I see them more often' – 62.5% of the responses). Certain respondents preferred to talk to mothers rather than fathers also because of mutual understanding ('because we understand each other better'). This answer was reported by 37.5% of the teachers (display marked 'yes'), while for the majority (62.5% of the respondents who marked 'no'), this category did not matter (see: Table 4).

Table 4. Mothers more than fathers/Mothers exclusively and mothers only

Why? (31.8% of teachers)	Yes	No
	%	%
Because they know children better	62.5	37.5
Because I see them more often	62.5	37.5
Because we understand each other better	37.5	62.5
Because we are of the same sex	3.6	96.4
Because they care more	23.2	76.8
Because they understand children better	25.0	75.0
Other reason?	1.8	98.2
No answer	0.0%	

Source: own research.

Similarly, the statement in which teachers reported that they feel more comfortable while talking about problems of pupils with fathers rather than mothers received the highest number of indications as negative categories (indicating marked as 'no') such as: 'because they know children better' ('no' was preferred by 100% of the respondents), 'because they care more' (also as many as 100% of the teachers declared 'no'), 'because I see them more often' (94.1% of the people surveyed chose 'no'), and 'because they understand children better' (also 94.1% of the respondents marked 'no' instead of 'yes'). The cafeteria 'because we understand each other better' had the highest number of teachers' responses among affirmative indications (52.9% of the respondents marked 'yes', while 47.1% marked the answer 'no' in this category).

A significant proportion of the teachers (82.4%) believe that parents would be willing to consider the completion of school with good results as important for both boys and girls.

Other respondents (17.6%) believed that parents would be more interested in the situation in which their daughter rather than their son finishes school with high scores. As an explanation for such a determination the respondents declared 'so that [girls] can be independent' (50% of the responses as 'yes' but on the other hand also 50% of the responses marked as 'no'). The opinions such as 'so that they can work' (80% of the responses designated as 'no') and 'so that they bring money to their family' (96.7% of the respondents marked an answer 'no') received the largest number of indications marked as negative categories. None of the surveyed teachers gave their affirmative answer in the category 'parents think it is more important for boys to finish school with high scores.'

Almost all respondents (86.1%) shared the opinion that mothers more often than fathers help their children with homework, whereas 1.7% of the teachers felt that it was primarily mothers who were engaged in helping children with their homework (cafeteria 'Exclusively mothers and mothers only'). These results may refer to specific social roles presented in teachers' views, the roles that are close to gender stereotypes. A small proportion of the respondents (12.1%) thought that fathers and mothers devoted their time to their children to an equal extent. Among these indications there were primarily male teachers' opinions.

Gender and teachers' opinions on school subjects – analyses of the study results (Poland)

For the question whether boys/girls are better at specific subjects, the Polish teachers provided opinions which are partly stereotypical (see: Table 5). A half of the respondents stated that boys perform better than girls in mathematics (55.7% of the recorded responses) and science (57.1%).

Table 5. In your opinion, which subjects are boys or girls better at?

In your opinion, which subjects are boys or girls better at?	Frequencies (%)							Measures	
	Boys exclusively and boys only	Boys more than girls	Equally boys and girls	Girls more than boys	Girls exclusively and girls only	Total	No answer	Mean	St. deviation
At mathematics	0.0	55.7	41.5	2.8	0.0	100.0	0.6	2.47	0.56
At language	0.0	1.1	55.1	43.8	0.0	100.0	0.6	3.43	0.52
At science	0.0	57.1	38.9	4.0	0.0	100.0	1.1	2.47	0.58
At arts	0.0	0.6	25.6	73.3	0.6	100.0	0.6	3.74	0.47
At sports	0.0	60.2	39.8	0.0	0.0	100.0	0.6	2.40	0.49
Which other subjects?	16.4%								

Source: own research.

A similar relationship can be seen with regard to arts, where in the view of the majority of the teachers (73.3%) girls are often more successful than boys. According to the respondents, only the category of arts is related to the predominance of girls (0.6% of the teachers believe that it is exclusively girls or only girls that are better than boys in the field of arts – for no other cafeteria did teachers choose such an indication). A half of the respondents believe that both boys and girls do just as well at languages (55.1% of the response rate). Physical education was another school subject analysed by the teachers. Most of the surveyed people (60.2%) marked the answer that boys are better than girls at sports (see: Table 5).

Another question in the survey referred to the assessment of differences in the way boys and girls deal with examinations. According to 48% of the respondents, both boys and girls can equally well manage their time (see: Table 6).

Table 6. Do you think that boys and girls differ in the way they deal with examinations?

Do you think that boys and girls differ in the way they deal with examinations?	Frequencies (%)							Measures	
	Boys exclusively and boys only	Boys more than girls	Equally boys and girls	Girls more than boys	Girls exclusively and girls only	Total	No answer	Mean	St. deviation
1	2	3	4	5	6	7	8	9	10
They can manage their time better	0.6	10.4	48.0	41.0	0.0	100.0	2.3	3.29	0.67

Table 6. Do you think that boys and girls differ...

1	2	3	4	5	6	7	8	9	10
They are more stressed out about achieving success	0.0	4.6	24.0	69.7	1.7	100.0	1.1	3.69	0.59
They can concentrate more	0.6	16.3	49.4	32.6	1.2	100.0	2.8	3.17	0.73
They are less interested in learning	2.9	72.3	20.8	4.0	0.0	100.0	2.3	2.26	0.58
They study harder	1.7	19.2	36.6	41.3	1.2	100.0	2.8	3.21	0.83
They are more supported by their family	0.0	2.9	83.9	13.2	0.0	100.0	1.7	3.10	0.39
They have less self-discipline	4.0	59.4	26.3	10.3	0.0	100.0	1.1	2.43	0.73
Other?	3.4								

Source: own research.

41% of the respondents stated that girls are better at time management than boys, whereas no one stated that girls exclusively and girls only manage their time better. Achieving success is more stressful to girls than boys (69.7), while 24% of the respondents stated that boys and girls are stressed out about achieving success to an equal extent. According to a half of the respondents, boys and girls equally well concentrate on task, whereas 32.6% stated that girls concentrate more than boys rather than the other way round (16.3%). In the opinion of 72.3% of the people surveyed, boys are more frequently less interested in learning than girls. None of the respondents agreed with the statement that girls exclusively and girls only are less interested in learning. According to 41.3% of the teachers surveyed, girls study harder than boys, while 36.6% marked the answer saying that boys and girls study equally hard for their success at examinations. The answers stating that girls only or boys only work harder received few indications (see: Table 6).

With regard to examinations, more support from the family is received equally frequently by girls and boys (83.9%), whereas according to 13.2%, by girls more than boys. According to 2.9% of the respondents, boys receive more support from the family than girls. 59.4% of the respondents stated that boys have less self-discipline than girls. Students of both sexes equally lack self-discipline in the opinion of 26.3%. In the case of 'exclusively girls and girls only', there were no opinions indicating less self-discipline, whereas according to 4.0% of the respondents, exclusively boys and boys only have less self-discipline. Another question referred to the frequency with which students display indiscipline and classroom management problems.

Boys more frequently than girls display disruptive behaviour (56.8%), provocative behaviour (57%) and neglect schoolwork (58%). They also more frequently damage school's assets by graffiti (63.8%). In social relations, boys also more frequently than girls tend to use violence (66.3%), resources abuses (68.6%) and sexually harass fellow students (51%). Boys and girls equally tell lies (69.9%), cheat and act dishonestly during tests (72.4%), and are late for classes (68.6%). None of the respondents stated that negative behaviour exemplified in the cafeteria refer exclusively to girls and girls only. According to the teachers surveyed, problematic behaviour to a small extent refers exclusively to boys and boys only (from 0 to 8.6%).

Conclusions

Both in Polish studies and the western approach, gender studies initially concerned the social situation of women. However, over the course of time a number of other problems and issues within this field have come into focus. Differences between men and women are analysed in terms of gender as a category related not only to physicality but also social standing, prestige and power. Gender stratification differentiates between men and women according to the number of possessed goods or access to resources which are considered valuable (income, prestige and power). Among other things, the system of gender stratification involves positioning women on lower levels of the social structure (lower salaries compared to men's, etc.).

Numerous studies show that teachers have different expectations regarding their students (as a result of different perceptions of gender), thus they contribute to the creation of socialisation tendencies by assigning boys and girls different tasks. Boys are expected to employ an individual approach to problem solving, be resourceful and independent, whereas girls' independence is limited and their dependence upon authority is reinforced. The stereotype of a girl who is 'careful, diligent, thorough, reliable, methodical and hardworking' as well as 'well-disciplined, composed, calm, well-mannered, humble, polite, kind, devoted and more grateful' in teachers' perception often creates an image of a child that is passive, compliant and not knowing her opinion. At the same time a stereotypical perception of a boy includes qualities such as 'unsystematic, less focused, less diligent and careful, undisciplined, overactive, aggressive and disruptive', boys being described by teachers in opposition to girls as 'the driving force in the class' (Gromkowska-Melosik 2011, p. 45).

The realisation of the idea of equal potential of boys and girls in the school context is a challenging task. Gromkowska-Melosik (2011, p. 55–56) points out that one of the main reasons behind this is the conviction – still constituting an integral part of the common awareness of parents and teachers – derived from essentialism that emphasizes the dissimilarity of men's and women's natures and their gender-designated tasks.

In the area of politics, the application of the gender category manifests itself in ensuring the proportional participation in power-sharing for men and women alike, as achieved by the introduction of the parity and quota systems. In turn, the educational system should incorporate it by eliminating stereotypical images of women and men in textbooks (presented types of behaviour and illustrations).

Nowadays it seems difficult and insufficient to present the social realities in the humanities or social studies without considering the gender perspective. The category of social and cultural gender has entered the canons of analytical tools, thus contributing to the emergence of various alternative paradigms based principally on biological differences between the sexes. Still, the analysis of gender differences in terms of access to education or professional success should always be placed in a wider context of social and economic differences.

The adoption of any interpretation of gender differences by teachers has major implications for educational purposes and school practice. Therefore it is so important for teachers to become acquainted with the issues of gender (during studies or training). Furthermore, addressing gender themes will allow teachers themselves to interpret the results of research on gender differences in all three aspects: psychological, socio-cultural and biological.

Bashkim Rrahmani, Majlinda Belegu
University 'Haxhi Zeka' Peja-Kosovo

The role of women as a crucial factor in developing post-war democracy in Kosovo

Introduction

Kosovo is one of the eight federal units of former Yugoslavia. It is a new state in the Balkans that derived from the process of the dissolution of the former Yugoslav federation. The process of dissolution of the federation was a nonconsensual process that caused many consequences, ruining, killings and other atrocities that were not seen in Europe since the Second World War. Slovenia and Croatia were the first to become independent states and it is Kosovo the last to proclaim independence and thus from this process in addition there are also the following states created: Monte Negro, Macedonia, Bosnia and Herzegovina and Serbia.

War in all territories of former Yugoslavia attacked all parts of population and women were not excluded in none of the territories from the attacks. And it is important to stress out that women were the most successful on developing reconciliation and peace activities after the world either as individuals or as organizations. Women were the most successful on linking communities and on building bridges between them. They established links between former federal units and they established links between communities within their own state entities. This has happened to Kosovo as well. History of women is the most powerful means in women emancipation (Lerner 2008, p. 11). It is their history that can improve and strengthen gender equality in these territories and broader as well. But it is not the aim of this paper to deal with the history in more details and it is not the aim of it to deal with the entire region. It is focused in Kosovo as a country where live different ethnic groups and where interact different ethnic cultures. Interaction of women of all different cultures and interaction between women and the institutions (both international and national/local)[1]. From June 1999 until Kosovo Independence (2008) efforts for improving the position of women in society were developed together and afterwards by the Kosovo institutions but of course monitored by international mechanisms.

The post war period can be divided in different phases from the emergence phase to democracy and institution building to the development phase. All these phases have their characteristics and during all of these phases the gender equality has changed in both ways: in their engagement and in their position in the society based on their and others activities and efforts.

The following data, taken from the Kosovo Agency for Statistics give some facts than can be used for various studies:

– the entire population of population at the end of 2011 resulted with 1,789,645 inhabitants;
– 61% of the population lives in the rural zones;
– illiteracy within women category is 5.07%;
– unemployment rate of women is 55.5% – men 40.5%
– 68% of women speak only Albanian;
– 33% of Kosovo Parliament are women;
– in 2010 80% of victims of domestic violence were women whereas in 2011 it has decreased to 77% (Kosovo Agency of Statistics 2013).

After war phases on gender issues development

Peace, humanitarian aid, reconciliation and similar were the first forms of activities that linked women associations more than any other possible forms. These were very fruitful, visible and successful especially in the areas with the mixed ethnic groups. Women groups and women associations start to implement various projects that in their content had the gender equality components in most cases. International donors (development agencies, private donors, etc.) while and when supporting local initiatives and projects asked for inclusion of gender perspectives[2]. This has shown to be important and to produce results in all fields where the pro-

---

1 In June 10, 1999, UN Security Council adopted Resolution 1244 that opened the door for international administration and the country was governed/administered by international civil administration and after some time by both Provisional Institutions of Kosovo and the International administration. In February 17 2008, Kosovo declared its independence and since then it has been recognized by more than 100 states.

2 Bashkim Rrahmani (the first author of this paper) has served as the Executive Director of the Foundation for Democratic Initiatives (FDI). FDI was a local Kosovo foundation that supported financially local NGOs and local initiatives in community development, peace, reconciliations, anti-corruption, etc. In all supported projects the foundation asked for allocation of determined resources for gender perspectives and for inter ethnic and inter cultural dialogue.

jects were implemented. Women through these initiatives: first, by implementing themselves these types of projects showed their strength; second, improved their position in society; third, gave a great contribution in linking communities and especially gave contribution to peace and reconciliation.

Women associations were among the first to enter into the areas that had characteristics of enclaves and with women community groups initiated dialogue that indeed was difficult to be developed after a war with a lots of killings, victims, atrocities, rapes, ruining, etc. But it is important to stress out that within UN mission there could be found prejudices and stereotypes about Kosovo society, especially regarding women. To a determined number of UNMIK one could see how they treated Kosovo as a traditionalist and patriarchal society.

> After the war there was tendency of marginalizing women from politics despite the fact that in Kosovo women were highly involved in the process of liberation, independence, and democracy

– Edita Tahiri, Deputy Prime Minister for Foreign Affairs and National Security[3]. Taking into the consideration the post war situation and difficulties that appear in such conditions; taking into the consideration the hate between Serbs and Albanians caused by the war; taking into the consideration the situation when everything was needed; taking into consideration the traditionalistic approach toward women; etc., the results achieved were quite big.

During this phase a big number of NGOs was created and they took the lead on developing the mentioned initiatives and projects at the same time showing Kosovo not to be treated as a strong traditional or patriarchal society. As a strong traditional society Kosovo was not even during the communist time.

Years 1999–2001 could be considered the years of emergency phase during which NGO activities were developed in all fields assisting international civil administration, assisting development agencies, assisting local institutions etc., on the implementation of their programs and strategies. By doing this, NGOs and especially women NGOs took the lead to overcome the barriers between communities that were split as a result of war. A lots of examples of success can be mentioned in this regard whereas it is important to stress out that there were Albanian Kosovo women NGOs to enter into Serb created enclaves without prejudices and established or re-established links between communities that were cut as a result of war and as a result of Serbian regime led by Milloshevich before the war. By doing this, women and their organizations and their networks have shown their strength and their abilities to touch and deal with the issues that were very difficult to be touched

---

More about the impact that projects had can be seen from the annual reports of FDI from 2002–2007 but also from all other donor agencies and bodies that were present in Kosovo.

3   See more at: The Kosova Women's Network (2011), *135 Facts & Fables*, http://www.womensnetwork.org/documents/ 20130120165559661.pdf (Accessed: 15.11.2013).

under those difficult situations. These women NGOs in addition assisted Serb and other minority women groups to create their nongovernmental associations so they could work together not only implementing projects but also on promoting values of their own communities, as well as working to improve their position in the society.

On the other side international administration together with the new local institutions and with the political parties developed and held long discussions about women representation at all levels of governance. Discussions were developed and even though there is no clear consensus within the society a quota was applied. A quota that gives 30% of women to be represented. Is this a real need or this serves more to promote women as decor? Is this something that ensures equality and proper representation? Is this something that under Kosovo circumstances improves women position? Is this something that guarantee the gender equality? There could be raised more questions related to quota and its implementation.

Arguments 'pro' and 'contra' could be found in various papers, studies, discussions etc., done in Kosovo and based on approaches, one may have, he/she may position himself/herself on this issue. We as authors of this paper stand somewhere between 'pro-s' and 'contra-s'. This because a need for better representation of women is apparent and crucial. If in 101,32 men there are 100 women[4] in Kosovo, then 30% is not enough in numbers but if that representation doesn't meet the proper criteria of quality then 30% is questioned. It is questioned because this goes only in favor of décor and by décor we cannot talk about the gender equality or women representation. Décor obviously doesn't ensure quality. But as a starting point obviously it is to be supported. We stand more for standards of equality on the representation of women, where women based on democracy standards and procedures get to the place that belongs to them as equal part of the society. If democracy standards and procedures are in place then there shouldn't exist a fear of discrimination. The fact that Kosovo's President is a woman doesn't mean that we have the gender equality and equal opportunities, because the current Kosovo President didn't undergo the normal process of elections. She became a President of the country as a result of an agreement reached between leaders of three political parties and this is known as 'Envelope President', since her name was taken out from an envelope as a proposal to be the Kosovo President. By stating this we do not have something subjectively against current president, but we stand that the process based on which she became President doesn't belong to democracy standards. And the case of current president is not an indicator that shows that Kosovo has reached that level of democracy where women are equal completely to men. If she entered into the process of elections and if she had been elected through the normal democratic election process and procedures, then situation would have been much more

---

4   See more at: The Kosova Women's Network (2011).

different. This was clearly not the case. Moreover three men and an Ambassador (all men) made an agreement to produce 'envelope president'.

Legal bases and mechanisms for gender equality

Kosovo as a new state is fulfilling international standards and the legislation system of Kosovo is in accordance with these standards. Thus Kosovo Constitution (article 71) promotes gender equality based on the international principles. Whereas among the other laws it is important to mention two very important laws regarding gender and gender equality:
– Law on Gender equality, June 2004
and
– Law Against Discrimination, September 2004.
These legal basis together with the international convenes created a good basis for creating mechanisms that can be used for implementing practically equality and non discrimination. The following are some of important mechanisms, as enumerated by Kosovo Agency of Statistics and that are being used in Kosovo nowadays:

Institutional mechanisms for gender equality:
Kosovo Parliament
– Informal Group of Parliamentary Women;
– Parliamentary Commission for Freedom, Human Rights, Gender Equality, Missing Persons and Petitions;
– Kosovo Government;
– Agency for Gender Equality/the Prime Minister's Office;
– Ombudsperson Institution/Unit for Gender Equality;
– Officers for Gender Equality in the Ministry;
– Intergovernmental Council for Gender Equality;
– Sector for Gender Issues-Ministry for Administering Local Government.

Mechanisms at the local level:
– Officers for Gender Equality at the Municipal Level;
– Municipal Committees for Gender Equality;

NGO mechanisms:
– NGOs;
– Shelters;

Governmental mechanisms that treat domestic violence:
– Unit for Domestic Violence-Kosovo Police Service;
– Division for Protection and Help of Victims-Ministry of Justice;
– Courts and prosecutors;
– Centers for social issues-ministry of labor social wellbeing.

The existing legal basis and the existing mechanisms have contributed to democracy and to better representation of women and consequently to equality in general. But it is obvious there is still a lot to be done. Legal instruments and mechanisms should be more used whereas the entire society should enter more deeply in a debate where quality should prevail instead of numbers and percentages. Priority should be given more to the quality and to the values rather than stressing out numbers and percentages that at the end of the day ore not clear indicators of real democracy. Moreover even if we rely in numbers/percentages still be do not have a proper women representation.

Conclusions

Kosovo has undertaken good steps in regard to gender equality and better gender representation. It has created solid legal basis and solid mechanisms on realizing equal rights and the protection when these rights are violated. It has created a good environment of interethnic and intercultural coexistence. It has started to promote gender equality and gender perspectives, but there are needs for more activities.

Kosovo needs to create accompanying instruments for law implementation, since laws are in force but they are to be implemented. Monitoring of law implementation and the democratic procedures need to be more monitored and monitoring mechanisms should be supported. Media should be more supported when promoting gender equality. Education programs should include gender perspectives and gender equality. Police and those that directly deal with the law implementation should be trained. Education programs should educate men in one side and on the other side women to ask and fight for equality, because their rights are not to be given by men. Equal rights belong to all equally. And Kosovo has to fulfill international standards first of all for its better development as a democratic country and on the other side these are obligations for Kosovo efforts for EU integration.

Onur Tutulmaz, Peter Victor
York University, Canada

Is there a gender Kuznets Curve for women's development?

Introduction

We would normally expect economic development to result in improvement in key social dimensions. If it did not it would hardly count as development. Women's development, by which we mean improvements in women's health, economic and social status, is one of these areas[1]. Some authors argue that contemporary development leads in the opposite direction. Eastin and Prakash (2013, p. 157) note that the existing literature '[...] tends to view development as either "good" or "bad" for gender equality *across* the development spectrum'. Taking issue with this view, Eastin and Prakash suggest that economic development is not a simple process and that its relationship to women's development corresponds to a non-monotonic Kuznets Curve. In section 2 we briefly review the theory of the Kuznets Curve and its environmental application. In section 3 we describe the newer gender Kuznets Curve (GKC) hypothesis which we assess theoretically in section 4 and empirically in section 5. Section 6 presents our conclusions.

Kuznets Curve hypothesis

Simon Kuznets's important work in 1955 was the starting point for studies examining the relationship between economic development and specific dimensions of development. He investigated the long and short 'swings'[2] of income inequality in the relation to the history of economic development. Kuznets also discussed some swings of other variables connected to economic development. The non-monotonic

---

1 We note that there are studies that focus on the negative effects of development (see: Tinker 1976; Tinker, Bramsen 1976).
2 Called 'Kuznets swings' in the literature.

relationship between economic development and income inequality was defined by Kuznets (1955, 1963).

According the hypothesized Kuznets Curve, as economic development proceeds, measured as growth in income level, income inequality first rises but after a turning point starts to fall. Represented by an inverse-U curve, this relationship defines the well-known Kuznets Curve (Figure 1).

Figure 1. Kuznets Curve

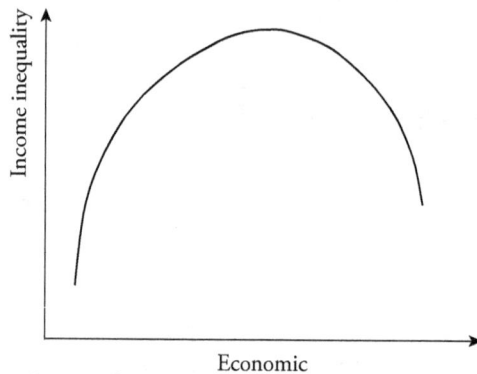

Source: Our presentation; for a similar and more complete figure, see Acemoglu and Robinson (2002).

Inspired by the Kuznets Curve, Grossman and Krueger (1991, 1993) showed a similar relationship between income and some measures of environmental quality. Grossman and Krueger, noticed the environmental pressure of developing economy is first rising but after some level of development it starts to fall. Shafik and Bandyophadyay (1992) studied the subject almost at the same time independently. This new relationship was called an Environmental Kuznets Curve by Panayotou (1993) and it has become widely examined and publicized.

Figure 2. Inverse-U form Environmental Kuznets Curve

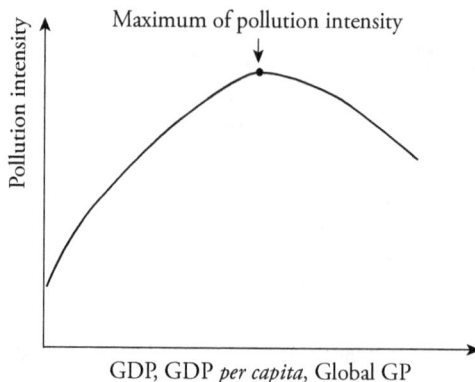

Source: Tisdell 2001, figure 1.

De Bruyn and Heintz (1999) use following EKC models in one general form:

$$EP_{i,t} = \alpha_{i,t} + \beta_1 \cdot Y_{i,t} + \beta_2 \cdot Y_{i,t}^2 + \beta_3 \cdot Y_{i,t}^3 + \beta_4 \cdot Z_{i,t} + e_{i,t} \tag{1}$$

EP: environmental pressure
Y: economic development variable (i.e. income)
Z: other variables
i, t: country and time index
α, β: constant term and coefficient parameters
e: error term

In equation (1), *EP* can be understood as pressure caused by economic development on the environment. As an explanatory variable, income or *per capita* income is consistently used in the literature. Different mathematical forms of the explanatory variable are used to determine the form of the relationship curve. *i* and *t* are used for country index and time index. α is a constant term which shows average environmental pressure when there is no important effect of income on the environment. β_k and *k* parameters show the relative weight of the explanatory variables. $Z_{i,t}$ represents others variable like population density, lagged income, and income inequality. $e_{i,t}$ is normally distributed residuals.

Figure 3. Inverse U and N relationships of the Environmental Kuznets Curve

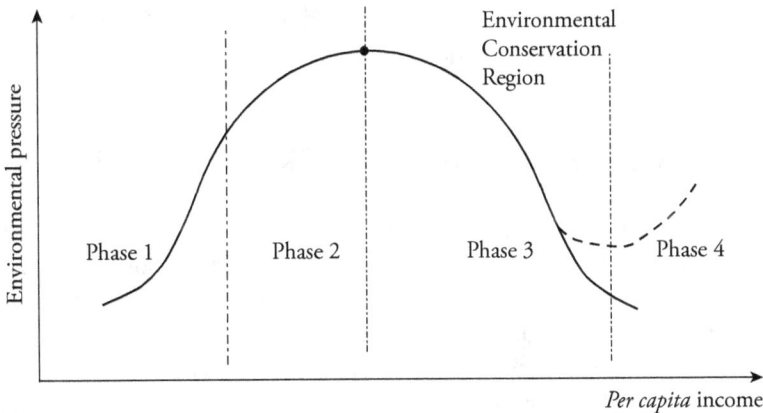

Source: De Bruyn and Heintz 1999, Figure 46.1.

The model given in equation (1) is used to examine 7 different forms related to the environment–economic development relationship (De Bruyn, Heintz 1999, p. 659). These different types of relationships depend on the estimated values of the parameters:

Parametric Conditions: (1a)

1. $\beta_1 > 0$ and $\beta_2 = \beta_3 = 0$ emissions increase monotonically with income
2. $\beta_1 < 0$ and $\beta_2 = \beta_3 = 0$ emissions decrease monotonically with income
3. $\beta_1 > 0, \beta_2 < 0$ and $\beta_3 = 0$ inverse-U form a quadratic relationship (EKC relationship)
4. $\beta_1 < 0, \beta_2 > 0$ and $\beta_3 = 0$ U form a quadratic relationship (inverse of EKC)
5. $\beta_1 > 0, \beta_2 < 0$ and $\beta_3 > 0$ give a cubic polynomial N form relationship
6. $\beta_1 < 0, \beta_2 > 0$ and $\beta_3 < 0$ give a cubic polynomial inverse N form relationship
7. $\beta_1 = \beta_2 = \beta_3 > 0$ give a straight line with no relationship between emission and income

There are different forms of relationship and the inverse-U form which is originally defined as the EKC relationship is only one of the possible seven forms. When the β_3 parameter is insignificant the quadratic form is confirmed and a positive β_1 with a negative β_2 gives the inverse-U relationship (De Bruyn, Heintz 1999, p. 659) as in Figure 2. In addition to (1a) conditions, it is noted that the absolute value of the positive β_1 should be greater than the absolute value of the negative β_2 for EKC relationship. If β_3 becomes signitficant, udner condition 4 given in (1a), the relationship can turn into an N-type relationship (as in Figure 3).

A Gender Kuznets Curve (GKC) hypothesis

It has become fashionable to consider whether the same non-monotonic relationship of economic development and income inequality and some environmental pressures can be extended to the other social issues such as human development and education (see: Ibourk and Amaghouss 2012). Recently, the Kuznets Curve idea has started to be applied to women's development as expressed by gender equality. One study by Eastin and Prakash (2013), detects an N type relationship between economic development and some selected criteria of women's development (Figure 4). This type of relationship is defined as the Gender Kuznets Curve (GKC).

Figure 4. Curvilinear (S form) relationships of gender Kuznets Curve determined by Eastin and Prakash

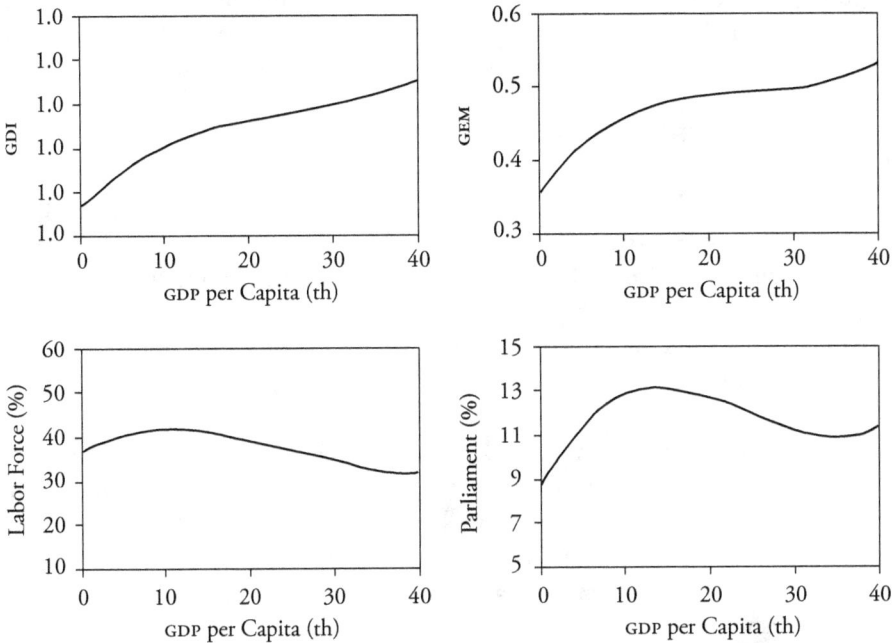

Source: Eastin, Prakash 2013; for the variables see text below.

Other studies (e.g. Kılınç and Yetkiner 2013; Forsythe *et al.* 2000) showing a relationship between economic development and gender equality also suggest a new type of Kuznets Curve. However, the GKC has not benefitted from the more general analysis brought to bear on other versions of the Kuznets hypothesis. This kind of scrutiny is conducted in the next section. Before that we present a general model for the GKC:

$$GD_{i,t} = \alpha_{i,t} + \beta_1 \cdot Y_{i,t} + \beta_2 \cdot Y_{i,t}^2 + \beta_3 \cdot Y_{i,t}^3 + \beta_4 \cdot Z_{i,t} + e_{i,t} \qquad (2)$$

GD: gender development related variable
Y: economic development variable (i.e. income)
Z: other (non-structural) variables
i, t: country and time index
α, β: constant term and coefficient parameters
e : error term

In equation (2) *GD* represents the gender development related variables. For the GKC models used in Eastin and Prakash (2013), these variables are Gender

Empowerment Measurement (GEM), Gender Development Index (GDI)[3], labour force participation rate for women and parliament participation rate for women (Figure 4). First two variables are a mixture of other measurements. We use the labour force participation rate and the employment to population rate to represent gender development (Figure 5) in our empirical application in part 5.

Theoretical discussion

To better understand the implications of the GKC we can first analyze the basic mathematical features of the curve suggested by the hypothesis. The Kuznets Curve relationship is a 'reduced' relationship. A reduced relationship tries to determine the shape of the total relationship between the 2 major variables represented in an equation by set on the both side of it. Therefore, adding structural variables transforms the main relationship from the general relationship to a more specific one. That is, the curve does not represent the reduced relationship anymore.

The main proposition of the Kuznets Curve hypotheses is the non-monotonic change in the variables investigated in relation to economic development (Acemoglu and Robinson 2002, p. 183). By contrast, the studies of the GKC tend to define the GKC as 'curvilinear' which is a weaker and in some respects a less interesting relationship than the conventional Kuznets Curve. The 'S-type' relationship is also used by eastin and Prakash (2013) to define that curvilinear relationship. It suggests temporary interruption in the path of women's development. It also suggests that the interruption can be a pause/stall (as Figure 4a, b) or a deterioration (as Figure 4c, d). However, these points constitute an important departure from the feature of non-monotonicity in the Kuznets Curve relationship. The inverse-U definition of the KC or EKC literature and N-form[4] Kuznets Curve relationship of EKC literature, which we analyzed in part 2, underline the sharp return and comeback that economic development activates after some level[5]. In contrast, the curvilinear or S-type relationship of the GKC suggests only a temporary interruption in the course of development.

Another important feature of the Kuznets Curve hypothesis is the more fundamental property of the whole hypothesis that makes the Kuznets Curve hypothesis one of the important tools of political economy. A political economy perspective clearly shows the polar sign of the relationship for society or economy. For example

---

3 GDI is very similar to the human development index (HDI) which has been calculated by the UNDP (United Nations Development Programme) for over 20 years; see: http://hdr.undp.org/en/statistics/hdi (Accessed: 23.07.2014).

4 As we underlined before the N-form curve is determined by statistically significant estimation of the cubic term. Otherwise estimation results generate the inverse-U form curve shape.

5 These sharp returns and changes of relationship are called '*de-linking*' and '*re-linking*' in EKC literature.

for the traditional Kuznets Curve (KC), income inequality is initially adversely affected by economic development. This relationship changes after a turning point. We can represent this relationship by (–, +) in terms of the consequence of economic development for income inequality. This effect is similar for the EKC which we can summarize as (–, +, –) in parallel manner. On the other hand, the implications of the GKC so far have been firstly positive for the society, followed by a reversal; and then changing again into a positive relationship which we can summarize as (+, –, +). As a result, this relationship proposes a different route compared with other Kuznets Curve hypotheses. GKC's main course is different from its predecessors which are shaped by the negative effects of economic development.

Data and empirical analysis results

Empirical analyses are generally conducted using econometric, statistical models. However, economic series showing a dominant nonstationary structure need very technical treatment which can be possible in various different ways. The GKC hypothesis, as discussed above is differentiated from other Kuznets Curve hypotheses, by proposing a temporary delay in the main path in terms of a stall or a temporary deterioration.

Inspection of this proposition from the raw series is comparatively easy. We present in Figure 5 the raw series of GDP *per capita* in terms of constant 2005$ US dollars, the labour force participation rate (LFPR) and employment/population rate (EMPPOPRATE) for women in 8 countries.

Despite the different economic development levels reached in these countries, the GDP *per capita* series show similar upward trends in Figure 5. Labour force participation rates of women have reached between 60% and 80% levels for the sampled countries except for Turkey which suggests a substantial structural difference from the other sampled countries. Interestingly, LFPR levels decreased for Poland compared to the 1992 level, which suggests the effects of an economic transition. Canada, Japan, Korea, Spain and US show these temporary stalls or recessions in women's development that the hypothesis suggests. Nevertheless, the economic significance of these delays are different and do not seem to be generalizable.

Although a complete econometric analysis is beyond the scope for this paper we present the econometric estimations conducted for quadratic and cubic forms of the model (see chapter 2) for a gender Kuznets Curve for comparison with the results of the recent study of Eastin and Parakash (2013).

Figure 5. Country analyses on GDP p/c, labour force participation rate (LFPR) and employment/population rate (EMPPOPRATE) for woman

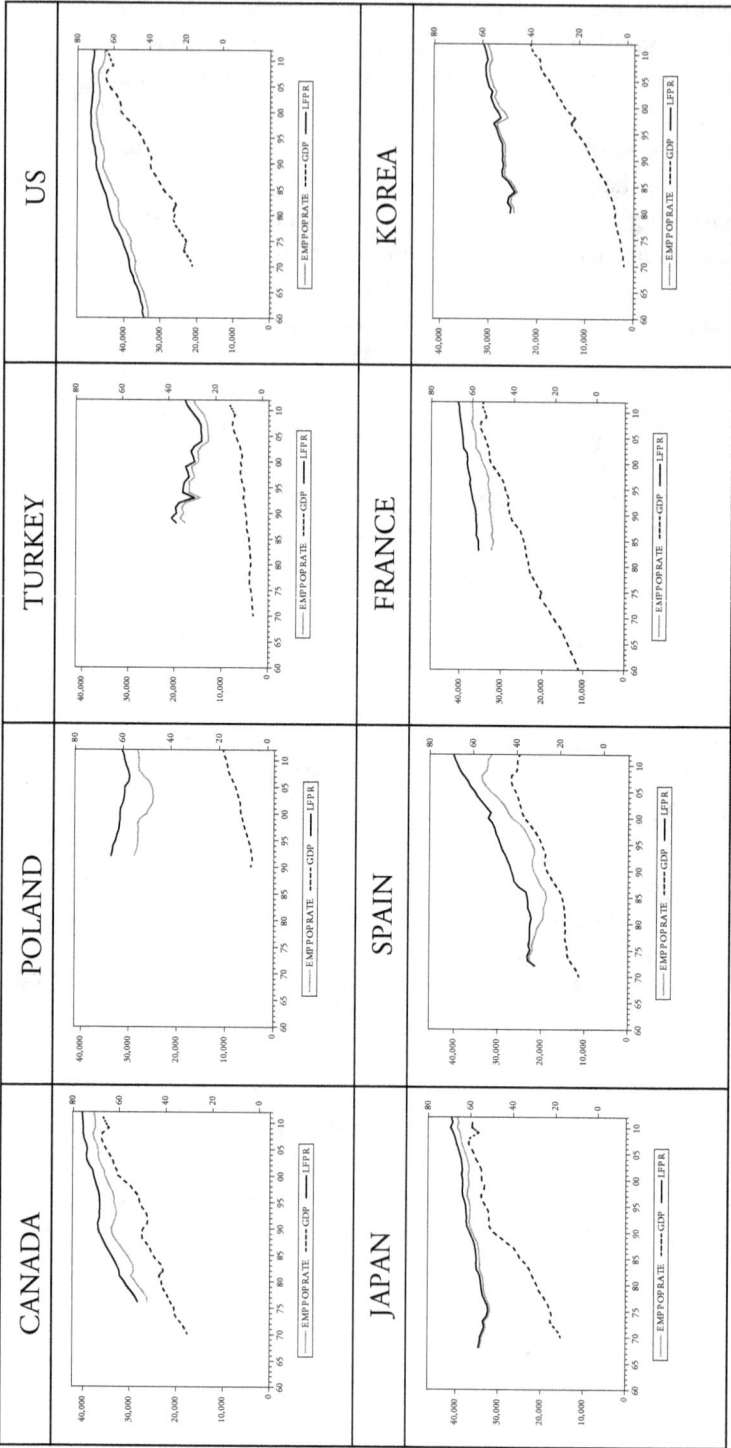

Table 1. Results of cubic GKC model estimations for sample countries[c], [d]

	CANADA	POLAND	TURKEY	US	JAPAN	SPAIN[a]	FRANCE	KOREA
β_1	0.001419 (2.74)***	0.030791 (61.91)***	0.032510 (15.52)***	0.002319 (19.45)***	0.006349 (35.65)***	0.006645 (14.52)***	0.005677 (12.09)***	0.014121 (25.43)***
β_2	$1.04\ 10^{-07}$ (2.91)***	$-4.73\ 10^{-06}$ (−36.49)***	$-7.58\ 10^{-06}$ (−11.49)***	$2.25\ 10^{-08}$ (3.20)***	$-2.48\ 10^{-07}$ (−18.44)***	$-4.88\ 10^{-07}$ (−10.54)***	$-2.03\ 10^{-07}$ (−6.44)***	$-1.13\ 10^{-06}$ (−14.33)***
β_3	-2.3810^{-12} (−3.97)***	$2.24\ 10^{-10}$ (27.53)***	$4.98\ 10^{-10}$ (9.81)***	$-8.69\ 10^{-13}$ (−8.65)***	$3.43\ 10^{-12}$ (14.11)***	$1.19\ 10^{-11}$ (10.61)***	$2.72\ 10^{-12}$ (5.19)***	$2.85\ 10^{-11}$ (10.74)***
R^2	0.94	0.88	0.83	0.98	0.93	0.94	0.94	minus
DW	0.26	0.65	1.23	0.60	0.57	0.21	0.77	
TP	minus $5712	$5109 $8968	$3083 $7044	minus +∞	$10861 $56975	$12821 $14518	complex	$10132 $16301
CI[b] (Johens.)	Yes	Yes	Yes	Yes	Yes	Yes	No	Yes

[a]: Employment rate data is used instead of LFPR data, since LFPR giving complex number turning points.
[b]: Cointegration inspection is conducted through Johansen tests for the cubic form models.
[c]: t-statistics are in parentheses: Significant at 10% level; **Significant at 5% level; ***Significant at 1%.
[d]: β coefficients stand for estimated income (Y) terms from Eq. 2; no unstructural variables (Z in Eq. 2) are used.

The estimations in Table 1 seem compatible with the analysis above and it is possible to draw some commonalities from the estimations. First of all, except for France, the cubic form of the gender Kuznets Curve models gives significant one or more cointegration vectors through formal Johansen tests conducted for cubic form models. Although all the models estimate all variables significant in the level of 1%, Canada and US models do not give meaningful results. Estimations for other countries, except for Japan, show a few second phase stalls (all under $15000 level). With $10861 and $56975 turning points, the estimations for Japan give an exceptionally wide second phase which still continues (Table 1).

Conclusion

The Kuznets Curve and its environmental application in the EKC hypothesis propose strong changes in social and environmental effects of economic development through the development path. This kind of Kuznets Curve development can be summarized as (−, +) and (−, +, −) in terms of the political economy perspective. The minus sign here shows increasing pressure or negative effects connected to economic development represented by the rising part of the inverse-U and N form of Kuznets Curves. In contrast, we shows that the gender Kuznets Curve hypothesis, as suggested in some recent literature, deals with an S-form[6] curve which has (+, −, +)

---

6 In terms of the shape of the relationship, the suitability of using S-type relationship might be another discussion.

effects for society. Here the normal way of development is positive and supports women's development. Nonetheless, economic development might also support the institutions that have a negative effect on women's development up to a point in which this might cause a stall or even a reversal in the development route.

Another substantial difference of the GKC hypothesis is its moderate definition of negativity in the second phase. A curvilinear S-form second phase can be a stall, as appears in Figure 4a, b, or can be recession, as appears in Figure 4c, d. The proposition of temporary delay in the route of women's development contrasts with to the turns and the strong change in the effects of economic development of KC and EKC hypotheses. Inverse-U and N form curves suggest that the negative effects of economic development for society and environment support also the institutions which can reverse the course after some level of development; yet, S-form curvilinear curve underlines the second phase negativities in the course of women's development which can cause temporary stalls or recessions in the course of development.

The empirical analysis conducted in our study supports the implications of the GKC hypothesis as stated above. Raw data of labour force participation rates for women show delays and recessions of various shapes. Despite the lack of unique features, this result supports the general implications of the GKC hypothesis presented by Eastin and Prakash (2013). Econometric estimations show cointegration for cubic models. Although the country estimations do not meet in a common point, the cubic model estimations give significant coefficients and comparatively narrow second phase recessions.

Bibliography

Acemoglu, D., Robinson, J.A. (2002), *The political economy of the Kuznets curve*, 'Review of Development Economics', 6(2), 183–202.

Ahn, H.N., Gilbert, N. (1992), *Cultural diversity and sexual abuse prevention*, 'Social Science Review', 66(3), 410–427.

Alberta Teachers' Association (2008), *Going to school in Alberta*, Edmonton, Alberta.

Archives of the Jewish Historical Institute, Kraków Association 68, letter No 1085/09.

Arcidiacono, C. (2012), *Sono caduta dalle scale... I luoghi e gli attori della violenza di gender*, Franco Angeli Editore, Milano.

Bajrami, A. (2011), *Sistemi Kushtetues i Republikes së Kosovës*, Artini, Prishtinë.

Barberi, M. (2011), *La società dei Peter Pan*, 'Mente & Cervello', 73, 24–31.

Bartosz, A. (2004), *Nie bój się Cygana. Na dara Romestar*, Fundacja Pogranicze, Sejny.

Cała, A., Węgrzynek, H., Zalewska, G. (2000), *Historia i kultura Żydów polskich. Słownik*, WSiP, Warszawa.

Chomczyński, P. (2006), *Wybrane problemy etyczne w badaniach. Obserwacja uczestnicząca ukryta*, 'Przegląd Socjologii Jakościowej', 1, 68–87.

Chybicka, A., Kaźmierczak, M. (eds.) (2006), *Kobieta w kulturze – kultura w kobiecie. Studia interdyscyplinarne*, Impuls, Kraków.

Czerniawska, O. (2011), *Andragogiczny wymiar wydarzeń osobistych i globalnych w badaniach biograficznych*, Wyd. AHE, Łódź.

Daci, J. (2011), *Të Drejtat e Njeriut-Botimi i tretë*, Julvin 2, Tirana.

De Bruyn, S.M., Heintz, R.J. (1999), *The environmental Kuznets curve hypothesis* [in:] J.C.J.M. van den Bergh (ed.), *Handbook of environmental and resource economics*, Edward Elgar, Cheltenham.

Dubas, E. (2001), *Kobiecość jako wartość – zadanie edukacji (dorosłych)* [in:] E.A. Wesołowska, (ed.), *Kobiety a edukacja dorosłych*, Wyd. ITE–PIB, Warszawa.

Dubas, E. (2011a), *'Uczenie się z biografii Innych' – wprowadzenie* [in:] E. Dubas, W. Świtalski (eds.), *Biografia i badanie biografii*, vol. II: *Uczenie się z biografii Innych*, Wyd. UŁ, Łódź, 5–11.

Dubas, E. (2011b), *Życie zdeterminowane historią. Uczenie się z biografii Innego – na przykładzie relacji Renee Villancher 'Moje skradzione życie'* [in:] E. Dubas, W. Świtalski (eds.), *Biografia i badanie biografii*, vol. II: *Uczenie się z biografii Innych*, Wyd. UŁ, Łódź.

Dubas, E., Czerniawska, O. (eds.) (2002), *Drogi edukacyjne i ich biograficzny wymiar*, Wyd. ITE, Warszawa.

Dybiec, A. (2007), *Weekend będzie należał do Romów*, 'Gazeta Wyborcza'.

Dzierzgowska, A., Rutkowska, E. (2008), *Ślepa na płeć – edukacja równościowa po polsku*, Fundacja Feminoteka, Warszawa.

Eastin, J., Prakash, A. (2013), *Economic development and gender equality: Is there a gender Kuznets curve?*, 'World Politics', 65(1), 156–186.

Eisenbach, A. (1988), *Emancypacja Żydów na ziemiach polskich 1785–1870*, PIW, Warszawa.

Faith-based arbitration (n.d.), http://www.nawl.ca/en/issues/entry/faith-based-arbitration (Accessed: 10.07.2014).

Ficowski, J. (1985), *Cyganie na polskich drogach*, WL, Kraków–Wrocław.

Forsythe, N., Korzeniewicz, R.P., Durrant, V. (2000), *Gender inequalities and economic growth: a longitudinal evaluation*, 'Economic Development and Cultural Change', 48(3), 573–617.

Fournier, P. (2002–2003), *The ghettoisation of difference in Canada: 'Rape by Culture' and the danger of a 'Cultural Defence' in criminal law trials*, 'Manitoba Law Journal', 29, 1,1–39.

Freeze, Ch.Y. (2002), *Jewish marriage and divorce in Imperial Russia*, Brandeis University Press, Hannover–London.

Futterman, M. (2003), *Seeking a standard: Reconciling child abuse and condoned child rearing practices among different cultures*, 'The University of Miami Inter-American Law Review', 34, 3, 491–514.

Galeotti, G. (2006), *Storia del voto alle donne in Italia*, Biblink, Roma.

Giddens, A. (2001), *Nowoczesność i tożsamość. 'Ja' i społeczeństwo w epoce późnej nowoczesności*, WN PWN, Warszawa.

Godlewska-Goska, M., Kopańska, J. (2011), *Życie w dwóch światach. Tożsamość współczesnych Romów*, Wyd. DiG, Warszawa.

Gonzalez Silva, S.M. (2012), *Per non avere dei bamboccioni*, www.italspageconomi.org/Resource/IncontroEconomi18-02-2012.pdf (Accessed: 17.07.2014).

Graff, A. (2001), *Świat bez kobiet. Płeć w polskim życiu publicznym*, W.A.B., Warszawa.

Graziani, C.A., Corti, I. (1996), *I diritti delle donne*, Giuffrè Editore, Milano.

Gromkowska-Melosik, A. (2011), *Edukacja i (nie)równość społeczna kobiet. Studium dynamiki dostępu*, Impuls, Kraków.

Grossman, G.M., Krueger, A.B. (1991), *Environmental impacts of the North American Free Trade Agreement*, NBER Working Papers, 3914.

Grossman, G.M., Krueger, A.B. (1993), *Environmental impacts of a North American Free Trade Agreement* [in:] P. Garber (ed.), *The U.S.–Mexico Free Trade Agreement*, MIT Press, Cambridge, MA.

Gruda, Z. (2010), *Mbrojtja Ndërkombëtare e të Drejtave të Njeriut, Botimi i pestë*, Furkam, Prishtina.

GUS (Central Statistical Office of Poland) (2012), Wyniki Narodowego Spisu Powszechnego Ludności i Mieszkań 2011. Podstawowe informacje o sytuacji demograficzno-społecznej ludności Polski oraz zasobach mieszkaniowych (*The results of National General Census in 2011. Basic information on the demographic and social situation of Polish population and house resources*), www.stat.gov.pl/cps/rde/xbcr/gus/lu_nps2011_wyniki_nsp2011_22032012.pdf (Accessed: 17.09.2013).

Hansson, E., Tuck, A., Lurie, S., McKenzie, K. (2009), *Improving mental health services for immigrant, refugee, ethno-cultural and racialized groups: Issues and options for service improvement*, The Task Group of the Services Systems Advisory Committee, Mental Health Commission of Canada, http://www.mentalhealthcommission.ca/SiteCollectionDocuments/Key_Documents/en/2010/Issues_Options_FINAL_English%2012Nov09.pdf (Accessed: 14.07.2014).

Henley, P. (2012), *Economic success makes Poland destination for immigrants*, BBC News Europe, http://www.bbc.co.uk/news/20714006 (Accessed: 14.07.2014).

http://biblia.deon.pl/rozdzial.php?id=2 (Accessed: 30.05.2014).

http://halakhah.com/pdf/moed/Rosh_HaShanah.pdf (Accessed: 30.05.2014).

http://halakhah.com/pdf/nashim/Yevamoth.pdf (Accessed: 30.05.2014).

http://halakhah.com/pdf/nezikin/Baba_Bathra.pdf (Accessed: 30.05.2014).

http://halakhah.com/pdf/zeraim/Berachoth.pdf (Accessed: 30.05.2014).

http://journals.sfu.ca/humanitas/index.php/humanities/article/view/17 (Accessed: 14.07.2014) .

http://hdr.undp.org/en/statistics/hdi (Accessed: 23.07.2014).

http://nawl.ca/en/issues/entry/faith-based-arbitration (Accessed: 14.07.2014).

http://o.canada.com/news/canadas-pediatricians-set-to-reveal-new-policy-on-circumcision (Accessed: 14.07.2014).

http://pl.globalvoicesonline.org/2014/03/unia-europejska-publikuje-obszerny-sondaz-dotyczacy-przemocy-wobec-kobiet (Accessed: 14.07.2014).

http://scholarship.law.duke.edu/lcp/vol73/iss2/10 (Accessed: 14.07.2014).

http://www.behavioradvisor.com/C-ChildAbuse.html (Accessed: 14.07.2014).

http://www.cbc.ca/news/health/selective-abortions-prompt-call-for-ultrasound-rules-1.128 2586 (Accessed: 14.07.2014).

http://www.cmaj.ca/content/184/4/387.full.pdf+html (Accessed: 14.07.2014).

http://www.cwhn.ca/sites/default/files//network-vol4no2EN.pdf (Accessed: 14.07.2014).

http://www.cygańskawyspa.pl/cms/aktualności/romsko-kobieta (Accessed:17.09.2013).

http://www.ilfattoquotidiano.it/2012/10/19/femminicidio-cento-vittime-nel-2012-donna-uccisa-ogni-due-giorni/ (07.12.2013).

http://intervistemadyur.blogspot.com/2009/08/intervista-con-lara-cardella-ventanni.html (Accessed: 14.12.2013).

http://www.jewfaq.org/women.htm#Mitzvot (Accessed: 30.05.2014).

http://www.jewishvirtuallibrary.org/jsource/Judaism/woman_commandments.html (Accessed: 30.05.2014).

http://www.jstor.org/stable/40176547 (Accessed: 14.07.2014).

http://www.juconicomparte.org/recursos/Cultural_Diversity_and_Sexual_Abuse_Prevention_uuh9.pdf (Accessed: 14.07.2014).

http://www.lawtimesnews.com/200509191106/headline-news/no-more-faith-based-arbitration (Accessed: 14.07.2014).

http://www.polonia.cc (Accessed: 14.07.2014).

http://www.romowie.com/index.php?newlang=polish (Accessed:17.09. 2013).

http://www.scripture4all.org/OnlineInterlinear/OTpdf/gen2.pdf (Accessed: 30.05.2014).

http://www.teachers.ab.ca/SiteCollectionDocuments/ATA/Publications/Albertas-Education-System/Going%20to%20School%20in%20Alberta.pdf (Accessed: 14.07.2014).

http://www.unaqualunque.it/a/2737/il-gioco-del-potere-delitto-d%27onore.aspx (Accessed: 13.12.2013).

http://www.unic.un.org.pl/kobiety_rozwoj_pokoj/konferencja.php (Accessed: 20.06.2014).

Ibourk, A., Amaghouss, J. (2012), *Measuring education inequalities: Concentration and dispersion-based approach*, 'World Journal of Education', 6(2), 51–65.

Immigration and ethnocultural diversity in Canada (2013), http://www12.statcan.gc.ca/nhs-enm/2011/as-sa/99-010-x/99-010-x2011001-eng.pdf (Accessed: 10.07.2014).

International perspective (2013), http://www.statcan.gc.ca/daily-quotidien/140107/dq14010-7b-eng.htm (Accessed: 10.07.2014).

Interviste madyur, http://intervistemadyur.blogspot.com/2009/08/intervista-con-lara-cardella-ventanni.html (Accessed: 14.12.2013).

Isztok, M. (2006), *Kobiety Romów*, www.jednota.pl/index2.php?option=com_content &do_pdf=1&id=483 (Accessed: 17.09.2013).

Ivchenko, J. (2007), *Historical analysis of the role of women in society*, 'Business, Finance, Law' 4, 25–28.

Jakimik, E.A., Gierliński, K.P. (2009), *Kobieta w środowisku romskim*, Związek Romów Polskich, Szczecinek.

Kale, R. (2012), *'It's a girl!' – could be a death sentence*, 'Canadian Medical Association Journal', 184, 4, 387–388.

Kameraz-Kos, N. (1997), *Święta i obyczaje żydowskie*, Cyklady, ŻIH, Warszawa.

Kapuściński, R. (2006), *Ten Inny*, Znak, Kraków.

Kiley, D. (2007), *Syndrom Piotrusia Pana. O mężczyznach, którzy nigdy nie dorastają*, Jacek Santorski & Co, Warszawa.

Kılınç, D., Yetkiner, H. (2013), *Does gender matter for economic convergence? The OECD evidence*, 'Working Paper', 2, Izmir University of Economics, Izmir.

Kirkey, S. (2013), *Canada's pediatricians set to reveal new policy on circumcision*, www.o.canada.com (Accessed: 14.07.2014).

[Kis O.] Кісь О., (2000), *Гендерні студії в Україні: стан, проблеми, перспективи*, Незалежний культурологічний часопис «Ї», http://www.ji-magazine.lviv.ua/seminary/2000/sem17-08.htm (Accessed: 14.07.2014).

Kosovo Agency of Statistics (2013), *Gratë dhe Burrat në Kosovë*, Kosovo Agency of Statistics, Prishtina, HP/Downloads/Grate%20dhe%20Burrat%20-%20Women%20and%20Man%202011%20(2).pdf (Accessed: 01.11. 2013).

Kristof, N.D., WuDunn, S. (2009), *Half the sky: Turning oppression into opportunity for women worldwide*, Alfred A. Knopf, New York.

Kuklińska, K.L. (2012), *Polskie singielki*, Dyfin, Warszawa.

Kulachek, A.I. (2001), *Issues of gender equality in nation-building: Ukraine and world experience / development of democracy in Ukraine*, Mat. Intern. Science. conf. – K., 29.

Kushtetuta e RepublikËs sË KosovËs (2008), http://www.mkrs-ks.org/repository/docs/Kushtetuta.e.Republikes.se.Kosoves.pdf (Accessed: 15.07. 2013).

Kuznets, S. (1955), *Economic growth and income inequality*, 'American Economic Review', 45(1), 1–28.

Law on Gender Equality (2004), http://www.kuvendikosoves.org/common/docs/ligjet/2004_2_al.pdf (Accessed: 12.07. 2013).

L'Italia: un Paese di Donne Infelici – Ecco la Ricerca, Il Corpo delle Donne (2012), http://www.ilcorpodelledonne.net/2012/11/litalia-un-paese-di-donne-infelici-ecco-la-ricerca (Accessed: 14.07.2014).

Legal experts recommend Canada legalize polygamy (2006), 'Vancouver Sun', http://www.canada.com/vancouversun/news/story.html?id=e20244cb-63b2-47f9-893e-390 453fa5067 (Accessed: 14.07.2014).

Lerner, G. (2008), *Vendosja e Grave në Histori*, 'Koha Ditore', 3, http://www.womensnetwork. org/documents/20130510160712665.pdf (Accessed: 07.09. 2013).

Lidia Poët (n.d.), http://www.fidapa.com/index.php?option=com_content&view=article& id=387:lidia-poet&catid=904:distretto-nord-ovest&Itemid=46 (Accessed: 13.12.2013).

Ludgate, S. (2009), *The compromise of Canadian Multiculturalism Policy: Group rights versus women's rights*, 'Journal of the Institute for the Humanities', 4.

Maciarz, A. (2004), *Macierzyństwo w kontekście zmian społecznych*, 'Żak', Warszawa.

Majewska-Kafarowska, A. (2010), *Narracje biograficzne a poczucie tożsamości kobiet*, Wyd. UŚ, Katowice.

Mazurek, E. (2013), *Biografie edukacyjne kobiet dotkniętych rakiem piersi*, OW PWr, Wrocław.

Mazzini, G. (2002), *Doveri dell'uomo*, Rizzoli Libri, Milano.

McIntyre, T., Silva, P. (1992), *Culturally different childrearing practices: Abusive or just different?*, 'Beyond Behavior', 4, 1, 8–12.

McMahon, K. (2005), *No more faith-based arbitration*, http://www.lawtimesnews.com/ 200509191106/headline-news/no-more-faith-based-arbitration (Accessed: 15.07.2014).

Mirga, A., Mróz, L. (1994), *Cyganie. Odmienność i nietolerancja*, WN PWN, Warszawa.

'National Post' (2011), *B.C. Supreme Court rules polygamy ban is constitutional, but flawed*, http://news.nationalpost.com/2011/11/23/b-c-supreme-court-rules-polygamy-law-is-consti-tutional (Accessed: 14.07.2014).

'National Post' (2012), *Internal dissent: Are some fetuses more equal than others?*, http://full-comment.nationalpost.com/2012/01/17/internal-dissent-are-some-fetuses-more-equal-than-others (Accessed: 14.07.2014).

Okin, S.M. (1999), *Is multiculturalism bad for women?*, Princeton University Press, Princeton N.J.

Pająk-Ważna E., Ocetkiewicz I. (2014), *Teachers and gender – a case of Poland* [in:] K.G. Karras, P. Calogiannakis, C.C. Wolhuter, N. Andreadakis (eds.), *Gender and Teachers. An International Study.*, Studies & Publishing, Cyprus.

Palla, M. (2006), *Mussolini e il fascismo*, Giunti Editore, Firenze.

Panayotou, T. (1993), *Empirical test and policy analysis of environmental degradation at different stages of economic development*, 'Working Paper', *P238*, Technology and Employment Programme, International Labour Office, Geneva.

Parca, G. (1973), *Le italiane si confessano*, Feltrinelli, Milano.

[Pasova T.] Пасова, Т. (2009), *Гендер – це свобода*, http://www.viche.info/journal/1351 (Accessed: 17.07.2014).

Renteln, A.D. (2005), *The use and abuse of the cultural defense*, 'Canadian Journal of Law and Society', 20, 1, 47–67, https://muse.jhu.edu/journals/canadian_journal_of_law_and_ society/v020/20.1renteln.html (Accessed: 14.07.2014).

Renteln, A.D. (2010), *Corporal punishment and the cultural defense*, 'Law and Contemporary Problems', 73, 2, 253–279.

Renzetti, C.M., Curran D.J. (2005), *Kobiety, mężczyźni i społeczeństwo*, WN PWN, Warszawa.

[Reznik G.O.] Резнік, Г.О. (2001), *Становище жінки в Українському суспільстві*, „Право", №8., С. 16–19.

Quarterly demographic estimates April to June 2013 (2013), http://www.statcan.gc.ca/ pub/91-002-x/91-002-x2013002-eng.pdf (Accessed: 10.07.2014).

Romanowski, P. (n.d.), *A short history of Polish-Canadians in Alberta*, Polish Heritage in Canada, Toronto, http://www.polishheritage.ca/page.aspx?page_id=89 (Accessed: 14.07.2014).

Selective abortions prompt call for ultrasound rules (2012), http://www.cbc.ca/news/health/selective-abortions-prompt-call-for-ultrasound-rules-1.1282586 (Accessed: 10.07.2014).

Scheppers, E., Dongen, E. van, Dekker, J, Geertzen, J., Deeker, J. (2006), *Potential barriers to the use of health services among ethnic minorities: A review*, 'Family Practice', 23, 3, 325–348, http://fampra.oxfordjournals.org/content/23/3/325.full (Accessed: 17.07.2014).

Semków, J. (1984), *Wiodące treści w programie andragogiki*, 'Oświata Dorosłych', 2, 65–69.

Shafik, N., Bandyopadhyay, S. (1992), *Economic growth and environmental quality: Time series and cross-country evidence*, 'Background Paper for the World Development Report', World Bank, Washington, DC.

Shaw, M. (2003), *International law*, Cambridge University Press, Cambridge.

Skibińska, E.M. (2006), *Mikroświaty kobiet, Relacje autobiograficzne*, Wyd. ITE–PIB, Warszawa.

Skuza, S. (2010), *Kobieta. Matka, córka, panna, żona, teściowa, synowa i wdowa w przysłowiach polskich i włoskich*, Poligraf, Brzezia Łąka.

Soroka, S., Roberton, S. (2010), *A literature review of public opinion research on Canadian attitudes towards multiculturalism and immigration, 2006–2009*, Government of Canada, Department of Citizenship and Immigration, Ottawa, http://www.cic.gc.ca/english/pdf/research-stats/2012-por-multi-imm-eng.pdf (Accessed: 17.07.2014).

Spinelli, B. (2008), *Femminicidio. Dalla denuncia sociale al riconoscimento giuridico internazionale*, Franco Angeli Editore, Milano.

State Archive in Kraków, Kr 7942, The Statute of Jewish Community of Kraków, approved with the rescript of High k.k. Governorship in Lviv on November 8, 1897 and 62931 on April 25, 1900 l. 5155, under the imprint of the Jewish Community – Print by Joseph Plessner and Co. in Podgórze, 1907 (APwK, Kr 7942, Statut gminy wyznaniowej izraelickiej w Krakowie, zatwierdzony reskryptem Wys. c.k. Namiestnictwa w Lwowie z dnia 8 listopada 1897 l. 62931 i z dnia 25 kwietnia 1900 l. 5155, nakładem Gminy wyzn. izr. – Drukiem Józefa Plessnera i Ski w Podgórzu, 1907 r.).

State Archive in Kraków, Kr 7942, The Statute of Jewish Community of Podgórze, approved with the rescript of High k.k. Governorship on January 19, 1898 l. 4758 (APwK, Kr 7942, Statut izraelickiej gminy wyznaniowej w Podgórzu, zatwierdzony reskryptem Wys. c.k. Namiestnictwa z dnia 19 Stycznia 1898 l. 4758).

State Archive in Kraków, Kr 7942, The Statute of the Kraków Association of Women for the support of Jewish widows (APwK, Kr 7942, Statut Krakowskiego Stowarzyszenia Kobiet dla Wsparcia Wdów Wyznania Izraelickiego).

Statistics Canada (2013a), Immigration and ethnocultural diversity in Canada, http://www.statcan.gc.ca/pub/11-402-x/2012000/chap/imm/imm03-eng.htm (Accessed: 14.07.2014).

Statistics Canada (2013b), International perspective, http://www.statcan.gc.ca/pub/91-002-x/91-002-x2013002-eng.pdf (Accessed: 14.07.2014).

Statistics Canada (2013c), Quaterly demographic estimates April to June 2013, http://www12.statcan.gc.ca/nhs-enm/2011/as-sa/99-010-x/99-010-x2011001-eng.pdf (Accessed: 14.07.2014).

Sulik, M. (2011), *Lekcja odwagi w kontekście sytuacji granicznych, czyli uczenie się z biografii Innego na podstawie wspomnień Janiny Bauman zawartych w opowieści pt. 'Zima o poranku'* [in:] E. Dubas, W. Świtalski (eds.), *Biografia i badanie biografii*, vol. 2: *Uczenie się z biografii Innych*, Wyd. UŁ, Łódź.

Szacka, B. (2011), *Gender i płeć* [in:] K. Slany, J. Struzik, K. Wojnicka (eds.), *Gender w spo-łeczeństwie polskim*, Nomos, Kraków.

Szarota, Z., Łaszyn, J. (2013), *Lustro społeczne czy krzywe zwierciadło? Autorecepcja dojrzałych kobiet* [in:] S. Rogala (ed.), *Kobieta i czas*, WSZIA, Opole.

'Szematyzm Królestwa Galicyi i Lodomeryi z Wielkim Księstwem Krakowskiem na rok 1873'.

'Szematyzm Królestwa Galicyi i Lodomeryi z Wielkim Księstwem Krakowskiem na rok 1875'.

'Szematyzm Królestwa Galicyi i Lodomeryi z Wielkim Księstwem Krakowskiem na rok 1879'.

'Szematyzm Królestwa Galicyi i Lodomeryi z Wielkim Księstwem Krakowskiem na rok 1892'.

'Szematyzm Królestwa Galicyi i Lodomeryi z Wielkim Księstwem Krakowskiem na rok 1897'.

'Szematyzm Królestwa Galicyi i Lodomeryi z Wielkim Księstwem Krakowskiem na rok 1898'.

'Szematyzm Królestwa Galicyi i Lodomeryi z Wielkim Księstwem Krakowskiem na rok 1899'.

'Szematyzm Królestwa Galicyi i Lodomeryi z Wielkim Księstwem Krakowskiem na rok 1900'.

Szmidt K.J. (2002), *Mądrość jako cel kształcenia. Stary problem w świetle nowych teorii*, 'Teraźniejszość – Człowiek – Edukacja', 3(19), 47–64.

The anti-discrimination law, 'Official Gazette of the Republic of Kosovo' (2004), http://www.gazetazyrtare.com/e-gov/index.php?option=com_content&task=view&id=77&Itemid=28 (Accessed: 02.08. 2013).

The Kosova Women's Network (2011), *135 Facts & Fables*, http://www.womensnetwork.org/documents/20130120165559661.pdf (Accessed: 15.11. 2013).

Tinker, I. (1976), *The adverse impact of development on women* [in:] I. Tinker, M.B. Bramsen (eds.), *Women and world development*, Overseas Development Council, Washington D.C.

Tinker, I., Bramsen M.B. (1976), *Women and world development*, Overseas Development Council, Washington, D.C.

Tisdell, C. (2001), *Globalization and sustainability: Environmental Kuznets curve and the WTO*, 'Ecological Economics', 39, 185–196.

Titkow, A., Duch-Krzysztoszek, D., Budrowska, B. (2004), *Nieodpłatna praca kobiet. Mity, realia, perspektywy*, Wyd. IFIS PAN, Warszawa.

[Tsokur O.] Цокур, О., [Ivanova I.] Iванова I. (2014), *Гендерна педагогіка – нова освітня технологія*, http://osvita.ua/school/method/upbring/1657 (Accessed: 15.07.2014).

Tyloch, W. (1987), *Judaizm*, KAW, Warszawa.

Ukrayina. Five years after Beijing (2001), Report on Ukraine to the provisions of the Beijing Declaration and Platform for Action approved by the Fourth World Conference on Women (1995–2000), 'Logos'.

Untermann, A. (2002), *Żydzi. Wiara i życie*, KiW, Warszawa.

Violence against women: An EU-wide survey. Results at a glance (2014), Publications Office of the European Union, Luxembourg, http://fra.europa.eu/sites/default/files/fra-2014-vaw-survey-at-a-glance_en_0.pdf (Accessed: 15.06.2014).

Vissandjee, B. (2001), *The consequences of cultural diversity*, 'Canadian Women's Health Network', 4, 2, 3–4.

Vissandjee, B., Kantiebo, M., Levine, A., N'Dejuru, R. (2003), *The cultural context of gender identity: Female genital excision and infibulations*, 'Health Care for Women Internatio-nal', 24, 2, 115–124, http://www.ncbi.nlm.nih.gov/pubmed/12746021 (Accessed: 17.07. 2014).

Wesołowska, E.A. (2002), *Drogi edukacyjne pięciu pokoleń – na przykładzie jednej rodziny w Polsce* [in:] E. Dubas, O. Czerniawska (eds.), *Drogi edukacyjne i ich biograficzny wy-miar*, Wyd. ITE, Warszawa.

Witkowska-Paleń, A., Maciaszek, J. (2010), *Kobieta we współczesnym społeczeństwie*, Drukarnia Diecezjalna w Sandomierzu, Stalowa Wola.

Wnuk-Olenicz, M. (2012), *Drogi edukacyjne słuchaczy Uniwersytetu Trzeciego Wieku*, Wrocław (unpublished doctoral thesis).

Wronko, A. (2013), *Status kobiety romskiej wczoraj i dziś*, www.romologia.net/romologica-net/ma-gazyn/2013-05/201305-art-status-kobiety-romskiej-html (Accessed: 17.09. 2013).

Zasada, M. (2013), *Drogi edukacyjne kobiet pochodzących ze środowisk wiejskich – konteksty społeczne i kulturowe*, Katowice (unpublished doctoral thesis).

Żbikowski, A. (1994), *Żydzi krakowscy i ich gmina w latach 1869–1919*, Żydowski Instytut Historyczny w Polsce, Instytut Naukowo-Badawczy, Warszawa.

Zbroja, B. (2004), *Gmina wyznaniowa w Podgórzu 1891–1939*, 'Rocznik Krakowski', 70, 58.

2
Women in public and domestic spheres

Katarzyna Dormus
Pedagogical University of Cracow, Poland

Towards full participation in public life – generational changes in the lives of Polish women

Since the end of the 18th century, Europe has been witnessing events and processes connected with the development of modern society characterized by: industrial development, urbanization, democratization and mass culture. One of the new phenomena reflected in this trend was emancipation of women. Women started to enter the public domain, to come out of the shadows of home life. This phenomenon was a result of changes in social and political conditions and growing self-awareness of women[1]. It was said that the 19th century 'discovered women' and the 'women issue' was considered a problem of vital social significance (Kizwalter 1990, pp. 1–9).

However, this was a long and tedious process. According to the French historian Michelle Perrot:

> Activity in the public space cannot be easy and obvious for women as they are destined to privacy – showing off or speaking too loud encounters criticism. However, women still engage in such activity in various ways, [...] They often refer to their traditional roles and then everything is fine – for example, when they participate in hunger riots or devote themselves to charity. Things get complicated when they try to assume male roles. The boundaries of politics seem most difficult to cross [...]. For a long time, politics has remained an unconquered area (Perrot 2009, p. 182).

Entering and functioning in the public domain was possible thanks to the efforts of three generation of Polish women living between the January Uprising and the World War II.

---

[1] Of course, women took part in public life before, but it was occassional and regarded individuals, notable persons, usually coming from the highest social strata.

The first one was the generation called the 'rebellious generation', 'fighter's gen-eration' or even 'heroic generation'[2] (Wapiński 1991, passim; Cywiński 1985, passim; Hulewicz 1939, p. 224), born in the 1860s, in the times of the January Uprising, its suppression and aftermath. Those event were part of general life experience of the mothers of the 'rebellious ones'. Political repressions and property seizure pushed many women from the landed gentry out of their existing lifestyle and forced them to struggle for life, often in a new urban environment. Lives of those women were marked by the tragedy of being unfit for such life, resulting mainly from lack of education and professional qualifications. Their daughters, i.e. the 'rebellious ones' learned from their mothers' fate and responded to the notion of women emancipa-tion proposed by positivists. (Hulewicz 1939, pp. 224–225).

For women, education became the starting point and the fundamental issue as this postulate 'encompasses everything: emancipation, promotion opportunities, work, creativity, satisfaction and requires a huge effort [...]' (Perrot 2009, p. 201).

The struggle for education focused on getting access to university studies. It carried on at general European level. Women were driven by two motives: hun-ger for knowledge (ideological motive) and desire to gain financial independence (material motive). It was most evident in Russia and in Poland, where women, unable to study in their home countries, headed for Western universities – mainly in Switzerland (Hulewicz 1939, pp. 195, 208). Initially, there were only a few Polish women coming to universities. The first Polish female student, Anna Tomaszewicz--Dobrska[3], appeared in Zurich as early as in 1870. 'After that, there is a huge time gap that proves how revolutionary those women were' – says Jan Hulewicz (Hu-lewicz 1939, p. 201).

The problems encountered by first female students included the need to break social and material stereotypes in their closest environment, because

> [...] even the wealthy families hesitate before sending their daughters to Switzerland or France as they do not want to bear costs of female emancipation whims (Cywiński 1985, p. 47).

Women also had to overcome the language barrier, make up for their educa-tion gaps and eventually, obtain financial resources for further studies. However, in the half of the 1880s, studies at foreign universities became very popular among Polish female students.

Students of such first generation were courageous, determined, pride and ambitious. They had to overcome various obstacles in life usually on their own. They studied for a long time as they often had to take breaks to make money.

2 The term 'rebellious ones' was used by Roman Wapiński and Bohdan Cywiński – they both refer to both women and men. The term 'female fighters' and 'heroic generation' was used by Jan Hulewicz.
3 After the studies, she returned to Poland and was the first practicing physician in Warsaw.

After completing their studies and returning to their home country, they worked as teachers, doctors, writers and editors, they engaged in social and educational activity (Hulewicz 1939, pp. 203–208).

After 'conquering' Western universities, another step was the struggle for access to domestic universities. Galicia was the battle arena with universities in Cracow and Lviv. In 1878, the Austrian Ministry of Religious Affairs and Public Education issued a regulation permitting women to be admitted to universities as guests as an exception. It opened a very narrow door to higher education for women and for a very long time, except single case of Ludmiła Kummersberg, did not encourage women to try to get to universities in Galicia (Hulewicz 1939, pp. 258–260; Perkowska 1994, pp. 11–12).

It was not until the Spring of 1894 when, on the initiative of Kazimiera Bujwid[4], wife of a renowned bacteriologist – professor Odon Bujwid, 54 applications from women asking for admission to studies were filed at the office of the Jagiellonian University. Only three of them were admitted, all of them being pharmacists (as they were considered duly prepared for studies): Stanisława Dowgiałło, Janina Kosmowska and Jadwiga Sikorska. However, since then, women's pressure on the authorities of the university had been growing constantly. Soon, a Faculty of Philosophy (1897) and Faculty of Medicine were opened for them. The Faculty of Law, due to the disapproval of both the Ministry of Religious Affairs and Public Education and university professors, remained unavailable for women, together with theology, veterinary sciences and fine arts (Hulewicz 1939, 260–265; Perkowska 1994, pp. 13, 15, 18–20).

Women entered the public domain not only through education, but also through patriotic and social activity. They gained their initial experience in charity work, which at that time began to lose its social gloss and became positivist 'grassroots work' (Mazur 2008, p. 380, 385). Participation of women in underground education and public education organizations was of vital importance. Their activities in those areas enabled them to gain organizational skills and experience in managing public activities. Engagement in work of patriotic nature also increased the social prestige of women (Żarnowska 2013, pp. 214–216).

Women cooperated with men in such organizations, however, over time, purely female structures, such as professional associations or self-help organizations, began to emerge. The growing ability of women to self-organize was their characteristic quality. Since 1891, every few years, women from all three partitions met during gatherings for women, initially underground and later openly. The biggest of such meetings took place in Cracow in Autumn 1905. It should be emphasized that such meetings had a nature of women's gatherings and not a female movement – it was all about gathering in one place as many Polish women as possible from all

---

4 Bujwid was also a member of the 'rebellious' generation: she was born in Warsaw in 1867.

partitions, social strata, presenting various interests and fields of activity (Sikorska-
-Kulesza 2008, pp. 81–96).

Female movements began to form slowly as well. In 1907, the Union for Polish
Women's Equality was established in Warsaw. It could be considered the first Polish
feminist organization. Its goal was to struggle for women's equality in political and
professional life and to gain full civil rights for women. This organization stemmed
from the common experience of the women's movement in the Russian and Austrian partition (Żarnowska 2013, p. 212). Female organizations also focused around
the editors of women's magazines: 'Nowe Słowo' in Cracow (1902–1907) and 'Ster'
in Warsaw (1907–1914).

Women were prohibited to establish political organizations in all parts of par-
titioned Poland. There were also very few women involved in political formations,
usually in the left wing. The only women that could be considered as a regular
politician was Róża Luksemburg.

Women did not have voting rights in any of the partitions (except some parts
of Galicia). However, they started to struggle for their election rights after 1905,
asking political parties to include the postulate of women's equality in their political programs. In Galicia, women tried to put direct pressure on the authorities by organizing manifestations, meetings, petitions or local election committees. In 1908 in Lviv, they even proposed their candidate for parliament – Maria
Dulębianka – a painter and close friend of Maria Konopnicka. Women's activities
in the area of voting rights did not meet the support of Polish politicians, besides,
they were limited to the upper social class of women only and were still in their
infancy (Żarnowska 2013, pp. 206–211).

The end of the 1880s and the beginning of the 1890s was the time when the
generation of the 'fighters' daughters' was born. Form many of them, the most
important experience in their lives was the 1905 revolution and participation in
school strikes and then World War I, which forced many women, especially in the
economic area, to assume male roles. The representatives of that generation saw
the dawn of the independent Poland in their prime age and influenced the shape
of the country. They drew from their mother's achievements. For example, they
used the education opportunities provided for them by their mothers to pursue
careers in science. The first female assistant professor (in histology) in Poland was
Helena Gajewska, who obtained her degree in 1920 at the Jagiellonian University
(Perkowska 1994, p. 178).

Female members of parliament and senate of the Second Polish Republic were
recruited mainly from the said generation. Irena Kosmowska became the deputy
minister of social care in the Lublin Government in November 1918. This is the only
case of a female member of the parliament in the history of the mid-war Poland.

Most of Polish women at that time did not see themselves as political activists. In the period of the Second Polish Republic, they occupied less than 2% of
seats in the parliament and 4% of seats in the senate. There were no women in the

governing bodies of political parties or chains of command, there were no female ministers or province governors. And although they established their own political associations, there were no female political parties. As far as the public activity is concerned, women focused on traditional areas, such as education, self-help and charity (Chojnowski 2000, pp. 40–41).

The experience of partitions left a scar in the mentality of both of the above mentioned generations. For them, public activities were always connected with the issue of independence and gaining the electoral rights in 1918 was considered a reward for their patriotic activity. The female movement in the territory of Poland in the late 19th and early 20th century and in the mid-war period was elitist. It was rooted in the world of noble intelligentsia. It defined its nature and limited the group of women ready for active participation in political life (Żarnowska 2000, p. 291; Żarnowska 2013, pp. 216–217).

The 'Generation of the Second Polish Republic' consisted of women who entered their adult age in a free country, where most of formal and legal obstacles for equality disappeared. Democratization of political life, easier access to education and professional career, as well as changing morality were favorable for women. Legalization of activities contributed to their spread and the range of forms of activity was much broader. Women could participate in the activities of their male peers (Wapiński 2000, p. 30–31, 36). During the period of the Sanation movement, female activists were even involved in paramilitary associations and actions for extending mandatory military service to women (Sierakowska 2009, pp. 42–43).

That generation was characterized by the increase of educational aspirations. The act on academic schools of 1920 granted equal rights to both men and women, although the reality was often different. Women wanted to study because a university diploma was a sign of prestige, enabled them to get better job and independence in private life. And although in 1887, 122 women commenced studies at the Jagiellonian University (9% of all students), in 1938, there were 1896 of them, making up 31% of all of the students (Perkowska 1994, pp. 22–23; Chojnowski 2000, pp. 40–41).

Acceptance for professional work of women was more and more common, although the choice of fields of professional work remained traditional – women usually worked as teachers. The increase of women's participation in public life resulted from taking up work in state and self-governmental institutions. The profession of a secretary and a clerk appeared. However, access to such jobs was not equal for women and some professions remained unavailable for them, for example criminal law. The 'pyramid' phenomenon was also common: the more prestigious the job, the less women doing it, the higher the position, the less women occupying it (Wapiński 2000, pp. 27–30, 32).

By the decree on the voting system dated 28 November 1918, women gained the right to vote. For young women, the active voting right was the opportunity to increase their engagement in public life. Anyone over 21 could vote. Women became the electorate that was worth soliciting. However, they failed to make the most of it, for example by putting pressure on political parties to formulate electoral programs attractive for women. Despite high voter turnout (higher than in many Western countries), women did not support other women – candidates for members of the parliament and the senate (Śliwa 2000, s. 49–51; Sierakowska 2009, p. 47).

Women were still feeling insecure in the area of politics. They did not establish any specific structures or develop a unique female plan of action. They had the tendency to 'stay in the shadow'. Similarly, the female movement remained conservative without any revolutionary ideas, fostering the so called 'traditional costume' (Sierakowska 2009, p. 46).

The Second Polish Republic brought changes leading to equalization of women's rights and constitutional standards set the direction of such changes. Amendments to earlier acts and new laws established after 1918 respected the gender equality principle.

> Formal equalization of women's rights was a necessary step in actual equalization of such rights – writes Michał Pietrzak – however, the exercise of their rights depended on many factors, first of all on overcoming stereotypes and mental barriers at both individual and society level. It required [...] educating the society. And it required much more time than twenty years of the mid-war period (Pietrzak 2000, pp. 90-91).

One could wonder if much has changed from the period between the World War II (another dramatic event that shattered our reality and women's awareness) to this day in the way women are active in public life. As far as education is concerned, there is undoubtedly an constant process of increase of educational aspirations going on. There are more and more female students and many fields of study are feminized. Barriers in professional careers are disappearing, although the problems of the 'pyramid' or pay-related discrimination still persist. The issue of unemployment appearing on the large scale after the transformation affects women in an especially painful way.

The parliamentary and political domain is similar to that of the Second Polish Republic. Although the number of women engaged in politics is on the rise, it is still not that much. Many women, despite their excellent education, usually occupy less prestigious positions in traditional areas of women's activity, such as social care, education and health (*Kobiety dla Polski* 2009, passim).

Polish women still have problems with creating a successful political organization. They have no good ideas or much influence in this area. The only female political party – *Women's Party* (Partia Kobiet), founded in 2007, is on the margin of political life. The Parliamentary Woman's Group representing the interests of the female lobby is not very effective or dynamic. The most active and most recognized organization is *Polish Women's Congress* (Kongres Kobiet Polskich), a social movement gathering women (not a female movement), whose activities focus on organization of congresses, directly referring to the tradition of women's gatherings of the late 19th and early 20th century. The activities of the above mentioned organizations is characterized by avoiding any relations with specific political parties, which is the preferred political approach among women. All of the above mentioned activities remain elite and are aimed at women from the middle class (Chołuj 2009, p. 432).

Prudence, conservativeness, limitation to traditional areas of activity, tendency to avoid political affiliations, reluctance to enter into open conflicts and elitism – all of them are characteristic features of the activities of Polish women in public life, especially in the area of civil and political life since their very beginning.

Dominika Urszula Popielec
Maria Curie-Sklodowska University, Lublin, Poland

A contingent of women in the Bilderberg Group

Introduction

The subject I would like to analyze is the participation of women in public life exemplified as the Bilderberg Group. Many of them, like Margaret Thatcher, Hillary Clinton, Condoleezza Rice or Melinda Gates, are very well-known in the world. On the one hand, one may think that Hillary Clinton and Melinda Gates would not have been known if not for famous husbands. But on the other hand, women like Margaret Thatcher and Hanna Suchocka marked their presence in the public sphere because of their the skills, experience, and an exceptional personality.

In this paper, I would like to present some hypothesis. First of all, the Bilderberg Group is an international forum which collects more influential women than earlier years (or earlier groups). Secondly, the Directing Committee as a part of the Bilderberg Group appreciates the potential of individual women and invites them to actively participation in the annual conferences. Thirdly, the contribution of these women is resulted from the fact that they occupy more governmental functions like prime minister, the high position in business and media often become CEO and major editor or journalist. I would also underline that women, who participated in the Bilderberg Group's conferences, have become more influential than ever before, and therefore in my opinion the Bilderberg Group helped to increase their impact in the public life.

The Bilderberg Group – historical outline

In this chapter, I would like to focus on the Bilderberg Group from historical perspective. The Bilderberg Group is an annual conference designed to foster dialogue between Europe and North America, which was founded in 1954 by Polish politician – Joseph Jerome Retinger. In short description about the Bilderberg Meetings we can read that

> Every year, between 120–150 political leaders and experts from industry, finance, academia and the media are invited to participate in the conference (Bilderberg Meetings, http://bilderbergmeetings.org/index.php, accessed: 29.11.2013).

Moreover, it occurs defined subdivision of the participants. Namely, we find out that

> [...] two thirds of the participants come from Europe and the rest from North America; one third from politics and government and the rest from other fields (Bilderberg Meetings, http://bilderbergmeetings.org/index.php, accessed: 29.11.2013),

but it has not been determined what percentage are women and men. In recent years, many women are invited to participate as a speakers during those sessions. This trend results from the fact that women are professionally more active than earlier. Moreover, it was underlined that these annual conferences are a 'forum for informal, off-the-record discussions about megatrends and the major issues facing the world' (Bilderberg Meetings, http://bilderbergmeetings.org/index.php, accessed: 29.11.2013).

In 1952 Retinger invited the elected politicians to discuss the further fate Europe and transatlantic cooperation. In this group were Alcide de Gasperi, Pietro Quaroni, Hugh Gaitskell, sir Colin Gubbins, Guy Mollet, Paul van Zeeland, Paul Rykens (Pomian 1994, p. 233). It was notable that relations with the United States require more attention and improved relationships. Their work led to the organization of first conference in 1954 in the Hotel de Bilderberg (Estulin 2009, p. 62). In that time, they discussed the issue of contemporary international relations: The attitude towards communism and the Soviet Union; The attitude towards dependent areas and peoples overseas; The attitude towards economic policies and problems; The attitude towards European integration and the European Defence Community (Retinger 1956, p. 10).

For many years the conference participants were men only. Comparing lists of guests in Steering Committee, one can see that there were fourteen men like Prince Bernhard of Netherlands, Retinger, Ball, Fergusson, Kraft, Fanfani (McGhee, p. 1). The composition of the participants definite about the uniqueness of the Bilderberg Group. Steadily expanded circle of the Bilderberg Group gave enthusiasm during the talks by sharing ideas and alliances. The invitations ware considered as a great honor and in later years became the dilemma of how diplomatically gave up one's candidacy. Retinger created the principle of selection of participants, according to which invitations were

> [...] sent to important and generally respected people who through their special knowledge or experience, their personal contacts and their influence in national and international circles could help further the aims set by Bilderberg (Sklar 1980, p. 168).

In creation of the lists intensely helped Denis Healey and Sam Watson, who, earlier than Prince Bernhard, decided about the selection of participants (Wilford 2003, p. 248). Two years later, Retinger created the key selection for guests. In his brochure we can find that

> [...] it has been our custom to invite representatives in the proportion of one-third politicians and one-fifth businessmen and trade unionists, the remainder being intellctuals, professional men, and other leaders of public opinion (Retinger 1956, p. 6).

He also pointed out that

> [...] we would choose the people to be invited to take part in our meetings, mostly guided by the nature of the subjects to be discussed, and using great care to preserve a strict balance (Retinger 1956, p. 7).

Retinger's activities were not accidental, but were a deep analysis as consistently implemented guidelines and political prudence. For those reasons, the European structures and the Bilderberg Group contributed to the development a later events, even in the European Union and transatlantic cooperation.

Powerful women in politics in the Bilderberg Group

In this chapter, I would like to focus on influential women, who can be classified into two important groups like politics and business. According to Retinger's principle of selection those groups form the basis of the Bilderberg Group. In those circles one can find: queens, prime ministers, ministers, secretaries of the state, businesswomen. I would like to underline that two decades earlier of functioning the Bilderberg Group, the guests were men only. This situation resulted from the dominant role of men in public life. For example, Prince Bernahard participated in annual conferences from 1954 to 1976 (Rockefeller 2002, p. 412).

Nowadays, first class of women in the Bilderberg Group are the female representatives of royal families from Europe. Queen Beatrix of the Netherlands, Prince Bernhard's daughter, has participated for many years (Traynor 2013, p. 1). Queen Sofia of Spain also attended in Bilderberg's conferences (Brooks 2010, p. 1). She was invited in 2009 as a participant (*Final List of Participants* 2009, p. 3).

Second class of women in the Bilderberg Group are prime ministers represented by Margaret Thatcher and Hanna Suchocka. Both of them were invited once, and were not, in that time, a prime minister. Thatcher was invited to a conference in Cesme in Turkey, which was in 1975 (*List of Participants* 1975). During these meeting participants disscussed about 'Inflation: its economic, social and political implications; recent international political developments; the present status and prospects to resolve the Arab-Israeli conflict and the effect on relations among NATO members; other recent developments affecting the relations among NATO countries. In that time, Margaret Thatcher became the Leader of the Conservative Party (Blundell 2010, pp. 136–137) and presented a free-market approach to state finances and the whole economic system (Blundell 2010, pp. 143–146). In this event, a political voice of Thatcher about economy has been noticed and probably her ideas were interesting during the discussion on inflation. Margaret Thatcher's Bruges speech in September 1988 was inspirational to found The Bruges Group in 1989[1].

Hanna Suchocka was not only Polish Prime Minister in 1992–1993, but also the Minister of Justice in 1997–2000 (Suchocka 2000, p. 25). She has been constantly associated with institutions and projects of the Council of Europe since 1990. Namely, Suchocka was the rapporteur on many international conferences, which were under the auspices of the Council of Europe. In 1997 she presented the report titled *The social charter and the states of Central and Eastern Europe*. A year after, she was invited to the Bilderberg Group's conference which took place in Ayrshire, Scotland. Suchocka spoke on the following issues like European Monetary Union or Europe's Social Model (*List of Participants* 1998). In her short, but substantive work, Suchocka presented arguments pro and against the European Constitution. She underlined that this kind of document would strengthen the subjectivity of the EU and would protect human rights (Suchocka 2000, p. 22).

In recent years, United States Secretaries of State like Condoleezza Rice and Hillary Clinton were also invited to the Bilderberg's conferences. Both of them participated in conference in 2008 in Chantilly, USA (Estulin 2009, p. 433). In this occasion, I would like to focus on Hillary Clinton, whose husband, Bill Clinton, participated in Bilderberg's conference in 1991 which took place in Baden-Baden (*Bilderberg Meeting Participants List* 1991). Hillary Rodham Clinton is well-known as First Lady of the United States, but she has achieved much more. Namely, Clinton was elected the first female Senator from New York in 2001 (Bernstein 2008, p. 587). In my opinion, the Steering Committee noticed her effectiveness, experience, and impact on American political life. Then, Hillary Clinton participated in Bilderberg's conference in 2008. Reflecting the agenda topics, I can conclude that Hillary Clinton was active during the panels about 'US Foreign Policy Without Change' and 'After Bush: The Future of US-EU Relations'[2].

European female ministers were also noticed by Steering Committee of the Bilderberg Group, and they have received invitations. In this context, I would like to mention Ewa Björling, who has been Trade Minister since 2007 and Minister for Nordic Cooperation since 2010 in the Swedish Government[3]. She has participated in Bilderberg's conference in St. Moritz in 2011[4]. During these meetings participants discussed about economic and national security in a Digital Age, a sustainable

---

1   See more on http://www.brugesgroup.com/about/index.live (Accessed: 29.11.2013).
2   See more: http://bilderbergmeetings.org/conferences.html (Accessed: 4.12.2013).
3   See more: http://www.government.se/sb/d/9542/a/87797 (Accessed: 4.12.2013).
4   See more: http://www.bilderbergmeetings.org/participants_2011.html (Accessed: 4.12.2013).

Euro, technological innovation in Western Economies[5]. I have chosen these areas of discussion because Björling could be active during the session because of her qualifications. Other ministers like Jutta Urpilainen, Dora Bakoyannis, and Emma Bonino also were invited to the Bilderberg Group's conferences. First of them, Jutta Urpilainen, is the Minister of Finance of Finland and the chairperson of the Social Democratic Party of Finland[6]. It is worth emphasizing that Urpilainen was elected as the first female chairperson of this party[7]. Urpilainen has participated in the Bilderberg Group's conferences in 2012 and 2013[8]. She might be active in sessions about 'Jobs, entitlements and debt', 'Can the US and Europe grow faster and create jobs?', 'Is vigorous economic growth attainable?', 'Sustainability of the euro and its consequences'[9]. The next female minister is Dora Bakoyannis, who participated in the Bilderberg's meeting in Greece in 2009[10]. She was Minister of Foreign Affairs of Greece in 2006–2009, which was the highest position ever held by a woman in the Cabinet of Greece[11]. She was included in Forbes list of the Worlds Powerful Woman together with 99 other female leaders in politics, business and philanthropy[12]. Her contribution in foreign affairs is: Greece's ratification of the European Union's Lisbon Treaty, support of France's Mediterranean Union plan, focusing on Mideast peace; and leading a conference on women entrepreneurs[13]. In my opinion, she was noticed by Steering Committee of Bilderberg Group for this reason. The last female minister, who will be presented in this article, is Emma Bonino[14]. She is an Italian politician, who has been Minister of Foreign Affairs since 28 April 2013[15]. She also

5   See more: http://www.bilderbergmeetings.org/conferences-10s.html (Accessed: 4.12.2013).
6   She was also a member of Committee for the Future, Foreign Affairs Committee, Finnish Delegation to the Nordic Council, Advisory Council of the Finnish Institute of International Affairs, Tax Subcommittee. See more: http://www.eduskunta.fi/triphome/bin/hex5000.sh?hnro=808&kieli=en (Accessed: 4.12.2013).
7   See more: http://www.hs.fi/english/article/Social+Democrats+choose+32-year-old+Jutta+Urpilainen+as+new+chair/1135237030682 (Accessed: 4.12.2013).
8   See: http://publicintelligence.net/2012-bilderberg-meeting-participant-list (Accessed: 4.12.2013) and http://publicintelligence.net/2013-bilderberg-meeting-participant-list (Accessed: 4.12.2013).
9   I quote topics of Bilderberg Group's conferences in 2012 and 2013; see: http://bilderbergmeetings.org/conferences-10s.html (Accessed: 4.12.2013).
10 Information is from http://info.publicintelligence.net/bilderberg-members-2009-press-release.pdf (Accessed: 4.12.2013).
11 Information is from http://web.archive.org/web/20081207032706/http://www.mfa.gr/www.mfa.gr/en-US/The+Ministry/The+Minister/Biography (Accessed: 4.12.2013).
12 She occupied 66th place in the ranking; see: http://www.forbes.com/lists/2006/11/06women_The-100-Most-Powerful-Women_Rank_3.html (Accessed: 4.12.2013).
13 Information is from http://www.forbes.com/lists/2008/11/biz_powerwomen08_Dora-Bakoyannis_QR52.html (Accessed: 4.12.2013).
14 Information about her participation is from http://www.polisblog.it/post/83101/bilderberg-cose (Accessed: 4.12.2013).
15 She is also a founding member No Peace Without Justice; see: http://www.theguardian.com/profile/emma-bonino (Accessed: 4.12.2013).

served as Minister for International Trade and European Affairs and before she was member of the European Parliament[16]. In BBC HARD talk Bonino has outlined situation of women in the contemporary world in following words: 'Is there a place where there is an easy life for women in power? If you know one, name it'.

Women of the media, business and science in the Bilderberg Group

In this part of my work, I focus on second group of women, who have been invited to the Bilderberg's meetings. I separated the politics of other spheres of public life because female politician are devoted most of the participants than other groups of women. I took into account the division proposed by Retinger. In this group, I collected female journalists, businesswomen, and female scientists.

Two female journalists, who participated in the Bilderberg Group's conferences, are Lilli Gruber and Vendeline von Bredow. First of them, Lilli Gruber, has been on the Bilderberg's conferences in 2013 and 2012[17]. Lilli Gruber is well-known as an Italian journalists and television persona. She is a television host in an Italian private channel La7[18]. Gruber also served as Member of the European Parliament from 2004 to September 2008[19]. She is also an author of books like *Chador, Figlie dell'Islam*, in which she describes a female emancipation in Islamic countries[20]. Lilli's sister asked her about dreams for the future and she answered

> So long as women's many abilities count for so little I will never stop supporting that issue. It's not only a question of justice, it's simply politically stupid to continue excluding women from the centers of power (Gruber 2008).

In my view, Lilli Gruber might discuss in following sessions: 'What can the West do about Iran?', 'Stability and instability in the Middle East', 'Current affairs: Syria'[21]. The second journalist, who is connected with the Bilderberg Group, is Vendelina von Bredow. In contrast to other women in the Bilderberg Group, she

---

16 See her biographical sketch on http://www.emmabonino.it/biography (Accessed: 4.12.2013).
17 See on http://publicintelligence.net/2013-bilderberg-meeting-participant-list (Accessed: 4.12.2013), http://publicintelligence.net/2012-bilderberg-meeting-participant-list (Accessed: 4.12.2013).
18 Her talk show 'Otto e mezzo'; information is from http://www.la7.it/ottoemezzo/?pmk=header (Accessed: 4.12.2013).
19 Information about her political activity is from http://www.europarl.europa.eu/meps/en/28368/LILLI_GRUBER_home.html;jsessionid=F991287ECD2F5CAC8E9E0D561D712302.node2 (Accessed: 5.12.2013).
20 See more: http://www.fembio.org/english/biography.php/woman/biography/lilli-gruber (Accessed: 5.12.2013).
21 See Bilderberg Group's agenda on: http://bilderbergmeetings.org/conferences-10s.html (Accessed: 5.12.2013).

was the reporter from 2011–2013[22]. Vendelina von Bredow is Deputy Europe Editor and Central and Eastern Europe Correspondent of 'The Economist'. Moreover, she worked for the 'Financial Times Deutschland' and 'Wall Street Journal Europe's'[23]. Furthermore, she took book leave from 'The Economist' between 2008 and 2010 to research and write the authorized biography of Gianni Agnelli[24], who attended to the Bilderberg Group's conferences. In my opinion, her function in the Bilderberg Group results from the knowledge of foreign languages and the experience in the media. I also believe that the writing the biography of Agnelli by Bredow was a significant factor.

I would like to present two businesswomen whose surnames are connected with the Bilderberg's participant lists. First of them, Melinda Gates is the wife of Bill Gates, who also participated in the Bilderberg's conferences. She is not only a wife of influential man, but also a businesswoman, philanthropist (Sellers 2008, p. 1) and co-founder of the Bill & Melinda Gates Foundation in 2000[25]. She was involved in the following projects: 'Launch HIV/AIDS prevention branch in India', 'Our original libraries work is complete', 'Launch alliance for green revolution in Africa'[26]. Melinada Gates characterized her own mission

> But ultimately, when I started to look at the role of philanthropy and what it can do to effect change, I realized it wasn't enough to just visit women in the developing world or to give them a tool like the vaccine; I had to use my voice on their behalf[27].

Another longstanding participant in the Bilderberg's conferences is Heather Reiseman who has attended since 2000. She is also a member of Steering Committee[28]. Reiseman is a Canadian businesswomen and the founder and chief executive of the Canadian retail chain Indigo Books and Music[29]. Similar to Melinda Gates she founded in 2006 the Indigo Love of Reading Foundation, of which she is chair, with a mission to enrich libraries in under-resourced public schools[30]. Reiseman with her husband donated 15 million dollars to Mount Sinai emergency care (Ballingall 2013). In this case, she is also a philanthropist.

The last group of women, which participated in the Bilderberg's conferences, are female scientists. In this context, I would like to mention Susan Athey, Hélène

---

22 Compare List of Participants on: http://publicintelligence.net/category/documents/bilderberg/bilderberg-participant-lists (Accessed: 5.12.2013).
23 See: http://www.economist.com/mediadirectory/vendeline-von-bredow (Accessed: 5.12.2013).
24 See from http://stateoftheunion.eui.eu/vendeline-von-bredow.html (Accessed: 5.12.2013).
25 See more about foundation on http://www.gatesfoundation.org/Who-We-Are/General-Information/History (Accessed: 5.12.2013).
26 *Ibid.*
27 See more on http://www.givesmart.org/Stories/Donors/Melinda-Gates (Accessed: 5.12.2013).
28 Currently, in Steering Committee of the Bilderberg Group are three woman and thirty men; compare on http://bilderbergmeetings.org/governance.html (Accessed: 8.12.2013).
29 See on http://www.chapters.indigo.ca/our-company/management (Accessed: 8.12.2013).
30 See more on http://www.womenofinfluence.ca/heather-reisman-2 (Accessed: 8.12.2013).

Rey, Anousheh Karvar, Marie-Josée Kravis. Three of them, except Anousheh Karvar, have been in this year.

Now, I will present Anousheh Karvar and Marie-Josée Kravis. Karvar has a doctorate in the history and sociology. In 2006–2008 she was a member of Board, Trader-Union Advisory Committee, OECD. Currently, she is responsible for international politics and social matters, fight against discrimination and promotion of diversity, relations with associations and intellectuals, reforms in public sector and government decentralization[31]. Karvar participated in Bilderberg's conference in 2012 and in my opinion, she could discuss about 'The future of democracy in the developed world', 'Is vigorous economic growth attainable?' Her professional experience was noticed by Steering Committee and she was invited in 2012. The second female scientist, who participated in Bilderberg's conferences, is Marie-Josée Kravis. She is an economist specializing in public policy analysis and strategic planning. Kravis has been associated with Hudson Institute since 1973. She directed Hudson's 'Corporate environment program' and the 'Europe and the World' study. Moreover, she has worked on studies of the economic development of countries such as Algeria, Morocco, and Mexico[32]. She and her husband, Henry R. Kravis, have participated in Bilderberg's conferences since 2000. In the history of the Bilderberg Group it is a unique situation when a marriage couple had been invited. It shows that both of them are influential people in public life, when taking into account their experience and professional achievements. In my observation, Marie-Josée Kravis in recent conferences might discuss about 'The Middle East', 'The world's economic problems', 'The new economy and its effects on society'[33].

Conclusions

This article shows the significant contribution of women in public life. I analyzed the subject from the perspective of the Bilderberg Group, which invited men only. This situation lead to lower activity by women in politics, science and in the media. For example, Margaret Thatcher and Hanna Suchocka were first female prime ministers, who were invited. In recent years, female ministers represent a significant percentage of visitors in Bilderberg's conferences. On the one hand, we observe women like Suchocka, Urpilainen, Bonino, who, by themselves, have gained their position in Bilderberg Group but one the other hand, we see women

31   See more on: http://www.weforum.org/global-agenda-councils/anousheh-karvar (Accessed: 8.12.2013).

32   See more on: http://www.hudson.org/learn/index.cfm?fuseaction=staff_bio&eid=Brd17 (Accessed: 8.12.2013).

33   These sessions are identical to her activity; compare: http://bilderbergmeetings.org/conferences.html (Accessed: 8.12.2013).

like Hillary Clinton, Melinda Gates, Marie-Josée Kravis, whose husbands are influential and have participated in Bilderberg's conferences as well. In my opinion, these women were invited because of their professional activity and experience. In these cases, the factor determining the invitation to the conference was not influential husbands, but these women's activities. These women are selected in accordance with the principle of Retinger.

Agnieszka Świątek
University of Łodź, Poland

Women's civic engagement and the communitarian personality model

The communitarian personality model

There are two main models of citizenship: the liberal personality model and the communitarian personality model (Weryński 2010). Communitarianism appeared in the 80s in the XX century. Its development was in 90's of the XX century (Łucka 2008). Communitarian approach has its source in such thinkers as: Arystoteles or JJ. Rousseau. Issue of discussion is who we could include to this trend (Gawkowska 2004). Surely we can classify here: Amitai Etzioni, Charles Taylor, Michael Walzer, Alasdair MacIntyre, Michael Sandel. Presented here only the main points of communitarianism will help to understand why it is so important for the development of civil society in our country to foster this model of citizenship.

According to communitarianism, the basic concept around which focuses the social life is the whole collective existence. Community exist, community interpenetrate and dominate in the life of the individual unit. We can say that our identity is shaped by community 'I'. We determine our 'I' through social practice, collective discourse and cultural background. Very important is a role of common meanings. The community is the common denominator for people to allows to understand the concepts which are so important for the continuance of each society: justice, freedom and tolerance. The awareness of the community role of is a kind of realization of concern for it (community) (Śpiewak 2004, pp. 5–15).

According to Walzer, theory of community is very important as criticism of liberal thought. Liberal theory misleads understanding of social life. Communitarians have the opinion that there are no individuals living outside the community. We can say that from the ontological point of view the community has priority over the individual. Family, which is the first community for individual, has the most important role in creation of identity. Relationship with the family is a fundamental element of society life. Everyone, coming into the world, becomes as a part of the community. Such a strong relationship with the family is the primary determinant of relationship between people.

Community needs to meet individual needs. This relationship between individual and community has to be beneficial for both.

> Cooperation, mutual aid, helping the handicapped, solidarity-based on the principle of subsidiarity and reciprocity – thus become the basic social values (Łucka 2008, p. 60).

So it is important to understand communitarians in category of the common good. According to liberals, the common good reduces freedom of the individual and it is difficult to define them. Communitarians agree with the second allegation but they emphasize that there are rights beyond the individual such as the legal system, culture, tradition, and those create the basis of self-esteem (Śpiewak 2004).

We can say that:

> According to liberal, citizenship is understood as the ability of individuals to create and to implement its own concepts of the common goods. For communitarians this concept simplifies the complicated relationship between the individual and society. Community of individuals is not only asinstrumental, as liberals want, but it is a place where their identity is formed (Koczanowicz 2005, p. 110).

This collective identity created by a common tradition, a community of values is the basis of building a civil society. The citizen is the one who is required to actively participate, care for the common goods and for local communities. It has therefore not only rights but also obligations towards the community to which he belongs (Karnowska 2011). We should remember that patriotism is understood as a concern for the cultural community, collective resources. The main principle of communitarianism is to give up even the particular interests for the community. Indeed, there is something like community of the nation and common history: 'Patriotism is a form of social obligation and discipline' (Śpiewak 2004).

In conclusion, communitarian model of personality emphasizes its commitment to the community. Communitarians respect the community, where they belong, starting from the family, the community and ending with the community of the state. They recognize that the formation of identity is related to the communities from which they have originated. Social activity for the benefit of the community is a natural consequence of belonging to it. We should know that without understanding the idea of the common goods it is not possible to explain communitarianism. At this time I will discuss a women's civic engagement focusing on how their attitude is fulfilling the principles of the concept of the communitarian personality model.

Women's civic engagement

Civic engagement is frequently understood as participation in elections (both active-vote, as well as passive-candidate), membership of political parties, sending petitions and queries to politicians, involvement in a third sector (Pacześniak 2009, p. 19). According to Putnam 'being a citizenship in community means to participate in all public sectors' (Putnam 1995, p. 133). Verba, Scholzmann, Bradym understands civic engagement as an active participation, which aim as influential to all by political institutions. It happens when we create public offices or when we choose people who create these public offices.

The fundamental issue in the literature is research of the experience of civil society in situations of voting (Sułek 2009, s.18).Unfortunately, as Raciborski writes, one cannot be deluded that the majority of our citizens are 'homo politicus' and the election is 'a procedure that is passionate for all' (Raciborski 2007, p. 334).

The level of voter participation in our country remains at a very low level (from 39,56% participation in local council's election in 2006 to 61,12% in presidential election in 2007):

> In Poland, however, the participation of women and men in the parliamentary elections (period 1997–2007), shows statistical differences in approximately 5–7% (women go to the elections more rarely than men) (Żukowski 2011, p. 14).

Table 1. Participation in elections

	The presidential election			The local council's election			The parliamentary elections: parliament			
Year	2000	2005	2010	2002	2006	2010	2001	2005	2007	2011
Poland	61,12	49,74	55,31	44,12	39,56	47,32	46,29	40,57	61,12	48,92

Source: own elaboration (http://www.pkw.gov.pl, accessed: 19.09.2013).

For the long time, the common concept in the development of democracy was that women vote in the elections under the influence of the most important men in their life environment (it can be a husband, father or a respected priest or neighbour). It has also impact on the participation of women taking the right to vote-stand. I can't describe the extensive issues to winning suffrage for women. Of course, we should more pay attention that in the period of III RP the small proportion of women in the parliamentary elections was presented and local government have been still relatively small.

Table 2. Percentage of women and men in the local elections for communal councils and in the parliamentary elections:

	Candidates		Elected	
	Women	Men	Women	Men
The local elections for communal councils (less than 20 thousand residents in 2006)	28%	72%	22%	78%
The local elections for communal councils (more than 20 thousand residents in 2006)	31%	69%	19%	81%
The local elections for communal councils (less than 20 thousand residents in 2010)	31%	69%	26%	74%
The local elections for communal councils (more than 20 thousand residents in 2010)	32%	68%	22%	78%
The parliamentary elections:2005	24,51%	75,49%		
The parliamentary elections:2007	23,08%	76,92%		
The parliamentary elections: 2011	43,54%	56,46%	23,91%	76,09%

Source: own elaboration (http://www.pkw.gov.pl, accessed: 19.09.2013).

Second most important aspect of civil activity of the women is their involvement in various non-governmental organizations (NGOs), which are a separate type of social organizations classified as the 'third sector'.

According to www.ngo.pl in Poland are 102512 non-governmental organizations (14.10.2013), which doesn't reflect the actual state. In 2012 in Poland registered more than 80 thousand non-governmental organizations: 11 thousand foundations and 72 thousand associations (excluding OSP – The voluntary fire department). We have to remember that the number of non-governmental organizations is smaller because a lot of organization are not active but are still registered in the database. That's why Klon-Jawor' Association estimated that function only 60––80% non-governmental organizations, and according to GUS from 2008, function 75% non-governmental organizations (Przewłocka, Adamiak, Zając 2012, p. 10)[1].

Third sector in Poland is characterized by people who work regularly monthly in 21% organization but don't have a contract. Only every fifth of organization (19%) hires full time employees (full-time or part-time) (Przewłocka, Adamiak, Zając 2012, p. 26).

---

[1] According to the Klon-Jawor Association, one in five (19%) assocations brings together less than 20 memebers, and nearly half association – between 20 and 50 members. At the same time 2% of the largest associations focused thousand or more members.

Table 3. Percentage of women and men among the groups involved in the activities of NGOs

Structure of the organization	Women	Men
Members of the organization	41%	59%
Management of the organization	41%	59%
Regular employees	55%	45%
Full-time employees	69%	31%
Volunteers	56%	44%

Source: own elaboration and Przewłocka, Adamiak, Herbst 2013.

Women are very important component of the functioning of NGOs. A lot of women who participate in group are full-time employees (69%), regular employees (55%) and volunteers (56%). The same person can be both: a member and an employee or volunteer and employee. The large percentage of women in the Third Section is often explained by the low salaries that men don't accept. The woman, however, choose to work part-time so that, they could both work and fulfil household duties.

The percentage of women in the structures of the official management of the organization (both being a member as well as being a part of the board) is at 41%. It increases when we exclude from the analysis the organizations in the field of sports (division is then 50% to 50% in the composition of the management). The field of the organization influence the composition of its members. Most women working in organizations are in charge in health care, social assistance and education where for every 6 females there are only 4 men. The least amount of women occupations are in sport organizations, where for every 3 females there are 7 men and one third of the management offices there is not one female (Przewłocka, Adamiak, Herbst 2013, p. 92).

These statistics do not cover completely the issues of women's civic engagement. It must be remembered, that the activity election also is manifested by participation in demonstrations, signing petitions, agitating in favour of a particular candidate, taking part in candidate's meetings. However, taking into consideration only the segment of social reality it should be emphasized that the condition of citizenship awareness in our country should provoke deeper reflection.

Women in the communitarian personality model

It is important to remember that social role of woman as mother play crucial educational role to next generations. They adapt the individual to live in society by socialization. Women's civic engagement has an impact on children's behaviour in the future.

Many economists when analyzing low level of entrepreneurial attitudes of Poles explain this with the historical conditions, the lack of examples of entrepreneurial activity in the closest family. Rarely, however, we recognize an analogy regarding learning about the citizenship position. Women are assigned to a social roles as: a house-wife, a mother, a babysitter. It has a fundamental impact on women's citizenship. Over the years, the situation of women has been changing. Women began to study, often to work in 'male professions'. Women have won themselves the right to vote (in Poland as parity on electoral lists, too). However, I should highlight the fact that it is always the most important in introducing changes is the mental changes. Social changes always take time. It is not enough to tell women about the possibility of candidate for parliament. Women must have the freedom to choose what they want. In this case it means a willingness to stand for election.

Research shows that women still do not believe that they are suitable for public offices (in 1997 this view was shared by 23% respondents, in 2013 by 21% responders – see: table 4). At a high level of management and politics dominate the desire to succeed at all costs, to ignore emotions, egocentricity and lack of empathy. Women feel that such action would be against them that's why they often avoid promotions (Piątek 2006).

Table 4. The reason of women's civic engagement

The reason of women's civic engagement	1997	2013
Women have a lot of household duties	71%	59%
In the public sphere dominated by men. That's why women have smaller opportunities	36%	43%
Women do not believe in their own strength and capabilities	23%	21%
Women are less interested in public life and professional careers	24%	19%
There is a lack of legal regulations to ensure greater participation of women in public functions	13%	15%
Women have worse qualifications and competences	8%	3%
Women are not suitable to act as responsible public functions	7%	2%

Source: own elaboration and Omyła-Rudzka 2013.

CBOS survey confirms that, in the opinion of Poles still the main reason for the lack of activity of women is too many household duties. However, the situation is improving as seen also by the percentage granted to this type of responses. In 1997 there were as many as 71% and in 2013 only 59%.

In the perception past 16 years, it is the greater percentage responses concerning the domination of men in the public sector (7 percentage points) and the lack of legal regulations giving women a greater opportunity to participate in public functions (2 percentage points). The situation of women is very complicated. Professor

A. Żukowski synthetically recognizes the reasons for unequal political participation of women in relation to men candidacy, obtain a mandate in three groups of factors:
- 'political factors' ('male' model of politics, the lack of the government's support of political parties, lack of cooperation between women's organizations, the type of electoral system);
- 'socio-economic factors' (feminization of poverty and unemployment, double duty 'work and family', restrictions on education and enhancing the professional qualifications);
- 'ideological and psychological factors' (the traditional role of women, the lack of trust in women's perception of politics by women as 'dirty' activity, negative stereotypes of women propagated by the media) (see: Żukowski 2011, p. 14).

We should add to this list also cultural aspects. There are extremely deep-rooted aversion to the admission of women to positions of power that is traditionally male occupy. There is the colloquial concept that women do not have good feature characteristics to perform this functions is a prejudice existing in the social life of generations: women know nothing about politics (Frątczak 2002).

In closing, it is worth to quote T. Bukciński's view on the importance of women's civil engagement in public life:

> It seems that just in the present situation, in which there are distortions, demoralization, mafia is in public and political life, feminist movements may play an important role, especially for restoration of civil and ethical character of the public sphere (Bukciński 1999, p. 194).

Women which realize the communitarian personality model in social life can become invaluable assistance in creating law-abiding community based on discussion and mutual respect. The women have invaluable contribution to the development of the welfare citizenship (Krzyżanowska 2012).

It is interesting that researches confirm that there is positive social mood present in the increased participation of women in public life. 47% of respondents would like to see increase number of female managers in government, in foundations and social organizations, 46% – in political parties, and 42% in the state administration. Only a low percentage respondents declare a desire to decrease the number of women performing important functions: from 3% to 8% (Omyła-Rudzka 2013). We should remember, that these are just declarations and social changes require time and overcoming deep-rooted stereotypes.

In conclusion, it should be emphasized that the low political and organizational activity of women is primarily caused by the motivation of interested. The crucial role play cultural factors. We should consider if the importance of women role in politics and business of NGOs that may influence changes in attitudes? Are women ready to 'get dirty hands' in politics? If agreeing to be the only employees, volunteers in non-governmental organizations they do not really create the communitarian personality model?

Out of range of considerations to this article was an area of informal, unorganized social activity. It involves the active support of the local community, for example, when someone supports a fund raiser for a sick neighbour, helps to create a playground on the estate or draws attention to the local vandalism. Without a doubt, this activity is also filling the communitarian citizen model. The role of women is invaluable here.

Paweł Łubiński
University of Warmia and Mazury in Olsztyn, Poland

The Women for Nation and the Women's Section of the National Movement as the examples of socially and politically engaged organizations

Introduction

In the face of the unending discussion about the meaning of the socio-political activity of women in the contemporary world, where the patriarchal model of social existence continues to dominate, a number of questions arise regarding women's situation and their place in such a model. What makes this discussion interesting is that it takes place in times when the activism, as well as the activation, of women in Poland coincides with the development of the social phenomenon of the National Movement. National and patriotic ideas and the promotion of a radical approach have caused this environment to attract a number of organizations supporting the ideas contained in the Declaration of the Ideology of the National Movement. Among these there are two women's organizations, i.e. the Women for Nation (Kobiety dla Narodu) and the Women's Section of the National Movement (Sekcja Kobiet Ruchu Narodowego).

Women's public activity

The discussion about the issues of women's movements and organizations, which originated in the 19th century in the wake of emancipation tendencies and the enlivened hope that women may achieve a stable position in the public (and with the time – political) sphere, became an important component of the socio-political public debate which continues to this day. The change of a certain way of thinking, as well as the status of women, did not, however, stabilize their position. Women continue to encounter numerous difficulties, both in fulfilling their needs, as well as in expressing their views (Miluska 2010, p. 115). When in 1989, a landmark year in Poland's history, the Round Table Talks were held, the over 50-person group representing both the government and the Democratic Opposition included only two women[1]. This does not mean that women are not politically engaged. Rather, it indicates their true position on the political scene which has for centuries been dominated by men. It is after the aforementioned date that a gender equality discourse began in Poland (Drewniak 2012, pp. 11–12). Many times the roles of women and men were explained by the biological traits related to their sexes. This was connected to the varied level of activity based on differences of character, skills and certain predispositions. Each biased judgement regarding female traits contributed to the deterioration of women's position. The limitation of women's influence on the public sphere was justified by their assumed weakness and the inability to act, which resulted in women being pushed into the private sphere (Chibowska 2012, p. 101) and the strengthening of the paradigm of the 'Polish Mother' (cf. Majewska-Opiełka 2010, p. 76).

Emilia Drewniak notes that at the time of the democratic revolution in Poland, the gender equality discourse was very limited in terms of the language and understanding on the part of men. The downplaying of women's role in public life and their influence on the occurring changes led to the creation of women's and feminist movements which included organizations incorporating Polish women, persons from the academic, legal and economic fields whose aim was to protect and improve the conditions of women in the public sphere. Emilia Drewniak indicates a number of non-governmental women's organizations from that time: Forum Współpracy Organizacji Pozarządowych, Demokratyczna Unia Kobiet, Fundacja OŚKA etc. (Drewniak 2012, p. 12).

Although both in the public sphere and on the broadly understood political scene, one may observe a 'social advancement' of women, certain fields (especially the ones of political nature) continue to be reserved for men. Even though women occupy a number of important positions in social, cultural or educational political departments, the areas such as finance, foreign affairs and matters of international (and national) security, as well as intelligence agencies, remain the domain of men (Miluska 2010, p. 119). However, researchers emphasize that the political phenomenon of women's 'emancipation' is an unavoidable process, supported by the increase in women's significance on the international political scene and the fact that they are gradually taking on the personality traits characteristic of men (Malendowski 2010, p. 141). The degree of the acceptance of the advancement of women is dependent on the national culture of a given country (Miluska 2010, p. 119).

A survey concerning the political representation of women, conducted in 2010 among 1,027 adult Poles (Fuszara 2010, pp. 1–5), indicates that 60% of the surveyed supported the civic initiative under which the number of women in elections to the

---

1   Prof. Anna Przecławska (pedagogue, researcher at the University of Warsaw) and Grażyna Staniszweska (activist of NSZZ 'Solidarność').

Sejm, the European Parliament or local governments must not be lower than the number of men. Looking at the sex of the surveyed, women were more likely (66%) to support the equal rights and political activity of the female part of the society than men (53%). Above the average support for this initiative was shown by persons aged 18–24 (68%), administrative workers (72%), housewives (67%) and students (68%) (Fuszara 2010, p. 1). This tendency can be interpreted in various ways (for instance, one may explain this state of affairs by the dominance of women in one of the surveyed professional groups or in a given age group), but other conclusions are important from the point of view of the nature and subject matter of this paper. Namely, the representatives of national movements view all emancipation and feminist tendencies as the results of ideological evolution toward the left wing (see: *Narodowo – subtelniej* 2013). The results of the above-mentioned survey show that the equality of rights (including activation) is supported by more practicing believers (69% of the surveyed who participate in religious practices a few times a week, supported the equal rights project), which is extremely important in the national-patriotic movement that has recently been experiencing a revival in Poland, than by the non-practising believers (52%). As noted by Małgorzata Fuszara (the equal rights movement – author's comment):

> [...] is also not connected with the declared political beliefs – in fact, supporters are less common among those declaring left-wing beliefs than among others – especially those who are undecided (Fuszara 2010, p. 1).

What is, therefore, the relation between women's representation in contemporary national organizations and the matter of women's engagement in the socio-political life, and how is their activity in the field of civic activity manifested?

The Women for Nation and the Women's Section of the National Movement

The National Movement, which has begun its socio-political expansion, is an entity incorporating many organizations devoted to a specific idea – the national idea. The National Movement includes peculiar (peculiar because of the unprecedented combination of the symbol of Polish identity with the status of women in the public discourse) women's organizations: the Women for Nation (KDN) and the Women's Section of the National Movement (SK RN).

The first, headed by Maria Piasecka-Łopuszańska, as described in the organization's official profile on a social networking website, is devoted to active women: students, workers, mothers, wives as well as successful women. Regardless of various interests, dreams and future plans, these women are united by the idea of 'Great Poland' predominant in the pre-war National Democracy movement from which it originated. The nature of the Women for Nation (noted above) is adequately captured by the slogan: 'Red and white colours suit the modern lady' ('Współczesnej damie do twarzy w biało-czerwonych barwach') (*Kobiety dla Narodu*, n.d.).

The second of the above-mentioned organizations is the Women's Section of the National Movement, headed by Anna Holocher. The SK RN employs the slogan 'The beautiful side of patriotism' ('Piękna strona patriotyzmu') (*Kobiety dla Narodu*, n.d.) and differs from the KDN mainly in the degree of affiliation with the National Movement. The SK RN is part of a larger project, a collective of national-patriotic organizations, i.e. the National Movement, whereas the KDN is independent of the Movement and merely cooperates with it, supporting the values advocated by its co-founders and leaders.

The conservative, traditional approach of the women from the KDN and the SK RN is often termed as 'right-wing feminism' in the public discourse (Jakubowski n.d.). The KDN organization itself presents an image of women in the society that runs contrary, for instance, to the 'Polish feminism' of the Congress of Women. The women of the KDN do not agree with the Congress's postulates: the introduction of gender quotas in elections, the unification of social roles regardless of gender or the liberalization of matters related to the Abortion Act, in vitro fertilization, birth control and sex education at school[2]. As noted by Grzegorz Jakubowski, the women of the KDN:

> [...] do not want women to replace men in all fields. They are in favour of a gender-based role division. They oppose homosexual marriage and children adoption by homosexual couples. They do not support the legalization of abortion (cf. Rejman 2013, p. 9) or the multi-culti policy. They support patriotic actions, defend football supporters and cultivate history. They fight for the children's rights (Jakubowski n.d.).

The SK RN focuses on social and ethical aspects of modern women, combining them with identity issues. It raises the issue of women working until the age of 67 years, the crisis of the family and the negative demographic situation, the deterioration of the traditional model of upbringing and educating future generations, the increase in VAT tax to 23% for 'children-related products' etc. Part of the SK RN's activity was adequately described by the leader of the organization during the 1st Congress of the National Movement which took place in Warsaw on 8 June 2013:

> Through our actions we wish to recreate the ethos of the mother, the guardian of the hearth who devotes her life to upbringing children and working for the good of the Nation (Holocher 2013b, p. 17).

---

2 Other postulates of the Congress of Women: promotion of culture and education in rural areas, institutional care for small children, equal parental custody rights, prevention of violence against women, equal salaries for women and men, facilities for the disabled and the professional activation of women, see: http//www.kongres-kobiet.pl (Accessed: 8.11.2013).

The KDN also emphasizes the role played by women in developing national awareness in former times and in the social activation (within the scope of the abovementioned issues) nowadays. Referring to the words of the mentor and the main ideologist of the National Democracy, Roman Dmowski, the spokeswoman for the KDN, Aleksandra Ceglarska, draws attention to the continuation of Christian tradition in Polish families and the role of women in the process of upbringing based on national values (Ceglarska 2013b, p. 3; cf. also: Cywińska 2013, p. 21). Dmowski perceived the positive aspect of women's conservative approach to children upbringing, cultivating religion and passing it on to the next generations, thanks to which 'families remained religious' (Dmowski 2002, p. 13). Unlike the feminists, the KDN fights for men, not against men, postulating the revival of the conservative opposition to left-wing activities, criticizing phenomena such as prostitution, sexual harassment and homosexuality (Sujka 2013, p. 12; Wasiukiewicz 2013, p. 10), violence in the family and the dictate of the minorities (Ceglarska 2013b, p. 3). Apart from social activity, the women of the KDN and the SK RN also conduct activities aimed at developing civic culture of Poles and their political engagement.

The examples of civic and socio-political activities

One of the civic and history-related activities is the KDN's campaign aimed at reminding Warsaw residents about the women who fought in the Warsaw Uprising. The campaign named '63 places of glory' ('63 miejsca chwały'), was launched on 1 August 2013 and served to present and reconstruct the life of the Home Army messenger Maria Cetys, who was shot by the Germans for her affinity with the Home Army. Similar topics were pursued in the film *Love epidemics (Epidemia miłości)*3 and the meeting: 'The more beautiful side of Solidarity. The history of women from anti-communist opposition in the 80s" ('Piękniejsza strona Solidarności. Historia kobiet z opozycji antykomunistycznej lat 80.'), both of which attracted great interest[4] (Ceglarska 2013a, p. 22). The SK RN also conducts activities aimed at commemorating the heroes who died in the fight for Poland's independence, bringing to light especially those events which did not make it to the social consciousness due to being ignored by the mass media. An example of the above is the participation of the women from the SK RN in the September commemoration of the 67 the anniversary of the Communist crime against the soldiers of the National Armed Forces in Barut, referred to as 'the Silesian Katyń' (Gąsiorek 2013, p. 17).

---

3 Maciej Piwowarczuk's documentary about the fate of people who got married during the Warsaw Uprising.
4 The meeting devoted to the activity and fight of women within NSZZ 'Solidarność'.

The engagement of women from women's organizations, cooperating with the National Movement, is largely manifested in campaigns for the dignity of the individual and the protection of human life from the conception. Numerous social actions, including religious ones, are dedicated to women struggling with existential, social or even moral issues. These actions often take the form of political demonstrations. Here the author would like to focus on the demonstration in a town in the Świętokrzyskie Voivodeship, where, following a Sunday mass, national female activists appeared with a banner presenting a local politician's negative stand on the citizens-initiated bill concerning the prohibition of eugenic abortion (We Ja 2013, p. 9). This demonstration had three dimensions: social – because it concerned the problem of abortion which has recently become the subject of many ethical debates and discussions; religious – because the protest took place in front of a church and concerned a matter expressly defined by Catholics as the right to kill unborn children; and finally political – because the demonstration concerned a member of the Polish People's Party and his moral relativism. Thus, from the perspective of the activists, the objective of the demonstration was achieved – women's activism sparked lively debate in the regional community and showed the true scale of the issue of abortion. This is also the aim of SK RN's actions under the bold slogans: 'Do not kill – rehabilitate!' ('Rehabilitować, nie zabijać!') (Holocher 2013c, p. 17), 'Catholics – defend life!' ('Katoliku, broń życia!')[5] (Holocher 2013a, p. 17), or the film 'October baby' (author unknown 2013).

Another example of socio-civic activity was the participation of women with nationalist views in the Poland-wide protest against the organized demoralization of children and young people: 'Hands off from our children!' ('Ręce precz od naszych dzieci!'). The protest involved members of the Right Wing of the Republic, Real Politics Union, All-Polish Youth and the Women for Nation. The action concerned the findings of the conference on the standards of sex education, co-organized by the Polish branch of the World Health Organization (WHO), according to which the development of a child's sexuality begins at its birth and thus sex education may be initiated as early as before the age of four. According to WHO's findings: children aged 9–12 should already know how to use birth control in the future, children aged 12–15 should be able to obtain birth control products on their own, while children older than 15 years old should be capable of taking 'a critical approach' to the cultural and religious aspects of parenthood and pregnancy (https://www.facebook.com, accessed: 10.11.2013). By protesting against these types of solutions, KDN women expressed their view on the sexualisation of children and their, as

---

5   This initiative involves: sending letters and asking for the support from various parishes, placing posters and banners with the slogan 'You cannot be a Catholic and support abortion at the same time' in public places; distributing leaflets which present the action's postulates, running workshops as part of religious education and posting the slogans on websites and social networking portals.

they term it, demoralization from the earliest years. Although there are many more such examples, the purpose of this paper is to present a certain general tendency.

Summary

The women's groups presented in this paper are an example of the self-activation and self-organization of civic forces in a situation which for many researchers constitutes a crisis of the institution of government and European structures, in the face of identity-related and economic issues. Regardless of whether one adopts a broader or narrower definition of civil society, it must be noted that the women of the KDN and the SK RN are making a voluntary and conscious 'attempt to organize themselves and cooperate despite the existence of the legal and democratic government' (Sepczyńska 2005, pp. 245–247), conducting their activities in the social, political and religious areas, the examples of which have been presented above. KDN and SK RN activity is focused on the defence of values such as: public activity (arising from the need to protect the highest values against feminist initiatives), womanhood (being an essential part of humanity), family (as the basic social unit), the Catholic Church (as the centre of morality and tradition), protection of life (from the conception), patriotism (as the women's concern for their homeland) and national pride (contrary to the syndrome of political correctness propagated by the media). The academic analysis of the correlation between the postulates of the KDN and the SK RN and their actual activities, the forecast of their development tendencies in the context of the dynamically changing reality and the development of the initiative of the National Movement, as well as the degree of the structural formalization of those organizations, pose a serious challenge to those sociologists, political scientists and pedagogues who wish to pursue the subjects discussed by the author of this paper.

Justyna Miko-Giedyk
The Jan Kochanowski University in Kielce, Poland

Social activity of female teachers in rural areas

Introduction

Social activity of teachers is directly linked to their role in society. Given the fact that a social role is a set of expectations of a society towards an individual, these expectations, in turn, influence and to some extent force a person to behave and act in a particular way (Parsons 1972, p. 306). Therefore, social activity of teachers is determined by changes in the perception of their role in society. Social activity of teachers in rural areas was of special importance as those areas were the most neglected and required special care of social activists. Over the years, social activity of teachers has undergone numerous changes – in terms of its extent and forms as well as its purposes. Despite many developments, both on a macroscale, i.e. social, economic and political changes, and on a microscale – local development, families and changes in people's awareness and mentality, social activity of teachers has retained its unchanged importance.

All the sources related to the job of a teacher refer to people doing this job either in the plural or in the singular masculine, but it is common knowledge that it is a strongly feminised prefession. It may be associated to the beginnings of the teaching profession which by the middle of the 19th century was typically 'masculine'. Only in the second half of the 19th century did female teachers acquire equal status in the profession as well as appropriate education. It was related to the establishment of seminars for teachers and the passing of laws which regulated the legal and professional situation of women. Moreover, it was commonly agreed that the 'caring' nature of the teaching profession was compatible with women's natural interests and passions (Woskowski 1997, pp. 203–204). Female teachers began to be employed in great numbers in schools also because of the fact that they were 'cheaper' and more obedient to men holding the position of head teachers (Renzetti, Curran 2008, p. 141–142). Since then there has been an increase in the number of female teachers. In the 1990s the percentage of female teachers in this professional group exceeded 70% (Woskowski 1997, pp. 203–204). In 2008, women employed as teachers accounted for 80.6% of all teachers (Raport 2009, pp. 13–15), whereas in 2010/2011 for 81.3% of them (Raport2012, p. 6).

This paper will address the issue of women teachers and their social activity in rural areas. To begin with, I will outline the changes which have occurred in the form and scope of teacher's social activity in the countryside, then I will move on to present the research conducted in the school year 2008/2009 in rural schools of the Kielce province, depicting the extent and form of social and cultural activities undertaken by female teachers.

The developments in social activities of teachers in rural schools

Over the years, social activity of teachers in rural areas has changed and reflected particular social needs. In the 19th century, when the teaching profession was still dominated by men, teachers' tasks included managing the area's development, familiarizing the local community with culture, helping people and giving advice in all types of difficulties, while serving as a moral model for the inhabitants (Dróżka 1991, p. 7). After the war, in neglected and backward rural regions teachers were the main organisers of education, which in many places in Poland (e.g. in western Poland) had to be built from scratch (Kwilecki 1960, pp. 37–38). They were the cultivators of civilizational progress, cultural and spiritual guides of the countryside, they performed its social tasks and fulfilled its cultural aspirations. Teachers performed numerous functions which were vital for many areas of social life, raised the level of education, contributed to the development of culture and economy. They were mainly expected to cultivate education and culture and carry out activities in various areas of social and economic life (Dróżka 1991, p. 8). Their social work strengthened crucial educational and cultural functions of schools in rural areas (Chałasiński 1969).

In the 1980s, rural areas still lacked skilled workforce, institutions, factories and social and cultural organizations which could take over certain tasks perfomed by education establishments. Due to this, teachers were expected to actively participate in the social life of the area, to cooperate with parents as well as institutions and social organizations which operated outside school. However, it did not mean that the teacher's role was perceived as a social mission. Female teachers were rather supposed to inspire, advise and organize various tasks. It was believed that by means of social activity they could contribute to a better exchange of information and views on different issues between the local community and the school. They could also influence public opinion and inspire inhabitants of rural areas to actively participate in transforming their own community (Dróżka 1991, pp. 83–84).

The range of social activity of female teachers in the 1990s was not as wide as it used to be. Female teachers mostly became involved intellectually in public issues. It mainly consisted of a critical analysis of problems and co-operation with the community by means of broadly understood educational work with children and teenagers at school (Dróżka 1999, p. 150; Dróżka 2002, p. 226). People referred to the history of education under the partitions and in the period between the two World Wars, when teachers sought to engage representatives of local communities in school life (Aleksander 1995, pp. 86–93).

In the 21st century, the importance of co-operation with the local community is stressed again and teachers are expected to initiate it, which can bring about numerous benefits for the education and upbringing of children and young people. Teachers are assumed to connect the network of schools with other educational institutions and engaging them in problems of the local community (Miłkowska-Olejniczak 2002, p. 278). Teachers are perceived as allies of the rural community and animators of communal co-operation (Mendel 2005, 23). Assuming the role of an ally and animator, the teacher acts as a negotiator between the local community and local authorities. This role remains opposed to local authorities. It involves seeking to overcome obstacles blocking educational growth, diagnosing them and making efforts to change the processes and the structures which have created them. Teachers work in alliance with their local community; irrespective of the aspirations and financial resources of the commune, they see the potential of individuals and groups. They organize networks of co-operation, relying on foundations found in the local community. They teach others to take political action, to defend the interest of individuals and groups threatened with the marginalisation. By the time the community becomes self-reliant, they act on its behalf, taking an active part in the civic life. They seek the roots of the most important problems in the community and indicate ways of solving these issues together. In this way, teachers can foster educational partnership (Mendel 2005, p. 23). Their role can be identified with being the leader of the local community. However, the basic difference between an animator and a leader is that the latter comes to the fore and leads the local community, whereas an animator is always in the middle of the community, acting in alliance, i.e. from the position on the same side (Mendel 2005, p. 24).

The contemporary complex reality requires teachers to go beyond the school environment and reach out to families and peer groups in order to become acquainted with the conditions in which a student is being raised (Miłkowska-Olejniczak 2002, p. 279). The co-operation with a student's family constitutes a very important, albeit difficult, aspect of the teacher's activities which aim at equal opportunities for students. The educational awareness of parents should be raised because, according to the research, among others S. Kawula, the quality and level of parents' awareness has a powerful influence on the development of children' educational aspirations, their school success, the choice of a profession and their social and professional starting point (Kawula 1996, pp. 348–356).

Teachers have an ingrained conviction that they are unable to influence education due to the lack of their own participation in developing the educational policy. As a result, they have a certain sense of helplessness, and with the passage of time they become accustomed to it as it is functionally favourable, particularly for those teacher who are not very active. This attitude is particularly hazardous. It is connected with the long-lasting process of nationalizing the initiative of the community. Replacing the initiative of the community with a state-run initiative leads to the failure of identification with the performed action (Kwiatkowska 2005, p. 222).

Social activity of female teachers is greater than the average activity in society, however, when their role in society is taken into account, it is not fully satisfactory. Female teachers are relatively little involved in local issues such as the improvement in living conditions of inhabitants in their own commune, issues of their professional environment, e.g. their working conditions (Sielatycki 2005). Such attitudes of teachers result from a wider social background. Teachers themselves point to such tendencies as the transformation of the Polish society from a community-oriented one to an individual-oriented one, from co-operation to competition, refraining from participation in the life of the local community and focusing on the family life. Those trends materialize in the threat of job loss due to a low birth rate, competition among teachers triggered by the new system of promotion, the loss of authority among students (Sielatycki 2005).

In the times of dynamic changes teachers are expected to facilitate the development and implementation of a new social order. They are assumed to prepare their students to live in new circumstances, to prepare them for new forms and methods of work organization, to manage their own lives, to shape their own growth (Appelt 2005, p. 6).

The social role of female teachers in rural areas has changed throughout history and it will continue changing. New developments in the teacher's role can be contributed to political, social, cultural and educational transformations in the country as a whole but also to the transformation of rural areas. This role has evolved: from familiarizing people with culture, organizing education as well as social, cultural and spiritual life, being the foremost authority in every walk of life, the promoter of civilizational progress, the intermediary between the school and the community, the initiator of a transformation in the local community, the co-creator, together with students and parents, of cultural and social values in civil democracy, through the pragmatist, to the teacher of success to 'customers of education establishments' as students are nowadays perceived. The role of female teachers from rural areas differs significantly from the role of urban teachers, which can be attributed to considerable discrepancies between those areas in Poland. Despite numerous efforts to bridge the gap between the conditions and the level of education in the countryside and in the city, rural education remains underprivileged and lags far behind the urban education. Therefore, the role and activity of female teachers in rural areas retains its particular importance for our country.

Social and cultural activity of female teachers in rural schools with regard to empirical research

In my article, I rely on empirical research conducted for my doctoral dissertation, concerning the role of teachers in assuring equal educational opportunities for students from rural areas. I wish to present the excerpt referring to the social and cultural activity of female teachers. For the sake of the research, this activity was assumed to be a response to cultural and social barriers deeply rooted in rural areas and mostly connected with the loss of traditional rural culture. This was in turn caused by the disappearance of the countryside and an inadequate acquisition of the patterns of universal culture, especially higher culture. These shortages had to be compensated for by the school. As schools have been closed down due to economic reasons, rural areas have been left without any social and cultural institutions and they have become culturally extinct. Young people have nowhere to meet, spend their leisure time or develop their interests (Strzemińska, Wiśnicka 2011, p. 25). This has deprived them of the opportunities to fulfill their dreams and ambitions, which is decisive in bridging the gap between the living standards in the city and in the countryside. These discrepancies cannot be compensated for by either higher education, working in high positions or the capital coming from a privileged background and affluence.

The research assumed that teachers engage in social and cultural activity by organizing special interest groups and extracurricular activities, school and community ceremonies, after-school trips with students. Furthermore, they establish co-operation between the community and cultural and educational institutions, establishments which pursue objectives of public interest; they propagate knowledge by means of promoting regional education which relies on the assets of the local environment.

The results of the empirical research have shown that social and cultural activity ranks first among other types of activities included in the research, both in the group of all teachers and in the group of female teachers who accounted for 91.7% (188 of the research sample). However, this activity is not widespread, it is located slightly above the average level (chart 1).

Chart 1. Social and cultural activity of female teachers against other activities

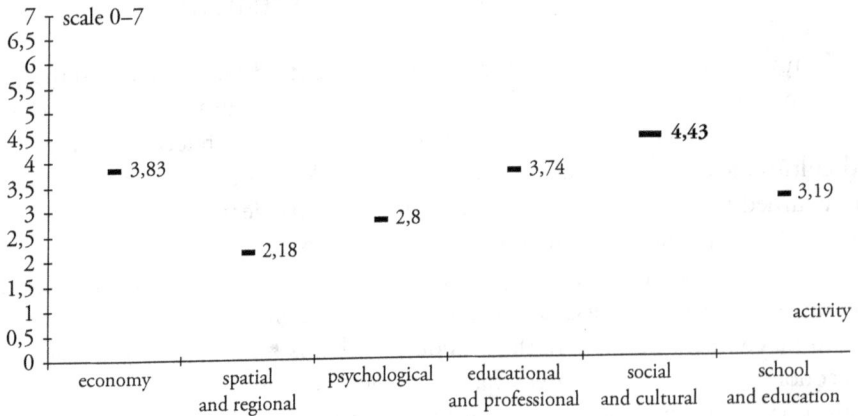

Source: own research.

A detailed analysis of the social and cultural activities has proved that 48.3% of the researched teachers run special interest groups in schools, whereas only 18.5% organize other extra-curricular activities. Many of the researched teachers (89.3%) organise school events and almost a half of them (48.8%) – out of school events. The majority of the researched female teachers (80%) organise excursions with students (class trips, visits to different cultural institutions – museums, theatres, music halls, etc.). A large proportion of the researched teachers cooperate with the community: 67.8% – with establishments pursuing objectives of public interest, 81% – with educational institutions, over 50% with other organizations and institutions in the local community. The majority of the researched teachers (82.4%) include elements of regional education in their teaching. The data is presented in chart 2.

Chart 2. Respective elements of social and cultural activity in the group of the researched female teachers

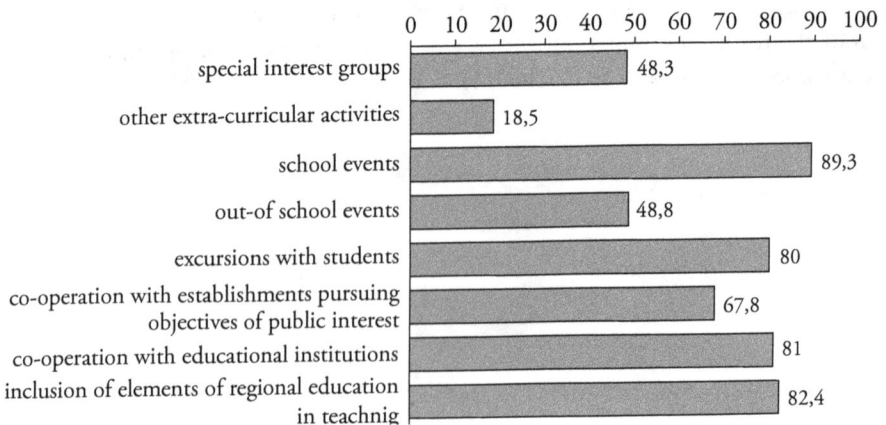

Source: own research.

Social and cultural activity is diversified in terms of the teacher's professional degree (Chart 3) and years of service (Chart 4). Trainee female teachers and those who had been working the shortest time demonstrated a considerably lower intensity in this type of activity than female teachers with higher professional degrees and with more years of service at schools.

Chart 3. Average intensity of social and cultural activity of the researched teachers in groups of promotion levels

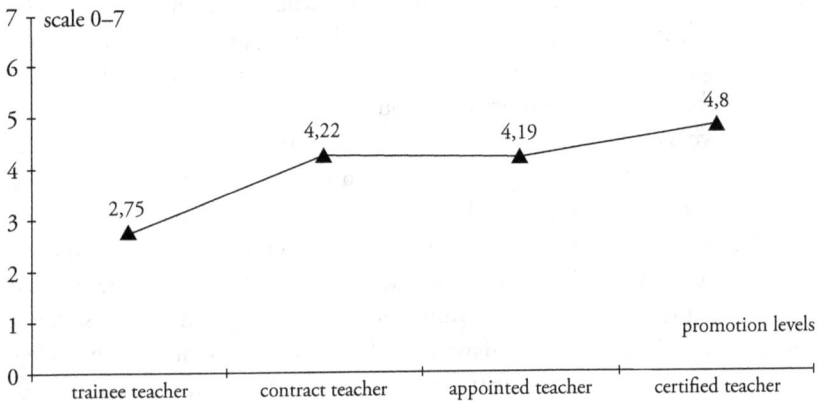

Source: own research.

Chart 4. Average intensity of social and cultural activity of the researched teachers in the groups of years of service

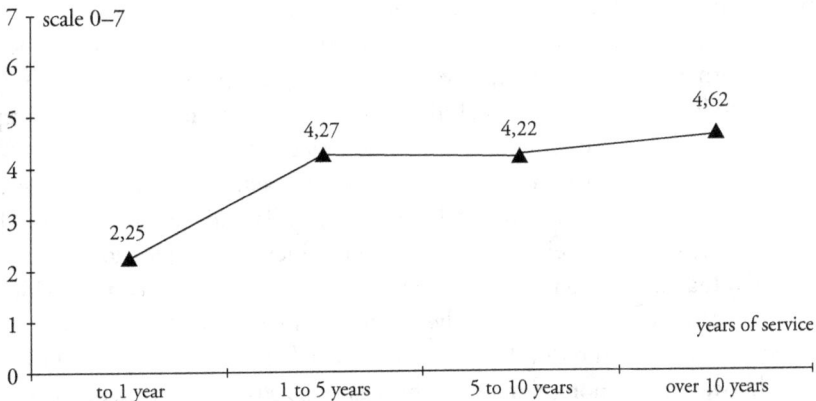

Source: own research.

Conclusions

Among the researched female teachers, social and cultural activity is the most often undertaken type of the enumerated activities. Despite the fact that its level remains slightly above the average, such results are encouraging as schools are often the only cultural and social institutions in rural areas. With schools closing down, rural areas experience institutional deprivation, which results in the shortage of cultural stimulation and places which could foster social and cultural development. Therefore social and cultural activity of female teachers is indispensable for the advancement of living standards of children and young people from rural areas. In this respect appropriate training for teachers is vital so that teachers can undertake such activities better and in a more conscious manner.

In recent years, the continual lowering of standards of university education has been pointed out as well as inappropriate training of future teachers. An increasing number of people graduating from university with a teaching degree claim that qualifications which they have acquired in the course of their studies are inadequate for current requirements (Kwiatkowska 2012a, p. 12). Teacher training in Poland remains retrograde, it is very traditional, despite numerous theoretical reflections on these issues. Those flaws are additionally compounded by delegating teacher training to non-pedagogical departments. Apart from pre-school and early primary school teachers, education departments in Poland do not train teachers (Dudzikowa, KnasieckaFalbierska 2013, p. 439). Furthermore, many universities still train teachers following the pattern of technical training (Kwiatkowska 2012a, p. 21). The teaching profession differs from technical professions in terms of its nature as it involves a lot of independent decision-making, often in a hurry, under time constraints, without any support, frequently in situations previously not experienced, with a shortage of data, in volatile conditions, under the additional pressure from the local community. Technical, skill-oriented training will not prepare future teachers for such requirements (Kwiatkowska 2012b, pp. 178–179).

The improvement in social activity of female teachers could be achieved by means of education which reinforces knowledge, skills and develops the teacher's personality. The cognitive reinforcement can be achieved by education which promotes individual intellectual activity and independence, as a result of which an individual is able to thik prospectively, construct a concept of themselves and of the world they act in. The development of the teacher's personality would lead to greater self-awareness among female teachers as well as the awareness of the sources where they can seek their professional empowerment (Kwiatkowska 2005, p. 171).

Teacher in-service training can play a crucial role in emphasizing the significance of social activity in the teaching profession. However, in recent years it has taken the wrong course (Day 2004, pp. 192–218). Instead of teaching teachers to be capable of a critical analysis of their profession, which involves challenging certain aspects of it and transforming it, teacher in-service training offers training that helps teachers achieve instrumental objectives. These objectives are achieved by means of 'tested and real' schemes of professional practice, legitimised by untested experience or uncritical acceptance of research results. It is connected with the direction of policy of teacher in-service training and leads to a situation where, despite greater current opportunieties, teachers in training have fewer chances for expanded learning and fewer possibilities to choose the knowledge they want to acquire (Day 2004, pp. 193–194).

Adrian Biela, Ewa Sierankiewicz-Miernik
Pedagogical University of Cracow, Poland

Volunteering as a form of social activity of women in early adulthood (based on the survey conducted among university students in Cracow)

Introduction

An essential element of civic society is a social capital, manifesting itself e.g. through social activity. Alongside the membership in social organizations and electoral participation, civic activity (also called public activity) also finds its manifestation in selflessly helping others – be it another human being or an animal (Łabędź 2008, pp. 54–68) – defined as volunteering.

Volunteering can be defined as 'a voluntary, gratuitous, conscious activity for the benefit of others, going beyond family, friends and colleagues related duties' (Nowosiadły 2006, p. 45). Its voluntary nature is intended to ensure that people in need, who are not able to handle difficulties by using their own resources of strength and potential thus becoming threatened with exclusion and social isolation, are taken care of.

Voluntary work can be done in relation to a number of entities or institutions acting on their behalf. The recipients could include e.g. people infected with HIV, addicted to psychoactive drugs, incarcerated in prisons or correctional facilities, having physical or mental disabilities, children, youths, adults, single mothers, homeless people, refugees or animals.

Givers, or volunteers, do not forget the main purpose of their activities, namely

> [...] placing the man and respect for the man in the centre of attention; focusing on the most vulnerable and the suffering; a civic sense of responsibility and participation in civil life; the meaning of service [...] and of sharing one's existence with the existence of others (Kostek 2010, p. 79).

As Stawiarska notes (Stawiarska 2011, p. 13), volunteering has an interdisciplinary character, consisting of three essential elements: a social dimension (volunteer

– charge relation), an individual dimension (psychological conditions and corre-
lates), and an existential dimension (a sense of meaning of life, self-realization).
The complexity of these dimensions leads not only to a change of situation and
development of a person receiving help, but also of a volunteer.

Volunteering as a value is a conscious reflection of that which is desirable,
a permanent conviction that

> [...] a specific behavior or an ultimate purpose of life is individually and socially prefer-
> able to alternative behaviors or ultimate states of being (Czerniawska 1995, p. 20).

K. Łabędź (2008, pp. 54–68) indicates factors determining stronger manifestations of civic activity and pro-social behaviors in society: the influence of the previous political system ideology (we could also mention the influence of the system of
education), the level of satisfaction with the current situation and the satisfaction
of needs, the desire to pursue one's interests, the level of trust in organizations or
institutions, and social awareness of contemporary societies.

The motives of pro-social behaviors and volunteering activities are complex.
They may be inspired by an altruistic motivation, resulting from the need to complement the value of one's life with altruistic work for others, a task-oriented motivation triggered by having experienced deprivation and callousness of professional
social services and a desire to neutralize this situation, or an ideological motivation
generated by religious experiences and family models of social service. There can
also be – though much less frequently – egoistic and affiliative motivation, where
pro-social activity results from the need to prove oneself, keep up with others, reinforce one's prestige in the eyes of others, acquire new skills that allow to get a job in
the former case, and in the latter – the need to be in contact with other people or the
environment of people thinking and feeling like us (Śliwak, Zdunek 2007, p. 111).

With the establishment of the European Year of Volunteering 2011, the issue
of voluntary activity has become a subject of a growing interest of theoreticians and
practitioners, which is highly valuable from a social point of view.

Study results show that the level of engagement in volunteering is not distributed equally within the Polish society; the key differences relate to educational
background, professional status, gender and age. Over the previous year, social work
was undertaken by one fourth of Poles with higher education and no more than one
seventh of those with basic or secondary education. An above-average activity can
be observed among the young (22% of volunteers are under 25) and students (29%)[1].

Other studies concerning the social activity of Polish citizens indicate that
women are more willing to engage in philanthropy and work for the benefit of
others; e.g. according to the data collected by the Central Statistical Office (2012),

---

[1] The study conducted by Millward Brown SMG/KRC on a random representative sample of
     1011 Poles aged 15 or more (Przewłocka 2013).

the percentage of women engaged in non-profit work is higher by 3.1% than in the case of men (27.4%; 24.3%).

The key role of education (obtained or being obtained) and gender has remained unchanged for years and they can be treated as significant characteristics of the pro-social commitment of the Polish society. Therefore, based on empirical data, below we present the conditions of undertaking volunteering by women in early adulthood and the image of their work with recipients.

Methodological notes

While diagnosing conditions and the course of voluntary activities of young women, the following aspects were taken into consideration:
- determining factors conditioning women's engagement in voluntary work: motives of commitment to voluntary work and people / factors / situations inspiring /promoting supportive activities ;
- place, time and forms of voluntary activity;
- wards and their needs (the problem areas of support by women – volunteers);
- types of support measures taken by the female respondents.

The study was conducted using a diagnostic survey in the period from December 2011 to March 2012 in Cracow. It involved 77 young women operating in various places, facilities, and organizations supported by volunteers. These included mainly foundations, university volunteering organizations, animal shelters, associations, nursing homes and orphanages.

A survey consisting of 25 conjunctive semi-open questions was used for collecting data. The respondents could choose more than one answer and also had the chance to express themselves freely.

Social and demographic characteristics of the studied women – volunteers

The studied women were aged from 18 to 25 years. The majority were between 21 and 23 years old (53 women – 68.8%) and studied pedagogical and psychological subjects. Almost one in four of the respondents was a student of the humanities (20 women – 23.3%), one in six studied natural sciences (14 women – 16.3%). A small percentage (5.8%) was represented by women studying science/technology and medicine (5 women each). It should be noted that an obtained number of study profiles exceeds the number of the studied people due to the fact that 8 women studied more than one faculty, with one being a student of three faculties.

Almost half of the women lived in a big city with the population of over 50 thousand residents (37 people – 48.1%). More than one in four respondents (27.3%) came from the countryside (21 people). The smallest percentage constituted the women living in small towns with the population of less than 50 thousand of residents (18 people – 23.4%). Concerning financial issues, their main sources of income were: parents' help (61 people – 79.2%), employment (25 people – 32.5%), educational scholarship (21 people – 27.3%), social scholarship (10 people – 13.0%), benefit (6 people – 7.8%), student loans (2 people – 2.6%) and a partner's income (one respondent).

The period of voluntary work measured at five intervals shows that the greatest percentage of volunteers were active for a relatively short time – up to a year (48.1%), this including mostly the youngest respondents. One in ten respondents (10.4%) worked as a volunteer from one to two years, a slightly larger (15.9%) worked from two to three years, and only 7.8% from three to five years. Nearly 1/5 of the respondents (18.2%) were active as volunteers for over five years, constituting a group that identified itself to the greatest extent with the idea of volunteering, and it can be assumed that this scope of engagement may also be present in their later lives, also after graduating.

Determinants of undertaking volunteering by the respondents

To understand the phenomenon of voluntary work for the benefit of other people, in considering volunteers' activities we cannot neglect factors determining those activities, such as: subjective reasons, factors or people inspiring one to engage in volunteering, and the favorable climate for the participation in voluntary work.

The most significant reasons behind becoming interested in pro-social activity include: *the chance to gain some experience* (41.6%), *mutual help of volunteers* (40.3%) and *the willingness to conquer the fear of the unknown* (37.7%). One in three students mentioned: *the possibility of self-realization* (33.8%) and *a better organization of support units* (29.9%), with one in four indicating: *the opportunity to gain knowledge and skills necessary for employment* (27.3%), *support from employed workers* (24.7%) and *a better working atmosphere* (22.1%); only one in twenty respondents indicated: *the possibility to gain recognition* (5.2%).

All our activities are motivated by something or someone. The respondents considered their *own initiative* (71%) and *the example of their volunteering friends* (33.8%) to be the key motivating factors. For one in ten respondents, *participation in student activities* (10.4%) and *Church's teaching* (9.1%) were significant. As many indicated *accidental nature of their involvement* (10.4%). A negligible percentage indicated: *their lecturers* (5.2%), or *family* and *the media* (1.3% each). Almost 8% of the women indicated other factors and people, such as: *a desire to gain experience in one's profession, high school, a priest teaching religion in secondary school, a secondary school teacher.*

The third determinant of getting involved in volunteering includes situations promoting such activities. The most frequent situation of such kind, activating pro-social activity of young women, is *being personally asked for help* (55.9%). Next, there is a conviction of *feeling like the only person that can help a particular person* (41.6%) and that fact that *a person seeking help is my family* (28.6%). For 1/4 of volunteers the situational impact took place when a person seeking help was *known to them* (27.3%) or *liked by them* (22.1%). They also place importance on *building self-esteem* and *having one's own resources* (19.5% respectively). The least important was *the possibility to impress someone* (1.3%).

Place and time of the support provided by volunteers

Analyzing the empirical data indicating the place of social work (cf. Figure 1) it should be pointed out that one woman in three works for *a foundation* (33.8%) or *an association* (32.4%). One in ten is engaged in taking care of and raising children – social orphans in *an orphanage* or participates in events organized by volunteering groups by *universities* or *the Polish Red Cross*. A slightly smaller number of respondents support *social welfare homes, Church*, or *the Polish Scouting Association* (7.8%; 6.6%; 6.2%). None of them indicated their *workplace* as the area for providing care and support.

Additionally, the women mentioned (in category: other) the following facilities: animal shelter (12 people), educational care facility (4 people), community and therapy centers (3 people), private volunteering (2 people), hospitals (2 people), Children's University (2 people), the Dun Bear Cub Foundation (2 people), as well as (single individuals): The Academy of Future, the Maltese Centre of Help for Disabled Children and Their Families, center for people with special needs, environmental inspectorate, schools, the Caritas Volunteer Center, the Polish Humanitarian Action.

Figure 1. Place of voluntary work*

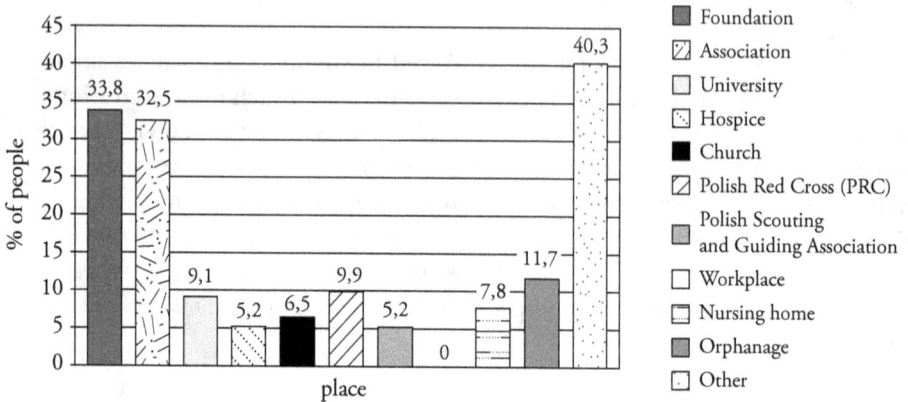

Source: own research.

* The question allowed for giving more than one answer, therefore the total amount value is greater than the number of the women studies, and the total percentage value exceeds 100%.

It is also important to specify the amount of time dedicated by volunteers to social activity. Within a week, one in four respondents (24.7%) claimed that they spent 1–2 hours working for others; one in five (19.5%) – two to four hours. 13% of the respondents spend four to six hours working for others, 6.5% – six to eight hours, and only 5.2% – over ten hours per week. The others indicated that the amount of time spent on voluntary work depends on their free time (13%) and their wards' needs (14.3%).

The subjects and character of volunteering

The wards of young volunteers include mainly *children* (62.3%) and *youths* (50.7%). One in five indicated *adults aged 18 to 60* (20.8%) as the recipients, as well as *elderly people* and *animals* (19.5% each).

As shown in the data presented in Figure 2, the subject of the majority of studied women's activity (44) is *an individual*, more than one fourth of them (21) conduct voluntary work for a *group*, and one in six (12) works with *society*. The least frequent is a comprehensive help provided for a *family* (declared by 10 respondents only), which might seem surprising in the light of growing needs for support and solving economic, social and educational problems of the family (especially in the context of ongoing changes within family and the economic crisis that started in 2008). However, this is understandable considering the fact that the specifics of systemic support for help require experience and professionalism that young volunteers still lack.

Figure 2. Forms of support activities

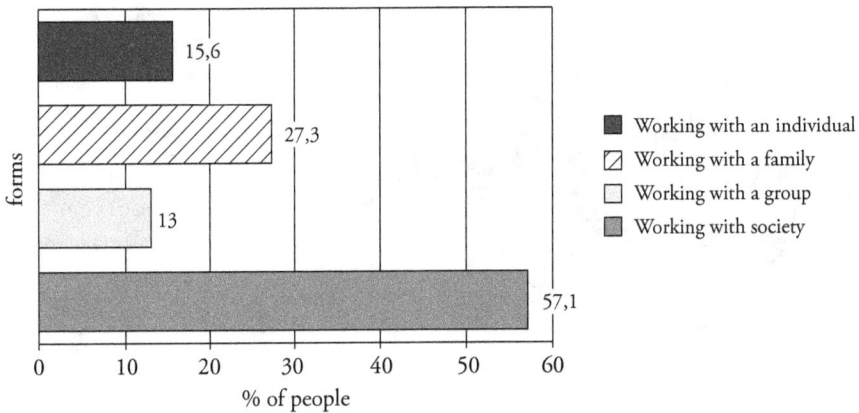

Source: own research.

* The question allowed for giving more than one answer, therefore the total amount value is greater than the number of the women studies, and the total percentage value exceeds 100%.

Educational and caretaking negligence in relation to children is a key area of support in relation to recipients of help, with 29 volunteers being active in this area (cf. Figure 3). For one in four of the volunteers, the recipients are *the poor* and *the seriously ill* (18–20 responses), for one fifth of the volunteers (16) – *people with physical disabilities,* for one sixth – *the homeless* and *casualties of fortuitous events* (12–13 responses). A relatively small number of women (8–13%) indicated *socially maladjusted people, the unemployed, mentally disabled* and *orphans* as the recipients of support. Other responses account for over 9% of choices made by the respondents. Their responses cover such problem areas as: *abandonment, problems with learning, poor care.* Two persons were unable to specify the area of their support activities, stressing the fact that their wards have various problems. Specific recipients of multifaceted activities seem to be two extreme age groups: seniors and children and young people.

Analyzing the scope of activities undertaken by the students in terms of volunteering (cf. Table 1), we can find out what forms of direct activities involving people in need are within the possibilities and competences of volunteers and what needs their wards have.

Figure 3. Problem areas of recipients*

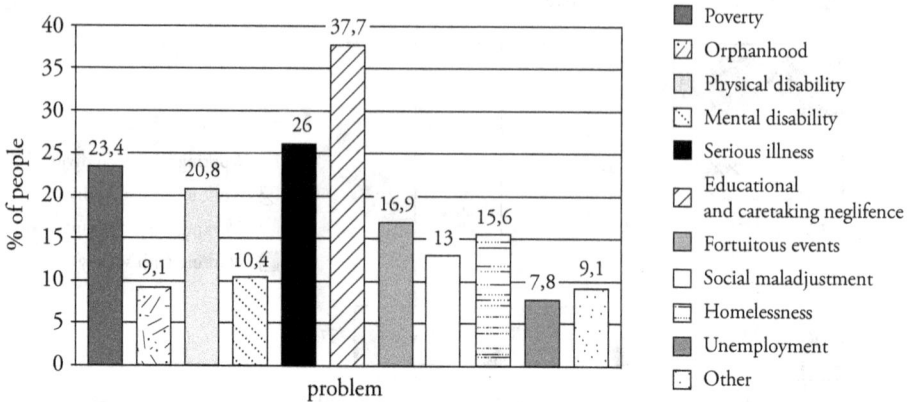

Source: own research.

* The question allowed for giving more than one answer, therefore the total amount value is greater than the number of the women studies, and the total percentage value exceeds 100%.

Nearly half of them have *conversations* with their help recipients. One in three goes for *walks* and *organizes fun activities*, whereas one in four h*elps with homework, aids and organizes support activities.* One in five volunteers sharing her time with others involves *organizing events.* One in five volunteers helps by *explaining, clarifying, fundraising and travelling with the recipients of support.* A somewhat smaller percentage of volunteers (10–13%) – are involved in *cleaning works* and *take care of their wards' personal hygiene. Informing about possible forms of support* oscillates around 6%. There is an equally small demand for *contacting institutions that could help a particular person* and *help in obtaining benefits or other forms of support.* One response – thus being close to a statistical error status – indicates *shopping.*

10% of the studied women additionally mentioned in more detail forms of support in relation to another person or an animal: *organizing free time for children and young people, promoting humanitarian values, expanding ecological knowledge in society, fulfilling dreams of sick children, conducting trainings, health care activities, taking photos and placing them on the Internet* (in the case of animals), and *animal socialization.*

Table 1. Support activities in relation to recipients*

Type of activity	No. of people	% of people
Conversation	36	46.8
Explaining, clarifying	12	15.6
Support	19	24.7
Taking care of the ward's personal hygiene	7	9.1
Walking	26	33.8

Cleaning works	10	13.0
Helping with homework	19	24.7
Play	26	33.8
Organizing support activities	20	26.0
Fundraising	11	14.3
Shopping	1	1.3
Organizing events (e.g. a concert for Santa)	14	18.2
Help in obtaining benefits or other forms of support	3	3.9
Informing about possible forms of support	5	6.5
Contacting institutions that could help a particular person	3	3.9
Travelling with wards	12	15.6
Other	8	10.4

Source: own research.

* The question allowed for giving more than one answer, therefore the total amount value is greater than the number of the women studies, and the total percentage value exceeds 100%.

Such a wide range of activities stems from the possibility to use a broad spectrum of methods, forms and techniques of influencing a ward's situation, as well as from the characterological diversity of help recipients or volunteers, and from the problem manifested when providing help. There is no single model of conduct because there is no single correct and approved strategy determining counseling, caretaking or corrective actions. Consequently, an ability to adapt to a changing mosaic of events and bio-socio-cultural conditions is a welcome trait for a volunteer.

Conclusion

A significant contribution to the functioning of volunteering is provided by students, especially students of social sciences (such as pedagogy) undertaking volunteering for a variety of reasons (from purely altruistic to egoistic). They are largely women aged from 21 to 23, active in a given area for no longer than a year, from one to four hours a week.

The studied women engaged mainly in support activities in foundations and associations supporting individuals that need help due to educational and caretaking negligence, serious illnesses, poverty, or physical disability. Wards include mainly children in need of psychological support (conversation) and other forms of activity, such as help with homework, walks, etc.

Though exiguous in nature, the conducted study nonetheless leads to a conclusion that factors such as age, gender and education are decisive for undertaking volunteering. However, it would be advisable to verify this thesis through comparative studies conducted among young people who are not students.

Monika Sulik
University of Silesia, Poland

The biographical dimension of femininity – andragogic references and contexts

Introduction

'Woman' and 'femininity' are concepts which in the ordinary common-sense meaning seem to be distinctive and clear, not requiring further defining. The issue related to femininity, or rather its lack in the social and scientific sphere has been, until recently, so significant and severe that it has become a kind of signpost for scientists and researchers to deal with these issues more broadly and more deeply. The silent presence of women in various areas of everyday life was *uncomfortable* not only for women themselves, but mostly for environments that are mature and consciously recognise the right and task of women associated with showing their perspective or emphasising their voice. One just cannot help but notice that in recent years the issue concerning the woman and femininity has been addressed with an increasing frequency and success, thereby providing the opportunity and space for the full occurrence of the perspective of both sexes in equal rights.

In literature, there are often voices and questions present similar to the ones of Natalia Kruszyna:

> What is this femininity then? This is one of the fundamental questions that seem simple and obvious, until we try to formulate an answer. Does one look for it in nature or in culture? Does it reveal itself in physiology or in the psyche? Is it the matter or the spirit? Harmony of body or chaos of desires? Deep knowledge or shallow pretence? Intuition exceeding the limits or stereotype restricting thinking? Goodness or curse?[1]

---

[1] http://www.mhk.katowice.pl/index.php?option=com_content&view=article&id=234&Item id=130 (Accessed: 8.03.2014).

At this point, one has to refer to a short story by Anthony de Mello:

> A woman in a coma was dying. She suddenly had a feeling that she was taken up to heaven and stood before the Judgment Seat.
> 'Who are you?' a Voice said to her.
> 'I am the wife of the mayor,' she replied.
> 'I did not ask whose wife you are but who you are.'
> 'I'm the mother of four children.'
> 'I did not ask whose mother you are, but who you are.'
> I'm a school teacher.'
> 'I did not ask what your profession is but who you are.'
> 'I am a Christian.'
> 'I did not ask what your religion is but who you are.'
> 'I'm the one who always helped the poor.'
> 'I did not ask what you did but who you are.' If you do not know who you are go back to the living and learn who you really are.
> When the woman got better she decided to discover who she really was.
>
> (Mello de n.d.)

This story seems to fit very much into the reflections presented in this text, it even disciplines them in the sense of involvement but it also lets one feel the vastness of the horizon of exploration in this matter. Creating an image of femininity in a general sense is rather arduous and even acrobatic abilities do not seem to help here in any way, thus, in this text, I wish to attempt to show different faces of femininity and the ways of searching for the essence of femininity through the prism of biographicity. It is a biographical perspective that allows to set off on a metaphorical journey, the purpose of which is to discover the essence of femininity in many contexts and dimensions.

The purpose of these deliberations is therefore not to create a unified picture or portrait of a woman, but to discover a variety of colours and shades, and thus the experiences of women who make up this portrait or picture, with the knowledge that after all *every person experiences himself/herself completely differently, constructing differently, because we are all different* (Sulik 2010, p. 169). I therefore wish at this point to share my research, teaching and biographical experiences connected with organising activities within the subject of andragogy and biography in education. I will show how one can undertake, in different ways, the realisation of one of the main ideas of andragogy, which is to encourage adults to engage in constructive self-reflection, to deepen their self-awareness.

Given the fact that my research interests are related mainly to feminological research, my reflection will above all cover biographical conditions for women's development and the feminine perspective of viewing the world. I will present my deliberations from three different perspectives, somewhat interpenetrating and complementary. Therefore, it will be a **research perspective** where I will introduce the research projects in which I have explored the concept of femininity, the projects that can become an inspiration for further personal explorations in this area. Another perspective is the **teaching perspective** mainly related to the classes and projects I have carried out in the classroom, the projects whose aim is to develop biographical competencies of participants but they also often touch the therapeutic dimension. And the third perspective, **autobiographical** one, where all personal experiences of women researchers mainly, but also experiences of participants of biographical research, shall echo.

The research perspective

When undertaking qualitative research, I did not sense, not even to the slightest extent, the significance that this research would have for me. For as a woman researcher, by getting closer to experiences of other women, I saw a chance to gain an insight into the mechanisms governing the lives of women and to re-evaluate my own experience, which seems to me invaluable (Mc Kinley Runyan 1992, p. 9). What became inspiring for me was the words of Małgorzata Bogunia-Borowska who compares the study of various aspects of everyday life to an Impressionist painting in which the brush strokes and paint applied to the canvas create a mixture of colours rather than the whole picture when viewed from a close distance. Therefore it seems necessary to make the compilation and comparison of these 'individual brush strokes' which only when viewed from an adequate comprehensive perspective will allow us to see the full picture (Bogunia-Borowska 2009, p. 8). And all this serves not only to encourage an andragogical and biographical reflection on ourselves but also on the world and others, to hear the voices of other women and to enable them to participate in various areas of everyday life with full rights.

One of my biographical projects which deals with women and femininity was the research topic entitled *Women in science. Subjective and socio-cultural conditions* (Sulik 2010). The narrative interview-based study of qualitative nature allowed me to create a sketch for a portrait of women in science but also to show the women's feelings and experiences. The narratives of the women involved in scientific and teaching work, while seeking fulfilment in many other areas, made it possible to present the biographies of women in science in the context of everyday life, in the context of obstacles, difficulties and uncertainties or in the context of what is elusive. It is the biographical perspective that allowed me to see, among other aspects, specific models of femininity developed by women in the scientific sphere or to show the women's academic careers. The undertaken studies have enabled me to show what is common in the experience of women seeking fulfilment in science, and not articulated by numbers and statistical calculations, but a voice, of these women, their timbre and tone. For only when the women themselves gave a personal meaning to their experiences, was it possible to understand the conditions for their development.

Another research project, still being underway, is entitled *The biographical dimension of femininity*. The aim of this project is to look into various areas of everyday life and tell about them in a female voice, through women's narratives. By studying different types of biographical works and materials one can also discover himself/herself. The task of persons involved in this project is to focus on the issues that are especially important, valuable or inspiring for them and to trace experiences of women related to a particular area in biographical materials. Thus, in this area the following works, among others, were created: *Woman as a wife of a famous husband and the First Lady; Woman and motherhood; Woman in travel; Woman with passion; Successful woman; Woman and cooking; Woman versus prostitution and sponsoring; Woman and war; Woman and disability; Woman on stage; Woman, infanticide mother, fallen angel; Woman and politics; Woman and fame; Woman and politics*, and many more.

The implementation of this project is related mainly to presenting important and interesting, even exciting experiences of women and personal meanings that women give to those experiences. In the women's narratives we also find many threads linked closely to andragogical issues, which is especially valuable when discussing these issues in the classroom.

The teaching perspective

At this point I would like, above all, to mention the qualitative research project that I have been involved in thanks to working with students for 12 years. The works I have gathered during the realisation of the *Biographical map of life* project are a moving example of how many functions and tasks this work can have from the andragogical and developmental point of view. Becoming aware of our own place in the world, redefining our own identity, discovering the conditions of our own life journey are just a few of them, and yet so significant. These projects are extremely meaningful and evocative, and the richness of forms and saturation with metaphor is the evidence of the extreme importance of pedagogical categories: creativity and imagination. When describing the feminine perspective in this sphere, it seems necessary to describe at least some of the works created in which femininity is articulated very vividly and clearly.

It turns out that many women described themselves, formed their own personal periodization of life based on their biographical experiences related to fulfilling their traditional women's roles in everyday life. Here are a few examples of this type of works:

– *A cookbook 'Pasta Unveiled'*: In the 'prologue' the author of the work wrote: *My life is like pasta. It takes different shapes, colours, it tastes different each time. Seasonings, sauces, additions make up pasta, whereas people, situations and events create my life.* The work constitutes a way to describe various stages of life by as pasta dishes, which in a very suggestive way become complementary to the described biographical experiences. For example, the author wrote about her eighteenth birthday in the following way:

The entry into adulthood – how does the eighteenth birthday taste? Bittersweet, that would be the answer to my question. We expect privileges, and together with those we get responsibilities. I chose a dish with spinach, because for me spinach may be both delicious and hard to swallow.

– **The map of life on the basis of the hair growth cycle**: When justifying such a choice of the way to present her biography, the author wrote: *Since I am a hairdresser, I will base my map of life on the hair growth cycle. The basic step in the search for common features between the biography and the life cycle of the hair is to divide human life into individual phases and distinguish common characteristics in each of them as well as to compare them with the structure and development of the hair. And so Levison divided life into four eras for which equivalents in hairdressing will be: childhood – a root that is the lower part of the hair, and its most important part is the matrix. The adulthood phase – a stem, which is part of the hair protruding from the scalp, divided into: 1) early adulthood – the hair root, anagenic phase, 2) the middle age (the middle part, length, catagenic phase, 3) late adulthood – the tip of the hair, telogenic phase.* Next, the author describes each of the phases in detail, extremely skillfully linking the sphere of life experiences with terms taken from the area of hairdressing.

Due to the nature of the undertaken reflections related to the search for the essence or shades of femininity, at this point it seems reasonable to me to present one of the works in full[2]. In my opinion, the work that deals a lot with the reflective and metaphorical 'painting of the female portrait' may at the same time become extremely inspiring, in terms of teaching, for people working with youth or adults.

The story of a painting[3]

Room: *The room is bright with windows wide open on sunny days. The air is filled with the smell of oil paints, solvents and fresh air, the windows are open and the room fills with the warm spring sunshine and crisp air. In the corners, on the floor, by the walls and on easels canvas, frames and other painting materials are placed. Among the*

---

2 At this point I would like to specifically thank both the authors of the works presented here as well as other people, female and male students who have taken the trouble to write and tell about themselves and their life, the effects of which I was given a chance to admire. Thank you very much.
3 Source: own research.

paintings and frames are the ones that are large, medium-sized, small and very tiny, completely finished, in the process of creation as well as the ones not yet started. A cat sits on the windowsill.

Canvas: The experienced hands (of the artist) rearrange the frames to finally choose the right one. Then they unroll the roll/bale of canvas to which a wooden structure is put. With skillful movements the hands stretch and fix the canvas to the frame to finally cut off the unnecessary material. The bale of the canvas is put back on its place – its task having been completed, it is time for an acrylic paint which will provide a foundation on which different, this time, colours of oil paints will be applied to create a painting. The canvas prepared in this manner is put in a dry place where it can dry easily. The cat observes everything with its emerald green eyes from its place at the back of an armchair. **The parents are expecting a child – me.**

Painting: Having finished its nap, the cat gets up from the bed, stretches and looks around. Not finding anything noteworthy, it jumps off the sill of an open window and disappears among lush greenery. Dry and ready to use the canvas – tabula rasa, a blank page ready to receive a form, to be filled with the content and meaning. Paints are squeezed out of tubes onto a palette, brushes wait ready to be used, the solvent (in a jar) exudes a peculiar odour. The fingers take the tool of creation, clear space in front of them... the cat has not returned yet. **My birth.**

The idea for a patch: Night. Behind the window a summer storm rages, when a branch snaps and hits the window almost breaking it – the cat runs across the room in horror – the knocked painting falls... Another morning, the cloudless sky promises a sunny day. The experienced hands pick the paining up from the floor, there is a tear in one of the corners of the canvas. After placing the painting in a well-lit area the artist starts mending it. Thin threads and several layers of pigment fix it and do not give a chance to guess the unfortunate event – still, the wound is there, giving the canvas and the paining a characteristic look. **When I was two and a half my father died. When I was four, my mother got remarried to my current dad.**

New painting: With the onset of summer both outside the window and in the painting, the painter reaches for another canvas which has already had time to dry and starts to work on it as well. Both paintings are to present the same place, scenery, but from different perspectives, showing different themes. **When I was eight years old, my younger sister was born.**

Landscape: After days of work both works slowly start to gain an expression that reveals their personalities. In the first painting, in the landscape there is a cleft hidden in the shade of the trees and in the midst of dense vegetation. At first glance it is difficult to notice. The cat basks in the warm sunshine on the windowsill. **One of the events that had a huge impact on me happened when I was in third grade of the secondary**

school. I will always be extremely grateful to two of my friends who listened to me and helped me – even, and perhaps especially, when I broke down during the eighteenth birthday party of one of them.

Life goes on: The theme of paintings as well as the landscape that they present change several times. Since the work in the painting is in progress, these changes are ongoing. Sometimes it is a new topic, sometimes another season showing its face in the colour of leaves, or the lack of them, and sometimes just a coincidence or fate, who knows, when the cat will mess something up or a stronger gust of wind will blow over a jar of solvent damaging a piece of the painting and the hand wielding the brush will have to start this part over again... My painting is still in the process of being created, and the phase of creating will end with my death. There are countless joys and sorrows ahead of me – whether scale pans will counterbalance each other or not is only for me to find out.

This work is an extremely peculiar and picturesque periodization of a woman's life – a student of pedagogy who, with an unusual excitement and sensitivity, painted herself and her life with words, or brushes as Milena Obrączka would say (Obrączka 2011, p. 174). This is another example of how a metaphor can be an unusual form of expression. A woman's act of painting is not just painting herself in a literal sense, but also painting with words, which like brushes show us everything that is invisible in women and associated with a certain mystery. A mystery of experiencing the self and the world, a mystery, a part of which I wanted to discover and reveal in this reflection.

The autobiographical perspective

Laurel Richardson wrote: 'creating stories and narratives has become a tool to give sense to my world through situating my specific personal experiences in a broader historical and sociological context [...]. I was sure that the research story was complete. Maybe not the only one I could tell, but completely sincere and reflecting my research experience honestly. I still believe it. After some time, however, I realised that it lacked my personal experience, my biography and that was the reason I wrote it' (Lalak 2010, p. 91).

Is it then possible to underestimate the fact that biographical studies provide a unique opportunity to meet another human being? Meeting them face-to-face, a very personal meeting, where we can experience the presence of another human being both verbally and non-verbally. Where we can feel invited to the meeting, experience co-participation, feel compassion, that is accompany in the journey. Finally, where we can feel we are travellers ourselves.

The research works anchored in biographical studies increasingly draw attention to showing the reflection of people participating in the studies and those conducting them. Even separate chapters attempt to present the reflection of the subjects and researchers after the study has been completed in order to further capture the personal experiences related to the research situation.

In my opinion, research projects or research reports supplemented with our own autobiographical references and reflections resulting from carrying out this research and after its completion, are extremely important and interesting from the point of view of the issues discussed in this paper. They make the content complete and make it possible to realise that the research situation changes and is a teaching opportunity for both participants in the study and the researchers. At this point a topic related to ethical aspects of biographical research as well as the level of involvement during research appears. But is it possible to participate in a situation or be part of a story of human life and not become involved? For it seems that not only are the narratives formulated by the respondents in relation to the topic that diligent researcher explore extremely important. Equally important is what happens to the capacity for reflection of the respondents during the research process itself. It is, after all, an important personal experience, which may also strongly influence the interpretation of the research material. It becomes a part of it.

I would also like to refer here to my personal experience as a researcher. When conducting the biographical research project related to the *subjective and socio-cultural conditions for development of women in science*, I also made an attempt to present personal reflections of the respondents as well as my personal reflections as a researcher, after the research was completed. Here is an excerpt of these thoughts: 'To me the conducted studies have a merit that cannot be overestimated in many dimensions. Although my main intention was to investigate the conditions for women's scientific development, the factors which determined the choice of their careers in science, in retrospect I can see what **wealth of meanings** the entire research process carried. For me, meetings and discussions with respondents provided not only a valuable cognitive material, but also, and often mainly, a response to the questions which bothered me, an opportunity for self-reflection, the ability to penetrate the intimate world of my interviewees. The contact with the women participating in the research – both in person and by mail, allowed me to explore the experiences of women in science, and almost **to touch** the areas of the world of science previously unknown to me. I will not forget either the atmosphere of these extraordinary meetings with the women scientists. The meetings held in an atmosphere of unusual cordiality. My interviewees were willingly sharing their insights and reflections. They allowed me to enter their world of autobiographical memories and experiences to which they gave personal meanings' (Sulik 2010, p. 188).

The words of the interviewees related to the research project in which they participated were extremely gratifying for me. Let me quote some of them[4]:

- '[...] *thanks to you I have wandered through all the years that were crucial in making decisions, in making life plans and wrestling with carrying them out'* (a woman with a doctoral degree, 54 years old, a representative of biology).
- '*I hope that my statement will help you explore the scientific problem at hand. This topic is really interesting for me and I will be glad to read your work. Good luck with your women's scientific activities'* (a woman with a doctoral degree, 33 years old, a representative of climatology.)
- '*Thank you for the opportunity for self-reflection'* (a woman professor, with a post-doctoral degree, 60 years old, a representative of philosophy).

As a researcher, but also as a tutor of biographical didactics, I wish to say with a strong conviction that the research projects I have had the opportunity to conduct are an unforgettable experience for me. The meetings with female and male students as well as my interviewees and narrators were a peculiar, multi-dimensional **journey for me in search of the essence, faces and shades of femininity,** a journey in the real but also in a metaphorical sense. A journey that will forever remain in my memory.

---

4 Source: own research.

Joanna Łukasik
Pedagogical University of Cracow, Poland

The identity of teachers
in the midlife transition period

> [...] *we 'discover' identity the moment it stops being 'given'*
> *and becomes 'set'* [...]
>
> Bauman 2007, p. 51

The identity of man

For the contemporary man, 'permanent change' has become inscribed in his life. As A. Giddens notes, this change

> [...] radically transforms the general nature of daily life and the most personal aspects of human activity. Modernity should be considered on the institutional level, but the transmutations occurring on this level are directly reflected in the life of the individual and, along with that, his identity (Giddens 2002, p. 3).

In the changing world, identity is not 'given' to the man along with the social origin (in the past, it was self-explanatory that an aristocrat was an aristocrat, a married woman was a married woman, and a blacksmith was a blacksmith (cf. M.J. Szymański 2013a). Rather, identity is 'set'; it is an identity which is yet to become and is supposed to be the result of one's own creation as well as various organized and unorganized, intentional and unintentional, institutional and personal influences of one's social environment (Jawłowska 2001, p. 51).

The above line of thinking makes room for M.J. Szymański's understanding of identity. He believes that

> [...] identity is a conviction construed in the course of one's life, through continuously made self-observations, self-assessments and external opinions of who one is, which is a consequence of various life choices, social roles, achievements, failures, and undertaken activities (Szymański 2013b, p. 195).

The author further argues that

> [...] identity can be construed consciously or incidentally, rationally or unreflectively, in a planned or chaotic manner, consistently and straightforwardly or else in a changing and convoluted way (Szymański 2013a).

To a considerable degree this depends on an individual's wisdom and strong will, as well as on people and institutions fostering his development. They influence an individual on various levels, inspiring activity, stimulating or hindering aspirations and desires. It is also worth emphasizing that in the process of construing identity it is important 'how, out of what, by whom and why it is construed'.

Therefore, there are numerous factors influencing the construction of identity. One of them is the cultural perception of roles. As Nowak-Dziemianowicz notes, such perceptions may well be subject to constant changes, yet they still impose different goals and expectations depending on one's gender (Nowak-Dziemianowicz 2012a, p. 246). This manifests itself in the following:

- Women pursue ready, set, culturally determined goals.
- Men are authors and creators of their own goals.
- Men can pursue any goals. Even if such goals are culturally considered 'female', such as raising and taking care of children, which inspires respect and recognition among others.
- Women fulfilling professional ambitions, striving for success, ambitious and professional have to additionally justify their activities by ensuring a successful family life.
- When constructing their identity, women need complementation and confirmation; they must be of need to others.
- Men construct their identity based on their own values and choices and they are self-sufficient in this process.
- The world presented to boys in the process of family socialization is given and open.
- The world presented to women in the process of family socialization is set and closed.
- The basic activity set for men is creation.
- The basic activity set for women is adaptation.
- Freedom in the family socialization discourse on the woman's role is conditional.
- Freedom in the family socialization discourse on the man's role is unconditional.
- The language of discourse in the socialization concerning woman's role is the language of duties and assessments.
- The language of discourse in the socialization concerning man's role is the language of possibilities and encouragement.
- Sanctions for the failure in the socialization process concerning social and professional roles are different depending on gender (Nowak-Dziemianowicz 2012a, pp. 246–247).

These premises indicate that the reasons behind cultural reinforcement and setting of women's roles can be found in the family socialization. This undoubtedly affects the construction of one's identity and the search for the answer to the question: 'Who am I?'.

The midlife transition period

Each period in one's life is unique due to some dominating role:

> [...] at the same time, in each of them there are the same reoccurring elements of I, allowing one to identify oneself on the one hand and differentiate oneself in different life periods on the other (Łukaszewski 2003, p. 264).

In the process of the identification and reconstruction of identity, people as active subjects gives meaning to events and processes taking place within them. They impose interpretations on successes and hardships which they undergo. Giving meaning to life is part of the man's orientation towards the future and follows from his system of personal meanings, created around his values, goals and fulfilled individual tasks' (Oleś 2000, p. 228). Interpreting life and giving it a sense of meaning, reminiscing about successes, achievements and failures, and analyzing one's life are characteristic features of the midlife transition period.

Middle age period (following Oleś, I have assumed the age between 35 and 55 years) is combined with a completely new perspective on the perception of life's tasks and problems. *Transition* (used by Oleś interchangeably with the term 'midlife crisis', understood as a transition) implies a significant qualitative change, a new outlook on life, and a new perspective on the future thanks to one's past experiences and the awareness of life's finality (Oleś 2000). In the transitional period, people apart from a sense of dissatisfaction with their present (previous) situation can also, as active entities, find a novel and innovative mode of reference to their dreams from the past and start realizing them in a novel way.

The numerous relevant works (Erikson 1997; Brzezińska 2004; Oleś 2000; Witkowski 2000, *et al.*) allow to accentuate several common elements (developmental tasks) characteristic of people in the midlife transition period. These include:
- developing and cultivating relationship and bonds with one's life partner;
- cultivating the development of family and house-keeping skills;
- generativity (productivity or creativity) – in Erikson's approach (Erikson 1997, p. 278) this means taking responsibility and engagement in the formation of a new generation, concern about the fate of a younger generation, taking care of and meeting the needs of young people, helping growing children become happy and responsible people, the need to be useful in one's professional work and other areas of life and to create something that will serve others; establishing

and sustaining a proper material standard of life, and a constant effort in developing professional career;
- forming a responsible civic and social attitude;
- altering (adapting to) the relationship with aging parents;
- learning a mode of spending free time by an adult which is typical of a given culture;
- accepting and adapting to characteristic middle age changes in physiology, identifying and accepting the fact of belonging to one's age category (Brzezińska 2004, p. 236).

The middle age crisis, according to a cycle-phase model, is a key moment of development. It is also a breakthrough moment in building one's new identity. Once again in his development the person is faced with a new task: to find orientation and anchor oneself in the world, to ensure security in a way different than before, in one's pre-individual existence (Fromm 1998, pp. 40–41). Thus constructing identity at this stage of life is an undertaking insofar as it

> [...] requires a constant effort and inclines one towards making one's shape the object of concern. On the one hand, it makes one look for a form that would allow to capture oneself, and correct this form from time to time, as we become more and more aware of ourselves (Malicka 1996, pp. 156–157).

In addition, it calls for 'self-sustaining activities' that follow from the concern for one's own shape (Malicka 1996, pp. 156–157). Constructing identity is therefore a self-discovery and a process of constructing oneself within the framework of a reflective project; it is conditional upon the person's capacity to 'keep a particular narrative going' (Giddens 2001, pp. 47 and 77), and his activity (what is important is what he does) (cf. Witkowski 1988)) as well as an internal ordering of interdependencies of meanings which we give to the past life events (Rosner 2003, p. 23). It is also related to the ability to make decisions (Goodwin, Wright 2011, p. 391), often intuitively, by reference to one's own categories, according to which one construes and interprets situations and makes decisions accordingly (Tyszka 1986, pp. 139–152), to make a choice (Tyszka 1999, p. 168) and carry out a self-project in accordance with them, along with bearing consequences and reflecting on their meaning.

The way in which one undergoes a transformation typical of the midlife transition period is also influenced by how he reviews his life. The person reviewing his life refers to the content of autobiographical memory, that is the information concerning himself in various moments of life, in various conditions, and in contacts with various people. This period is the time of fundamental rebuilding of the concept of self and constructing a new life structure. This structure involves a certain model of activity of a subject and his relations with the environment as well as the beliefs concerning the world and one's role within it, feelings, aspirations, values and expectations.

Methodological assumptions

This article presents a very brief and fragmentary overview of research results of everyday life experiences of 6 female teachers in the midlife transition period (more: Łukasik 2013). The teachers were selected from among 47 participants of the competition for a diary, journal or report entitled: *A month in the life of a teacher*. The competition lasted from March to December 2009 (cf. Łukasik 2011).

In the presented study the sample selection criteria included: sex (women), the stage of development in life (midlife transition), and the account of everyday life experiences spanning any given month (a full month, 'day after day', working days and work-free days). Flick believes that the sample selection for a qualitative study does not involve merely 'selecting cases and materials, but also making choices *within* such cases and materials' (Flick 2010, p. 67). When searching for data in documents,

> [...] we do not make a selection of people or situations in order to create a set of data through their methodical study; instead, we use already existing materials which we select for the purpose of analysis. The order is therefore reversed: first we have some materials, then we choose from among them, then we move on to employ particular research methods (Flick 2010, p. 66).

A deliberately selected sample of participants of qualitative studies should be diversified, which best allows to 'capture variability and diversity of a studied phenomenon' (Flick 2010, p. 59). Consequently, there were differences in terms of the number of children the women had, their life environment, their financial situation, their place of work, and the subject they taught. The category of difference concerned first and foremost their family situation which is vital in experiencing everyday life after work. The similarities included: sex, professional stabilization, and the fact of being married.

Owing to the assumed qualitative research orientation, in the empirical part we cannot formulate any conclusions or propose a thesis as to the existence of any tendency in the social dimension. The study results are therefore fragmentary and can refer primarily to the women under analysis.

Following Bauman's belief that 'along with the discovery of identity, the "reflective subjectivity" comes into the world' (Bauman 2007, p. 52) and that the man, whether he wants it or not, has to learn to decide who he is and who he wants to be – 'and the world being in a constant state of flux, decisions need to be constantly retaken' (Bauman 2007, p. 52) – I have made the construction of teachers' identity in the midlife transition period the subject of further analysis.

The identity of women in midlife transition period in the light of studies

Tadeusz Tomaszewski thinks that 'just as meaningful as the question: "What is the man like?" is another question: "What is the man being like from time to time?"' (following: Łukaszewski 2003, p. 262). The question involves an assumption that, alongside constant things, there also exist: changeability, temporality and situational aspects of life experiences, all of which help us build our identity. The specific nature of life in the contemporary world, as well as entering new stages of development, force one to attempt changes oriented towards constant self-redefinition, a dynamic determination of one's place, priorities, the construction of one's identity, reorientation (Szymański 2013a), openness, and flexibility (Kwiatkowska 2005, p. 29). It becomes possible only for conscious, reflective and active individuals, striving for self-realization (Szymański 2013a).

Analyzing everyday experiences of teachers in the context of redefining identity in reference to their developmental activities, we can note that they consciously cultivate relationships and bonds with their life partners, creating and introducing rituals and intimate situations that help one give again a sense of meaning to the relationship. They redefine frameworks that allow to sustain relations and encourage family development.

Productivity and creativity of women are the two aspects especially pronounced in the accounts of everyday life. They manifest themselves in professional and extraprofessional activities (including artistic activities), and result from the characteristics of this stage of development: responsibility, commitment to the formation of a new generation (both in terms of professional work and own children), and the need to be useful both at work and in other areas of life and to create something that can serve others.

Family and work are regarded as especially important by women in the midlife transition period. Their purpose in life is to leave something behind for others. A sense of duty and mission, a desire to leave behind a permanent mark in other people's life and memory, motivate teachers to engage in unconventional and additional professional activities. The understanding of the purpose and sense of work, and the identification with a unique mission of teacher's profession gives special value to their work. At this stage of their lives, women have considerably more time for work (their own children do not require care or much engagement in caretaking or educational activities, as they are already 'grown up') and more relevant experience. They can use it for professional activities that are the confirmation of responsibility for educating and bringing up pupils, and result from the willingness to give them something meaningful and to leave a permanent mark.

In the case of the discussed teachers, professional work and life activity have a significant influence on the unique individual shape of identity (cf. Witkowski

1988). This activity undoubtedly fosters the creation and reinforcement of identity. After all, the preservation of identity is reinforced by the activities that strengthen integration, content and independence of the subject. This consolidates the structure of the subject, becoming a relatively constant element sustaining and protecting identity (Węgrzecki 1966, pp. 80–81).

Professional and extraprofessional activity of the studied teachers is therefore a decisive factor preventing a minimalism of desires, reduction of effort, regress and marginalization (Kwiatkowska 2012). It also follows from a good adaptation to a new, changing reality.

Experiences (past and present) and analyses of one's life in midlife transition period lead to breaking schematic rules of life according to a single, required and desired pattern. Professional experience are to a considerable extent a component of the subjects' identity. They become a basis for building family relations, an element allowing self-identification and building one's self-esteem, or a natural course of events not analyzed at the time of their occurrence. Reflections on everyday life experiences show to what extent the teachers perceive themselves through the prism of their professional roles (Miluska 1996). As Henryka Kwiatkowska notes, 'in teacher's profession, as in no other profession, it is hard to differentiate between that which is individual, which refers to a teacher as a person, and that which is professional, and which points to a teacher as a representative of the profession. If happens that the way a teacher functions professionally faultlessly 'lives on' the kind of person she is' (Kwiatkowska 2005, p. 287).

Conclusion

Self-reflection on life experiences facilitates the search for oneself and the change. Every day the subjects undertake numerous activities aimed at self-improvement and the improvement of the surrounding reality, both non-professional and professional. Despite various tensions and problems they 'carry out their identity project' (Giddens 2002, p. 275), oscillating between an image of the conscious past, the present and the imagined future, creating a coherent and meaningful structure, within which the process of self-understanding occurs (Kwiatkowska 2005, p. 33 and seq.). The extended reflection on oneself, one's life and accomplishment recorded in the journals, as well as the ordering of experience and life events, and accompanying them thoughts captured in the narratives, led the teachers to reflect upon themselves, their concern to be differentiated from others, and their submersion in the current of experiences. Writing a journal became for them an amazing moment of conscious self-experience, shaping their identity and the content of their everyday lives. It also confirmed the transition from submitting to duties towards the conscious building of one's identity, individual autonomy and independence.

The midlife transition period in which the teachers were captured was for them the time of intensified reflections on themselves, a critical evaluation of past events and accomplishments, creating and recreating identity, and redefining their concept of 'who they are'.

Halina Rusek
University of Silesia, Poland

Identification of young female inhabitants of Zagłębie with the region

Introduction

When talking about Silesian Province we rarely mean the same thing. Indeed, one of the distinguishing features of this administrative unit is its 'unusual', 'enormous', 'unheard of' diversity, described in various aspects and recalled because of different needs, not only of cognitive, but often of political character. In scientific and popular literature much attention has been devoted to this issue, in particular the origins of the multiculturalism of this region, originally formed in effect of administrative decisions. The Silesian Province is a multicultural space as, unlike most of other regions, its cultural and even ethnic diversity resembles a colourful mosaic. In common thinking and publications the Silesian Province is most frequently associated with Katowice industrial agglomeration which has heterogeneous borders rather than with its other integral parts, from Zagłębie[1], through Częstochowa and Podbeskidzie regions, up to the Cieszyn Silesia. Therefore, the Silesian Province is a specific region, distinguished as an administrative unit with specific industrial specialization (Kwaśniewski 1993, pp. 75–86). A sociological concept of a region which is an area whose residents have developed a strong sense of identity, experience it on daily basis, feel bonds with their own group, at the same time distancing from groups inhabiting different areas (Szczepański, Ślązak-Tazbir 2010) is not appropriate in the case of such a complex entity. The Silesian Province is a multicultural region which consists of several historically developed regions or their parts, as described above. Unity of culture, values, norms, and identity develops in effect of a process which takes much longer time than a few dozen years of belonging to one administrative unit, as is the case with the Silesian Province.

---

[1] The term 'Zagłebie' used herein refers to the geographical name 'Zagłębie Dąbrowskie' (in English: 'Dąbrowa Basin').

However, a long-term process of cultural patterns diffusion, their penetration from one local community to another, from one culture to another, results in reducing the sharpness of boundaries between regions or sub-regions. Zagłębie is one of the regions of historical and cultural significance, and administratively, one of sub-regions that make the Silesian Province.

Dąbrowa Basin – non-Silesia

Identification with Zagłębie is not an easy task due to several reasons. The first one is connected with the fact that Zagłębie has always stayed in the shade of Upper Silesia and the aspirations of the inhabitants of the latter to consolidate their cultural and even political and economic autonomy which was manifested in the rise of Silesian Autonomy Movement and fairly high position of this group in the political sphere are significant. Inhabitants of Zagłębie have never had such ambitions. Besides, Zagłębie is located on the border of two strong cultural centers: Silesia and Malopolska, the fact that does not facilitate the emergence of own cultural identity, original patterns and lifestyles.

Most Poles are not able to distinguish between Silesia and Zagłębie. Primarily, mass media are responsible for such a perception of the region by using the abbreviated term 'Silesia' or 'Silesian' when referring to the whole province. This is a common tendency in the statements of public figures, especially politicians. A quotation from the most popular regional daily, *Dziennik Zachodni*, is as a good illustration of this phenomenon: 'Sosnowiec is in Silesia, all mines are in Silesia, and even Bielsko-Biala has something in common with Silesia' (Zasada 1012). Meanwhile, the region called Dąbrowa Basin almost never had anything in common with Silesia – in the course of its history it had administrative connections with Silesia only three times: for the first time after the third partition of Poland when the so-called New Silesia was formed, for the second time during World War I, and for the third time since 1939, when initially the Śląsko-Dąbrowskie Province was formed, followed by the Stalinogrodzkie Province, and finally the Katowickie Province. In terms of culture, this region is most strongly connected with the Małopolskie Province where up to this day the influence of Małopolska on cultural identity of Zagłębie is evident. The present administrative division has little in common with the past tradition and cultural affiliations – the Silesian Province consists, almost in half, of the lands that have never been Silesian (Krajewski 2009. pp. 17–19).

It is hard to think of Dąbrowa Basin as of 'my place' or 'my little homeland' when the boundaries of this sub-region are not entirely defined. There are two concepts of that. According to the first one the region is made of the towns of : Sosnowiec, Dąbrowa Górnicza, Będzin, Czeladź, and Wojkowice. According to the other one, much broader concept, Zagłębie is made of Sosnowiec, Dąbrowa Górnicza, Będziński, Zawierciański, Myszkowski and Olkuski districts and Ożarowice commune in the Tarnowskie Góry district. The broader concept, favoured by most researchers, is based on historical considerations articulated already in 1939 in *Prze-wodnik po Zagłębiu Dąbrowskim* (*Guidebook around Dąbrowa Basin*) (Kondracki 199, pp. 1–3, 7).

Sosnowiec, informal capital of Dąbrowa Basin, always in the shade of Silesian towns, was perceived as a provincial town with no own history at all. Such an opinion has rested upon Sosnowiec since communist times. Apart from that, in the commonly known conflict between Silesia and Zagłębie Sosnowiec has always stayed right in the center of it – other towns in Zagłębie have never been so nega-tively perceived. Actually, Sosnowiec used to be a provincial town once however it played some important episodes in history.

Although Dąbrowa Basin has a rich past, it is poorly elaborated and document-ed. Historians agree that as a separate region it was established in the late eight-eenth century, at the time Będziński District was formed and incorporated into the Piotrowska Governorate. The region shaped from the turn of the eighteenth and nineteenth centuries on, when zinc ore, iron, and especially coal were discovered on this typically agricultural area. Growth of industry – ironworks, brickyards, and mines significantly accelerated in the nineteenth century with the construction of a railway line, in particular the Warsaw-Vienna Railway, resulting in the rapid inflow of German, French, Belgian, Austrian and Russian capital to the region. Until mid-nineteenth century the region did not have any official name. It was only in the 1850s when the term 'Zagłębie' first appeared and an officially sound-ing name: Zagłębie Węglowe w Królestwie Polskim (Coal Zagłębie of the Polish Kingdom) was used in 1856 on the *Geognostic map of the Coal Zagłębie of the Polish Kingdom*. With the passing of time, the name gained popularity in the press and in everyday speech. In the 1880s the name 'Dąbrowa Basin' emerged. Since then it was used in the press, on maps, and in professional mining journals. Therefore, as early as before World War I, a significant industrial center, neighbouring the Prussian Silesia and the Russian Empire grew in South-Western part of the Polish Kingdom. It differed from Silesia in terms of language, law, as well as political, economic and social conditions. In independent Poland the former administrative division was maintained and Będziński District, i.e. the area of the previously mentioned Dąbrowa Basin was incorporated in the typically agricultural Kieleckie Province.

After World War II the urban districts of Będzin, Czeladź, Dąbrowa Górnicza, Sosnowiec, Zawiercie and rural districts – Będziński and Zawierciański were incor-porated into the Śląsko-Dąbrowskie Province existing since 1950. In 1995–1999, these administrative units were incorporated into the Katowickie Province and since 1998 they have been part of the Silesian Province (Nita 2009, pp. 15–17).

The problem of the identity of the Zagłębie region, perceived already in the past, nowadays exists mostly as a dispute on the relationship of this identity with a much wider concept of Silesian identity, often evoked in public discourse and by inhabitants of Silesia themselves. In this context it might seem that the separateness of multicultural sub-region of Zagłębie, although evident, is vague and not particularly attractive to researchers. From this perspective Zagłębie could be considered a region without its own history, tradition, with no clear political image, or, if any, a thoroughly leftist ne. Contrary to such opinions, the identity of the Zagłębie region does exist and is based on strong pillars. The first one and of highest importance is a proletarian character of the sub-region, the existence of a specific mining and industrial tradition, which links Zagłębie with Silesia. Other, more important for the identity of Zagłębie features include intellectual character of towns and existing in the past a large, significant in economic and cultural terms, Jewish community. These two indicators of the identity of Zagłębie are however rarely mentioned and if so they remain in the shade of the first one, namely the proletarian character (Wódz, Wódz 2009, pp. 2–4). Historians point out that, just as in Upper Silesia a conflict existed between Poles (Silesians) and Germans, in Zagłębie it was evident rather among Poles, Russians, and Jews. What distinguished these two regions from each other was the presence of own intelligentsia in the towns of Zagłębie and its lack in Upper Silesia (Woźniczka 2008, p. 11).

In the 1970s, Zagłębie played an important role, both in the region and in the whole country, of a strong industrial center where state authorities, with Edward Gierek as First Secretary of the Central Committee of the Communist Party directed particularly large funds for various investments. However, recent years have witnessed a considerable economic decline of Zagłębie. Restructuring of heavy industry, carried out for over a dozen years throughout the province, has hit Zagłębie particularly strong.

The present has turned out to be very difficult for the whole Silesian Province. This industrial region is transforming into a post-industrial one, the process accompanied by the inherent to it question: what is, or should be a vision for the whole province and its individual components, large and small towns, and agricultural areas? Some administrative units cope with finding answers to this question better than others. Based on various considerations one can get the impression that the capital of Zagłębie, Sosnowiec is included in the latter group. Studies conducted in the recent two years by researchers from the University of Silesia demonstrated depopulation of towns throughout the whole province. Since 1999, i.e. the year when the province was established, the population decreased by ca. 300 thousand inhabitants. From 2001 to 2011 the population of Katowice decreased by 16.5%, and of Sosnowiec by 16.2% (Minorczyk-Cichy 2013). Most often it is young people who leave their hometowns, primarily in search of better paid jobs. However, middle aged and elderly people do so as well, moving to the outskirts of towns or returning to their homeland, most often the Małopolskie Province. The job market in Sosnowiec shrank – four of the five mines, steel works and textile factories were closed.

The data included in *Diagnoza społeczna* for 2013 (*Social diagnosis for the year 2013*) confirms rather poor social and economic condition of Zagłębie and

Sosnowiec. The entire Silesian Province, besides the Mazowieckie, Opolskie and Wielkopolskie Provinces, belongs to regions where the level of life is highest. This concerns primarily satisfaction of housing needs, health care, and participation in cultural life to meet the needs in terms of housing, health and participation in culture. However, in Sosnowiec and the sub-region of Sosnowiec in the past eight years, and in particular over the last two years, the quality of life has deteriorated. Sosnowiec residents have included their town among the ones where life is toughest – Sosnowiec together with Włocławek, and Wałbrzych have been positioned top three towns in this category. The following indicators were used as criteria in the survey: the level of civilization (Sosnowiec: 23rd position among 28 towns and cities; the sub-region Sosnowiec: 18th position among 58 units), social welfare (Sosnowiec 19th position; sub-region of Sosnowiec 26th position), financial well-being (Sosnowiec 24th position; sub-region of Sosnowiec: 15th position), pathologies (Sosnowiec: 25th position, sub-region of Sosnowiec: 24th position), social capital (Sosnowiec 27th position; sub-region of Sosnowiec 38th position), physical well-being (Sosnowiec: 15th position; sub-region of Sosnowiec: 31st position), psychological well-being (Sosnowiec: 20th position; sub-region of Sosnowiec 22nd position), life stress (Sosnowiec 18th position, sub-region of Sosnowiec: 44th position) (Czapiński 2013).

Females in the Silesian Province

The above remarks and analyses, in my opinion, clearly demonstrate that Dąbrowa Basin as a sub-region of the Silesian Province, which currently undergoes difficult economic, political, and cultural transformations, is not an attractive place to live and accomplish one's plans and aspirations. Such a conclusion might result from official evaluations and statistical data. However is it really so? Is an objectively difficult situation of the region reflected in the reasoning of its inhabitants? Research on this issue has rarely been carried out, although in recent years studies on that subject have become more frequent. However, the opinions of female inhabitants, who constitue a distinct social and research group on this issue are unknown.

Women represent 51.7% of the inhabitants of the Silesian Province (total number of inhabitants amounts to 4 626 357), of which 47.7% are in the working age and 68.8% in the retirement age. Female inhabitants of the Silesian Province are better educated than men, which is evidenced by the following comparisons:

- university level education:

14.2% men
17.5% women

- post-secondary and secondary level education:

30.3% men
34.4% women

- first-level vocational education: 31.9% men
   19.1% women
- junior secondary school and primary school education: 17.8% men
   22.9% women

No education or incomplete education:
elementary: 0.7% men
   1.0% women

On the job market the situation of female inhabitants of the Province is much worse than that of men. Women make a bigger group of the unemployed: among the 186 200 registered unemployed are in Silesian Province 56.1% are women. They are also among the professionally less active population group:

professionally active: 49.6% men
   43.1% women
working: 43.9% men
   37.6% women
professionally inactive: 45% men
   52% women

The share of women in local government bodies of the province also reflects the situation typical for the whole country:

councilors of local government bodies
2 346: municipal councils (in total)
622 women (26.5%)
469: councils of cities and towns assigned with district rights (in total)
115: women (24.5%)
396: district councils (in total)
84: women (21.2%)
47: Silesian Province council (in total)
15: women (31.9%)[2].

The above numbers indicate poor involvement of women in the political life of the Silesian Province, which is however not a surprising conclusion but rather a confirmation of the well-known truth. However, this issue deviates from the main topic of this study.

2 Rocznik statystyczny Województwa Śląskiego 2012, wwwstat.gov./cps/rde/katow/ASSETS_ ROCZNIK_2012 (Accessed: 14.07.2014).

Female inhabitants of Zagłębie on their region –
preliminary study report

The 'identification' term is most often used synonymously with the 'identity' term and as such it has been used in the present study. Identification – regional identity, also referred to as 'local identity', is one of the dimensions of collective identity and cultural identity which interlocks with it, constructed by individuals and social groups within a specific socio-cultural system. Cultural identity translated into identification with a particular cultural universe, a particular set of ideas, beliefs, a system of values, and a system of cultural behavior patterns. Regional identity and its sense is associated with the perception and feeling of cultural diversity and often that of the language one of the own region, identification with regional customs and traditions, and is associated with a sense of relationship with its inhabitants perceived as 'own folks', and the knowledge of its history. This identity is based on the regional tradition, which refers to a clearly defined territory, its unique social, cultural (symbolic), economic, and even topographical features which distinguishing it from other regions (Szczepanski, Śliz 2010, p. 69).

On the basis of the presented concept of identification / regional identity, in September and October 2013, a questionnaire survey was conducted among young female inhabitants of Zagłębie. Those were pilot studies conducted as a forerunner of the further, in-depth research, at that time at the conceptualization stage, on the dimensions and changes of the identity of various groups of inhabitants of Dąbrowa Basin as a region in part still industrial and in part post-industrial. In contrast to the Upper Silesia, this type of research in Dąbrowa Basin is rare and rather contributive.

One hundred and twenty female inhabitants of Zagłębie (aged 18 to 35), students of universities located in the region, were given a questionnaire consisting of questions on the respondents' perception of the region where they live. Sixty evaluated questionnaires were used for the preliminary analysis of the results.

The program of the study includes several indicators of regional identity, which have been considered as particularly clearly characterizing this type of identification:
– a sense of attachment to the region expressed as a declaration and determination of the strength of this relationship;
– autostereotype, i.e. simplified characteristics of the inhabitants of the region in response to the question: what they are like? and therefore 'what are we like?;
– knowledge of the region as a territory, as well as social and cultural space;
– perceiving, or not, by young females, the place of their residence as a 'small' or 'private' homeland.

The research issue is supplemented with questions on opinions on the latest processes happening in the region.

For the purpose of this report several problems have been selected as the illustration of the research project.

The first is the sense of attachment to the place of residence. According to the responses given by female inhabitants of Zagłębie, the opinion that such attachment is strong but not very strong (46.7%) prevails, 23.3% of the respondents feel very strong attachment with the region, the same number of respondents claim rather weak, and just two respondents a very weak one. Quite strong attachment with the region is not equivalent to a very good or at least good knowledge of it. Only 5% of the respondents find their knowledge on the past and present of Zagłębie very good, 38.8% perceive it as an average one, and 36.7% as a poor.

Responses given to the next question confirm that respondents have only an average knowledge of the region. To the question asking what particular towns belong to the region most respondents (86.7%) gave the right answers however of those 50% were able to name not more than two or three towns, usually the main towns of the region: Sosnowiec, Będzin, and Dąbrowa Górnicza. About 37% of this group of respondents mentioned more cities and towns, in their responses referring to a broader, less popular perception of the actual size of the region.

More than a half of the surveyed young female inhabitants of Zagłębie are well aware of socio-economic and cultural degradation of the region (53.3%) and consider unemployment, particularly among young people, shortage of apartments, and a general lack of prospects for young people, as well as modest leisure opportunities as chief manifestation of such a degradation. Despite such a large number of dissatisfied respondents more than half of them think that Zagłębie is a region which gives young people opportunities for fulfilling of their ambitions, life plans, and needs. According to the respondents, women have in this respect same opportunities as men (78.3%). This result confirms my conviction that only distant echoes on the discussion concerning discrimination of women on the job market, in politics, and public life in general reach Zagłębie. Female inhabitants of Zagłębie, not only the young ones, stay on the margin of life, and as can be seen, rather fail to protest against it. One of the reasons for such a situation this is a stereotype, firmly fixed in the region, and especially in the neighboring Upper Silesia, that a woman acts best as a guardian of the household. However, the emergence of certain organizations and activities of several socio-cultural institutions may promise a breakthrough in this regard. This issue requires more attention and space than possible within the frames of this elaboration.

A factor often taken into consideration in research on local identity is the perception, by respondents, of other inhabitants of the region, i.e. a specific kind of stereotype. The contents of the stereotype which has a positive resonance can be regarded as an expression of a positive assessment of the local community and a strong sense of belonging to it. The responses of young female respondents usually included a brief description of the inhabitants of Zagłębie as listing of the traits of their character, attitudes, and/or behaviors. 33.3% of the respondents positively views fellow inhabitants of the region, perceiving them as hospitable, hardworking, attached to families, friendly, open-minded, proud, attached to their place of residence). 15% of respondents perceive inhabitants of Zagłębie only negatively, viewing them as fierce, intolerant, ill-mannered, arrogant, and unwilling to help. 16.7% of the replies include a description based both on positive and negative aspects and in several cases descriptions which can be called neutral: entertaining, confident, busy, and traditionalists. Approximately 17% of respondents did not give any answer the above discussed question. Therefore, if on the basis of the obtained data we attempted to determine the strength of attachment with the home region, we could consider it average.

Strong identification with the place of residence can be associated with the perception of such a place as 'own', close, associated with home, 'one's place on earth.' In order to learn the attitudes of female inhabitants of Zagłębie on that, they were requested to finish the sentence: '*When I think of Zagłębie, I think of...*' Most replies were quite laconic, containing only few words. A dozen or so respondents (33.3%) included in these brief responses direct references to their region as a place close to them and 'their' space, e.g.: I think of 'my home', 'childhood', 'my little homeland', 'the place where I was born and still live', 'my place, family, and my family's future', 'my native land, and primarily memories from early youth', 'family, home, friends'. In the quoted responses it is fairly easy to discover references to a well-known concept of a 'small', 'local' homeland proposed years ago by Stanisław Ossowski. Probably a lot of places in Zagłębie make homeland for the inhabitants of this region, although the region itself, as seen by S. Ossowski should be defined rather as ideological homeland (Ossowski 1984, p. 26).

More responses (35%) include connotations of a neutral character: when I think of Zagłębie I think of... 'Sosnowiec, greenery', 'football matches', 'the region where I live, my university, industry'. In individual cases strongly positive connotations appear, however totally devoid of any emotions: I think of... 'relatively clean air as compared to Silesia' or 'huge development possibilities' which are strongly positive associations but deprived of any emotions: I think of ... 'as a clean environment compared to Silesia', 'major development opportunities.' 28.3% of respondents expressed strongly negative connotations: 'I think of painted, devastated blocks of flats', 'trains that run late', 'Leaving here and Poland', or 'bankrupt mines and shut-down mills'.

The presentation of selected, partial results of the study is not sufficient to make outright summaries and conclusions of a general nature. However test results constitute good grounds to verify the issues of the research and pose further questions. Identification of young female inhabitants of Zagłębie with their region in the context of the presented results seems to be quite strong on the level of declarations or subjective judgments, but rather poor in respect to the knowledge about the region. For half of the respondents Zagłębie is a good place to accomplish life plans and ambitions and for the other half the region from where it is best to get away, move to another place. A small group of respondents clearly associates Zagłębie with their small homeland and almost the same number of respondents thinks about their region in neutral terms however only a bit less numerous groups thinks of Zagłębie in negative terms. This ambivalence is evident in regard to almost all indicators of regional identity, which have been included in the research. Indeed, identification with this region is not easy. This identification is based primarily on the awareness of a common fate, and historical and social memory based on which a distinct character of a region emerges. Regional education is an important tool in shaping of such awareness. However no data exist that would demonstrate how it is accomplished in the schools of Zagłębie region. Although 'Silesia Schola', the Association of Regionalist Teachers, in 2013 conducted research on the implementation of regional education in the schools of the Silesian Province, only the region of Upper Silesia was covered with the study. It turned out that among the seventy-five communes covered with the research this issue is dealt with only in twenty one schools (Pustułka 2013). As the situation in the region of Zagłębie may look similar an assumption can be made that regional education in Zagłębie has a long way to go. However, since researches take it for granted that the knowledge of own roots and the history of the community is a necessary tool for a modern, somewhat lost in the global space human, then it seems there is no retreat from that.

Grzegorz Libor, Dorota Nowalska-Kapuścik, Monika Szpoczek-Sało
University of Silesia, Poland

Global consumer trends and local models of consumer behavior among women – a study of the Lipiny case

Introduction

'[Today] Globalization and consumerism are the dominating perspectives on contemporary societies' (Bogunia-Borowska, Śleboda 2003, p. 9). They are believed to play the main role in the social and economic development, being the core regulator of human life, as well as the driving force of economy and economic situation. Today's technological development in the area of communication and technology allows consumers to get access to contemporary lifestyle, contributing to unification of the promoted consumer behavior models across national boundaries.

Similar situation can be observed in Poland, which is experiencing a strong saturation and influence of western consumer models that are not always compatible with the domestic market of needs and opportunities.

The goal of this article is to present the models of consumer behavior among women – residents of Lipiny (a district of Świętochłowice) in the context of dominating global trends. Basic literature on the analyzed subject, as well as research material gathered during the author's own studies were used in this article.

Globalization and regionalism in consumerism – determination of (co)dependency

Let us assume that the contemporary world is a civilization of consumerism. Much attention is paid today to consumption of goods and services. Of course, consumption and consuming have always been one of the most important aspects of human life, however, in recent years, we have been witnessing redefinition of their role and meaning. Consumption is no longer considered in the context of buying and using specific goods and services only or in order to satisfy real demands. Today, it is rather considered to be a social act; a symbolic message, a way of life, conveying not only a promise of relief, but also quite the contrary – of remaining in the permanent state of begging for more. According to Bauman

> [...] for consumers in a consumer society, being on the move – in pursuit, in search, failing to find or not finding 'yet', is not something bad, but a promise of pleasure or even pleasure in itself. For them, reaching the goal [...] becomes their doom (Bauman 2000, p. 99).

This contemporary escalation of consumption seems to convey a message saying that by choosing the right elements from the world of consumerism, people are able to manifest their social status, happiness and individuality. It happens because individuals are given an impression of free maneuvering and choosing from many, often contradictory elements that can shape or complement their identity. We can choose from a number of offers, grouped in universally desired – or undesired – fashions and trends.

The notion of 'trend' itself should be understood as 'the direction in which something is developing in a given time'. The sociological definition emphasizes that it is 'a visible regularity of changes over time, illustrated by a social index' (Marshall 2005, p. 404). From the point of view of consumerism and consumer behavior, a trend is therefore a change of course in a consumer's life style. The process of formation of specific trends is rooted in economic, demographic, social, technological, political or legal activities. Not going into details of trend typology, it is worth to emphasize what seems most important from the perspective of this discussion: trends can be considered with regard to both their global and/or local scale.

Reference to globalization and regionalism requires a few words of explanation. In recent years, there has been a huge interest in everything encompassed by the notion of *globalization*. The fact that over less than two decades (from 1980 to 1998), the number of publications containing the word 'global' or 'globalization' in the title only increased by eleven times, shows how much interest this issue has attracted (Bogunia-Borowska, Śleboda 2003, p. 18).

According to Sztompka,

> [...] the notion of globalization has entered common language. Every day, politicians, editors and journalists refer to globalization being either as a source of troubles of contemporary world or – on the contrary – as a chance to overcome our troubles (Sztompka 2002, p. 582).

The term *globalization* itself is nothing but 'spread of customs, values and technologies in such a way that they affect human lives all over the world' (Albrow 1997, p. 88). For ordinary consumers, it means a possibility to choose and pursue consumer behavior models that appeared in other social and cultural environment and which, through mass media (recently – the Internet), seem to be a tempting alternative to traditional standards and codes of conduct. Of course, such alternatives are neither uniform nor organized, i.e. concurrence and divergence appear.

Contact with foreign models does not mean their automatic assimilation, for various reasons: some do not want to follow global trends, other are not able to do so, for example for economic reasons.

> Some of us become fully *global*, whereas others are stuck with their regionalism, which is not pleasant or even bearable in a world where globalized people dictate the rules (Bauman 2000, p. 7).

Such situation gives rise to important dilemmas and a research question we will try to address: what is the nature of consumer behavior models among women from Lipiny: are they consistent with global proposals or rather lean towards local solutions?

Consumer models among women from Lipiny – research

Lipiny is a district of Świętochłowice, located in the north-western part of the city. It was established in the 18th century and saw its peak in the 19th century, resulting from industrial boom in the region. In its heydays, the population of Lipiny was three times higher than today and the town was ahead of most of other Polish regions in terms of development. In that times, there was a high demand for heavy industry products all over Europe and Lipiny thrived on rich deposits of coal and zinc. After depletion of the deposits in Lipiny together with a global industrial crisis, the district witnessed economic, environmental and social degradation. The fate of other industrial districts was similar. After 1989, the district become the symbol of poverty and alcoholism in Silesia. Fortunately, many companies, especially from the transport, construction and automotive industry, have appeared in Lipiny, giving job to many people and making the district more civilized[1].

The demographic structure of Lipiny is as follows: its population equals 7404, making up 13.2% of the total population of the town. The population of the district is young in terms of demographics. Lipiny is the third district in Świętochłowice in terms of unemployment rate. Here lives almost 1/5 of all of the unemployed registered in the whole town. 34.3% residents of Lipiny are beneficiaries of the Social Welfare Centre.

Research on consumer behavior of female residents of Lipiny were carried out from June 2011 to April 2013 on a group of 60 women receiving support from the Social Welfare Centre in Świętochłowice, as well as residents who displayed the qualities of local leaders during the research.

---

1 See: *Świętochłowice – Lipiny* [on-line], http://slaskiemiasta.pl/swietochlowice/lipiny (Accessed: 29.05.2013).

Methods used in the research were as follows: participant observation and free-form interviews carried out during visits at the respondents' homes. The researchers also actively participated in the life of the local community, making their presence something completely natural and accepted. Thanks to the trust gained during the research period, women spoke freely about their private issues and allowed the researchers to participate in their lives. Sometimes, the researchers were invited to various family meetings.

In order to confront the observations made, interviews with social workers, teachers and local entrepreneurs were carried out. On the basis of the materials gathered, four types of women were distinguished, with special attention paid to the problem of consumer activities:

TYPE ONE – The Polish Mother

Those women put their needs last. In the first place, those women try to satisfy the needs of their families and children. They use their financial resources to pay for food and bills. In their free time, they look for extra jobs to make fulfill the dreams of their children and to ensure a better life future for them. One of such examples is Basia, a 40-year-old married mother of 2 adolescent sons. The income of her family is as follows: husband's pension – PLN 600, fixed benefit – PLN 80, financial aid from her children's school – PLN 200. Sometimes, she and her husband manage to make extra PLN 200 monthly. When she was asked what she spends the money on and what are the priorities, she replied: rent, bills, food, books, school materials and medications, if there was any money left (it is worth to add that both she and her husband should take medications regularly because of their health problems). When she was asked what does she do in her free time, she replied: my children attend free sports classes and music classes.

TYPE TWO – The Partying Mother

She puts her needs first and spends money for what she wants. As soon as she gets money from the Social Welfare Centre, she goes shopping (cosmetics, clothes), usually to the bazaar. The needs of her children are put last as the Partying Mother claims that her children are guaranteed free breakfasts and lunches at school and are provided with clothes from the Social Welfare Centre. She spends her free time in clubs, pubs, discos and cafes with her friends. When asked what her children are doing in her free time, she says that they take care of each other. One of such women is Beata, mother of eight children, who says that she needs to blow off some steam as long as she is still young and their children are grown up enough to take care of themselves anyway. She buys only the most important food products for their children, such as milk, cereals or jam – things that her children like most and don't have them at school.

TYPE THREE – The Alcoholic Mother

This is a very common type – not only in Lipiny, but also in other communities with high poverty and crime rate. Such mother spends the money she gets on alcohol. She tries to keep her drinking habit in secret so that the social workers cannot find out about her problem. Her children are left alone, she forgets about their needs. She spends her free time with her friends, at home or hiding away, often in front of TV. One of the examples is Anna, a married mother of two children. The family gets money from the benefits received from the Social Welfare Centre, financial aid from children's school or occasional work. However, she claims that she does not drink or drinks only occasionally. She does not pay the rent as she claims she cannot afford it. She spends her free time with her friends. She says she does not drink denatured alcohol, but some of her friends do.

TYPE FOUR – The Sly Mother

This type of woman has some common features with the Polish Mother. However, the Sly Mother is able to make the most of the support institutions. She 'specializes' in getting money from social welfare and various support centres. She does not work, she claims that she does not need to and that the government is there to help her. Her husband usually works illegally or is paid the minimum wage. She spends her free time at home, taking care of her children, or meets her female friends to discuss various forms of family support with them. She usually lives in a well-equipped council or social flat (washing machine, TV, computer with access to the Internet etc.). She usually arranges her visits with social workers beforehand and allows them to visit one room only, hiding the most valuable items in other rooms. Her children are not allowed to speak of what they have. One of the examples of such mothers is Halina, a married mother of five children. Her family income comes from: earnings of her husband, who works for the minimum statutory wage, but actually gets twice as much under the table, family benefit for the children, designated benefits, housing allowance, as well as school financial aids. Her children attend school in other, better districts. As she states, the school, to which her children go has better teachers, better food and more support (children are given free food packets and their lunches consist of two meals). Her children attend two children's shelters and a community centre. They do not wear second-hand clothes.

TYPE FIVE – The Freelance Woman

The Freelance is another category we are able to distinguish. She lives alone, without a family or a partner. She either receives pension or earns money by doing occasional jobs, e.g. cleaning or collecting scrap metal. She spends her free time with her neighbors, they often watch TV together. She buys necessary products only. A Freelance Woman has never been employed, she receives support from her partner or parents. One of the examples of such type s Eugenia, a 53-year-old women living in a council flat consisting of two rooms. Until 2011, she was supported by her partner, who was a scrap metal collector. After his death, she was left alone without the right to any social benefits. She does not receive any support from the SWC. She says that the social workers told her to register at the Employment Agency, which she did and was given a job in waste sorting, but she does not want to work in dirt. She lives off the generosity of her neighbors. She draws electricity for her flat illegally, she has been charged for that and may do time in prison. She spends her free time at her neighbors, watching TV or sleeping.

TYPE SIX – Miss Independent

This is usually a woman with low income, raising children on her own. She believes she does not need any support as there are others who need it more. She tries to ensure the best education possible for her children. She tries to earn additional income e.g. by cleaning or babysitting. She pays her bills in the first place and spends the remaining money on food and entertainment for her children so that they do not feel any worse than their peers. She usually shops at discount stores, where prices are much lower than in grocery stores. She leads a rather modest life. At the beginning of each month, she pays her bills. She usually goes shopping on foot to save money. She tries to buy discount clothes only. Her son attends a technical secondary school in another town. She always buys new school books for him. She invests most of her money in her son (once a week he goes bowling or goes to the movies with his friends). In her free time, she usually stays at home or attends a free computer course.

TYPE SEVEN – The Pensioner

She lives off a retirement pension that she uses to pay all her bills. She tries to spend any money left wisely. She also supports her non-working children and grandchildren. She participates in projects aimed at seniors. Once a week she goes to a pensioner's club. She also attends mass every day. She shops in grocery stores as she claims they are cheap and one needs to support local business. She is nostalgic about the times when the cultural and social life in Lipiny was thriving. She talks about various shops that used to be in the district a long time ago. One of the examples of such type of women is Aniela, who lives together with her grandson. She has not bought any new clothes for herself or anything new for her apartment for years. She tries to support her grandson so that he has better opportunities in the future. She buys herself cigarettes and claims that it is her only luxury.

TYPE EIGHT – The Working Woman, not afraid of any work

A woman belonging in this category is working full time and lives in the best part of Lipiny – Matylda housing estate. Her apartment is neat and tidy. She takes good care about self-development: she attends computer courses, aerobics and language courses. She spends her free time going to a theater or cinema. She shops in shopping malls. A model example of that type is Genia – a 50-year-old accountant who lives in Lipiny because she feels an emotional connection with this place. She spends her free time travelling with her family. Once a week she attends sports classes with her friends, computer courses and goes to a theatre or a cinema once in a month. She always spends her summer vacation away from home.

On the basis of the material gathered, we were able to identify not only where the women from Lipiny usually go shopping, but also the products they usually buy. Women from Lipiny usally shop in corner stores, where they buy milk, sugar, flour, bread, jam, cereals, meat, sweets, vegetables and fruit.

Conclusions

To sum up our research, we may state that one of the main deciding factors in the absorption of global trends by a local environment is the nature and characteristics of residents. In the case of Lipiny discussed in this article, social problems experienced by its residents, women in particular, defined not only their needs and priorities, but also (and maybe in the first place) the resulting behavior, including consumer behavior. The nature of the persons participating in the interview, as well as their approach to family and professional life were also of significance.

However, in most cases consumer activity concerned basic goods and services, rarely luxurious ones. Also, in most cases the place of consumer activity was Lipiny itself with its stores and shopping malls. Moreover, a large part of women from Lipiny spent their free time in a similar manner, which contributed to the strengthening of local bonds, but also aggravated the existing problems. On the other hand, in many cases the financial resources were used to improve the situation of the closest relatives – children – and to improve their future opportunities. Such type of consumer activity, however, is not only a local trend in Lipiny. In a global world, switching the financial resources from family budgets to education and development of children is becoming more and more evident trend as well.

Bibliography

Albrow, M. (1997), *The Global Age. State and society beyond modernity*, Standford University Press, Standford.

Aleksander, T. (1995), *Optymalizacja pracy dydaktyczno-wychowawczej szkoły poprzez wykorzystanie sił społecznych środowiska lokalnego* [in:] A. Jopkiewicz (ed.), *Edukacja i rozwój. Jaka szkoła? Jaki nauczyciel? Jakie wychowanie?*, Wyd. WSP, Kielce.

Appelt, K. (2005), *Style funkcjonowania nauczycieli w sytuacji zmiany społecznej*, 'Forum Oświatowe', 2(33), 5–23.

Ballingall, A. (2013), *Gerald Schwartz and Heather Reisman donate $15 million to Mount Sinai emergency care*, http://www.thestar.com/news/gta/2013/12/05/gerald_schwartz_and_heat-her_reisman_donate_15_million_to_mount_sinai_emergency_ care.html (Accessed: 4.12.2013).

Bauman, Z. (2000), *Globalizacja*, PIW, Warszawa.

Bauman, Z. (2007), *Tożsamość ze sklepu. Tożsamość ze spiżarni* [in:] A. Gromkowska-Melosik (ed.), *Kultura popularna i (re)konstrukcje tożsamości*, Wyd. WSH, Poznań–Leszno.

Bernstein, C. (2008), *Hillary Clinton*, Prószyński i S-ka, Warszawa.

Bilderberg Meetings, http://bilderbergmeetings.org/index.php (Accessed: 29.11.2013).

Bilderberg Meeting Participant List (1991), http://publicintelligence.net/1991-bilderberg-meeting-participant-list (Accessed: 4.12.2013).

Bilderberg Meetings (1998), *List of Participants*, http://publicintelligence.net/1998-bilderberg-meeting-participant-list (Accessed: 4.12.2013).

Bilderberg Meetings (2009), *Final Lists of Participants*, http://www.publicintelligence.net/?p=1971 (Accessed: 4.12.2013).

Blundell, J. (2010), *Margaret Thatcher. Portret Żelaznej Damy*, Zysk i S-ka, Poznań.

Bogunia-Borowska, M. (2009), *Codzienność i społeczne konteksty życia codziennego* [in:] M. Bogunia-Borowska (ed.), *Barwy codzienności. Analiza socjologiczna*, Scholar, Kraków.

Bogunia-Borowska, M., Śleboda, M. (2003), *Globalizacja i konsumpcja. Dwa dylematy współczesności*, Universitas, Kraków.

Brooks, A. (2010), *What are the Bilderberg Group really doing in Spain?*, www.independent.co.uk/news/world/europe/what-are-the-bilderberg-group-really-doing-in-spain-1991021.html (Accessed: 4.12.2013).

Brzezińska, A. (2004), *Społeczna psychologia rozwoju*, Scholar, Warszawa.

Brzezińska, A., Appelt, K. (2000), *Tożsamość zawodowa psychologa* [in:] J. Brzeziński, M. Toeplitz-Winiewska (eds.), *Etyczne dylematy psychologii*, Wyd. Fundacji Humaniora, Poznań.

Bukciński, T. (1999), *Sfera publiczna* [in:] E. Pakszys, W. Heller (eds.), *Humanistyka i płeć III. Publiczna przestrzeń kobiet. Obrazy dawne i nowe*, Wyd. UAM, Poznań.

Ceglarska, A. (2013a), *Kobiety dla Narodu – Sierpniowe Panny*, 'Polska Niepodległa', 1, 22.

Ceglarska, A. (2013b), *Myśli nowoczesnej Polki*, 'Polska Niepodległa', 8, 3.

Chałasiński, J. *et al.* (1969), *Młode pokolenie wsi Polski Ludowej*, vol. 6: *Nauczyciele i uczniowie*, Warszawa.

Chibowska, A. (2012), *Uwarunkowania partycypacji politycznej kobiet w Polsce*, Elipsa, Warszawa.

Chmura-Rutkowska, I., Ostrouch, J. (2007), *Mężczyźni na przełęczy życia. Studium socjo-pedagogiczne*, Impuls, Kraków.

Chojnowski, A. (2000), *Aktywność kobiet w życiu politycznym* [in:] A. Żarnowska, A. Szwarc, (eds.) *Równe prawa i nierówne szanse. Kobiety w Polsce międzywojennej*, Wyd. DiG, Warszawa.

Chołuj, B. (2009), *Dlaczego organizacje pozarządowe? Preferencje organizacyjne w drugiej fali ruchu kobiecego w Polsce* [in:] A. Janiak-Jasińska, K. Sierakowska, A. Szwarc (eds.), *Działaczki społeczne, feministki, obywatelki... Samoorganizowanie się kobiet na ziemiach polskich po 1918 roku (na tle porównawczym)*, vol. 2, Neriton, Warszawa.

Cybal-Michalska, A. (2006), *Tożsamość młodzieży w perspektywie globalnego świata. Studium socjopedagogiczne*, Wyd. UAM, Poznań.

Cywińska, M. (2013), *O wychowaniu narodowym: rodzice i nauczyciele*, 'Polska Niepodległa', 1, 21.

Cywiński, B. (1985), *Rodowody niepokornych,* Editions Spotkania, Paryż.

Czapiński, J. (2013), Diagnoza społeczna 2013, www.diagnoza.com (Accessed: 15.07.2014).

Czerniawska, M. (1995), *Inteligencja a system wartości – studium psychologiczne*, Trans Humana, Białystok.

Day, Ch. (2004), *Rozwój zawodowy nauczyciela. Uczenie się przez całe życie*, GWP, Gdańsk.

Dmowski, R. (2002), *Kościół, naród i państwo*, Ostoja, Krzeszowice.

Domański, H. (1996), *Na progu konwergencji. Stratyfikacja społeczna w krajach Europy Środkowo-Wschodniej*, Wyd. IFiS PAN, Warszawa.

Drewniak, E. (2012), *Wpływ kobiet na politykę państwa na przykładzie Polski i Hiszpanii*, Promotor, Warszawa.

Dróżka, W. (1991), *Nauczyciel w środowisku wiejskim. Działalność społeczna i samokształcenie*, Wyd. WSP, Kielce.

Dróżka, W. (1999), *Rola i pozycja społeczna nauczyciela w środowisku wiejskim – na podstawie pamiętników młodych nauczycieli* [in:] M. Meducka (ed.), *Wokół 'Syzyfowych prac'. Problemy edukacji wiejskiej w Polsce w XIX i XX wieku*, Kieleckie Towarzystwo Naukowe, Kielce.

Dróżka, W. (2002), *Nauczyciel. Autobiografia. Pokolenia. Studia pedeutologiczne i pamiętnikarskie*, Wyd. Akademii Świętokrzyskiej, Kielce.

Dudzikowa, M., Knasiecka-Falbierska, K. (2013), Sprawcy i/lub ofiary działań pozornych w edukacji szkolnej, Impuls, Kraków.

Erikson, E.H. (1997), *Dzieciństwo i społeczeństwo*, Rebis, Poznań.

Estulin, D. (2009), *Prawdziwa historia Klubu Bilderberg*, Sonia Draga, Katowice.

Final Lists of Participants (2009), http://www.publicintelligence.net/?p=1971 (Accessed: 4.12.2013).

Flick, U. (2010), *Projektowanie badania jakościowego, WN PWN, Warszawa.*

Frątczak, J. (2002), *Przemiany społeczno-polityczne a udział w działalności stowarzyszeniowej* [in:] A. Wachowicz (ed.), *Przemiany orientacji życiowej kobiet zamężnych. Studium socjologiczne*, Wyd. Fundacji Humaniora, Poznań.

Fromm, E. (1998), Ucieczka do wolności, Czytelnik, Warszawa.

Fuszara, M. (2010), *Badania opinii publicznej na temat politycznej reprezentacji kobiet*, http://www.pl.boell.org/downloads/partycypacja_polityczna_kobiet_badania.pdf (Accessed: 7.11.2013).

Gąsiorek, A. (2013), *Barut – Polana Śmierci*, 'Polska Niepodległa', 5, 17.

Gawkowska, A. (2004), *Biorąc wspólnotę poważnie? Komunitarystyczne krytyki liberalizmu*, Wyd. IFiS PAN, Warszawa.

Giddens, A. (2001), *Nowoczesność i tożsamość. 'Ja' i społeczeństwo w epoce późnej nowoczesności*, WN PWN.

Giddens, A. (2002), *Socjologia*, WN PWN, Warszawa.

Gliński, P., Kościanowski, A. (eds.) (2009), *Socjologia i Siciński. Style życia. Społeczeństwo obywatelskie. Studia nad przyszłością*, Wyd. IFiS PAN, Warszawa.

Goodwin, P., Wright, G. (2011), *Analiza decyzji*, Wolters Kluwer, Warszawa.

Grisold, C.P. (2011), Heather Reisman, http://www.womenofinfluence.ca/heather-reisman-2 (Accessed: 8.12.2013).

Grzegorek, G., Piegza, M. (2002), *Lipiny 1802–2002. Zarys dziejów osady, gminy, dzielnicy*, KorGraf, Katowice.

GUS (2012), *Wolontariat w organizacjach i inne formy pracy niezarobkowej poza gospodarstwem domowym*, http://www.stat.gov.pl /cps/rde/xbcr/gus/GS_wolontariat_i_inne_formy_pracy_niezarobk_2011.pdf (Accessed: 17.07.2014).

Holocher, A. (2013a), *Katolik nie zabija!*, 'Polska Niepodległa', 2, 17

Holocher, A. (2013b), *Kobieta XXI wieku*, 'Polska Niepodległa', 3, 17.

Holocher, A. (2013c), *Rehabilitować – nie zabijać!*, 'Polska Niepodległa', 4, 17.

http://bilderbergmeetings.org/conferences.html (Accessed: 8.12.2013).

http://bilderbergmeetings.org/conferences-10s.html (Accessed: 5.12.2013).

http://bilderbergmeetings.org/governance.html (Accessed: 8.12.2013).

http://bilderbergmeetings.org/index.php (Accessed: 29.11.2013).

http://publicintelligence.net/category/documents/bilderberg/bilderberg-participant-lists (Accessed: 5.12.2013).

http://stateoftheunion.eui.eu/vendeline-von-bredow.html (Accessed: 5.12.2013).

http://web.archive.org/web/20081207032706 (Accessed: 4.12.2013).

http://web.archive.org/web/20081207032706/http://www.mfa.gr/www.mfa.gr/en-US/The+Ministry/The+Minister/Biography (Accessed: 4.12.2013).

http://www.bbc.co.uk/news/world-24672373 (Accessed: 4.12.2013).

http://www.bilderbergmeetings.org/participants_2011.html (Accessed: 4.12.2013).

http://www.brugesgroup.com/about/index.live (Accessed: 29.11.2013).

http://www.chapters.indigo.ca/our-company/management (Accessed: 8.12.2013).

http://www.csw.umk.pl/zukowski-partycypacja-wyborcza-kobiet (Accessed: 17.07.2014).

http://www.economist.com/mediadirectory/vendeline-von-bredow (Accessed: 5.12.2013).

http://www.eduskunta.fi/triphome/bin/hex5000.sh?hnro=808&kieli=en (Accessed: 4.12.2013).

http://www.emmabonino.it/biography (Accessed: 4.12.2013).

http://www.europarl.europa.eu/meps/en/28368/LILLI_GRUBER_home.html;jsessionid=F991287ECD2F5CAC8E9E0D561D712302.node2 (Accessed: 5.12.2013).

https://www.facebook.com (Accessed: 10.11.2013).

http://www.fembio.org/english/biography.php/woman/biography/lilli-gruber (Accessed: 5.12.2013).

http://www.forbes.com/lists/2006/11/06women_The-100-Most-Powerful-Women_Rank_3.html (Accessed: 4.12.2013).

http://www.forbes.com/lists/2008/11/biz_powerwomen08_Dora-Bakoyannis_QR52.html (Accessed: 4.12.2013).

http://www.gatesfoundation.org/Who-We-Are/General-Information/History (Accessed: 5.12.2013).

http://www.givesmart.org/Stories/Donors/Melinda-Gates (Accessed: 5.12.2013).

http://www.government.se/sb/d/9542/a/87797 (Accessed: 4.12.2013).

http://www.hs.fi/english/article/Social+Democrats+choose+32-year-old+Jutta+Urpilainen+as+new+chair/1135237030682 (Accessed: 4.12.2013).

http://www.hudson.org/learn/index.cfm?fuseaction=staff_bio&eid=Brd17 (Accessed: 8.12.2013).

http://www.la7.it/ottoemezzo/?pmk=header (Accessed: 4.12.2013).

http://www.mfa.gr/www.mfa.gr/en-US/The+Ministry/The+Minister/Biography (Accessed: 4.12.2013).

http://www.mhk.katowice.pl/index.php?option=com_content&view=article&id=234&Item id=130 (Accessed: 8.03.2014).

http://www.pkw.gov.pl (Accessed: 19.09.2013).

http://www.polisblog.it/post/83101/bilderberg-cose (Accessed: 4.12.2013).

http://www.theguardian.com/profile/emma-bonino (Accessed: 4.12.2013).

http://www.weforum.org/global-agenda-councils/anousheh-karvar (Accessed: 8.12.2013).

Hulewicz, J. (1939), *Sprawa wyższego wykształcenia kobiet w Polsce w wieku XIX,* Gebethner i Wolff, Kraków.

Jakubowski, G. (n.d.), *Kobiety dla Narodu. Prawicowe feministki w ofensywie,* http://grzegorz-jakubowski.natemat.pl/64257,kobiety-dla-narodu-prawicowe-feministki-w-ofensywie (Accessed: 8.11.2013).

Jamieson, L. (2008), Od rodziny do intymności [in:] P. Sztompka, M. Bogunia-Borowska (eds.), *Socjologia codzienności,* Znak, Kraków.

Jawłowska, A. (2001), *Tożsamość na sprzedaż* [in:] A. Jawłowska (ed.), *Wokół problemów tożsamości,* Wyd. LTW, Warszawa.

Karnowska, D. (2011), *Spór o wspólnoty. Idee komunitarystyczne we współczesnej polskiej myśli politycznej,* Wyd. Adam Marszałek, Toruń.

Kawula, S. (1996), *Studia z pedagogiki społecznej,* Wyd. WSP, Olsztyn.

Kizwalter, T. (1990), *Procesy modernizacji a emancypacja kobiet na ziemiach polskich w XIX wieku* [in:] A. Żarnowska, A. Szwarc (eds.), *Kobieta i społeczeństwo na ziemiach polskich w XIX w.,* Instytut Historyczny UW, Warszawa.

Kobiety dla Narodu, https://www.facebook.com/KobietyDlaNarodu/info (Accessed: 8.11. 2013).

Kobiety dla Polski. Polska dla Kobiet. 20 lat transformacji 1989–2009. Raport (2009), Fundacja Feminoteka, Warszawa, http://www.kongreskobiet.pl/Content/uploaded/files/sytuacja_kobiet_w_polsce/raport-kobiety-dla-polski-polska-dla-kobiet-20-lat-transformacji-1989-2009.pdf (Accessed: 11.07.2014).

Kobiety z Ruchu Narodowego przeciwko feministycznej propagandzie (22013), www.pch24. pl/kobiety-z-ruchu-narodowego-przeciwko-feministycznej-propagandzie,13903,i.html (Accessed: 10.11.2013).

Koczanowicz, L. (2005), *Wspólnota i emancypacje. Spór o społeczeństwo postkonwencjonalne*, WN DSWE TWP, Wrocław.

Kondracki, J. (1991), *Zagłębie Dąbrowskie. Co to takiego?*, 'Ekspres Sosnowiecki', 5.12.

Kostek, M. (2010), *Wolontariat w hospicjum impulsem do zmian w człowieku?*, TN KUL, Lublin.

Krajewski, J. (2009), *Niezwykła granica*, 'Nowe Zagłębie', 1, 17–19.

Krzyżanowska, N. (2012), *Kobiety w (polskiej) sferze publicznej*, Wyd. Adam Marszałek, Toruń.

Kwaśniewski, K. (1993), *Elementy teorii regionalizmu* [in:] K. Handke (ed.), *Region, regionalizm. Pojęcia i rzeczywistość*, SOW PAN, Warszawa.

Kwiatkowska, H. (2005), *Tożsamość nauczyciela. Między anomią a autonomią*, GWP, Gdańsk.

Kwiatkowska, H. (2012), *Ze sfery zdziwień, pozoru, banalizacji, paradoksu bycia pedeutologiem* [in:] M. Dudzikowa, R. Bera (eds.), *Dążenie do mistrzostwa...*, 'Rocznik Pedagogiczny', numer specjalny z okazji XXV-lecia LSMP pod patronatem KNP PAN, 91–99.

Kwiatkowska, H. (2012a), *Pedeutologia*, Łośgraf, Warszawa.

Kwiatkowska, H. (2012b), *Teoriopoznawcze implikacje związku teorii z praktyką w kształceniu akademickim nauczycieli* [in:] B.D. Gołębniak, H. Kwiatkowska (eds.), *Nauczyciele. Programowe (nie)przygotowanie*, WN DSW, Wrocław.

Kwilecki, A. (1960), *Rola społeczna nauczyciela na Ziemiach Zachodnich w świetle pamiętników nauczycieli osadników*, Instytut Zachodni, Poznań.

Lalak, D. (2010), *Życie jako biografia. Podejście biograficzne w perspektywie pedagogicznej*, Żak, Warszawa.

List of Participants (1975), http://publicintelligence.net/1975-bilderberg-meeting-participant-list (Accessed: 4.12.2013).

List of Participants (1998), http://publicintelligence.net/1998-bilderberg-meeting-participant-list (Accessed: 4.12.2013).

Łabędź, K. (2008), *Determinanty aktywności publicznej w Polsce współczesnej* [in:] K. Łabędź (ed.), *Bariery aktywności publicznej*, Wyd. Adam Marszałek, Toruń.

Łucka, D. (2008), *Utopia czy rzeczywistość. Komunitaryzm w USA*, 'Magazyn Obywatel', 1(39), 58–61.

Łukasik, J.M. (ed.) (2011), *Z codzienności nauczyciela*, Black Unicorn, Jastrzębie Zdrój.

Łukasik, J.M. (2013), *Doświadczanie życia codziennego – narracje nauczycielek na przełomie życia*, Impuls, Kraków.

Łukaszewski, W. (2003), *Wielkie pytania psychologii*, GWP, Gdańsk.

McGhee, G.S., *Memorandum of Meeting of the Bilderberg Steering Group 1954*, http://pl.scribd.com/doc/148742424/Memorandum-of-Meeting-of-the-Bilderberg-Steering-Group-December-6-and-7-1954-in-Paris (Accessed: 4.12.2013).

McKinley Runyan, W. (1992), *Historie życia a psychobiografia: badania teorii i metody*, WN PWN, Warszawa.

Majewska-Opiełka, I. (2010), *Czas kobiet*, Rebis, Poznań.

Malendowski, W. (2010), *Kobiety w polityce. Czy światu grozi matriarchat?* [in:] T. Wallas (ed.), *Między historią, politologią a medioznawstwem*, WN WNPiD UAM, Poznań.

Malicka, M. (1996), *JA to znaczy kto? Rzecz o osobowej tożsamości i wychowaniu*, Znak, Warszawa.

Marshall, G. (ed.) (2005), *Słownik socjologii i nauk społecznych*, WN PWN, Warszawa.

Mazur, E. (2008), *Ku aktywności w życiu publicznym – kobiety w organizacjach dobroczynnych* [in:] A. Janiak-Jasińska, K. Sierakowska, A. Szwarc (eds.), *Działaczki społeczne, feministki, obywatelki... Samoorganizowanie się kobiet na ziemiach polskich do 1918 roku (na tle porównawczym)*, vol. 1, Neriton, Warszawa.

Mello de, A. Kim jesteś?, www.poema.pl/publikacja/8779-kim-jestes (Accessed: 14.07.2014).

Mendel, M. (2005), *Animacja współpracy środowiskowej na wsi* [in:] M. Mendel (ed.), *Animacja współpracy środowiskowej na wsi*, Wyd. Adam Marszałek, Toruń.

Miłkowska-Olejniczak, G. (2002), *Na pomoc dziecku i rodzinie, czyli o przygotowaniu nauczycieli do pracy wychowawczej w środowisku lokalnym* [in:] E. Kozioł, E. Kobyłecka (eds.), *W poszukiwaniu wyznaczników kompetencji nauczyciela XXI wieku*, Wyd. UZ, Zielona Góra.

Miluska, J. (1996), *Tożsamość mężczyzn i kobiet w cyklu życia*, Wyd. UAM, Poznań.

Miluska, J. (2010), *Kobiety w przestrzeni publicznej* [in:] T. Wallas (ed.), *Między historią, politologią a medioznawstwem*, WN WNPiD UAM, Poznań.

Minorczyk-Cichy, A. (2013), *Śląskie się wyludnia. Uda się to zatrzymać?*, http://www.dziennikzachodni.pl/artykul/999580,debata-dz-slaskie-wyludnia-sie-nie-powstrzymamy-tego-sprobujmy-choc-zahamowac,id,t.html?cookie=1 (Accessed: 21.07.2014).

N.N. (2013), *Presentation of the anti-abortion film 'October Baby'*, 'Polska Niepodległa', 7, 22.

Narodowo – subtelniej. W Imieniu Dam (2013), http://narodowcy.net/archiwa/6803-narodowo-subtelniej-w-imieniu-dam (Accessed 7.11.2013).

Nita, M.E. (2009), *Historia podziałów*, 'Nowe Zagłebie', 1, 15–17.

Nowak-Dziemianowicz, M. (2012a), *Inni, różni, odmienni. Dziewczynki i chłopcy w nowoczesności*, WN PWN, Warszawa.

Nowak-Dziemianowicz, M. (2012b), *Inni, różni, odmienni. Dziewczynki i chłopcy w wychowaniu rodzinnym i edukacji szkolnej* [in:] R. Kwiecińska, J. Łukasik (eds.), *Zmiana społeczna. Edukacja-polityka oświatowa-kultura*, Wyd. UP, Kraków.

Nowosiadły, A. (2006), *Szkolenie przygotowujące wolontariuszy do pracy w świetlicach*, -PARPA, Warszawa.

Obrączka, M. (2011), *Słowa jako pędzle. Kolory w powieści Virginii Woolf 'Fale' i przekładzie Lecha Czyżewskiego*, 'Przekładaniec', vol. 24, Kraków, 174–184.

Oleś, P. (2000), *Psychologia przełomu połowy życia*, TN KUL, Lublin.

Omyła-Rudzka, M. (2013), *Kobiety w życiu publicznym*, CBOS, Warszawa.

Ossowska, M. (2002), *Motywy postępowania. Z zagadnień psychologii motywacji*, KiW, Warszawa.

Ossowski, S. (1984), *Analiza socjologiczna pojęcia ojczyzna* [in:] S. Ossowski, *O ojczyźnie i narodzie*, PWN, Warszawa.

Pacześniak, A. (2009), *Wpływ Unii Europejskiej na aktywność obywatelską w Polsce – dobrodziejstwo czy przekleństwo?* [in:] R. Morawski, T. Jemczura (eds.), *W kierunku samoorganizacji społecznej. Społeczeństwo obywatelskie w działaniu*, Wyd. PWSZ, Racibórz.

Parsons, T. (1972), *Szkice z teorii socjologicznej*, PWN, Warszawa.

Perkowska, U. (1994), *Studentki Uniwersytetu Jagiellońskiego w latach 1894–1939. W stulecie immatrykulacji pierwszych studentek*, 'Secesja', Kraków.

Perrot, M. (2009), *Moja historia kobiet*, Pax, Warszawa.

Piątek, K. (2006), *Być kobietą w Polsce, w XXI wieku. Blaski i cienie* [in:] E. Jurczyńska--McCluskey, K. Piątek (eds.), *Między tradycją a nowoczesnością. Współczesna kobieta polska z perspektywy socjologicznej*, Katedra Socjologii ATH, Bielsko-Biała.

Pietrzak, M. (2000), *Sytuacja prawna kobiet w Drugiej Rzeczypospolitej* [in:] A. Żarnowska, A. Szwarc (eds.), *Równe prawa i nierówne szanse. Kobiety w Polsce międzywojennej*, Wyd. DiG, Warszawa.

Pomian, J. (1994), *Józef Retinger. Życie i pamiętniki pioniera Jedności Europejskiej*, Pavo, Warszawa. *Przegląd i ocena głównych tez* [in:] P. Socha (ed.), *Duchowy rozwój człowieka. Fazy życia, osobowość, wiara, religijność*, Wyd. UJ, Kraków.

Przewłocka, J. (2013), *Co wiemy o wolontariuszach w Polsce*, http://www.mragowo.pl/phoca-download/pliki-artykuly/album_1393_220_1/2_Co_wiemy_o_wolontariuszach.pdf (Accessed: 17.07.2014).

Przewłocka, J., Adamiak, P., Herbst, J. (2013), *Podstawowe fakty o organizacjach pozarządowych. Raport z badania 2012*, Stowarzyszenie Klon/Jawor, Warszawa, http://www.ngo.pl/PodstawoweFakty_2012_raport/ebook/content/PodstawoweFaktyNGO_2012_KlonJawor_raport.pdf (Accessed: 11.07.2014).

Przewłocka, J., Adamiak, P., Zając, A. (2012), *Życie codzienne organizacji pozarządowych w Polsce*, Stowarzyszenie Klon/Jawor, Warszawa.

Pustułka, A. (2013), *Pierwszy raport z frontu: gminy skąpią na edukację regionalną*, 'Dziennik Zachodni', 25.03, p. 6.

Putnam, R. (1995), *Demokracja w działaniu*, Fundacja im. S. Batorego, Warszawa.

Raciborski, J. (2007), *Zachowania wyborcze Polaków 1989–2006* [in:] M. Marody (ed.), *Wymiary życia społecznego. Polska na przełomie XX i XXI wieku*, Scholar, Warszawa.

Raport. Nauczyciele w roku szkolnym 2010/2011 (2012), J. Zarębska (comp.), Wydział Informacji i Promocji – Zespół Informacji Pedagogicznej ORE, Warszawa, http://www.bc.ore.edu.pl/dlibra/docmetadata?id=279&from=&dirids=1&ver_id=&lp=1&QI=DF3F E5F8D8852412CFCE7A71275C22A8-19 (Accessed: 11.07.2014).

Raport. Nauczyciele we wrześniu 2008 roku. Stan i struktura zatrudnienia (2009), J. Zarębska (comp.), CODN, Warszawa.

Rejman, E. (2013), *Stop aborcyjnej nowomowie*, 'Polska Niepodległa', 5, 9.

Renzetti, C.M., Curran, D.J. (2008), *Kobiety, mężczyźni i społeczeństwo*, WN PWN, Warszawa.

Retinger, J.H. (1956), *The Bilderberg Group*, http://pl.scribd.com/doc/169401263/Bilderberg-Group-Essay-1956-by-Retinger (Accessed: 21.07.2014).

Ręce precz od naszych dzieci!, https://www.facebook. com/events/458612624237108 (Accessed: 10.11.2013).

Rockefeller, D. (2002), *Memoirs*, Random House Publishing Group, New York.

Rocznik Statystyczny Województwa Śląskiego (2012), www.stat.gov/cps/rde/katow/ASSETS_ ROCZNIK_2012 (Accessed: 14.07.2014).

Rosner, K. (2003), *Narracja, tożsamość i czas*, Universitas, Kraków.

Różańska-Kowal, J. (2009), *Motywacja zachowań prospołecznych i antyspołecznych nieletnich*, Impuls, Kraków.

Ruch Narodowy. Sekcja Kobiet, https://www.facebook.com/SekcjaKobiet/info (Accessed: 9.11.2013).

Sellers, P. (2008), *Melinda Gates goes public*, http://money.cnn.com/2008/01/04/news/news makers/gates.fortune/index.htm (Accessed: 4.12.2013).

Sepczyńska, D. (2005), *Społeczeństwo obywatelskie* [in:] S. Opara, D. Radziszewska-Szczepaniak, A. Żukowski (eds.), *Podstawowe kategorie polityki*, Instytut Nauk Politycznych UWM, Olsztyn.

Sielatycki, M. (2005), *Młodzi i starsi obywatele w polskiej szkole. Uwagi na rozpoczęcie Europejskiego Roku Edukacji Obywatelskiej w Polsce*, http://www.ereo.codn.edu.pl/index. php?option=com_content&task=view&id=21&Itemid=58 (Accessed: 23.07.2014).

Sierakowska, K. (2009), *Samoorganizowanie się kobiet w II Rzeczypospolitej: dążenia, szanse, realizacje* [in:] A. Janiak-Jasińska, K. Sierakowska, A. Szwarc (eds.), *Działaczki społeczne, feministki, obywatelki... Samoorganizowanie się kobiet na ziemiach polskich po 1918 roku (na tle porównawczym)*, vol. 2, Neriton, Warszawa.

Sikorska-Kulesza, J. (2008), *Trójzaborowe zjazdy kobiet na ziemiach polskich na przełomie XIX i XX wieku* [in:] A. Janiak-Jasińska, K. Sierakowska, A. Szwarc (eds.), *Działaczki społeczne, feministki, obywatelki... Samoorganizowanie się kobiet na ziemiach polskich do 1918 roku (na tle porównawczym)*, vol. 1, Neriton, Warszawa.

Sklar, H. (1980), *Trilateralism: the trilateral commission and elite planning for world management*, South End Press, Boston.

Słownik języka polskiego, www.sjp.pwn.pl (Accessed: 17.07.2014).

Socha, P. (2000), *Stadialny rozwój sądów moralnych w koncepcji Lawrence'a Kolberga. Przegląd i ocena głównych tez* [in:] P. Socha (ed.), *Duchowy rozwój człowieka. Fazy życia, osobowość, wiara, religijność*, Wyd. UJ, Kraków.

Stawiarska, P. (2011), *Wolontariat hospicyjny – perspektywa interdyscyplinarna*, Difin, Warszawa.

Strzemińska, A., Wiśnicka, M. (2011), *Młodzież na wsi. Raport z badania*, Warszawa, http://www.rownacszanse.pl/books/18702_mlodziez_na_wsi_raport.pdf (Accessed: 11.07.2014).

Suchocka, H. (2000), *Jaka konstytucja dla Europy? Problem konstytucji europejskiej z punktu widzenia kraju przygotowującego się do przystąpienia do Unii Europejskiej*, Litar, Hamburg.

Sujka, P. (2013), *Leczenie homoseksualizmu*, 'Polska Niepodległa', 8, 12.

Sulik, M. (2010), *Kobiety w nauce. Podmiotowe i społeczno-kulturowe uwarunkowania*, Wyd. UŚ, Katowice.

Sułek, A. (2009), *Doświadczenia i umiejętności obywatelskie Polaków* [in:] P. Gliński, A. Kościański (eds.), *Socjologia i Siciński. Style życia. Społeczeństwo obywatelskie. Studia nad przyszłością*, Wyd. IFiS PAN, Warszawa.

Świętochłowice – Lipiny, http://slaskiemiasta.pl/swietochlowice/lipiny (Accessed: 17.07.2014).

Szczepański, M.S., Ślązak-Tazbir, W. (2010), *Region i społeczność lokalna w perspektywie socjologicznej*, 'Górnośląskie Studia Socjologiczne. Seria Nowa', vol. I, Wyd. UŚ, Katowice.

Szczepański, M.S., Śliz, A. (2010), Dylematy regionalnej tożsamości, „Śląsk", 10.

Sztompka, P. (2002), *Socjologia. Analiza społeczeństwa*, Znak, Kraków.

Szymański, M.J. (2013a), *Socjologia edukacji. Podręcznik akademicki*, Impuls, Kraków.

Szymański, M.J. (2013b), Wykład inauguracyjny wygłoszony 27 września 2013 r. na uroczystości otwarcia roku akademickiego 2013/2014 w Wyższej Szkole Pedagogicznej ZNP.

Śliwa, M. (2000), *Udział kobiet w wyborach i ich działalność parlamentarna* [in:] A. Żarnowska, A. Szwarc (eds), *Równe prawa i nierówne szanse. Kobiety w Polsce międzywojennej*, Wyd. DiG, Warszawa.

Śliwak, J., Zdunek, M. (2007), *Wolontariat – bezinteresowne działanie na rzecz potrzebującego człowieka* [in:] J. Śliwak (ed.), *Psychologiczne problemy zatrudnienia osób niepełnosprawnych*, Wyd. Norbertinum, Lublin.

Śpiewak, P. (2004), *Poszukiwanie wspólnot* [in:] P. Śpiewak (ed.), *Komunitarianie: wybór tekstów*, Fundacja Aletheia, Warszawa.

Traynor, I. (2013), *Queen Beatrix of the Netherlands abdicates in favour of son*, 'The Guardian', http://www.theguardian.com/world/2013/jan/28/queen-beatrix-netherlands-abdicates (Accessed: 4.12.2013).

Turowski, M. (2011), Liberalizm po komunitaryzmie? Filozoficzne koncepcje jednostki, wspólnoty i państwa jako źródło krytyki społecznej i politycznej, Wyd. Adam Marszałek, Toruń.

Tyszka, T. (1986), *Analiza decyzyjna i psychologia decyzji*, PWN, Warszawa.

Tyszka, T. (1999), *Psychologiczne pułapki oceniania i podejmowania decyzji*, GWP, Gdańsk.

Wapiński, R. (1991), *Pokolenia Drugiej Rzeczypospolitej*, Ossolineum, Wrocław.

Wapiński, R. (2000), *Kobiety i życie publiczne – przemiany pokoleniowe* [in:] A. Żarnowska, A. Szwarc (eds.), *Równe prawa i nierówne szanse. Kobiety w Polsce międzywojennej*, Wyd. DiG, Warszawa.

Wasiukiewicz, A. (2013), *Podświadomość i problem grzechu*, 'Polska Niepodległa', 3, 10.

We Ja (2013), *Po pikiecie narodowców w Strawczynie: grożenie sądem, utrata pracy*, 'Polska Niepodległa', 7, 9.

Węgrzecki, A. (1966), *Zarys fenomenologii podmiotu*, Ossolineum, Wrocław.

Weryński, P. (2010), *Wzory uczestnictwa obywatelskiego Polaków*, Wyd. IFiS PAN, Warszawa.

Wilford, H. (2003), *The CIA, the British left, and the Cold War: calling the tune?*, Routledge, London.

Witkowski, L. (1988), *Tożsamość i zmiana. Wstęp do epistemologicznej analizy kontekstów edukacyjnych*, Wyd. UMK, Toruń.

Witkowski, L. (2000), *Rozwój i tożsamość w cyklu życia. Studium koncepcji Erika H. Eriksona*, WIT-GRAF, Toruń.

Wódz, K., Wódz, J. (2009), *Jaka tożsamość?, Jaki region?*, 'Nowe Zagłębie', 1, 2–4.

Wolicka, E. (1988), *Osobowa tożsamość i odrębność w perspektywie hermeneutyki dialogicznej* [in:] J. Kłoczkowski, S. Łukaszewicz (eds.), *Tożsamość, odmienność, tolerancja a kultura pokoju*, Instytut Europy Środkowo-Wschodniej, Lublin.

Woskowski, J. (1997), *Feminizacja zawodu nauczycielskiego* [in:] W. Pomykało (ed.), *Encyklopedia pedagogiczna*, Fundacja Innowacja, Warszawa.

Woźniczka, Z. (2008), *Kształtowanie się tożsamości Zagłębia Dąbrowskiego – perspektywa historyczna (zarys problemu)* [in:] M. Kaczmarczyk, W. Wojtasik (eds.), *Wokół tożsamości regionalnej. Zagłębie Dąbrowskie i jego sąsiedzi*, Wyd. WSH, Sosnowiec.

Żarnowska, A. (2000), *Obywatelki II Rzeczypospolitej* [in:] A. Żarnowska, A. Szwarc (eds.), *Równe prawa i nierówne szanse. Kobiety w Polsce międzywojennej*, Wyd. DiG, Warszawa.

Żarnowska, A. (2013), *Ruch emancypacyjny i stowarzyszenia kobiece na ziemiach polskich przed odzyskaniem niepodległości – dylematy i ograniczenia. Wprowadzenie* [in:] A. Janiak-Jasińska, K. Sierakowska, A. Szwarc (eds.), *Kobieta i rodzina w przestrzeni wielkomiejskiej na ziemiach polskich w XIX i XX wieku*, Wyd. DiG, Warszawa.

Zasada, M. (2012), *Jak odróżnić Śląsk od Zagłębia? (Poradnik Regionalny)*, 'Dziennik Zachodni', 29.06.

Żukowski, A. (2011), *Partycypacja wyborcza kobiet — wyzwania i dylematy*, Towarzystwo Naukowe Organizacji i Kierownictwa Dom Organizatora w Toruniu, Toruń.

3
Women and violence
Legal, social and cultural contexts

Zofia Szarota
Pedagogical University of Cracow, Poland

Oppression *versus* liberation
Awareness of domestic violence victims' rights

Women are citizens.

In a contemporary world, such statement is a truism. However, as recently as a hundred or even fifty years ago, it caused consternation among many of the then-contemporary male citizens.

Women are the focal point of international discourse concerning social change, in the debate on fundamental human rights and freedom. Promoting and protecting women's rights is an integral part of UN and EU's human right policy. Why is that? It is because women are still considered a minority group and their full emancipation is a condition for, and goal of, social change.

Being aware of one's rights is the key to freedom and personal dignity. Polish women were granted civil and political rights in 1918. Are they able to enjoy them fully and consciously? This article provides the answer to this question from the perspective of women – victims of domestic violence.

Reflection upon the history of human and civil rights

The beginning of the idea of human rights dates back to the ancient Eastern civilization. For example, the Code of Hammurabi of the 17th century BC stated that the purpose of power is to uphold justice and protect the weak from the evil deeds of the strong. Philosophical reflections of the classical Greek antiquity is full of utopias and ideas of a perfect state, as well as rights, obligations and virtues of its citizens. There were many prominent predecessors contemplating human and civil rights of the time, including Solon (ca. 635–560 B.C.), who introduced democratic reforms in the Athens, philosophers: Plato (ca. 427–347 B.C.), Aristotle (384–322 B.C.) and from outside the European cultural heritage area – Confucius

(551–479 B.C.). The ideas of natural rights from the Greek philosophical thought were adopted and developed by the Romans, e.g. Cicero (106–43 B.C.) and Seneca the Younger (ca. 4 B.C.–65 A.D.) (Osiatyński 1998, pp. 28–30).

The ideas of protection of human freedom were also present in the Medieval times, when the firsts legally binding Acts were created, including Magna Carta Libertatum of 1215.

In the Renaissance and later cultural movements, the concepts of organization of the state, as well as civil rights and duties were raised e.g. by: Thomas More (1478–1535) in *Utopia*, Tomasso Campanella (1569–1639) in *City of the Sun*, Thomas Hobbes (1588–1679) in *Leviathan*, Gerrard Winstanley (ca. 1609 – after 1676) in his pamphlet entitled *The Law of Freedom in a Platform: Or, True Magistracy Restored*, John Locke (1632–1704), e.g. in his work entitled *Two Treatises of Government*, Montesquieu (1689–1755) – author of the theory of separation of powers among a legislature, an executive and a judiciary in *The Spirit of the Laws*, Voltaire (1694–1778), Jean-Jacques Rousseau (1712–1778) in *Social Contract*, Immanuel Kant (1724–1804), as well as writers calling for women's rights, such as Nicolas de Condorcet (1743–1794) postulating the right of women to education and Olympe de Gouges (1748–1793), a playwright, publicist, feminist, revolutionist, paradoxically decapitated during the French Revolution.

Olympe de Gouges, referring to (and even mocking) the French Declaration of the Rights of Man and of the Citizen of 1789 in her own Declaration of the Rights of Woman and Female Citizen wrote:

> This revolution will only take effect when all women become fully aware of their deplorable condition, and of the rights they have lost in society (de Gouges 2000).

She claimed that

> Woman are born free and remain equal to man in rights. [...] All citizens including women are equally admissible to all public dignities, offices and employments, according to their capacity, and with no other distinction than that of their virtues and talents (de Gouges 2000).

To emphasize her opinions, de Gouges used the following argument: 'Women have the right to mount the scaffold, they must also have the right to mount the speaker's rostrum'. In her Declaration, she called for women's rights to freedom, equality, property, security, opposing oppression, to create laws, freedom of belief and speech, equal access to professions, honors and functions. She demanded the right for women to join military service. She postulated gender equality in families and churches (de Gouges 2000). Her postulates remained on paper only, she was executed by guillotine on 3rd November 1793.

Despite growing feminist movements before 1900, women did not have voting rights in any of the European countries. Women were granted passive voting rights in Wyoming, USA (1869) and New Zealand (British territory) (1893).

Another non-European country to recognize civil rights of women, however in a limited and restricted scope – was sovereign Australia (1902). As far as Europe is concerned, women were granted rights for the first time in Finland (Grand Duchy of Finland at that time) – on 1st June 1906, then in Norway (1913), Soviet Russia (10th July 1918). In the same year, more countries introduced the category of female citizen in their legislature, mainly Austria, Austria, Germany, Poland, Hungary, Estonia, Latvia and Lithuania. After two years (in 1920), USA joined the group of countries recognizing female rights. The last country in Europe to grant such rights was Liechtenstein (*Wommen's Suffrage*) in 1989 and Swiss Canton of Appenzell-Innerrhode Canton in 1989 (*Postęp dla wszystkich...* 2010, p. 3).

The last countries to grant voting rights to women were Kuwait (2005) and United Arab Emirates (2006). Women from Saudi Arabia and Brunei still do not have any civil rights.

Polish women managed to win their civil rights. They were granted to them by a Decree of the Chief of State – Józef Piłsudski dated 28th November 1918 on system of election for the Legislative Sejm (Dekret Tymczasowego Naczelnika Państwa... 1918) after Poland regained independence. Those rules were confirmed in the March Constitution of 1921 (Dekret Tymczasowego Naczelnika Państwa... 1918) which also granted women the right to hold any public office and married women were given the right to be a party to civil and legal proceedings (Malec 2009, p. 12).

Human and civil rights as women's rights

Human rights are natural, inherent – they exist regardless of the will of any authority and belong to any human being since birth, they are part of people's humanity. Human rights are inalienable – people cannot waive or give up such rights. Human rights are inviolable – no one can deprive a human being of their rights, they must be respected at all times and the state is responsible for protection and enforcement of such rights (Juchniewicz, Kazimierczuk 2006, p. 116).

Civil rights, however, can be understood as

[...] rights granted to an individual by the law of the country of that person's nationality. Other than human rights, civil rights are related to being a national of a given country. Laws and civil liberties of a given country determine the status of a citizen in that country (Kulig 1996, p. 191).

In the contemporary world, human rights have been divided into four categories, the so called generations of human rights.

The first generation are natural, inalienable and inviolable human rights rooted in human dignity, regardless of state legislature. They include civil and political rights, the most 'classic' rights of human beings: right to life, personal liberties related to protection of personal inviolability, freedom of thought and religion, right to property, equality before the law, political rights related to freedom of speech (Garlicki 2003, p. 88).

The second generation of rights includes economic, social and cultural rights, ensuring physical and spiritual development, as well as social security being a guarantee of participation of an individual in social life (social participation) at a proper level. Decent economic and social conditions are to help an individual be a citizen, an active member of local community and the country they live in (Kruszka 2008, p. 56). They include e.g. the right to work, health care, education and participation in culture, to social security.

Third generation rights are the so called collective rights – rights of nations and social groups. They require cooperation between countries and reflect general human solidarity and brotherhood. This category include e.g. the right to peace, the right of nations to self-determination, the right to clean natural environment, common world heritage, right to communication, development and humanitarian help. (ref. Malinowska 2004, p. 16).

The youngest group of rights are the emerging rights of the so called fourth generation, including international rights regulating e.g. the right to nationality and minority rights (religious and sexual minorities).

Rights of women in the contemporary world

Human rights have been the subject of numerous international documents, conventions and agreements, the most important of which make up the so called International Bill of Rights. Among them, special attention should be paid to the Universal Declaration of Human Rights UN of 10th December 1948 which states the following:

Article 1
All human beings are born free and equal in dignity and rights. They are endowed with reason and conscience and should act towards one another in a spirit of brotherhood.

Article 2
Everyone is entitled to all the rights and freedoms set forth in this Declaration, without distinction of any kind, such as race, colour, sex, language, religion, political or other opinion, national or social origin, property, birth or other status. Furthermore, no distinction shall be made on the basis of the political, jurisdictional or international status of the country or territory to which a person belongs, whether it be independent, trust, non-self-governing or under any other limitation of sovereignty (The Universal Declaration of Human Rights 1948).

The set of laws adopted by the UN also includes laws that relate especially to the principle of equality and protection of women: Convention for the Suppression of the Traffic in Persons and of the Exploitation of the Prostitution of Others dated 1949, ILO Equal Remuneration Convention of 1951 concerning the principle of equal remuneration for the same type of job; Convention on the Political Rights of Women (1952) ordering its signatories to respect active and passive voting rights of women and holding the same public offices as men; Discrimination (Employment and Occupation) Convention (1958); Convention against Discrimination In Education (1960), Convention on Consent to Marriage, Minimum Age for Marriage and Registration of Marriages (1962) combating gender discrimination at work; as well as International Covenant on Civil and Political Rights and the International Covenant on Economic, Social and Cultural Rights (1966) and Declaration on the Elimination of Discrimination Against Women of 1967 (see: Równe prawa dla kobiet i mężczyzn 2003).

A more contemporary list of documents begins with the Resolution No. 34/180 of the United Nations General Assembly of 18th December 1979 – Convention on the Elimination of All Forms of Discrimination against Women, called **the international bill of rights for women** (*Postęp dla wszystkich...* 2010, p. 5). Other UN documents in this list include: Declaration on the Elimination of Violence against Women (1993) and Resolution A/54/4 of the United National General Assembly – Optional Protocol to the Convention on the Elimination of Discrimination against Women dated 6th October 1999.

The UN organized four world conferences concerning women's rights. The first one took place in 1975 during the International Women's Year in Mexico, the second on was held in Copenhagen in 1980, the third one – in Nairobi in 1985, and the fourth one – in Beijing in 1995. Since 2000, New York has been hosting sessions of the United Nations General Assembly every 5 years, summing up the previous actions and setting new goals in the area of protection of women's rights (see: *Postęp dla wszystkich...* 2010, pp. 16–19).

The European Community has also drawn up a number of documents concerning social inclusion of women and equality of their rights (http://ms.gov.pl). Those are:

– Recommendation No. R (1985) 4 of the Committee of Ministers on Violence in the Family dated 26th March 1985,

– Recommendation No. R (1990) 2 of the Committee of Ministers on Social Measures Concerning Violence within the Family dated 15th January 1990,

– Recommendation No. 1450 (2000) of the Council of Europe on Violence against Women in Europe,

– Recommendation No. Rec.(2002)5 of the Committee of Ministers on the Protection of Women against Violence dated 30th April 2002,

– Convention on preventing and combating violence against women and domestic violence (2011, pp. 2, 3), stating that: 'realisation of *de jure* and *de facto* equality between women and men is a key element in the prevention of violence against women' by 'aspiring to create a Europe free from violence against women and domestic violence'.

Protection of human and civil rights in Poland is guaranteed by: the Constitution, the Civil Code, the Criminal Code, the Labour Code, the Family and Guardianship Code, common courts, the Supreme Administration Court, the Constitutional Tribunal, the Human Rights Defender, as well as non-governmental organizations.

Although there is a number of provisions of international law, women's rights are violated constantly. According to WHO's report entitled *Global and regional estimates of violence against women: Prevalence and health effects of intimate partner violence and non-partner sexual violence* (2013), over one third (35%) of women in the world experience physical or sexual abuse. It is therefore a macro-pathology, a global problem, even an epidemic. Undisputable data show the scale of this problem. Domestic violence is experienced by 37% of women in Africa, the Middle East and South-Eastern Asia; 30% of female population of Latin and South America; one fourth of European women and 23% of American women. Women who are most at risk of physical abuse are aged: 40–44 (37.8%) and 35–39 (36.6%) (WHO 2013, p. 24).

According to the UN, over 600 million women live in countries, where family violence is not considered a crime. In 2000, the United Nations adopted eight general Millenium Development Goals to be achieved by the year 2015, including promotion of gender equality, women's empowerment and social promotion, elimination of gender inequality in access to all levels of education by 2015, as well as improving health status of pregnant and parturient women.

Analysis of OECD's Report shows that the quality of life of women is still much lower than that of men. They perform unpaid work much more often (maintaining a household and looking after children) and devote much more time to it than their partners (twice as much in Poland – men: 157 minutes, women – 296 minutes daily[1]). They also receive lower remuneration for professional work (OECD 2013, p. 120). Access to offices and managerial, decisive positions for women is limited (see: Sulik 2010). Misogyny is still rampant.

---

[1] Average for countries associated within OECD is ca. 32 hours of unpaid work for women and ca. 21 hours of unpaid work for men. The best male-female ratio concerning household chores is in Denmark – 186 minutes of unpaid work for men and 243 minutes for women.

Awareness of women's rights – victims of domestic violence, results of study

The subject of the study[2] was awareness of the female respondents, victims of domestic violence, of their rights. The aim of the study was to determine the level of awareness of rights and knowledge of institutions and support organizations for women experiencing domestic violence, as well as to create an educational project to increase such awareness. The research questions were as follows:

1. What is the level of awareness of rights relating the area of family and professional life of the respondents?
2. What institutions defending human rights are known to the female respondents?
3. What factor play the most important role in formation of legal awareness in women?

Collective case study (multi-case study) (Stake 2009, p. 623) with an in-depth interview consisting of 28 conversation topics was implemented. The study included crisis intervention centers[3] of Małopolska province in southern Poland and was carried out on 15 women aged 24–47. The choice of respondents was intentional – those were women with a history of crisis intervention, victims of domestic violence.

They were characterized by the following variables:

1) education level of the respondents: primary – 1, vocational – 7, secondary – 2, higher – 5;
2) family setting: 13 married women (including two abandoned by their husbands and two married for the second time), one living in a cohabitation, one divorced; children: six women with two children, four women with one children, three women with five children, one woman with four children, one woman with no children;
3) labor market situation: eight professionally active women (including one employed on 0.5 FTE basis, one employed on 1.5 FTE basis and one in managerial positions), seven women were not active on the labor market;

---

2 On the basis of contribution studies carried out under my supervision: *Kobieta wobec praw i wolności obywatelskich* (B. Warchał), *Świadomość praw obywatelskich kobiet doświadczających przemocy w rodzinie* (D. Wojtysiak), *Świadomość praw obywatelskich kobiet przeżywających kryzysy* (A. Maryon), *Poziom świadomości praw obywatelskich u kobiet doświadczających przemocy domowej* (R. Mucha), auditing students of postgraduate studies, Pedagogical University of Cracow, Kraków 2013.

3 Crisis intervention centers provide psychological, pedagogical and social support for people in difficult situations, such as family violence. The centers provide psychological support in the first place, but one can also use legal counseling or pedagogical consultations. CICs have hostels offering shelter for individuals and families forced to leave their homes or for whom it would be dangerous to stay at home.

4) perpetrators of violence: husbands in twelve cases and partner in one case, in addition: family members in three cases and partner's mother (mother-in-law) in one case;
5) type of abuse: mental abuse was experienced by all of the respondents, eleven of them were victims of economic abuse, ten of them experienced physical abuse and there were two cases of marital rape.

Table 1. Characteristics of the respondents

Woman and her age	Variables				
	Family situation	Professional status	Education	Type of abuse	Perpetrator
W1, 47	married for the second time, five children (one adult, other at the age of 14–6, one disabled child)	inactive	primary	physical, mental, economic	husband
W2, 47	married, two children (22 and 17-years-old)	1.5 FTE	higher	mental	husband
W3, 44	married, five children (including three underage children, 16-, 14- and 11-years old)	inactive	vocational	physical, mental, economic	husband, mother-in-law
W4, 41	married, two sons (age 17 and 12), the older son is disabled	inactive	vocational	mental, economic	husband
W5, 40	married, two daughters (age 13 and 9)	active	secondary	physical, mental	husband
W6, 39	divorced, four children (age 15–19)	0.5 FTE	vocational	physical, mental	husband
W7, 38	married for the second time, five children	inactive	vocational	physical, mental, economic	husband
W8, 37	married, son (6-years-old)	active	higher	physical, marital rape, mental, economic	husband
W9, 37	married, two children (age 11 and 9)	inactive	higher	physical, mental, economic	husband
W10, 35	abandoned by her husband, two children (5- and 2-years-old)	inactive	vocational	mental, economic	father, brother
W11, 34	married, no children	active, managerial position	higher	physical, marital rape, mental, economic	husband
W12, 33	married, two children at early school age	active	vocational	physical, mental, economic	husband

W13, 29	abandoned by her husband, son (6-years-old)	active	secondary	mental, economic	direct relatives
W14, 28	husband (moved out), daughter (4-years-old)	active	higher	mental	husband, direct relatives
W15, 24	partner, 6-month-old son	inactive	vocational	physical, mental, economic	partner and his mother

Source: see note 2, p. 215.

After combining the above data, we may present a specific average characteristics of victims of domestic violence. Those are mothers in relationships experiencing all kinds of humiliation and experience mainly from their husbands/partners, they have no social support and have poor awareness of their rights:

– [...] *it is hard to expect anything from life when one is left alone and is dependent on others* (W13, 29).

    – *The fact that my husband is abusing me is not an infringement, but a violation of my right. I am not allowed to say anything, I have to do everything he wants or he wouldn't like it. I don't have any money, he says that he is the one making many so he is to decide. I would like to find a job, but how? My husband knows his rights, when he was called by the social welfare, he went there with a representative. I don't know if it is allowed, but I think so, because my husband did it* (W7, 38).

Despite the fact that women's rights are regulated by law, victims of violence – with one exception (W11, 34) are hardly aware of their existence. And one can use and enforce all their privileges and rights only while being aware of such rights and privileges. Therefore, it is necessary to raise social awareness of gender equality, especially among women. However, such process should start with diagnosis of the state of awareness of rights among the respondents – victims of domestic violence.

According to the results of in-depth interviews, the respondents have a very low awareness of their first and second generation rights. The only right identified by all of the respondents was the right to work.

It should be remembered that all of the respondents are victims of domestic violence and maybe that is why they do not see the problem of permanent violation of their right to personal freedom and immunity, to property, to personal dignity and privacy. The largest number of rights were identified by respondents with the highest level of education.

Table 2. Awareness of one's rights[4]

Rights		Number of indications
First generation rights	Right to personal immunity	9
	Right to life	8
	Right to personal freedom	5
	Voting rights	5
	Right to property (own money)	4
	Right to privacy (in the context of personal data protection)	4
	Right to personal dignity	3
	Right to freedom of conscience and religion	2
	Right to defense	1
Lack of awareness of any first generation rights		2
Second generation rights	Right to protection of health, medical leave	9
	Right to holiday leave	7
	Right to maternity leave after giving birth to a child	6
	Right to free health (medical) care	5
	Right to use psychological and legal help	5
	Protection of pregnant women	4
	Right to minimum wages	4
	Right to divorce	2
	Right to protection at work	1
	Right to retirement pension	1
	Right to equal treatment at work	1
Other	Children's rights protection	1

Source: see note 2, p. 215.

The respondents were able to identify only a few documents (legal acts) regulating the issue of human and civil rights in Poland; Constitution was referred to six times, moreover, one person mentioned the Labor Code, the Act on combating gender discrimination, the Act on combating violence, stressing that she was informed about those documents by the employees of a crisis intervention center. Single respondents also pointed to the Human Rights Declaration and Convention on the Rights of the Child. However, a typical answer was similar to the ones quoted below:

> – *What are civil rights? I don't know any regulations, I'm not interested in politics at all. Besides, there are laws, but people have to struggle anyway* (K1, 47);

---

4 Original answers of the respondents have been used.

– The government and employers don't give a damn about our rights. And the relatives... I wonder why make such laws if nobody obeys them. (K14, 28);

– My husband has left me with debts and small children, I don't have a job or anything. I think this is a violation of my laws, but I don't know, maybe I'm wrong?? (K6, 39).

Most of the female respondents were not able to identify any institutions, organizations or persons that could help them free themselves from the violence they experience. The answers included suggestions concerning the current situation of women receiving institutional support: crisis intervention centers – 11 times, Police, court and social support centers – 8 times each, local commission for solving alcohol-related problems and prosecutor's office – four times. Media (the Internet, radio, TV, leaflets, brochures) were also mentioned four times. In four cases, the social support network was created by sisters of the respondents as those who 'made them realize' their situation, friends and prenatal physicians were mentioned three times. Mental health clinics, the Church (as the community of people) and court officers were mentioned three times.

The studies show that the ignorance of the respondents – victims of violence – is remarkable. They were not able to associate the so called Blue Card[5] procedure, in which they actively participate, with their right to personal immunity, non-violence and respectful treatment. They cannot identify the scope of family duties divided between partners. They are not able to enforce the right to money they earn working hard and honestly. They experience jealousy, harassment, humiliation and beating.

Their social, economic and political emancipation is the mean and purpose of social change. It is a difficult task as the perception of social roles of the respondents is deeply rooted in traditional values. The image of a woman was shaped in a society, where relations between genders were defined by patriarchy. The respondents follow the family role models functioning in their families of origin: a woman economically dependent on her husband taking care of the house and children.

– I do the housework, that's the way it should be. My mom did everything at home and nobody ever helped her and she is okay. A woman should count on herself, there's nobody who can help her (W4, 41).

All the respondents believe that personal freedom can be achieved through employment, however, six of them did not find the courage to take up any job.

– [...] I think that my rights are violated permanently, mostly by my husband. I wanted to go to work, but he didn't let me. He says that he is the one making money and I need to stay at home. I don't understand it, I am educated. Yes, I have never worked, but maybe I should? Besides, I have no experience, It will never happen, so why are we talking about

---

5 Procedure of dealing with victims and perpetrators of domestic violence established by the Police in Poland together with instructions for victims of violence, including seeking support (since 1998).

*this in the first place? I'd love to work, it is my dream, I believe that a woman should work
and pursue her career. Maybe then she can gain respect? The children will grow up one day
and what I am going to do then? Women who work have other goals and challenges to face*
(W9, 37).

The respondents display the so called 'Stockholm syndrome', lowered self-
esteem, subordination, resignation, learned helplessness, manifested by inability
to make independent decisions and perceiving oneself as helpless in confrontation
with the perpetrator and life.

*– My dad used to beat my mom. He drank a lot, he was aggressive. I decided to go
to a college, get education. I wanted to run away from everything my home was. I always
thought that when I finish my college I will manage by myself. During the studies, I met my
future husband. I was in year two and he was already defending his master's thesis. I was so
much in love with him, he was so smart, intelligent and caring. I remember that he pulled
my arm once because I didn't want to go for a walk, it hurt. He apologized and everything
was fine. However, it happened again after our marriage. I know that I shouldn't repeat my
mom's mistake and I should leave him, but I can't, I don't want to* (W9, 37).

Despite their suffering, they expect they husbands and partners to be the heads
and supporters of their families. They believe in traditional division of household
labor:

*– The role of women is to look after the house and men have to make money. Those are
the roles of women and men. It had been so for ages until recently, now the world is turning
upside down* (W4, 41).

The respondents are at the beginning of their road to self-awareness, awareness of their rights, to emancipation, however, some of them will never reach personal freedom, as effective change requires personal commitment and some of the
respondents are not yet ready to begin working on themselves and change their
position.

Prevention and therapy: social education

Educational actions aimed at making women aware of equality of rights should
be carried out at three levels – elementary, secondary and tertiary prevention.

In the area of elementary prevention, we should strengthen educational, system, organizational, political and economic actions, as well as prevention schemes.
Cooperation between social forces, from the government to local self-governments,
from physicians, police officers etc. to social workers and women's right organizations is necessary. Legal instruments have already been established, however, it is
necessary to monitor the gender equality policy on an ongoing basis. Social education should use all the tools available – social campaigns, city lights, billboards,

spots in mass media. The society should be subject to universal legal, civil and human right education. The issues of human and civil rights, including women's rights, should be promoted more – in kindergartens and schools through themed plays using education toys, during general education classes or civics classes, by encouraging schools to take an interest in civil rights by organizing various knowledge competitions and contests. Teaching materials and books should emphasize issues of gender equality and educate both girls and boys in this matter – it will raise girls' awareness and boys' respect for their rights. Such actions should increase the general awareness of civil rights in the nearest future.

Secondary prevention should be aimed at care and compensation in the identified families and environment at risk through: improvement of family's social and financial situation, overcoming social isolation of families, promoting normal emotional and communication patterns within families, education, counseling, creating an environmental network of family support institutions and incorporating the already existing institutions in such network. Persons at risk of discrimination and violence should receive free access to legal and psychological aid, as well as necessary financial support. It is very important to prepare educational offer for those at risk of becoming victims of violence and – in a broader context – gender discrimination, informing them about their rights. Control over Blue Card procedures and enforcement of provisions regarding protection of victims should be strengthened as well.

Actions in the area of tertiary prevention are of preventive and therapeutic nature. They should be aimed at breaking the victim-perpetrator relation. They are aimed both at victims and perpetrators of violence. Apart from normal therapeutic work (group therapy, support groups, raising self-esteem, promoting independence, promoting active employment among women and having one's own financial resources), one should ensure that continuing education in the scope of human and civil rights becomes a part of each contact with specialist institutions, including support institutions.

Activities in this area should also include professional training for support workers with regard to proper approach to victims and perpetrators of violence (physicians and other healthcare workers, Police, psychologists, pedagogues, social workers, family assistants, counselors, court appointed guardians etc.) with regard to equality and non-discrimination.

In accordance with the individualization principle – therapies for specific victims (and perpetrators) should employ different, case-specific methods of work and prevention.

To sum up: violence – a tool of oppression and consent for helplessness and powerlessness should be opposed. Victims should be taught how to stand up for their rights, they should receive support in order to liberate themselves from oppression.

Fernando Barragán Medero
University of La Laguna, Tenerife, Spain

Women in a violence-free society: An educational programme[1]

Multiculturality and the culture of women

A least two gender cultures coexist in every culture: the feminine one, and the masculine one. No human culture is homogenous. The term *multiculturality* implies that various cultures coexist but that one of them prevails over the rest, thus giving rise to private cultures and public cultures. Public cultures can be represented in the educational syllabuses, whereas private cultures remain excluded from them. Private cultures are perfectly organised to be preserved and perpetuated despite the generally lacking political powers. This is the most common way in which curricular politics and issues have generated exclusion, assimilation and segregation.

Patriarchy, gender, and sexuality

As Lagarde clearly explains,

> Patriarchy is a power arrangement, a way for men and masculinity to dominate. And it is based on the supremacy of men and masculinity over the inferioritisation of women and femininity. It is also an order of domination of some men over others and of alienation between women [...] The resulting world is asymmetrical, unequal and alienated, androcentric, misogynistic and homophobic (Lagarde 1994, p. 397).

1 We would like to thank the funding and cooperation of the European Commission (Directorate-General for Justice, Freedom and Security) and the Regional Government of the Canary Islands, the Regional Department of Employment and Social Affairs (the Institute of Women and the Directorate-General of Youth of the Canary Islands) in relation to the 'Educación para el presente sin violencia: Construir una cultura de paz' project. The above institutions do not necessarily agree with the opinions and points of view herein expressed; nor do the authors of this document agree to the points of view of the above mentioned institutions.

From a similar theoretical position and, aiming to maintain the 'strong meaning of the term gender' to imply the fundamental aspect of power there is to it, patriarchy is defined as

> [...] the power to assign spaces, not only practically, placing women in submissive places, but also symbolically, that is to say, naming and valuing those places as 'feminine'. That way, Patriarchy would be the 'all powerful' androcentric fate that is misinterpreted as being simply 'all powerful'. Gender would be the operation and result of assigning restrictive spaces to what is feminine while masculinity is the construed form of the centre as something that has no limits other than the negative, the abject and the valueless (Tubert 2003, p. 22).

Violence and heterocentrism

Gender-based violence constitutes an illegitimate expression of power exerted over other people, but it can be distinguished from other forms of violence thanks to one peculiarity: it is generally selective, that is to say, it is primarily targeted to women, pubescent girls and little girls. Violence against women, pubescent girls and little girls constitutes an unbearable and unacceptable type of human cruelty, and that is way there is a strong and firm commitment to eradicate it from educational centres.

Heterocentrism is a way of understanding the world based on the assumption that heterosexuality is the dominant and hegemonic form of expression of the sexual experience, assumption that has not been proven to this day. 'In sex, there is not one only happiness', explains Yukio Mishima (Mishima 2010, p. 13). Heterosexuality has never been the central or only form of human behaviour – not in history nor within different cultures – heterosexuality has thus, been encouraged, made obligatory and used as a means of control of patriarchal masculinity, and it has been a key element for the prevalence of gender-based violence. From the perspective of ecofeminism (Puleo 2011), the ethics of the care that we consider to be the opposite of violence are set out.

Planning, implementation and assessment of the educational programme for a violence-free present

Within 1998 and 1999, the Daphne Project[2] was implemented in Spain, Denmark and Germany. Its main goal being the preparation of curricular resources

---

2　The funding of the European Commission, Directorate-General of Family and Justice has made possible the Daphne Project.

focused on preventing violence (Dalgaard 1999; Barragán, De la Cruz, Doblas 2001; Herschelmann 2001).

Critical assessments of the results achieved by the aforementioned project have led us to outline a new educational approach to gender-based violence and interculturality through the 'Educación para el presente sin violencia: Construir una cultura de paz'[3] project.

Methodology

Problem and goals

The problem addressed lies in the preparation of intervention programmes aimed to teenage population with two main purposes: to raise awareness about the use of different forms of expression of violence, and to achieve a reduction or the eradication of all expressions of physical, psychological and sexual violence. Additionally, the programme should also have a preventive purpose and make participants understand how violence is an inappropriate response to conflict solving.

This programme will have to overcome the reservations caused by previous educational interventions – even existing educational interventions – which were characterized by their sexist and segregating nature. This nature relates to sexuality and diversity cultures: immigration and disability.

The **first objective** is to plan, implement and assess an educational programme based of the action research model that has the ability to raise a greater and more general awareness against any type of violent expression, in order to significantly reduce the regular demonstrations of violence. This programme should be adjustable – transferable – to all countries of the European Union.

The **second objective** is to prepare a programme targeted to the primary prevention of gender-based violence.

The **third main objective** is to test to what extent the action research methodology can be an alternative to solve a problem shared by all countries within the European Union. This is done through its simultaneous implementation in

---

3 This was initially planned by Fernando Barragán, from the Departamento de Didáctica e Investigación Educativa de la Facultad de Educación de la Universidad de la Laguna, Spain, and has counted on the participation of: Estudios Educar en la Diversidad, de la Universidad de La Laguna, Spain; Kinderschutz-zentrum, Oldenburg, Germany; Centro di Iniziativa Democratica degli Insegnanti, Milan, Italy; researcher Janne Hejgaard, Copenhaguen, Denmark; Instituto de Sexología, Málaga, Spain; and GEISHAD, Grupo Educativo Interdisciplinar en Sexualidad Humana y Atención a la Discapacidad, A.C. Mexico. It has received funding from the European Commission (the Directorate-General for the Family and Domestic Affairs); and the Regional Government of the Canary Islands (the Regional Department of Employment and Social Affairs, Directorate-General of Youth and the Institute of Women of the Canary Islands).

four countries, thus obtaining a transnational perspective. All failures and successes observed during the implementation of the programme are also taken into account.

Action research as an alternative for educational programmes

Action research has proven to be the path to follow when working in programmes aimed to prevent gender-based violence and interculturality, as we have been able to observe from the results of a series of European programmes (Barragán, Tomé 1999; Barragán, De la Cruz, Doblas 2001; Barragán 2006).

It has been pointed out from a critical emancipatory paradigm that:

> Every action research has two central objectives: to improve and to create interest. Regarding improvement, action research notes three distinct areas: first, the **improvement of a** given *practice*; second, the **improvement in the** *understanding* **of the practice** within the participants; third, the **improvement of the** *situation* in which such practice takes place. *Creating an interest* amongst the participants goes hand in hand with the *improvement process*. Those who participate in the practice object of study need to take an active part in each one of the stages of the action research process – planning, action, observation, reflection. As the project action research develops, it is expected for more and more participants or people affected by the practice to show an increasing interest in it (Carr, Kemmis 1988, p. 177).

Among the characteristics of the action research within a curriculum, it is pointed out that it can be of use in the improvement of certain problematic social situations (Mckernan 1999, pp. 50–51). It is also noted that it is described as 'emancipatory' due to the fact that it 'attempts to make those who suffer from repressing or unfair practices free' (McKernan 1999, pp. 52–53).

It is also relevant to acknowledge some of the limitations that have been observed in relation to the connection between third-wave feminism and critical emancipatory action research. Weiner points out the criticism of positivist paradigms in research as long as rationality, objectivity and truth are concerned. These are dominated by the values in practical experiences oriented to cooperative practice, one that is democratic and non-repressing, and that is organized in relation to decision making. It will never be possible to consider science as a certain true, but as the uncertainty of the doubt, from our point of view (Weiner 2004, p. 639).

Weiner goes on explaining a crucial aspect – a limitation that we entirely agree upon:

> [...] however, what critical action research has seemed to be unable to tackle up till now is the gender specificity and other social positioning, as related to the strategies chosen, as well as the types of resistance generated in order to achieve the expectation of a potential transformation (Weiner 2004, p. 639).

The process of selecting the participants

Through 'criteria-based selection' (Goetz, LeCompte 1988, p. 93) we have been able to set up the basic criteria for our project: four educational centres in each country, a teaching staff of a minimum of 5 female and male teachers in every centre; the size of the centre – urban and suburban centres in big and small cities; teaching staff specialized in different fields of expertise; and the required percentage of immigrant and disabled students (aged 12 to 18). Initial expectations were soon exceeded: 32 educational centres took part in the programme, adding up to 143 male and female teachers and 2,847 male and female students.

Table 1. Direct participants

Number	Country					Total
	Germany	Denmark	Spain	Italy	Mexico	
Schools	9	11	5	6	1	**32**
Teaching staff	12	27	63	40	1	**143**
Students	229	470	1,682	446	20	**2,847**

Source: the action research project 'Educación...', see: note 3, p. 225.

It is important to note, in regards to multicultural inclusion, that we have worked with immigrant students coming from over 30 countries, both EU (Belgium, France, Germany, Portugal, Sweden, etc.), and non-EU (Argentina, China, Lebanon, Palestine, Kurdistan, Turkey and Uruguay, amongst others). The central matters are which women and cultures are studied and how feminine cultures are represented in multicultural societies, and which women groups we refer to. As for cultural groups, Inuit culture in Denmark and Sami culture in Finland, Norway and Sweden are represented.

Diagnosis, action plan and implementation

Identifying the needs and planning the actions

The action research project 'Educación para el presente sin violencia: Construir una cultura de paz' has been implemented in primary and secondary education centres in Spain, Germany, Denmark and Italy, with Mexico as a special participant. From 2002 to 2005, the abovementioned countries – excluding Mexico – have experienced severe governmental budget cuts and a 'progressive loss' of the state of welfare. They have also been in a state of public emergency due to the implementation of policies that openly oppose 'equality' and immigration. Following this project, the programme was also successfully implemented with the participation of groups of prisoners (Barragán, Rivadeneira, Gómez, Herrera 2013).

The insights of the teaching staff

An analysis of the ideologies amongst the teaching staff was carried out, namely regarding gender-based violence and interculturality. The methodology used was that of debate groups (Ibáñez 1994), more specifically, the *analysis of explicit content* (Vallés 1997, p. 384). Sessions were recorded using Soundforge v.6 software.

Among the most relevant data, and in relation to **masculinities**, we would like to highlight that the teaching staff understands the importance of discussing the position related to the male gender and its links to the problems of coexistence, violence and relations between different cultures.

The *change in women* also makes the discussion on male gender relevant. Men are still reluctant to and little interested in gender equality. It is the male members of the teaching staff, paradoxically enough, who criticize the patriarchal model with a stronger conviction. There is awareness on the fact that the patriarchal model is close to its extinction and that it gives way to new acceptable forms of being a man. They also remark the feeling that 'men are in a state of great confusion, feel lost and out of place'.

As long as **interculturality** is concerned, it is pointed out that the presence of people coming from different cultures has not yet become a problem itself. When discussing the topic in depth, teachers does not seem to have ideas on how to deal with it, and they acknowledge as strategic the issue of being able to come to an understanding from different cultures and unequal positions. This discussion is triggered following the debate on the ban on the veil imposed to Muslim female students in French educational centres.

Pedagogical itineraries are put into use, allowing the teaching staff to divide the contents into subsequent units depending on the particular needs of specific groups and centres. The forms of organization chosen by the staff have been varied: several male and female teachers develop the same topic in order to carry out a group analysis, they share groups, they reschedule school hours, and different groups share the same classes. They additionally organize tutorial classes as a complement to all the above mentioned, which proved to be highly efficient.

Development and implementation within the syllabus

The initial proposals of a comprehensive curriculum where reviewed on a later stage through methodological triangulation and data analysis processes. Theoretical content was included responding to the needs pointed out by the teaching staff during their assessment. Their critiques and suggestions to change activities were also taken into consideration.

The new version of the curriculum now consists of three parts: first, *A theoretical and practical guide for the teaching staff*, including chapters such as sex, gender and syllabus; gender-based violence, masculinities and interculturality; gender-based violence and education; emotional education; from culturality to transculturality; the culture of peace and fair treatment; adolescence and learning; a new conception from the action research model; general goals; contents; methodology and evaluation. The second part, a *Guide to work with the students*, consisting of 9 lessons and introduction, goals, activities, bibliography, Internet resources, and specialized magazines. This is complete with a glossary containing terms and two appendices with the *Activities registering page and tools for evaluation.*

Have the objectives of the project been achieved?

The results presented in the above mentioned sections of the programme prove that the objectives have been satisfactorily covered.

We have been able to confirm that 'methodological rigour' has made possible the planning, implementation and assessment of a programme to prevent gender-based violence resulting in the production of a manual addressed to both teaching staff and students that fulfils the requirements to favour an increase in awareness of our everyday expressions of violence. It also helps reduce expressions of violence and has a great value as a preventive tool in all ranges of age it has been tested for.

All the requirements regarding the functioning of the action research methodology have been met, and we can now confirm that its use within a European context is possible. Several countries have participated, adding up to a significant amount of educational centres. This provides a new dimension to the action research methodology.

Issues arising from new educational approaches: an attempt to explaining the problems and suggesting improvements

Comparing the evaluation of other programmes, the results attained by our programme are highly satisfactory. However, some questions remain: Why is it that some students do not significantly reduce their use of violent language? Why is it possible to observe a noticeable improvement in the relationship between local and immigrant students?

Among the non-desired results – that we refer to as malign – we believe it important to state that, although a high percentage of participants claims not to use psychological violence, there remain some students that are not willing to renounce it (the proportion of male students is higher in this sense). We must, therefore, emphasize the connection between language and culture and conduct a 'more thoroughly analysis with the students' about the effects of psychological violence because 'considering it normal' makes the change more difficult. It is also a matter of concern that *'girls defend the use of violence'* – even extreme violence: this can be frequently observed in educational centres.

Research and education: processes and results

Approaching interculturality has made it possible to create an atmosphere of respect and thirst for knowledge about the different cultures coexisting in the classroom. Cultures of our own countries that are subject to invisibility and the development of multicultural skills have also been covered.

The evaluation presented by teachers clearly expresses that the atmosphere in the classroom has experienced a significant improvement thanks to working on activities related to interculturality. A clear example is the fact that sexist and xenophobic prejudices – normally translating into the expression of various types of psychological violence – existing among the students are 'discussed openly'.

We would also like to mention two basic aspects of the programme highlighted by the students in their evaluations: the results of the concepts of violence and interculturality both prior to the programme and after it, and the results of the self-assessment on what they had learned about the 9 proposed topics.

Regarding the changes in the concepts, 49.2% of the students have experienced an improvement – a majority of male students.

Table 2. Changes in the concept students had of gender-based violence
and interculturality (percentage by gender)

	GENDER		
One or two points above	Male	Female	Total
More than two points*	29.1%	26.2%	27.5%
	22.4%	20.9%	21.6%
Σ	51.5%	47.1%	49.2%

* 0 points – minimum score / 20 points – maximum score (**n = 538**)

Source: the action research project 'Educación...', see: note 3, p. 225.

The students' topic-based self-assessment of the knowledge acquired show the average mark achieved for each one of the topics – displayed from the highest to the lowest marks: **creating a culture of peace** (average: 8.08), **masculinities** (average: 7.93), **interculturality, gender and xenophobia** (average: 7.83), **violence in daily life** (average: 7.25), **families, power relations and violence** (average: 6.96), **masculinities and homophobia** (average: 6.73), **emotional education in men** (average: 6.58), **sexual violence** (average: 6.51), and – lastly – **interculturality, gender and violence** (average: 5.95).

Plausibility and meta-evaluation qualitative criteria – use following conventional orthodoxy – were deemed of the highest quality.

We would like to highlight that the criteria of *dependency,* a relevant aspect that represents the ability to respond, has been proven thanks to the fact that the procedures for implementing and assessing the project, the gathering up of data, as well as the triangulation processes, make it possible for a response, namely because of the

> [...] vitality of the facts and *habitats* in which the social programmes take place. In the words of Heraclitus: No man ever steps in the same river twice (Santos 1990, p. 161).

We should remark, regarding the deontological code, that, since the beginning of the project, **ethics** have been conscientiously respected at all times in relation to the 'negotiation' of the use of the results, reports and publications. Anonymity has also been kept whenever it has so been requested. All critiques received throughout the assessment processes have been taken into consideration too.

The preparation of the programme and the learning process amongst students

The first undeniable conclusion we have come to is that there has been an increase in the levels of awareness in relation to gender-based violence expressions, along with a reduction in its regular demonstrations. Besides this, participants have acquired conflict-solving and affection-developing skills. It has also been positive to give visibility and a voice to immigrant students, fact that made it possible for a non-violent 'confrontation' of the issue to take place.

We have reached a second and equally important conclusion: there is an 'emergency' situation within a critical sector of students that we can call 'students that defend the change', motivated by and related to the topics covered by the project and the ability 'to see beyond the school boundaries' and acknowledge the pedagogical value of European initiatives as a way of solving common social problems. This group is also critic towards the policies implemented in their own countries, towards the teaching staff and the use of information and results from the assessment of their participation in research projects.

The third conclusion is the preventive value of the programme in participants aged from 12 to 18 years old. The programme is, therefore, genuinely useful as a pedagogical and transformational resource in social projects related to repressing conducts practiced by individuals of a given gender.

Katarzyna Gajek
University of Łódź, Poland

Power, violence and resistance strategies in women's lives – the examples of gender discourses and women experiencing violence

Introduction

The purpose of this paper is an analysis of power, violence, and strategies of resistance to them, from the perspective of gender discourses as well as interpersonal relationships between men and women.

The social construction of discourses is subject to various restrictions and is regulated by specific procedures, the implementation of which allows expressing one's views. In fact, there are privileged groups that have authority and access to the freedom of expression and the protection of their own interests and dominated groups that are not allowed to speak. These assumptions will be the starting point for the reflection on the discourses constructed in the area of gender. Symbolic resources produced by the dominant male discourse serve to maintain the social order and shape a specific vision of the world. This vision has been challenged by feminist discourses which postulate the redefinition of the reality.

Discourses play an important role in shaping the reality that reflects the social order created within them. In the context of socio-cultural conditions, it is thus possible to trace relationships between people living in a heterosexual relationship. The dominant vision of the world reinforces the belief in the naturalness of the control of a man over a woman. Therefore, what can become a tool of taking this control is violence which ensures, *inter alia*, the protection of authority. However, oppression and the infliction of pain and suffering provokes the reaction of women's passive and/or active resistance.

Gender discourse and power-knowledge

The concept of discourse is extremely diverse in terms of its scope of meaning and content, which is why it has become blurred. Definitions created in different fields of knowledge refer to various ways of understanding this category. The linguistic tradition recognizes discourse as a fragment of language, larger than a sentence, and analyses conducted in this paradigm relate to the research on more extensive linguistic wholes as well as the use of language in specific social contexts. The philosophical perspective of discourse situates it at the junction of communication and cognitive processes and the moral dimension. The essence of the research has become the rules of reaching the statements deemed to be true and the issues of rationality and legitimacy. On the other hand, the sociological point of view emphasizes the process of the social construction of discourse as well as its importance in the creation of social reality (Krakowiak 2008, pp. 50–52).

The production of discourse in society is governed by specific procedures and is subject to external and internal constraints. Their task is to ensure the control, selection, organization and redistribution of meanings whose creation is the essential function of discourse (Foucault 2002, pp. 7–26). Therefore, not everyone can have access to generating knowledge which would validate certain statements or actions resulting from them. The openness of discourse is controlled by specific conditions and imposed rules and only when one obeys them she or he is allowed to speak (Foucault 2002, pp. 26–27). The privilege or the right to speak reinforces the dominance of certain groups, allowing them to reject or ignore utterances of others. The discourses that are widely accepted because of their obvious character are considered to be true and they constitute the 'regime of truth' of a given society. The symbolic resources produced and legitimized by different types of rationality (such as religion or science) become the content of beliefs and shape the perception and understanding of the world, which makes them a form of having control over individuals.

An example of the discourse which has acquired a dominant position in culture is the idea of 'natural' male supremacy. This position has been solidified for centuries, first by religious discourses and then by the discourse of emerging science. Men, as the originators of science, had access to creating the discourse that provided them with specific symbolic resources to interpret the reality. The privilege to speak enabled them to exclude women from the participation in the discourse. The lack of different ways of describing and understanding the world enhanced the social structures and the impact of men on the social, cultural, economic and political developments. This situation was reproduced in many areas of life, also with the participation of women who referred the way in which they were seen by men (created self-definitions) to dominant symbolic resources present in culture. They took part, often unknowingly or against their will, in their own oppression, accepting the limits imposed on them.

The relegation of women to the marginal position deprived them of the chance to take control and be capable of decision-making and thus to have impact on the course of their lives. It reduced their possibilities of making choices and limited their rights, while imposing duties upon them. Their inferior status was linked to discriminatory practices (e.g. in the area of law), and to reduced economic, educational, professional or recreational opportunities. Women were also vulnerable to social pressures and economic crises (see: Mahler 1993, p. 193).

Michael Foucault drew attention to the interplay of power and knowledge. He felt that

[...] there is no relationship of power without the field of knowledge correlated with it, and there is no knowledge which does not assume and does not create a relationship with power (Foucault 1998, p. 34).

Power-knowledge, defined by him as a political technology, is dispersed, therefore it is ubiquitous in human life. Furthermore, its discursive form has a productive character, which signifies the production and at the same time subjectification of subjects.

M. Foucault believed that governance is not a property (one cannot own governance, it is not a fixed attribute or privilege) but a strategy. Power is the relationship between the governing and the governed forces and the effects of domination can manifest themselves in relationships since people have certain dispositions, while they also take concrete action, perform maneuvers and use tactics designed to achieve the intended purpose. Furthermore, power cannot be simply imposed on those who do not exercise it – it exists in them and through them, blocking them at the same time (Foucault 1998, p. 33).

Each relationship of forces is a relationship of power which should be distinguished from the category of violence. The essence of power is built on a relationship of forces, and the only subject and object of force is another force. Violence does not create a force but it can go hand in hand with it or be a consequence of it. According to this assumption, a relationship of forces goes beyond violence which affects the specific entities, destroying them or changing their form (Deleuze 2004, p. 99). Power-knowledge is a strategy used to influence another subject that acts or is able to act, which distinguishes it from violence. Accordingly, the power-knowledge relationship may exist only in case of free entities that have the capacity to respond. Power-knowledge and freedom both determine and oppose each other (Foucault 1982, pp. 219–222). Freedom may lead to a consent to and acceptance of power-knowledge or strategies of resistance to it. M. Foucault states that there are three known varieties of struggles (Foucault 1982, p. 212): against domination (serfdom), against exploitation (subordination) and against those aspects that are associated with the subject itself and make it submit to others (the struggle against forms of subjectivity and subjectification).

The marginal position of women in society can provoke them to respond in two ways (Mahler 1993, p. 194). It can trigger conformist attitudes, characterized by passivity, the acceptance of the status quo and the adaptation to it or an escape from the reality. On the other hand, it can evoke the pursuit of emancipation, oriented at gaining autonomy and taking action to improve one's situation. In addition, it should be noted that the process of social control that uses orders, prohibitions and penalties is conducive to the stability of the social order as well as the norms and values which dominate it (cf. types of power: disciplinary, sovereign, pastoral, *inter alia,* Foucault 1982, 1998). Due to the spatial expansion of societies and the enormous complexity of human relations, power is dispersed. The internalization of knowledge and meanings it produces introduces internal control mechanisms aimed at discipline and self-control of individuals (Foucault, 2000, p. 249).

Feminist discourses are part of a strategy of resistance to the male, dominant discourse, and recognized from the perspective of the causative bodies (which is contrary to the concept of Foucault) may also be an example of the manifestation of freedom of women. The reinterpretation of the reality from the women's point of view has enabled the creation of new, alternative symbolic resources. The emancipation of women as well as the redefinition of the social order related to it have entailed a violation of a certain status quo, which was not without significance for the shaping of the social reality. Power-knowledge present in the feminist discourse has legitimized efforts to eliminate gender inequalities and advocated a social, economic and political change. It has thus had impact on the individual and collective action that has led to the sequence of significant transformations.

The resistance discourse has challenged the male dominance in relationships between the sexes and therefore also the control of the man over the woman, a husband over his wife. Formal equality, an increase in women's participation in public life, their access to education and professional activity have undermined the foundation of the traditional division of social roles and have given rise to egalitarian aspirations concerning a family.

Violence experienced by women

The discourses analyzed above point to the dominance of the patriarchal system (but also the evolution of the social system) which creates certain dependence within family relationships. Socio-cultural resources are the foundation of the privileged position of men who have the socially accepted right to impose their will, even despite some opposition of other family members. Their control over resources also allows them to influence the behavior of others.

Considering the relationships of forces in this context, they will be identified with the relation of subjects (forms) who remain in a hierarchical system. One of the parties has the power to govern and influence the behavior of the other person and impose its own behaviour, which makes the other party take specific action or prevents it from taking it. With this understanding, we move away from an anonymous, impersonal being and dispersed power delineated in M. Foucault's concept and get closer to the category of violence, which – recognized as individual human experience – is connected with the idea of active and acting human beings.

As for violence, physical strength and mental domination are revealed in supervising, controlling or attacking behavior which take different forms. These actions are deliberate, premeditated, consistent and instrumental in nature. The purpose of these practices is the infliction of harm and control or the protection of authority. Imposing one's will or the method of interpretation and meaning on other people, controlling space, forcing other people to behave in a specific way or to perform specific actions causes pain and suffering (physical and/or mental), it damages and destroys people, leading to oppression, subordination, exploitation as well as limited freedom, self-agency and independence of the individual.

The rapid progression of relationships between family members, which brings about physical and psychological suffering, is the evidence of the occurrence of family violence, also known as domestic violence. People who resort to violence can be both adults and children, their objective is to gain, confirm and/or enhance the sense of control over others. Violence against the loved one is related to an asymmetric relationship as well as the unequal distribution of power. Treating another human being as an object sanctions the use of force against them, exercising control over them, which leads to intimidation, manipulation and disregard for needs and rights of that person.

Focusing on the intimate relationship, Lenore E. Walker noticed that in the early years of the development of the phenomenon of violence, certain events occur in a cyclic manner. The cycle of violence consists of three repetitive phases of varying duration and intensity: the tension building phase (frustration, stress, poor communication, escalating anger and emotional disorders), the acute battering episode (acts of violence triggered by certain events – a quarrel, struggle, anger, fear, anxiety) and the honeymoon phase (hostile, silent attitude or regret, remorse, guilt felt by the perpetrator, promise of improvement, decreasing tension or anger, reconciliation, hope for a change) (Walker 2009, p. 85 and the following pages; see also Rajska--Kulik 2007, pp. 19–20). Similarly, Kevin Browne and Martin Herbert (Browne, Herbert 1999, p. 98) developed a 'beating cycle' with interactions based on violence in partner relationships. The Polish Alliance of People, Institutions and Organizations Helping the Victims of Domestic Violence 'Blue Line' presents a vicious circle of violence in its training materials and newsletters (Mazur 2002, pp. 33–34).

The literature on the subject of violence points to the battered woman syndrome as a subcategory of PTSD (Post-Traumatic Stress Disorders) (cf. Walker 2009, p. 41 and the following pages). Women categorized in this way experience threats, coercion and constant criticism, they are isolated, bullied, accused, humiliated and/or ignored. Their partners manipulate their guilt, try to convince them that they suffer from a mental illness or use their children to exercise control over them (cf. Rode 2010, p. 52). The result of such experiences is low self-esteem, the withdrawal from social interactions and learned helplessness. Lenore E. Walker, analyzing the battered woman syndrome, revealed that its development occurs in two phases. The first of these is characteristic of the initial stage of the relationship, when in response to acts of violence the woman reacts with an active or passive rebellion (e.g. an escape) or in active defense (e.g. hitting back, throwing objects). After some time, when she realizes that her actions do not bring desired results and the situation becomes increasingly difficult, she grows overwhelmed by a sense of helplessness, often associated with depression, numbness, reduced interest in the world and anxiety reactions. The acceptance of the experienced violence, defined as the learned helplessness syndrome, is the second phase of the battered woman syndrome (Walker 2009, p. 71 and the following pages; see also: Rajska-Kulik 2007, pp. 14–16). Judith Lewis Herman (2002, p. 101) believes, however, that the concept of learned helplessness cannot be applied to the situation of battered women. They are not resigned and apathetic, they take numerous, though unsuccessful, attempts to stop the violence, and thus change their situation. Women have learned, however, that they are constantly observed and their efforts will lead to repression because they will be treated as acts of insubordination. The lack of effect means that with the passage of time they limit their activities to those that ensure their own protection and survival (e.g. meeting the partner's expectations, submission), and not a definite change in the situation.

Richard J. Gelles (Gelles, Straus, Steinmetz 1988) enumerated the coping strategies used most often by women confronted with violence, they are as follows: avoiding the aggressor for some time, refraining from raising sensitive issues in conversations, refraining from talking about violence, demanding from the partner that he stop using violence (coercing the promise), using threats (e.g. filing an application for divorce or calling the police) or violence in retaliation, hiding or leaving the house for several days.

Lee H. Bowker (1983, after: Salber, Taliaferro 1998, pp. 12–14), on the basis of the study of a thousand women regularly beaten by their partners, identified key strategies they used to stop physical violence:
- talking to the perpetrator about what he did and about their sense of injustice and suffering caused by his behavior in order to cause him to feel guilty;
- obtaining a promise from him that he will change his behavior and refrain from using violence;
- threatening: a woman threatens the abuser that she is going to notify the police, leave home, divorce him or make a complaint in the workplace;
- hiding: a woman during the escalation of violence, in order to temporarily avoid an act of aggression, runs out of the house, hides in another room, shuts herself

in the bathroom, basement or closet (most often it becomes a pretext for another attack);
- passive defense: during the attack a woman instinctively protects her body with her hands, arms, feet or appliances which are within her reach;
- avoidance: factors such as increasing stress and strain or impaired communication allow a woman to predict the impending threat of violence;
- defensive fight: violence can trigger aggressive behavior of a woman who may respond with scratching, kicking, biting, pushing away the attacker, throwing objects at him;
- degrading strategies: a woman's behavior oscillates towards complete surrender to the will of the perpetrator of violence, including humiliation, because the manifestations of her enslavement indisputably prove his dominance, giving him the satisfaction.

None of the above-described strategies used by battered women led to breaking the cycle of violence. Some defensive actions, such as calling the police or deciding to take legal action against the aggressor caused short-term effects. They prevented acts of violence for certain time, caused a decrease in the frequency of their occurrence or minimized their severity.

When analyzing the phenomenon of violence, it may be noted that exercising constant control, usually by means of injunctions, prohibitions and penalties which bring about suffering, is the basis for changes in the way of interpreting the world. The existing knowledge becomes inadequate and new experiences cannot be integrated with the previous ones, therefore they require a reinterpretation of the situation and a reconstruction of one's own identity. Again, one needs to make sense of events and build a new, coherent picture of the reality, based on other meanings that will become the foundation of schemes of actions to be used in solving future problems. Living in a relationship based on violence is associated with the continual use of certain strategies of resistance that normalize the existence. This requires a redefinition of the past and the present, a reorientation of values and objectives and the establishment of new priorities. Constant control and acts of violence lead to total subordination of one's existence to another person, a focus on the perspective of 'here and now' and avoidance of risks. They are also associated with a significant reduction of potential opportunities. The interiorization of new symbolic resources and the conviction that there is a continuous supervision result in self-control, similar to the ideas regarding J. Bentham's Panopticon (Foucault 1998, p. 241).

Conclusion

Both in the feminist discourses and in the actions undertaken by women experiencing violence, we can observe the use of resistance strategies aimed at liberation from the domination of men who, by exercising control, have a huge impact on the social, cultural, economic and political life. Their privileged position relegated women to a secondary role and was conducive to their exploitation. This dependence, which lasted for many years, led to the internalization of the dominant vision of the world by women who themselves also participated in the reproduction of the social order. The liberation from male supremacy required a reinterpretation of the reality, changes in the content of beliefs and an inner struggle for the reconstruction of women's own identity, questioning the socially desirable norms.

The effects of the dominance may manifest themselves in interpersonal relationships and the use of violence is an extreme case of maintaining control. Violence involves the strength (physical, mental) of one of the parties which is used in order to weaken the other partner and determine new frontiers of his or her potential. However, the ability to take action is the basis for the strategy of resistance which provides a chance to change the situation.

Małgorzata Halicka, Anna Szafranek
University of Białystok, Poland

The living space of elderly female victims of intimate partner violence in view of court acts

Introduction

In recent years, the issues of domestic violence involving the elderly have been of increasing interest to researchers. Both empirical research and statistics indicate that, in spite of the problems with diagnosing it, this problem is becoming increasingly important (Halicka, Halicki 2010). A report, developed for the UN Secretary General for the 64th General Assembly, stressed that it is a global and universal issue (Report of the Export Group Meeting 2009). Furthermore, the extension of human life expectancy means that the number of elderly will increase and that they will be in danger of abuse and neglect, including from their intimate partner. This problem should be analysed and its scale estimated. This will help in the search for methods of preventing violence against the elderly, who are particularly prone to be victims of violence, because of the difficulties they face in daily life (Halicka, Czykier, Sidorczuk 2010).

In order to raise the awareness of the problem in Polish society, the Institute for Psychology of Health issued in 2009 a handbook, which stressed that although the scale of the problem of violence perpetrated by one's closest (spouse, children, grandchildren) is not known, it is assumed that one in ten people experience it, while one in three elderly (aged 65 or more) had contact with someone of their age, who was a victim of violence (Dąbrowicka 2009). This data may indicate that the actual scale of the problem may be significantly higher than is assumed. Therefore, new research initiatives have been taken up in recent years, as well as new social programs, such as the 'Starszy Pan, Starsza Pani' in Warsaw (Kuźmicz 2007), aiming to improve the knowledge of the problem, as well as increasing the awareness of this issue.

Apart from national initiatives, Polish researchers have taken part in international research projects concerning violence against the elderly, particularly elderly women. Two projects may serve as an example, which involved as partners the Department of Sociology of Education and Social Gerontology and the Department of Andragogy and Educational Gerontology at the University of Białystok. Below are presented some of the results of one of these projects, which relate to the living space of elderly (60+) female victims of intimate partner violence. It should be noted that the living space of these women has been restricted to their household and their marital relations. We were interested in finding the answers to the following questions: What is the everyday life of these women like? Where does the violence stem from? What forms does it take? How does law enforcement (police, courts, prosecutors) deal with marital violence against elderly women? These problems were analysed in cooperation with partners from Austria, Germany, Portugal, Great Britain and Hungary, as part of two international research projects: 'Intimate Partner Violence against older Women' (IPVoW) and 'Mind the Gap! Improving Intervention in Intimate Partner Violence against older Women'.

Intimate Partner Violence against older Women

'The Intimate Partner Violence against older Women' (IPVoW) project was realised from January 2009 to December 2010 and aimed to gain insight into the problems of intimate partner violence against elderly women. For that purpose, interviews were conducted with people who work with both victims and perpetrators of violence in various institutions. We would like to stress in particular, that we also managed to interview the victims.

Results have shown that only a small group of elderly victims seek help. Elderly women are less aware of existence of support systems and less capable of making use of them than younger women. We noticed that law enforcement and social aid institutions have a poor understanding of the complexity of the problem of violence against the elderly, especially elderly women. Many professionals within law enforcement and social aid confirmed that they lack the appropriate knowledge of the specificity of old age, which influences the way problems of violence among the elderly should be handled. Therefore the next project focused on improving the ability of law enforcement and social aid professionals to effectively cope with situations of violence within the living space of the elderly, particularly elderly women.

Mind the Gap! Improving Intervention in Intimate Partner Violence Against older Women

'The Mind the Gap! Improving Intervention in Intimate Partner Violence Against Older Women' projects lasted from March 2011 till February 2013 and, as was already mentioned, aimed to improve the ability of law enforcement and social aid organisations to deal with cases of intimate partner violence against elderly women, as well raising social awareness regarding violence and its victims.

We analysed court files, in order to better understand how law enforcement institutions handle cases of intimate partner violence against elderly women. In accordance with the assumptions of the project, the analysed cases were those concerning intimate partner violence against women aged 60 or more.

A total of 70 cases where analysed in Poland. These were cases presented before the District Court in Białystok as crimes of domestic violence (violation of art. 207 of the Penal Code). Most of the cases were reported by elderly from urban areas (53 cases amounting to 75.7% of all analysed cases), with much fewer reports from inhabitants of rural areas (17 cases, 24.3%). The victims were aged 60–81, when their cases were reported.

The results of 'The Mind the Gap! Improving Intervention in Intimate Partner Violence Against Older Women' project (concerning the analysis of selected problems in Polish court files) will be the basis of this work.

Acts and types of violence in court files

Analysing the court files we noticed that in many cases violence was present in a relationship from the very beginning. The earliest reported acts of violence took place as early as 1946 and the latest in 2000–2011. The violence was usually one-sided (i.e. perpetrated by the male intimate partner). Although there were two cases (constituting 2.9% of all cases), where both the victim and perpetrator were in a situation of mutual violence. This may point to the victim attempting to defend herself. This data also shows how few women try to prevent acts of aggression against them.

Violence perpetrated against elderly women usually took the form most difficult to detect – emotional abuse. It is noticeable that all of the victims reported this type of violence. As is detailed in table 1, there were also numerous reports of physical violence, economic abuse, chasing away from home and sexual abuse.

Table 1. Forms of violence against elderly women*

Forms of violence	answer	N	%
1	2	3	4
Physical violence	yes	65	92,9
	no	5	7,1
Sexual abuse	yes	7	10,0
	no	63	90,0
Emotional, verbal and psychological abuse	yes	70	100,0
	no	0	0

Table 1. Forms of violence...

1	2	3	4
Financial abuse	yes	39	55,7
	no	31	44,3
Overbearing control	yes	3	4,3
	no	67	95,7
Sexual abuse	yes	0	0
	no	70	100,0
Stalking	yes	0	0
	no	70	100,0
Deliberate neglect	yes	1	1,4
	no	69	98,6
Chasing away from home	yes	21	30,0
	no	49	70,0

Source: The project 'The Mind the Gap! (...)'.

* Does not sum up to 100% because the victims could report many forms of violence perpetrated against them.

Most victims experienced physical violence and thus it is important to inquire about the forms it took. Many women reported that their intimate partner used various forms of physical violence. Most frequently they suffered beating (74.3%), yanking (61.4%), pushing (52.9%) and kicking (30%). It seems worth noting that none of the perpetrators used a gun as of the last reported incident, although some of them used other items as weapons. Usually this would be a knife, axe, cane or other household item.

A vast majority of perpetrators were under the influence of alcohol during the last reported incident. Only three of them (4.3%) were sober at the time. On the other hand, 91.4% of the women were sober at during the last incident, in 2.9% of the cases it was not possible to ascertain (based on the court files) and in 5.7% of cases there were conflicting testimonies (e.g. the perpetrator claimed that his wife was under the influence of alcohol, which she denied). It is difficult to decide in these cases, because the police did not test them for alcohol.

It is worth noting that in most of the analysed cases (over 50%) violence resulted in injury: 21.4% of the victims suffered moderate injury, 15.7% suffered severe injury and 14.3% minor injury. While 38.6% of the women reported no injuries, it does not necessarily mean that they suffered none. However, there were no cases of death dues to injury in the analysed cases.

In many of the cases it was possible to ascertain that there was a high risk of severe, even potentially lethal situations in a violent relationship. As many as 94.3% of the perpetrators threatened the victim with death, or with suicide, 44.3% threatened to 'completely destroy' her and 22.9% strangled or attempted to strangle the victim.

During the last incident 60% of the victims had an eye-witness. Usually these were their (victim's and perpetrator's) children (47.1%), or other family members (15.7%). In 10% of the cases the witness was a neighbour and in 2.9% they were the victim's children. In the vast majority of cases (95.7%) the incident took place in the victim's and perpetrator's home. It is worth noting that in 34.3% of the cases the victim was verbally threatened by the suspect in the presence of police or other officials.

Usually (70% of cases) it was the victim herself who notified the police of the last recorded incident. Frequently it was the family that notified the police (20%) or the Commission for Solving Alcohol Problems (7.1%). Because in so many cases the violence is long term, it is important to answer the question: did anyone know earlier about the problem of intimate partner violence in the family? In 97.1% of the cases there were other people who knew about the situation; 94.3% of the victims told other family members, 77.1% reported to law enforcement agencies and 71.4% told their neighbours. There were also other people or institutions who knew about the violence in a given relationship. These were people from the victim's social circles (44.3%), representatives of social aid institutions (35.7%), health care professionals (30%), institutions dealing with domestic violence (22.9%), the Commission for Solving Alcohol Problems (11.4%). There were also single cases where people or institutions who knew about the situations. They were: the priest (1.4%), probation officer (1.4%), a shelter for female victims of violence (1.4%). Only 2.9% of the women were left completely alone with their problem.

Victims of violence

When the case was reported to the police the female victims were aged 60–81. Women aged 60 formed the largest group – 51.4%. There were also a few victims aged 62, 64 and 65 – 7.1%.

Almost 76% of the victims lived in urban areas, while 24.3% lived in rural areas. It is worth noting, that there were no cases, where the victim was the perpetrator's carer at the time of the last reported incident. However, in 3 cases (4.3%) they were themselves in the care of the perpetrator. Close to 43% of the women suffered from chronic somatic diseases, 7.1% were physically disabled, 6% were mentally ill, 2.9% had dementia, and 1.4% had an addiction problem. Half of them had health problems at the time of the last reported incident, which made it more difficult for them to defend themselves from aggression.

Almost all of the victims (94.3%) were not employed when their case was reported to the police. Only 5.7% were. Almost all of them received a retirement pension and only 4.3% receive a social aid benefit. Only one of the victims (1.4%) seemed to be financially dependent on the perpetrator. This may be the reason why they received no financial aid from institutions, either because they did not apply for it or were refused due to too high incomes.

A vast majority of the victims lived with the perpetrator and were married to him. However, there were also cases of couples who were in separation or even divorced, who continued living in one household. This is an occasion to state the question why victims would not fully separate from the perpetrators. One of the causes may be the deficiencies of Polish law, which is not sufficiently efficient in evicting the perpetrators. Usually it is the victim, who is forced to leave the apartment she shares with the perpetrator. In many cases women have nowhere to move to, so even many years after the divorce they continue living with their tormentor.

Table 2. Cohabitation and the relation of victim to perpetrator

Form of cohabitation		N	%
Married, cohabiting		59	84,3
Partners, cohabiting		2	2,9
Other	Divorced, cohabiting	5	7,1
	Separated, cohabiting	4	5,7
Overall		70	100,0

Source: The project 'The Mind the Gap! (...)'.

Most of the victims (80%) did not wish to separate from the perpetrator at the time of the last reported incident, only 20% took steps towards that aim. Similarly, only 20% of the women attempted to separate from the perpetrator in the past, while 80% never made such attempts. This may also be a reflection of the fact that it is the victim who has to leave the common household. On the other hand, victims remain with the perpetrator, because they keep hoping that something will change – that the husband will show more respect for them and stop being violent.

At the time the last incident was reported to the police the victims' marriages or relationships had lasted from 7 to 57 years, but most commonly it was 32, 33, 40, or 42 years. In 10 cases it was impossible to ascertain, based on the available documents.

Over a half of the victims did not live with the perpetrator alone. In 55.7% of the analysed another family member lived with them. Usually they were children, or children with grandchildren, sometimes the victim's mother. The remaining 44.3% lived with the perpetrator alone. This was reflected in the presence of eye--witnesses to the violence.

At the time of the last reported incident most of the victims (78.6%) did not receive any form of support from institutions dealing with domestic violence. Those who did mostly received help from a Crisis Intervention Centre (17.1%), there were also a few cases were help came from the district constable (2.9%) or probation officer (1.4%). Only 8.6% of the victims received help from institutions dealing with the problems of the elderly, more precisely a Social Aid Centre (in all cases). It is worth noting that 90% of the women received no such help. This data indicates that most of the victims probably never looked for help in solving their problems. This may also be caused both by a feeling of shame and lack of knowledge about institutions, which provide the necessary help in difficult situation, particularly to victims of violence.

Only 14.3% of the victims received long-term medical aid (table 3). In 17.1% of cases it was impossible to ascertain if they received long-term medical help, while in 68.6% of cases it is known that they did not. Those who did were in most cases treated for various forms of cancer, but there were also women treated for neurosis, or receiving psychiatric help.

Table 3. Receiving long-term medical aid

Answer	Form of long-term medical aid	N	%
Received aid	Diabetic treatment	1	1,4
	Treatment for neurosis	2	2,9
	Oncological treatment	3	4,3
	Treatment for depression	1	1,4
	Orthopedic treatment	1	1,4
	Psychiatric treatment	2	2,9
Did not receive help	–	48	68,6
No information	–	12	17,1
Total		70	100,0

Source: The project 'The Mind the Gap! (...)'.

Perpetrators

In all of the analysed cases the perpetrator was a man of Polish origins (i.e. not an immigrant). Because in some cases violence started shortly after marriage, the age of the perpetrators at the time of the first recorded incident was 25–76. However, most of the perpetrators were at least 50, when the victim first reported an incident. At the time of the last reported incident the perpetrators were aged 52–82. Most were aged 59 (12.9%), 60 (14.3%), 61 (11.4%), or 65 (10%).

At the time of the last recorded incident, none of the perpetrators were in the care of the victim, or any caring institution. It should be noticed that 4.3% of them were the carers of their victims. 38.6% of them suffered from serious somatic illnesses, 14.3% were physically disabled, 5.7% suffered from dementia and 2.9% were mentally ill. All of them abused alcohol, which led to the escalation of violence.

Only 7.1% of the perpetrators were employed at the time of the last recorded incident, because they had passed retirement age and were of poor health. Most of them (80%) received a retirement pension, while 10% received a social aid benefit. It should be stressed that 10% of the perpetrators seemed to be financially dependent on the victim. This dependency may reflect the perpetrators unwillingness to undertake gainful employment in earlier years, leading to lack of a retirement pension and thus being unable to provide for themselves. In the case of alcohol addicts, it would be foremost the need to buy alcohol, often stronger than the need for food or sleep. This financial dependency coupled with the need to drink or being under the influence of alcohol, may lead to frustration, aggression and finally violence.

It should be noted that 92.9% of the perpetrators had an earlier history of violent behaviours, while 28.6% were even punished by court for intimate partner violence. Usually this was a single sentence, but there was one case of a perpetrator with two sentences. This explains why victims may be rightfully wary of notifying law enforcement agencies. Data on the recurring of criminal behaviours point to mistakes made in the rehabilitation process, which often leads the perpetrator believe that he can continue his violent behaviour with impunity.

In most cases the result of earlier sentences was probation or imprisonment. Usually the perpetrators were sentenced for domestic abuse. It is noteworthy that the perpetrator's behaviour often deteriorated (i.e. he returned to violent behaviours or violence increased) when probation ended.

Courts

In 64 cases (91.4%) the investigation ended with the case being brought before court. In 6 cases there was no trial, because: one of the perpetrators died, 3 victims were reconciled with the perpetrator during the investigation, one asked for mediation and one wanted her husband to be put into medical rehabilitation, not sent to prison. However, in all 70 cases, an act of prosecution was presented and all perpetrators were charged with domestic abuse.

In 11 cases (which was 17.2% of all cases presented before court) the court dismissed the case (in 7 cases conditionally). In the remaining 53 cases (82.8%) the perpetrator received a sentence. Usually the cases were dismissed without a sentence, because the victim stated (usually during the first hearing) that she was reconciled with her partner, his conduct improved significantly and is correct and therefore she no longer wishes him to be tried. The perpetrator would confirm this statement and declared that he wanted to further improve his conduct. In the remaining 53 cases the perpetrator was found guilty and sentenced to jail (11 cases) or put on probation (42 cases).

As is shown in table 4, perpetrators were most frequently (18.6%) sentenced to 12 or 18 months imprisonment. Less frequently (8.6%) they were sentenced to

24 months in prison, or to shorter (4–8 months) terms. As it was mentioned, all of these sentences were conditional. The period of probation for these sentences was 2–5 years, most frequently 3 years (16 out of the 42 perpetrators put on probation). In 9 cases, the period of probation was 2 years, 8 men were under observation for 4 years and a further 9 for 5 years.

Table 4. Sentence and its length

Sentence in months	N	%
4	1	1,4
6	2	2,9
8	1	1,4
10	3	4,3
12	13	18,6
18	13	18,6
20	3	4,3
24	6	8,6
N/A	28	40,0
Total	70	100,0

Source: The project 'The Mind the Gap! (...)'.

Immediately after the court case, 11 perpetrators were put in prison for 6 to 24 months. Almost a half of them (5) were sentenced to 12 months imprisonment, 2 were sentenced to 12 and 18 months imprisonment, one to 10 months and one to 24 months.

Research results and conclusions

A national report on the problem of intimate partner violence against elderly women was created based on our results, as well as an international report on the same topic, including the similarities and differences between partner states.

As was already mentioned, the IPVoW showed that the work of law enforcement and the judiciary should be improved and its representatives should be allowed to participate in training sessions on gerontology, as well as violence against the elderly and working with older people (Halicka, Halicki 2012). Therefore, during the Mind the Gap! Project a training and research session was organised (on 26.10.2012 in the District Court in Białystok) for representatives of law enforcement, the judiciary and social services. It is only regrettable that so few prosecutors and judges decided to take part. Information posters were prepared for a campaign aiming to draw attention to the problem of violence against elderly women. A handbook was developed for the police and social services. Its main task was to make them more aware of changes brought on by ageing, which mean that work with elderly female victims of intimate partner violence needs to take different forms. It also covered strategies used both by perpetrators and victims. It showed what kinds of behaviour can be expected during an intervention in a domestic violence situation.

These materials pictured not only the complexity of the problem of violence against the elderly, but also drew attention to the insufficient knowledge of gerontology among members of judiciary, law enforcement and social aid agencies, who should constantly improve their knowledge concerning work with the elderly – both victims and perpetrators (Halicka, Halicki, Kramkowska, Laskowska, Szafranek 2013). It should be remembered that elderly female victims of intimate partner violence are often characterised by a feeling of shame, leading them to be less inclined (compared to younger women) to share their experience with police officers and aid workers (Kramkowska, Szafranek, Żuk 2012). Therefore, it is worth going to the trouble of teaching law enforcement officers, members of the judiciary and social aid workers about the humanistic approach and empathy towards the elderly. The main goal is a better understanding of the needs of elderly victims of crime (particularly victims of domestic violence).

It would be also well to improve the cooperation between various institutions conducting investigations in cases of violence against the elderly. Many people working with elderly victims and perpetrators of violence stressed the lack of communication skills and communication between various institutions of law enforcement and social aid. Finally, the main goal of institutions supporting victims should be communication and cooperation with each other, in order to give the elderly not only a decent, but also safe life in old age.

Jolanta Maćkowicz
Pedagogical University of Cracow, Poland

Violence against elderly women from the victimological perspective Case study

Introduction

According to statistics, elderly women, usually wives, mothers and grandmothers, fall victim of domestic violence most frequently. This 'first place' proves that the scale of this problem, hidden behind a wall of science, shame and helplessness, is very large. Statistics show that women abuse (regardless of their age) is a serious social issue.

According to the report published by the European Agency for Fundamental Rights entitled *Violence against Women* (FRA 2014) in the EU, 1/3 of European women have experienced violence. What is surprising is the fact that countries with the highest Gender Equality Index had the highest rate of violence which, according to the authors of the report, proves that in such countries women find the courage to speak up against violence more often. The data on seeking help by victims are equally surprising. Only 26% of Polish women claimed that they reported physical and sexual abuse to the police or support organizations. This is very alarming as it turns out that only 1/4 of the victims report their situation and try to seek help. On the other hand, however, in Poland the reporting rate is much higher than in most of the EU countries as the EU's average is only 14%.

According to WHO's data (2013), one third of women are physically or sexually abused by their partners on a global scale and in some region, this rate is as high as 38%.

Domestic violence against elderly women reaches similar prevalence rates. Studies carried out under Daphne project (Konwencja o zapobieganiu i zwalczaniu przemocy wobec kobiet i przemocy domowej 2011) in five countries (Austria, Belgium, Finland, Latvia and Portugal) on a group of 300 women aged 60–97 show that 28.1% of the respondents experienced various forms of abuse over the last year.

The most common form of violence was emotional abuse, economic abuse made up 10% of the cases and negligence – 5.4%. The least common forms of violence against elderly women was physical and sexual abuse (2.5–3.1%), whereas the rate of sexual abuse was slightly higher than physical abuse. Most of the women did not report their problem to any institutions and did not speak about it with anyone. The main reason for their silence was that they did not believe it could change anything. (Luoma, Koivusilta, Lang *et al.* 2011).

Historic and cultural contexts

The problem of violence against an elderly woman (**Granny Battering**) was described for the first time in a British scientific magazine in 1975, so this is not a recent phenomenon (Baker 1975, after McAlpine 2008).

For centuries, violence against women was a cultural tradition cultivated since the ancient times. Later legal regulations allowed husbands to use violence against their wives as well (Pospiszyl 1994).

For example, until the 18th century, legislation in most European countries allowed husbands to whip their wives. They could exercise this right if their wives were disobedient, lazy, wasteful, neglectful or jealous. Husbands were not only allowed to do so but they even had to pay a fine if they did not beat their wives in case they undermined their family honor. In 19th century, the flagellation right was changed to the so called 'rule of thumb' (in British and American legislation), allowing husbands to beat their wives, but only 'with a stick not thicker than a thumb'. It was not until 1870 that this law was abolished (Pospiszyl 1994, p. 64).

In Poland, the situation of women was similar, they were beaten and humiliated in all social strata and according to the then-contemporary literature, in 15th century the court in Cracow ruled that a husband has the right to 'punish' his wife with a 'rod or a whip, but no other tool' (Tazbir 1997, p. 168). The lower the social status of a woman was, the worse her situation. 'The most tragic was the situation of peasant women, among which beating was a method of terminating pregnancy' (Tazbir 1997, p. 169). So women were men's servants and could be severely punished for even the slightest wrongdoing.

Those deeply rooted 'rules' of treating women have centuries-long tradition and are still supported by many. An although we may speak about significant evolution of equality of rights and positive changes in protection against violence, the statistics are stubborn, even despite that today victims have the right to seek support.

The problem of violence against women in a relationship cannot be considered without a reference to patriarchal system of power, where males play the dominant role in the society and culture. Cultural gender constructs, ascribed social roles and expectations are rooted in different socialization. (Butler 2008; Lipowska-Teutsch 1995). Victims of long-term abuse are women of both low social and economic status, as well as highly educated women, although the latter are more aware of their rights.

Victim dependence mechanisms

What happens to a victim who remain in a battering relationship for many years? There are specific dependence building mechanisms. Those include methods of weakening the victims and depriving them of relations with other people, aimed at making the victims fearful and helpless, as well as destroying their self-esteem in relations with others (Herman 1998, p. 88) The key mechanism is the 'brainwash' – although it has been used for decades in various areas of social life, this is such an effective tool of influence (over one's attitude, needs etc.) that often the subjects of brainwashing are unaware of any manipulation whatsoever. The techniques of perpetrator's control include: isolation, degradation, monopolization of attention, threatening, demonstration of power and occasional indulgence (see: Ogólnopolskie Pogotowie dla Ofiar Przemocy w Rodzinie).

However, regardless of the above mechanisms, additional factors, such as victim's education and economic situation are of importance (although indirectly). Such factors could help in creating the opportunity to change the victim's situation or attempt to do so. In other words, educated and independent women are much more likely to break from such toxic abusive relationship than women that are completely dependent (also economically) on the perpetrators. However, the situation of an elderly female victim of domestic violence (even if she is financially and functionally independent) encounters a number of internal barriers, such as: Protecting Family, Self-Blame, Powerlessness, Hopelessness, Secrecy (Beaulaurier *et al.* 2008). Attention should be drawn to emotional dependency on perpetrators (partners/husbands or children). A strong, long-term emotional bond between the victim and the perpetrator, as well as the feeling of shame in family and neighborhood settings seem to be the most common barriers in disclosing the problem and seeking help and in the longer perspective, they tend to develop internal barriers that become inextricable for the victim.

Elderly women have difficulties in protecting themselves against domestic violence because their family home is usually the only place they could and want to live in. Victims are afraid that any possible complaints would make their lives even worse. They remain silent as they are ashamed to speak about their humiliation or they even believe that they deserve it. In many cases, elderly women have limited ability to walk or contact other people. Sometimes they are afraid to report violence in fear of being put in a retirement home. For many people this is like getting 'out of the frying pan into the fire'.

Victims of domestic violence from the perspective of *life course approach*

In studies on domestic violence, it seems necessary to adopt the ***life course approach*** perspective. Attention should be paid to relations between types of abuse (physical, mental, sexual, economic abuse, neglect), direction of abusive relation (parent-child, husband/partner-wife/partner, adult child-elderly parent, grand-child-grandparent) in various stages of life, as well as the frequency of violence (occasional, regular). Such long-term perspective will allow us to look at violence in various stages of life and at various roles (victim, perpetrator or witness) and forms. (Williams 2003; Tobiasz-Adamczyk 2009; Payne, Gainey 2010).

Period of life

Childhood	Adult age	Old age
victim	victim	victim
victim	perpetrator	victim
–	–	victim
Victim	–	victim
	victim	victim
	No violence	

Source: Tobiasz-Adamczyk 2009, p. 21.

Violence can be experienced at any age, from childhood, through adult life to late old age. When it comes to transmission of violence between generations, the roles switch from being a victim in one's childhood (when a child is abused by parents), through being a perpetrator in one's adult life, using violence against one's own children and elderly parents. Perpetrators repeat the model behavior they are familiar with to become victims of abuse in their old age again.

In the case analyzed in this study, an elderly women became a victim in her adult life and old age. She had not experienced violence before, however, her husband fell victim of parental violence in his childhood in various forms.

Methods

The main goal of the study is to present the acts of violence from the perspective of a victim, to get to know their way of thinking, emotions and various barriers experienced by women who fall victim to domestic violence.

The method used in the qualitative study paradigm is case study.

The main research technique was an autobiographical and narrative interview with an elderly woman – a victim of violence. Such interview is used when the researcher tries to get familiar with the process of development of individuals or origin of the problem, resulting in hearing a life story or a part of it. Telling one's story stimulates reflections over one's past in the context of all previous experience. (Kvale 2010; Pilch, Bauman 2010). For the purposes of this article, the author analyzed the case of Elżbieta[1], a 63-year-old woman and a victim of domestic violence. The results will be presented in the form of a description. In order to confirm the accuracy of interpretation of the materials gathered, such description will be accompanied by fragments of the story (using the original words) presented in italics.

Elżbieta is a 63-year-old woman with secondary education, living in a big city, unemployed because of her age and health problems. Elżbieta has an adult son and two grandchildren. She had been living together with her husband in a common apartment. She is currently living alone as her husband is doing time in jail for abusing her.

Analysis of study results

The woman in question is a victim of marital abuse. Suffering, fear, despair, helplessness, as well as physical abuse accompanied her for many years. It was not until 40 years after marriage that Elżbieta decided to talk about her experience.

'[...] *after 40 years of marriage, I finally decided to call the police for the first time in 2010; I wish I had done this earlier; I had always believed that maybe something will change, maybe if we get our own apartment...*'.

Elżbieta fell victim to violence for the first time very early, even before marriage. The woman was a victim of violence from the beginning of her relationship, she experienced all kinds of family abuse, from physical violence, through emotional and sexual violence, to neglect and financial abuse. Physical abuse had various forms: pushing, dragging, face slapping, kicking, not calling medical help or depriving the victim of sleep.

'[...] *he was hitting me, spitting on me, pouring water over me, turned off heating at night*' '*he was aiming for the most sensitive spots on my body to make me feel pain*' '*he (husband) was clearly enjoying it, sometimes when he abused me and I cried, he was laughing*', '*he kicked my stomach so bad, just after my surgery, he did not have any sympathy, next week I had to go to the ER because of bleeding... as the cause was unknown... and it was because he kicked me and my wounds opened again*', '*when he walked in the kitchen, he usually kicked me or threw something at me*'.

---

1 The name of the person has been changed.

Physical abuse was accompanied by emotional abuse, such as criticizing his wife's opinions, behavior, feelings and appearance, name calling and humiliation

'[...] *he was mocking me,*' '*he was always calling me names, he was screaming as soon as he came home*', '*when my family called us, he never handed the phone over to me, he was always hanging up or calling names, I sometimes asked him why he was doing this and he always told me to fuck off, to mind my own business*'.

The perpetrator used emotional abuse – emotional blackmailing, arguments, humiliation, threatening – making the victim lose faith in herself. Physical abuse had the form of mocking and name calling. The perpetrator mocked the appearance of the victim, depreciated her lifestyle and personal qualities, also when the victim was very sick

'*I went to the surgery, he heard our conversations and was angry at me that I go from one doctor to another and looking for God knows what (...). He didn't even show up at the hospital*' '[...] *when he came, he opened the balcony door and told me that I stink, that I rot, that I am no longer a woman, that I am deprived of everything, that I am worthless now*'.

The victim also experienced sexual abuse. Neglecting the victim is another sign of domestic violence in Elżbieta's relationship.

'[...] *after 7 days in the hospital, you know, everything was cut out, my ovaries and whatnot, it was such hell, because you know it's cancer, he didn't even ask once if I had anything to eat*', '*I could not get to the oncology ward, you think he drove me there? He didn't even ask if I needed anything*'.

The perpetrator was abusing his victim financially for many years of marriage, using economic abuse:

'[...] *he crashed his car once, I believed in what he told me as I was not there, the case ended in a court and he got a high fine and did not admit it; I accidentally (...) found it and paid the fine [...] well, if there's a fine, you have to pay it, he did not care at all*', '*he came to me for money and I said it was his duty to pay it and he said to me that he already spent his wages drinking [...] so I gave him the money again*'.

The victim was experiencing abuse regularly for the period of around 40 years.

Emotions and behavioral patterns

Violence against the victim in question was accompanied by strong emotions, from fear, sadness, grief, shame, to regrets and blaming herself for her situation, contributing to nervous breakdown and helplessness. Intense experiences had been making mental trauma of the victim even worse for years. The woman could not accept the fact that her husband is abusing her, all she felt was overwhelming sadness:

'I felt like my heart was going to burst,' 'I could never accept that', 'the worst thing was I could never count on him when I was sick or in trouble.'

The initial incidents of aggression did not made the victim alarmed – *'I didn't even realize it, it was only after our marriage when things got really bad'*. When the tension in the family began to increase and conflicts intensified, the victim tried to avoid any situations that could escalate such conflicts. She did what she could to control the situation – she fulfilled her duties and tried to please her husband:

'[...] her colleagues from work visited him at home [...]. Of course, I made them some tea and something to eat and then I went to another room'. 'I tried to do my best, thinking that maybe if everything gets better, then maybe it will stop, there will be no more mocking and name calling'.

Elżbieta often wondered how to stop her husband from abusing her. When violence escalated, the victim started to become aware of her situation more and more often:

'I started to realize what is going on, I saw his behavior and the way he was humiliating me and pushing me around'.

The victim was experiencing more and more terror, shame, anger and helplessness. What is typical of women who fall victim of domestic violence, despite her negative experience, the victim was also feeling more and more guilty for her situation

'[...] my mom always told me that in marriage, both spouses are always to blame for what is happening and I thought that maybe I am doing something wrong, behaving badly and so it went on'. '[...] everything was building up'.

Elżbieta still believed that her husband's behavior can change

'I believed that maybe something will change when we get our own apartment, that maybe later on... and then he started using his methods, he did not take a word from anyone'.

Breaking the silence

Breaking the silence is always very difficult for victims of domestic violence, especially for women who fall victim to marital violence. As women do not believe in the support system for victims of violence, they do not report their abuse for many years. To make things worse, cultural attitudes towards women still foster the belief in hierarchy of power in marriage. Acceptance of long-term violence makes women even more submissive and increases social acceptance and tolerance for violence

'[...] *we have not become fully aware of it yet, in rural areas many believe that the man is the lord and the master and women must shut up and do what they are told*'.

For the most of her period of marriage, Elżbieta lived in constant fear, shame and did not believe that law and procedures could be effective. She had been torn by regrets and feeling of guilt and shame for 40 years:

'*I have always been so compassionate and thinking of him as my husband and me as his wife and I was afraid of what people or my family would say. This is what mattered and when the police was standing in the hall, it was horrible when people looked at me and talked about me. It was all very traumatic for me*'.

The victim tried to get help from her siblings, but in vain, so she became convinced that she is alone with her problems – '*when I needed help, I was alone* [...] *my family let me down so much*'. She did not receive any help from her son, the victim quickly stopped trying to get help from him as she was afraid that she could lose contact with her son and his wife – '*I don't even talk to him about it as I can see it is depressing for him* [...]'. She did not want to put her son in more trouble – '*I can see that it is very painful for him and sometimes he tells me: mom, my stomach cramps every time I am about to see you*'.

Finally, after 40 years of marriage, thanks to specialist support, the victim decided to break the silence

'[...] *after group meetings, my mind began to change, I became aware of some facts*', '*I wish I had done that earlier*', '*now I think in a completely different way, I am no longer afraid of what people or my family say,* [...] *my reactions are not different although it still hurts very much.*'

Becoming aware of her situation and the opportunity to get real support made Elżbieta certain about her decision to disclose the violence, as well as strengthened her attitude:

'*I already know where to go, whom to talk to when I need to solve my problems. My lawyer from the social welfare has been very supportive; he gave me some good pieces of advice, for example he told me to claim my maintenance,* [...] *initially, I didn't even want any maintenance from him, because I had thought that if he hates me so much and did so much harm to me, I don't need anything from him*'.

Discussion and summary

The analyzed case presents a typical method of victim's behavior, resulting primarily from the level of victimization, at which the victim is. There are many reasons why the victim had decided not to report domestic violence earlier, for example intimidation, learned helplessness or hope for a change. In order to understand them, we have to look closer at the nature of relations between the perpetrator and the victim. At some level of experiencing violence, the victim tried to seek help or some support among her family, but in vain. Her family, instead of helping her, showed a typical behavior resulting from the popular stereotype that 'nobody should interfere with private family life, even if there is violence involved'.

In the analyzed case, conflicts, arguments and various forms of violence that brought suffering to all members of the family were followed by family disorganization and its eventual breakdown. The causes of violent behavior of the perpetrator are defined by both individual and environmental factors. The perpetrator of violence is a male with basic education and alcohol problems. According to the victim, the perpetrator also experienced domestic violence as a child, which could be the cause of his behavior as an adult. For many years, the victim felt a strong sense of guilt resulting from the belief that she is the one responsible for violence, she thought of herself as of someone who has no control over their life.

To sum up, the above analysis of experiences of a female victim of domestic violence allows us to see the situation of violence 'from the inside', to get familiar with the causes of behavior of the victim – a woman who had been stuck in a toxic relationship for 40 years, experiencing severe humiliation, pain and overwhelming fear. Her life story clearly shows the way that victims think and barriers that women, wives and mothers have to overcome to break the silence and seek help.

A victim of violence repeats a specific behavioral pattern, resulting mainly from the level of victimization such person is at. A thorough analysis of the victim's situation from a victimological perspective should be the basis for preventive measures (in both individual and general context), overcoming stereotypes and shaping the right attitudes towards violence. It is essential that victims are not left alone with their problems, that they receive support in their closest environment in order to break the silence and take steps aimed at combating violence.

Dorota Kamińska-Jones
Nicolaus Copernicus University, Toruń, Poland

The figure of the Indian woman-victim as a pretext for colonialism and imperialism

Introduction

The aim of this paper is to analyse British attitudes towards Indian women, describing ways in which they were victimised and how this victimisation was used to support ideas of colonialism and imperialism. The British officially settled in India from 1600 – with the establishment of the East India Company – until 1947 when they handed over power to local authorities. During these three and a half centuries they changed their attitude both to their own presence in the country and to the people of India. This can be divided into two main phases. The first one covers the period from the beginning of their presence on Indian soil to around 1800, and the second from that time until their final departure from India. This second period can be further divided into two phases: from 1800 to 1858 – when India was formally incorporated into the British Crown, and from 1858 until 1947 – when they were part of the Empire. The main focus is on the period between the 19th and the beginning of the 20th century.

Problems and questions of the study

The main issue is to investigate the representation of Indian women as victims in the source texts and visual depictions. The typical components of such descriptions will be indicated along with reoccurring patterns. It is vital to question what factors influenced the formation of such a vision of womanhood – when and why it was constructed. The next issue is to single out the different social groups that employed such rhetoric. The question is: what was the goal of each group and what solutions did they offer? What, therefore, was their contribution to the development of colonialism and the upholding of imperialism? Did they really mean to improve the lot of women or did they, perhaps, have other goals?

British attitudes towards India and Indian women

In the first period of the their presence in India, the British were mainly traders, interested in doing business and making money. They did not have more serious territorial ambitions and the wars that they fought were mainly aimed at protecting their interests rather than conquering new lands. Many of them became interested in India, often adopting the local lifestyle. Relationships with local women were common and, moreover, actually recommended in guide-books for the newly arrived. Travellers and artists who had settled in India raved about Indian women. Those men who had direct contact with local women and either married or took them as concubines enthused over their charm, warmth, kindness and love. In their memoirs, these men repeatedly mentioned that these were the most wonderful women that men could possibly imagine (see: Kamińska-Jones 2012). Travellers and artists who did not have nearly as close relationships with Indian women saw them, in turn, mainly through the prism of their own aesthetic categories and found in them reminiscent of either ancient beauty or picturesque figures. The conservative attitude prevalent during the last two decades of the eighteen century was characterised by an appreciation of Indian civilisation. Two of the biggest admirers of India included Sir William Jones[1] and William Robertson[2].

The situation began to change from 1800 when the British began to pursue a more expansionist policy and conquered more and more areas of the country. An imperial attitude towards India began to emerge. The wealth of the nabobs (British adopting the lifestyle of the Indian elite) and widespread corruption caused a change in the way the company was managed. Prime Minister William Pitt's Indian Act (1784) separated the Company's civil service and military from its trading wing and raised salaries. The Act's goals were to curb corruption by separating the East India Company's two conflicting functions: that of trading and that of ruling the Subcontinent and to give the government a more direct role in controlling India. To India were brought officials who were to conscientiously perform their duties. This Civil Service was educated in the British manner and likely to conduct itself with 'honour and industry'. This Civil Service was indoctrinated with a sense

---

1 Sir William Jones (1746–1794) was an Anglo-Welsh philologist and scholar of ancient India, particularly known for his proposition of the existence of a relationship among Indo-European languages. He, along with Henry Thomas Colebrooke and Nathaniel Halhed, founded the Asiatic Society of Bengal.

2 William Robertson (1721–1793) was a Scottish historian, minister in the Church of Scotland, and Principal of the University of Edinburgh.

of imperial responsibility and ingrained with a sense of Britain's greatness (Bearce 1961, p. 39). The Company's racial policies also changed. The earlier open-minded approach was replaced by a new one consisting of separation from the people with whom they lived. The growing policy of racial segregation was one of the causes of the Sepoy Mutiny in 1847. What was considered to be the first spurt of Indian independence was brutally suppressed. A year later, the East India Company was disbanded and India was incorporated into the British Empire. The British government, after formally taking over control, introduced its administration as well as reforms on a large scale in India until the time when they officially left.

Since 1800, along with the change in attitude towards India came a noticeable change in attitude towards Indian women. Closer relations with the residents of India were banned as they constituted, in the eyes of the British, a threat to their race. Interracial relationships would lead to union at the most basic level of the family and would result in mixed offspring. British ladies were encouraged to travel to India to provide a mainstay of 'Britishness' and British domesticity. For those who could not afford to maintain a British wife, brothels were established. Indian woman became more and more 'other'. They gradually ceased to be a wonderful companion for life, and started to become a more and more unwilling victim. 'To speak of the state of women in India is to disclose a picture of sorrow such as is found nowhere else on earth [...]' – this is a typical statement of this time. 'Her degradation and sorrow are a load upon her existence from the cradle to the grave' (Godbey, Godbey 1892, p. 70). In literature from this period we find very many descriptions of the misery of women centred around several core issues. The same patterns repeat over and over again consisting of several key elements: the position of women in the house, bad social practices and a degenerate culture, belief in superstition and the worship of monstrous and cruel gods. The main reasons for the low status of women in Indian culture were perceived as the cruelty of local men and the religion. Liberation was supposed to come in the form of conversion to the Christian religion and the British government.

The Indian woman – a victim of culture and local men

An Indian woman's life was dependent on her parents, and then her husband. The parents did not consult her on the choice of a future spouse. They also married her off early, usually during childhood. After the wedding, she no longer had any freedom, but was shut in the house at the behest of her husband, devoted to him and the children. Not being able to read or write, she only learned to cook and listened to the stories of the deities transmitted orally by the other women of the household. She was cut off from the outside world, shut in the *zenana* – the women's section of the house. The segregation of the sexes was considered as 'a great evil' and 'failure' (Fuller 1900, p. 86, 87). A woman served her husband in the most servile manner, was his slave and could not eat with him; she always had to be ready for his orders – he was her god. It was emphasised that the most terrible aspect of the lives of women in India was how they were treated at home, almost like domestic slaves. When a spouse died before her and she became a widow then a life of real misery began. Widows were often even suspected of causing the death of her husband, had to get rid of everything and live in self-mortification ever after. This attitude is in some sense a consequence of the custom of *sati* – death on the funeral pyre of her husband. It was believed that religion and the social system forced her into this – as a widow she was to have a terrible life whereas if she burned alongside her husband she would meet with recognition, praise and gain the status of the sacred.

A woman while being her husband's servant was also his victim. Local men were portrayed in two ways. On the one hand, they were depicted as cruel tyrants, holding their women in confinement and bullying them. On the other hand, they were shown as weak, effeminate, listless and totally unsuitable to govern their own country. Social evil was responsible for such traits focusing on women, the young age of marriage, the prohibition of re-marriage for widows, lack of education, and hence the belief in superstition and the excommunication of women from the public sphere. So the wheel was closed.

A victim of religion

Women, as already mentioned, were also seen as victims of religion. As Mrs. Sherwood[3] claimed

> [...] as religion (...) has more influence on the female mind than on that of men, so the abominable administrators of a corrupt worship have a much stronger and more detestable influence over the minds of the weaker than stronger sex (after: Dyson 1978, p. 96).

Hinduism was openly criticised for being full of cruel practices such as human sacrifice. Such practices were contended by the critics to be in honour of the goddess Kali, who demanded them: 'to this horrid deity the mothers of India have offered their daughters through many ages of darkness and misery' (Godbey, Godbey 1892, p. 72). Sometimes there were detailed descriptions of the performance of blood sacrifices involving women and children.

> A young woman pregnant with her first child, was selected, and brought in front of the shrine. She was then beheaded with one blow of a sword so that the head rolled

---

3 Mary Martha Sherwood (1775–1851) was a prolific and influential writer of children's literature in 19th-century Britain. She composed over 400 books, tracts, magazine articles, and chapbooks. Sherwood was also passionately involved in education; she established a number of schools both in England and in India, where she lived for 11 years from 1805, and where she became an evangelical Christian.

up in front of the image, on which the blood of the victim was also sprinkled (Mateer 1871, p. 198).

They provided an example of the cruelty of this pagan religion which, in their opinion, was Hinduism. Images of the goddess Kali, one of the most terrifying in the eyes of the British, appeared frequently in both descriptions and illustrations. Artists had often not seen the image of the goddess with their own eyes and depicted her on the basis of descriptions, giving her a slightly different look than she had in reality. Particular attention was given to scary details, such as the decapitated head given in sacrifice or held out by her. She could also be portrayed as devouring children. The faithful were depicted in humble or fearful demeanour, worshiping and making full sacrifice to the cruel Kali. 'This terrible image is habitually worshipped by thousands of poor ignorant mothers of India' (Mateer 1871, p. 200). In his book, Anthony Ramsen Cavalie put this illustration on the first page, as a kind of introduction to the Indian world, while setting the tone for the reader (Cavalie 1899, p. XI).

Not only, however, in honour of Kali were such sacrifices made. In relations from India we can find many stories of how an Indian mother had to sacrifice her little daughter. They doped her with opium or another drug and threw her into the river (Fig. 1) or left her in the jungle to starve to death or be devoured by wild animals. This custom, according to the authors, was stronger than any natural feelings towards the child, which showed the terrible impact of religion on society and especially on women. They had to do this for religious reasons as well. It was also written that before the introduction of British law everywhere in India children were murdered (Godbey, Godbey 1892, p. 72). On one of the presentations we see on the left side children dying in the arms of their Indian mothers, and on the other side – mothers happily travelling towards the tent guarded by the British, symbolising the Empire and its care for women and children. The vision of Indian mothers murdering their children was so widespread in the West that it even became the theme of a children's song:

> See that heathen mother stand
> Where the sacred current flows
> With her own maternal hands,
> Mid the waves her babe she throws
> Send, Oh send, the Bible there,
> Let its precept reach the heart;
> She may then her children spare-
> Act the tender mother's part (Forbes 1986, WS-2)

The horror of idolatry was also emphasised.

> It would be difficult to imagine anything more painful to the mind of a Christian than the busy scene of idolatrous worship and superstitious ceremonial. [...] Pilgrims [...] eagerly bent on devotional observances, which take them further away from God, instead bringing them nearer to Him, in the end leaving them in hopeless darkness, if not in despair (Cavalie 1899, p. 50).

The drama of worshipping statues particularly concerned women, because they brought up children and conveyed to them the belief and value system from birth. 'What a sad picture have we here' – wrote John Liggins.

> A poor pagan Hindoo mother kneeling before a hideous image of Ganesa, the god of wisdom and teaching her child to worship it. No wonder that the little creature starts back and is afraid to lift up his hands. He may well be frightened by such a monster; but it is not possible that he can ever love it (Liggins 1867, p. 8) (Fig. 2).

Indian women were called 'the poor idolatrous females in bondage' (Chapman 1839, p. 175).

Women were also particularly vulnerable to the effects of evil spirits and demons. Some Indian deities were considered to be the incarnation of the devil, and their demonic nature was emphasised. There were long descriptions of the temples of devils and demons where terrible ceremonies would take place. The names of some of them were depicted in horrific terms, such as Ammen, mentioned by Samuel Mateer, who indignantly states that the name means 'mother' – an 'awful desecration of the sacred term!' (Mateer 1871, p. 200). According to the authors,

> [...] these malignant spirits, male and female, of various names and antecedents, are supposed [...] to possess women [...] and to kill children (Mateer 188-, p. 19–20).

The woman as a victim – Liberal and Utilitarian approach

The image of a woman as a victim was used by both Liberals and Utilitarians. These two groups originated with James Mill (1773–1836) – a Scottish historian, economist, political theorist and philosopher, who turned his attention to India in 1806, when he began his work on *The History of British India* (published in 1817.) He was convinced that Indian civilisation was at a lower level of development than European[4]. He took one of the criteria to be the plight of women. 'The condition of women is one of the most remarkable circumstances in the manners of nations. Among rude people, the women are generally degraded; among civilised people they are exalted (Mill 1826, p. 445). He maintained that women in India 'are held in extreme degradation' (Mill 1826, p. 450). Descriptions of the tragic situation

---

4 This matter was dealt with in detail in Book II, *Of the Hindus*, Chapter 10 *General Reflections* (Mill 1826, Vol. II, p. 135–206), see: http://oll.libertyfund.org/titles/840 (Accessed: 15.07.2014).

of women aimed to support the main thesis of the inferiority of Indian culture compared to the British. Somehow one of the responsibilities of the more civilised nations was to civilise those standing lower in the hierarchy. James Mill was convinced that India desperately needed Britain. He considered India as a tabula rasa on which the British inscription would remain forever. But the use of women's status as an index of civilisation easily led to promoting reforms for women on instrumental grounds rather than for the women's sake (Strobel 1991, p. 50).

The woman as a victim – the missionaries' approach

Missionaries exploited the image of women as victims mainly to justify spreading the mission in the country. They believed that Christianity alone was able to liberate women from oppression. They often contrasted the plight of Indian women with their happiness upon changing their religion.

A major role in spreading Christianity among Indian women was played by women missionaries. Initially, they were mostly the wives of missionaries, but as time went on, more and more professional women missionaries to come to India to help Indian women to 'find the truth'. The significant role of women in this mission was due to the fact that for the large part Indian women lived separately in the houses *(purdah)*. The parts of the house designated for women were not accessible for men unrelated to them. Therefore, for male missionaries, this world remained out of bounds. So, female missionaries had greater room for manoeuvre. In their memoirs, and those of other women who had the opportunity to enter the female part of the house, many descriptions of the situation of women and the conditions prevailing in the *zenana* can be found. Often we discover the opinion of how disappointing it was when the harems of popular imagination were confronted with reality. 'I was glad to see *zenana*' said Fanny Parkes[5], 'but much disappointed: the women are not ladylike (Parkes 1850, p. 60).

Spreading the good news and the liberation of women could be carried out with the support of colonial rule. Female missionaries were, therefore, not only a force supporting imperialism, but they themselves constituted a strong colonial and imperial force that promoted British values through its activities. Education was also aimed at teaching according to Christian values. 'It is precisely the womanhood of India [...] the protectress and zealous adherent of traditional heathenism' (Richter, Moore 1908, p. 329). The female missionaries saw the chance to spread the Christian faith in India via women precisely because it was they who raised children and so shaped the next generation. Therefore, this was a campaign on the very basis of Indian civilisation and culture. This influence on women resulted in

---

5 Fanny Parkes (née Frances Susannah Archer) (1794–1875) was a Welsh travel writer.

deep changes within the family, and hence the society as a whole. An important aspect of the colonisation of Indian women was also the 'civilising' of the domestic sphere, and thus the whole society, which had the effect that India would be safer for British citizens. This aspect of power gained momentum particularly from the mid-nineteenth century, when the country was considered to be part of the Empire, in other words one of the organisms of the state.

Sometimes it was even written that Hindus came to the missionaries of their own accord to ask for enlightenment and to be shown the 'truth' and the 'true religion' (Liggins 1867, p. 10), and that the wiser people of this country appreciated the civilising role of the missionaries and the Empire. 'India is highly indebted to these disinterested and large-hearted followers of Christ, for her present prosperity' – wrote Mary Carpenter[6] quoting Indian man.

> Fortunately for India, she was not forgotten by the Christian missionaries when they went about to preach the Gospel. While, through missionary agency, our country has thus been connected with the enlightened nations of the West [...] I cannot but reflect with grateful interest on the day when the British nation first planted their feet on the plains of India, and successive steps by which the British Empire has been established and consolidated in this country. It is to the British Government that we owe our deliverance from oppression and misrule, from darkness and distress, from ignorance and superstitions. Those enlightened ideas which changed the very life of the nation, and have gradually brought about such wondrous improvement in native society [...]. Are not such considerations calculated to rouse our deepest gratitude and loyalty to the British nation and Her Most Gracious Majesty Queen Victoria? Her beneficent Christian administration has proved to us not only political, but social and moral blessing, and laid the foundation of our national prosperity and greatness; and it is but natural that we should cherish towards her no other feeling except that of devoted loyalty (Carpenter 1868, pp. 73–74).

So it was India who asked for enlightenment and the British – government and missionaries – were so wonderful that they took on the burden of introducing order in India and saving her women.

The woman as a victim – the governing officials' approach

Like the missionaries, the governing officials also employed such rhetoric. They depicted themselves as introducing order and bestowing protection upon Indian woman. There was a shift towards the rhetoric of how white man rescued from oppression the dark-skinned woman (Spivak 1988, p. 93), the victim of local men and culture. Cruel and barbaric practices were reported such as *sati* and they, as representatives of a more civilised culture, were rightly outraged by the cruelty. *Sati*

---

6 Mary Carpenter (1807 –1877) was an English educational and social reformer.

became an alibi for the colonial civilising mission. Such a horrible oppression of Indian women was a sign of the degradation of India as a whole (see: Mani 1998). The Hindu woman, as a passive victim of her own culture and men, begged the British for her own liberation (Fig. 3). The introduction of formal colonial rule was thus to provide them with deliverance and safety. Britannia accepted 'foreign' women under her wings and afforded them shelter from their own barbaric culture and cruel men. This idea is perfectly captured in an illustration reproduced in 'Punch' magazine (1890.10.18, p. 182). At the foot of a personified Britannia falls a terrified Indian woman as if seeking help. Above her rises the ominous shadow of an Indian man, giving the impression that this is a torturer approaching his victim. Britannia, however, raises her hand in a caring, yet authoritative gesture against the impending man. The imposition of foreign governments were thus presented as necessary, and one which allowed protection for local women. The British introduced a number of laws aimed at improving the status of women. The first of these was the prohibition of Sati in 1829, followed by the Hindu Widow Remarriage Act of 1856 and the Age of Consent Act of 1891.

The woman as a victim – the approach of the women reformers and feminists

For their own purposes the rhetoric of Indian women as victims was used by British women reformers with feminist awareness and feminists. Mary Carpenter (1807–1877), mentioned above, a renowned 19th century social reformer began wide-ranging efforts to improve the lot of women on a grand scale. 'For the first to the last day of residence in India, the point which most painfully strikes the mind is the position of Indian women' – she wrote. 'May many more English women arise, who shall devote themselves to the glorious and blessed work of raising their Eastern sisters to fill their place in society.' 'The devoted work of multitudes of English-women [...] shows what our sex can do: new light, the rapid progress of civilisation' (Carpenter 1868, p. 74, 83). For them the main justification for British rule was to cleanse local societies of social evils affecting women. Many British feminists were characterised by an imperialistic attitude. The feminists fighting for their social rights emphasised their usefulness for the Empire as activists for improving the condition of their Indian 'sisters'. Many of them justified women's equality on the grounds that, as women, they contributed to the survival and continued prosperity of the British Empire. The conviction that Indian women represented a special feminist burden was one expression of middle-class British 'imperial feminism'. Bourgeois feminists exhibited interests in Indian women and a sense of responsibility for their colonial sisters (Burton 1991, p. 47). They spread the ideas of universal 'sisterhood' but it was not a sisterhood of equals. British women showed themselves to be among the better ones and of higher standing up in the hierarchy of races, whose aim was to help tormented sisters in other parts of the Empire, at lower levels of development. Indian women in their opinion were in need of salvation by their British feminist sisters. The Empire was essential to bring the help they required.

The Indian woman as a victim was also the concern of American women's activists. One of the most critical in terms of the status of women in India was Katherine Mayo (1867–1940). In her famous book *Mother India* (1927), and others on this subject like *Slaves of the Gods* (1929), *Volume Two* (1931) or *The Face of Mother India* (1935) she criticised the social position of women in India. She was of the opinion that India needed Western rule and was a strong supporter of the Empire. For her, only a foreign government could guarantee an improvement in the lot of women. So she strongly opposed India's independence.

Conclusion

As mentioned previously, the vision of Indian women as victims was used by various groups for their own purposes, but in each of them was the important aspect of colonialism and, later on, the maintenance of the Empire. Indian women in the nineteenth century rarely spoke up for themselves. They were presented as silent victims, and no one asked their opinion. Gradually, however, they began to assert their voice. In the twentieth century, increasing numbers began to represent themselves alone, without the need for liberation or the protection from foreign invaders. They have taken up the fight for themselves in their own country.

Fig. 1. A child committed to the river by its mother [J.E. Godbey, A.H. Godbey (1892), *Light in darkness, or, Missions and missionary heroes : an illustrated history of the missionary work ... taking up principally the work in India, Burmah, Siam, China... being a history of these countries ... to which is added the adventures of missionaries among the uncivilized races of the world ...*, Imperial Pub. Co. St. Louis, MO, p. 72]

Fig. 2. J. Liggins (1867), *The Oriental picture gallery*, Hurd and Houghton, New York, p. 8

Fig. 3. Burning a Hindoo widow [J. Peggs (1832), *India's cries to British humanity, relative to infanticide, British connection with idolatry, ghaut murders, suttee, slavery, and colonization in India; to which are added, Humane hints for the melioration of the state of society in British India*, Simpkin and Marshall, London, p. 112]

Muhammad Mumtaz, Muhammad Shahbaz Arif
GC University Faisalabad, Pakistan

Honor killing in international law with a special reference to the situation in Pakistan

Introduction

The honor killing is a primeval concept and has prevailed since the Greek times. It means killing of a woman by the members of her family in the name of shame or respect. The logic behind the honor killing is that the victim has brought dishonor upon her family in society. The actions of the victim that can lead to an honor killing may include sex, love or marriage with someone without the consent of the family or when a woman has her own relations outside the family or when she breaks the arranged marriage which was planned by the family. A woman can fall victim to an honor killing by her family due to diverse reasons which are common in our society, for example when she refuses to enter into an arranged marriage, when she is sexually assaulted, when she seeks divorce from an abusive husband or when she commits adultery (Mitra, Bachchan 2004).

It has been estimated that in the Middle East and Asia more than 20,000 women are killed on the pretext of honor every year. This ratio may be higher in Pakistan, India and Afghanistan than in other countries. In Arab societies the woman is either considered a 'factory for producing children' either a 'nobody'. In certain societies women are not allowed to take part in any social events or activities of their tribes (Irfan 2008).

Honor killings are an old tradition in all societies, it is not a new phenomenon. History shows that the honor killing has been practiced for centuries all over the world.

Major causes of honor killings

There are various causes which are involved in honor killings:

- Choosing a life partner; a woman can fall victim to an honor killing in society due to her insolent behavior, when she chooses her life partner against the will of her family.
- When she is not satisfied with her domestic life or household life and she goes out and engages in conversations with other male members of the society.
- When she rejects decisions of her father or other dominant family members. A woman can fall victim to an honor killing, when she chooses her profession, career, school or job herself. Such types of decisions made by women in traditional societies cause strong reactions from their families.
- A change of religion may be another cause for an honor killing of a woman – when she changes her religion for the purpose of marriage or due to other reasons.
- Rape is also a cause of honor killings. When a girl is raped, it is considered a shame for the tribe or her family.
- Seeking divorce is considered another cause of honor killings in most of the Muslim societies, especially in the tribal areas of Pakistan.
- Honor torture is also very famous in some societies, such was the case of Mukhtaran Mai in Pakistan, she was sexually tortured because of honor of the tribe and revenge was taken on her.

The honor killing is not a national issue, it is a universal issue. It has been reported that honor killings have been committed in most of the Muslim countries, however many Muslim jurists and scholars have condemned this crime.

The countries where the perpetration of honor killings is recurrent are the following: Syria, Palestine, Egypt, Afghanistan, Pakistan, India, Bangladesh, Jordan and Turkey.

There are also certain countries which have legalized the honor killing:

- Jordan, where under article 340 of the criminal code the honor killing was exempted from the punishment if it was committed by blood relatives. However, due to huge pressure from women's organizations it has been declared an offence.
- Brazil, where the honor killing was legal until 1991 and the killing of one's wife was not defined as an offence. The wife was considered the property of her husband.
- Morocco, where the Criminal Code (2003) of Morocco improved the status of women and expressly declared the honor killing an offence. Before that this crime was not seriously dealt with.

Modes of honor killings

There are different modes which are used for honor killings, including; shooting, strangling, axing, clubbing, stabbing, electrocution, slitting the throat, beheading, burying alive and logging etc.

There are different reasons for the increasing number of honor killings, such as the lack of awareness, tribal system, brutal attitude of society towards women, poverty, lacunas in the criminal justice system and the availability of weapons (Warraich 2005).

The measures taken by the international community

Several steps have been taken by the international community regarding the worst crime against women which is commonly called the honor killing. The landmark step taken by the international community was the approval of the Convention on the Elimination of All Forms of Discrimination against women (CEDAW). It was the most important and effective document for women's rights and it is usually called the international 'Bill for women' (Haile 2007).

The State parties to the CEDAW are also bound to take effective measures in order to control the violence against women. The CEDAW has a specific body which monitors reports and progress regarding women's rights. Although the CEDAW does not deal specifically with the honor killing, its purpose is to eradicate all kinds of violence against women (UNICEF, 2000).

Article 1 of the UN Declaration on the Elimination of Violence against Women proclaims:

> the term 'violence against women' means any act of gender-based violence that results in, or is likely to result in, physical, sexual or psychological harm or suffering to women, including threats of such acts, coercion or arbitrary deprivation of liberty, whether occurring in public or in private life (Vitoshka 2010).

Another important declaration is the UN Declaration on the Elimination of Violence against Women (1993). This declaration has defined more specifically the definition of violence against women and states that any act which physically or sexually amounts to harm to women is termed as violence against women.

Several steps have been taken at the European level to tackle the honor killing; the most important step is the European Convention for the Protection of Human Rights and Fundamental Freedoms (1950). This convention strengthens the idea of the right to life, security of person and the eradication of slavery in a more comprehensive manner.

Similarly, the International Covenant on Civil and Political Rights also gives the guarantee of the right to life, security and liberty in its article 6. The life of any man or woman cannot be taken in any situation (Barlas 2004).

The Universal Declaration of Human Rights also ensures the protection of women in its article 5 which states that no one shall be subjected to torture or inhuman treatment. This article covers the dignity of women as well.

The measures taken by Pakistan

Pakistani women are also facing the tradition of the honor killing, as in other countries. There are different methods that are being used in case of violence against women such as beating, murder and other forms of torture. The honor killing is being committed in nearly all parts of Pakistan, especially in tribal areas (Jehanzeb 2004).

In Pakistan women who choose to marry on their own terms are threatened with the old tradition of the honor killing. In most areas of Pakistan the Jirga System has banned the registration of reports of honor killings at police stations and declared that this is our custom and the tradition of tribes that is not allowed to be violated by anyone. In these areas girls have no right to choose whom they will marry (Saleem 2003).

Although the honor killing has been declared an offence under the Pakistan Penal Code, the government is not seriously considering its implementation in its true spirit. According to section 308 the offence of the honor killing is a compoundable offence. The *Wali* or the plaintiff has the right to withdraw the criminal case and forgive the accused (Mumtaz 2012).

The constitution of Pakistan also gives protection to the man and woman. According to article 9 of the constitution, everyone has the right to life and it cannot be violated in any circumstances. The Supreme Court has issued the decision that legally and morally no one is allowed to take the life of anyone in the name of *Ghairat* – honor.

There is no doubt that Pakistan has signed different conventions and treaties regarding violence against women and in this respect the Women Protection Act was passed which grants more rights to women. Nevertheless, at the national level the government is not thinking seriously about adopting effective measures which can prevent this evil or violence against women.

In the light of the above discussions the following **recommendations** are made:
– Respect for the right to life;
– Awareness programmes of women's legal rights;
– Steps should be taken at national and international levels to adopt necessary, effective legislation;

– Victim support centers should be established widely;
– The government should adopt legislation which makes the honor killing an offence.
– Bails should be discouraged by the courts in the cases of the honor killing.

Conclusion

It is clear from the above study that the honor killing is a worldwide issue. Men fully dominate women in several parts of the world, including Pakistan. The right to life is recurrently being violated in the name of the honor killing. Women are suffering in the name of honor and respect of the family. Although the honor killing has been declared an offence against humanity, unfortunately it has not been eradicated. It requires time to take momentous measures at national and international levels. Strict substantive and procedural legislation is required in order to wipe out this appalling crime. The mindset that favors violence must be changed through economic and education reforms, because the root cause of the honor killing is the lack of awareness of women's rights in the community.

Malwina Misiąg
University of Rzeszów

Patriarchal culture – the source of violence against women

Introduction

The starting point for the analysis of the problem was the scale of domestic violence, harmful for the most important legally protected values such as health and human life, freedom, public safety, etc. To illustrate the scale of the problem one must point to the fact that in Poland in 2013 there were 86,797 people injured due to domestic violence (there were 61,047 Blue Card forms filled in), of which 58,310 were women (over 67%)[1]. Similar data is presented in the European Union Agency for Fundamental Rights Report from 2014 which indicates that one out of three women in Poland was sexually molested, one out of ten was a victim of stalking and 19% fell victim to physical or sexual violence. It is clear that domestic violence mostly harms women. However, this problem has been seen as such only recently. The feminist movement has helped immensely in organizing structures which provide assistance to women affected by domestic violence. M. Kostash described the birth of women's liberation movement as follows:

> [...] analysis and practice which were developed by the feminists so laboriously are a reflection of their own experiences in the male-dominated left. To be precise, that their work and intelligence is coarsely used by male management who is, in turn, preoccupied with power and strengthening their own position, that their sexuality is being used in the name of false ethics of 'free love', that their 'female' flair for cooperation rather than hierarchy, for combining sensibility and intellect and substituting violence with sensitivity is treated with contempt by men, and also, which may be the worst of all, that women themselves accept this exploitation, abuse and contempt as if it was perfectly natural. (Kostash 1988, p. 3–4).

---

[1] See: Przemoc w rodzinie – statystyka policyjna (2013), http://statystyka.policja.pl/st/wybra -ne-statystyki/przemoc-w-rodzinie/50863,Przemoc-w-rodzinie.html (Accessed: 24.04.2014).

The socialization of women – establishing the basis of oppression

Researchers dealing with the analysis of the problem of violence against women all agree that the explanation according to which men resort to beating because they are aggressive and frustrated 'by nature' is not sufficient since it does not explain all the situations in which violence occurs. It is the different socialization of boys and girls that serves as the key to understanding men's violence against women – being a victim of violence is a part of women's cultural role, being the perpetrator is a part of men's cultural role. Since the early stages of socialization culture has imposed on women the belief that according to patriarchal standards home and family are their natural places in society.

Lipowska-Teutsch writes that in order to understand the phenomenon of violence against women, one must consider the process of socialization which shapes their identities and social roles.

> Girls are expected to be caring and sensitive to other people's problems, to take care of their appearance, but not to take initiative in sexual contexts. Excessive independence, tendency to dominate, aggression and competiveness are not perceived as positive qualities. Thus, a conviction that the only success that should matter in female life is creating a happy household and bearing children develops in women (Lipowska--Teutsch 1997, p. 49).

They are expected to be able to keep the man at home with their charming behaviour. Such an intense training of passivity and dependence is a serious obstacle for women in developing an effective self-defense.

The patriarchal structures of society are usually not associated with violence since as claimed by K. Millet: 'it undergoes socialization in such a perfect way that using the force seems to be unnecessary' (Millet 1982, p. 83). Violence more often tends to be perceived as an indication of social pathology, and if it still happens to occur somewhere nowadays, it is treated as an individual deviation. And yet, maintaining the control in a patriarchal culture would be incomplete and unsuccessful if the survival of the fittest was not used as an effective means of threatening, especially in crisis situations (Millet 1982, p. 69).

A precise description of the process of women's socialization in a patriarchal society was provided by J.M. Bardwick and E. Douvan. The authors observe that even in their early childhood girls are less physically active, less inclined to open aggression, more sensitive to pain, less interested in genitalia and distinctively exceeding boys in the verbal, cognitive and perceptive areas. Moreover, girls' greater psychical maturity allows them to react more quickly and precisely to the stimuli coming from the outside. Their self-determination and affirmation depend on others, and, being proficient in reading social demands, they become conformists. Their gratification is found in good marks at school, in parental love, in teachers' fondness towards them and in peer relationships. They become complaisant and especially prone to cultural modeling. They develop an attitude of passivity which is especially demonstrated in their academic achievements, mainly due to their good behaviour and memory. The search for their identity and for the inner criteria of their self-esteem is much delayed in girls as it does not start until adolescence. Then their femininity proves to be an attribute that must be deserved, which is a problem especially difficult due to girls' ambivalent feelings towards their bodies. An adolescent girl must create her inner female 'I' accepting all the functions and complaints of a mature body; the physical changes require the change of requirements imposed on her by the culture. Teenagers – potential heterosexual partners – start to be punished for their excessively obvious accomplishments and rewarded for being attractive for the opposite sex. However, their attractiveness cannot be conspicuous: it may threaten their friendship with other girls. Thus, the girls learn that they will probably be punished for the successes preceded by rivalry. Even competitive and independent girls – who might have felt normal up to this point – upon entering adolescence undergo their first great crisis connected with searching pleasure deriving from physical 'femininity' and developing psychological 'femininity'. However, since their self-esteem comes from others and they describe themselves using categories of interpersonal relations, most girls undergoing the stress of the incomplete female identity agree to the new criteria of socialization, thus learning their new social roles. At this moment of changing priorities such characteristic features as independence, aggression and competitiveness are rejected since they threaten heterosexual relationships (Bardwick, Douvan 1982, pp. 165–186).

It is at this point that a new image of the woman is shaped – the one of a victim whose social role is focused exclusively on the needs of the opposite sex partner and on the consequences of unfulfilling those needs. The loss of love and being exposed to any critical evaluation become extremely painful. Due to the lack of objective and independent achievements, girls and women estimate their value on the basis of other people's reactions, recognizing their own identity only within the relations they have with the society as daughters, wives, mothers. When asked what makes them happy, they usually say: when I love and am loved, when I make other people's happiness possible, when I have a satisfactory family life and healthy children, when I know that I have been able to create a happy relationship. In their youth, similarly to their childhood, women have as much recognition for themselves as is shown to them by the people they emotionally interact with. For many women this attitude lasts for their whole life. The measure of their self-esteem is the personal success: this is how they perceive their life purpose. If they are unable to create a romantic relationship, their inner 'I' becomes fragile and oversensitive. Only the women whose position is secure, who have developed their identity and self-esteem through love, are able to allow themselves to risk and search for the unusual, untraditional, 'male' achievements. They become the models all female goals and efforts are compared to, since the culture gives the priority to male productivity (Bardwick, Douvan 1982, p. 165–186).

The whole socialization in a patriarchal society pushes women into a space where they are unable to undertake roles or goals which may threaten heterosexual relationships, as their self-esteem is based on them, while agreeing to the position of dependence and submission in functioning interpersonal relations.

The woman's imperfection – religious and philosophical justification of female nature's limitation

The inequality in the treatment of men and women is largely based on the authority of the Holy Bible interpreted in a peculiar way. As stated by L. Kocik in his reflections on the genealogical 'imperfection' and 'inferiority' of women, having created the first man – Adam, God said that since it is not good for a man to be alone, a being submitted to him must be created. The Bible's authority was also used to legalize and institutionalize extremely patriarchal family structures since it was written that after the exile from the Paradise God informed the woman that she was to be under her husband's power and it was his right to rule over her. This was the beginning of the patriarchal family, based on the traditional interpretation of the Holy Bible, in which the man was the lord of life and death (Kocik 2002, pp. 73–75).

Women's inequality was also theoretically justified in the views of numerous scholars. For example, A. Schopenhauer claimed that a woman is not destined to great works. Her nature is not active, but passive (see: Kocik, p. 74). A sophisticated theory of women's intellectual inferiority was also created by S. Freud. His view on the development of female character shaped by the anatomical differences was aimed at assessing the qualities, interests, attitudes and emotions from the angle of physical difference. To express his contempt for the lesser intellectual abilities, greater vanity, predispositions to neuroses and passiveness of women, S. Freud used the terms 'male' and 'female' as symbols of the contrasting pairs of values: one part was assigned all the positive features, while the other part – only the negative ones. Such assumptions led to specific practical consequences, excluding women from the participation in cultural, creative and political activity due to the alleged shortcomings in their nature (see: Giddens 2012, p. 130).

Until recently wife beating was an institutionally regulated and commonly accepted form of relations between spouses. Its universality may be reflected in popular proverbs such as 'Spare your wife the rod, let her liver rot' or 'Thee who loves well, beats well'. They usually reflect the misery of a woman beaten and bullied by her husband and give him full power over his wife.

Some of the folk songs sung during wedding receptions stress the fact that by marrying a woman her husband takes over all the protective duties that used to belong to her father. As her guardian the man gains the right to punish his wife, for example by flogging her, which used to be treated as a recommended educational measure (Kocik 2002, p. 78).

According to psychologists, violence against women, especially domestic violence, is a pathology which is deeply rooted in Polish customs and traditions. Its existence is commonly known, and yet people seem not to be aware of it since it is a taboo subject.

The respect for traditions is also common among the judiciary people. The police euphemistically talks about 'family disagreements' not worth their intervention. Until the 10th of October 2010[2] the court demanded from the victims to undergo forensic examination at their own expense, not to mention the fact that any twisted arm was not impressive enough for the judge. There is more understanding for the perpetrator who, for example, claims: 'I have never beaten my wife to harm her'. Psychologists describe it as the cultural background of violence and criminologists estimate that the number of registered cases of domestic violence is just a fraction of the dark number of acts of violence happening within four walls.

The feminist interpretation of female oppression

Feminist theories point to numerous conditions of female oppression, and due to the strong impact of patriarchal and sexist culture they have a universal meaning.

D. Duch-Krzysztoszek in her reflections on power in the family writes that the most important credit that should be given to the feminism is drawing the attention to the role of culture in shaping the power relations – the concept of the social-cultural sex (gender) and cultural sex differentiation (sex-gender system) based on it. It is the cultural constructs of femininity and masculinity connected with the models of wife and husband, mother and father, that play an important role in shaping the relations between the sexes. The sex-related stereotypes which assign women to family life and men to the public sphere cause a great inequality between men and women. Burdened with free labor, women have limited access to paid work and material resources of power, whereas gaining full equality of sexes is not possible without establishing the equality of men and women in the public space, while women's presence on the job market that is equal to that of men is not possible without redistributing the work and care within the family (Duch-Krzysztoszek 2007, pp. 37–38).

---

2   See: The Minister of Health Regulation from 22 October 2010 on the format of medical certificates concerning the causes and types of injuries caused by the use of domestic violence ('Journal of Laws' 2010, no 201, entry 1334).

According to R.P. Tong, radical feminists believe that the system of biological and cultural sex is the basic reason for oppression of women. A. Jaggar and P. Rothenberg interpret this definition in different dimensions, among other things claiming that the oppression of women is most widespread because it exists in almost every known society, being the most difficult form of oppression to eradicate as well as causing the most suffering. A. Echols notes that some radical-cultural feminists believe that the differences between biological and cultural sex derive not as much from biology as from socialization or rather from the fact that women have been living for a long time as subordinates in a patriarchal society (Tong 2002, pp. 65–67).

K. Ślęczka writes that according to cultural feminists men have power: over women, children, animals, nature and their power is used for exploitation. In order not to lose it, they reach for oppression and humiliation of subordinate groups, terrorizing them with regularly repeated acts of violence. Due to this fact they also rule in the hearts and minds of the oppressed. Thousands of years of the patriarchy enabled the establishment of such ideas and beliefs about the world and some of the subordinate do not want any change, do not consider rebellion and often even under the patriarchal oppression feel the satisfaction coming from the prevailing order (Ślęczka 1999, pp. 411–412).

K. Millet – the precursor of radical-libertarian feminism – notices that the patriarchal violence is also often displayed in acts of sexual aggression. The statistics involving rapes are only partial since the 'shame' prevents women from taking their case to court and taking part in a trial. During the rape the feelings of aggression, contempt, dislike and the wish to destroy one's psyche reach their patriarchal peak (Millet 1982, p. 85).

Feminists also agree that the basic cause of rape as well as the most widespread form of human oppression is sexism. They claim that women have always been beaten, forced to have sex, raped, sexually molested and abused, and the image of a woman in cultural messages, especially in mass culture, presents them as the sex which can only find, according to its nature, fulfilment through sex, and, thus, through giving birth to children, nursing and raising them, caring for the household and private needs of family members. Strengthening the stereotype of women as the objects of men's sexual needs, sadistic by nature, may be especially attributed to pornography, which often suggests apparent female masochistic tendencies. Pornography is the quintessence of something pervading the whole culture, art and science, although appearing in it in a more oblique way. A woman is always seen as an object, not a subject, and it is usually a sexual object. It can clearly be seen in the way women are portrayed in advertisements (Ślęczka 1999, p. 412), where the perfectly thin bodies of models appearing on magazine covers become the standard for the whole female kind. And no one has openly voiced the commandment: 'Thou shall shape thy limbs and body in the image and likeness of 'a sexy celebrity'. Women simply know what is expected of them, they know what it means to be a beautiful woman (see: Tong 2002, p. 71). The ubiquitous sexism, therefore, serves as a pre-model of every previous prejudice, including racism and class prejudice, informing women that their female role obliges them above everything else to fulfill male expectations.

The patriarchal ideology, as claimed by K. Millet, furthermore exaggerates the biological differences between men and women, assuming that men will always have the dominant, that is male, role whereas women will always have the subordinate, that is female, one. This ideology is so strong due to men being able to rule in such institutions as universities, the Church, family, every one of which forces women to be subordinate to men (Millet 1982, pp. 69–70). 'If a woman refuses to acknowledge the patriarchal ideology and shows her mistrust towards it by rejecting her 'femininity' – men will use constraint to achieve the effect which was not granted by the conditioning she underwent. Bullying, as observed by K. Millet, is a usual measure in patriarchal systems. A conscious woman knows that if she wants to survive, she should behave 'in a feminine way', otherwise she may be subjected to 'various cruel and barbarian actions' (Ślęczka 1999, p. 70).

K. Millet also describes exercising economical supervision as an effective method of the patriarchal rule. In a traditional society women did not have a legal status of a person and were sentenced to economical inexistence since they did not possess anything or did not earn their own money. However, they always worked and usually performed arduous and routine activities. The fact that women are and have always been a workforce is not a subject of the dispute, however, there is still the matter of remuneration. In modern society women have gained economical rights, however, they are not paid for the so-called 'female jobs' which are performed by two-thirds of the female population. The remaining one-third of women who are paid for their work earns less than men. It is of utmost importance in the advanced financial management where the autonomy and prestige is dependent on the possessed assets. Generally speaking, women's financial position is the permanent function of their basic oppression, thus having a significant impact on the economical violence against them (Millet 1982, p. 79). It is also of considerable importance for women in order to undertake actions aimed at leaving their perpetrator.

Conclusion

Nowadays the problem of violence against women is in the centre of attention not only of feminists but also of public authorities. In 2011 the Council of Europe accepted the Istanbul Convention[3] on preventing and combating violence against

---

3 See: Konwencja o zapobieganiu i zwalczaniu przemocy wobec kobiet i przemocy domowej (2011), http://ms.gov.pl/Data/Files/_public/ppwr/akty_prawne/miedzynarodowe/konwencja-re-o-zapobieganiu-i-zwalczaniu-przemocy-wobec-kobiet-i-przemocy-domowej.pdf (Accessed: 15.07.2014).

women and domestic violence and Poland began working on its ratification. The representatives of the government and science institutions as well as of non-governmental organizations have held talks about the gender theory and the legitimacy of ratifying the convention for Polish law. The convention is of great significance for the functioning of the interdisciplinary teams for preventing domestic violence, which have existed since 2010[4], since the answers to the recommendations held in the draft of the EU resolution involving the prevention of violence against women can be found in the actions of the teams. Their main concern is that the elimination of violence against women is not possible by taking single actions but by a number of infrastructural, legal, judicial, executive, cultural, educational, social and health-related operations as well as any other actions connected with the services which may greatly increase the knowledge about the problem and limit the violence with its consequences[5].

In conclusion, it is worth mentioning that there are numerous studies concerning the problem of violence which may help analyze the problem of violence against women as a social phenomenon and problem. However, the existing publications do not contain any instructions on how to successfully eliminate violence from family and interpersonal relations, nor do they present any universal, timeless forms and methods of prevention.

---

4 See: Ustawa z dnia 10 czerwca 2010 roku o zmianie ustawy o przeciwdziałaniu przemocy w rodzinie oraz niektórych innych ustaw,Dz. U. z 2010 r. Nr 125, poz. 842, http://isap.sejm. gov.pl/DetailsSer vlet?id=WDU20101250842 (Accessed: 15.07.2014).

5 See: European Parliament Report from 31 January 2014 with recommendations to the Committee of Women's Rights and Gender Equality on combating violence against women, http://www.europarl.europa.eu/sides/getDoc.do?pubRef=-//EP//TEXT+REPORT+A7-2014-0075+0+DOC+XML+Vo//PL#title1 (Accesed: 15.07.2014).

Fernando Barragán Medero, Antonio Llorens de la Cruz
University of La Laguna, Tenerife, Spain

Masculinities and quality of life: an educational programme promoting a new model of interpersonal relationships within prisons[1]

Introduction

The role of women in patriarchal societies is mainly characterized by their being subject to men since the moment they are born. This characteristic is common to all patriarchal societies, regardless of the specific culture, religion or social and economic status. To a lesser or a greater extent, family and social environment impose a set of rules of conduct to women, thus putting limits to the development of their personality. This way, women are made to accept certain rules in order to avoid potential punishment or social rejection. Culture is the learned, shared knowledge (Spradley 1980) and, in that sense, we must bear in mind that gender is but a social construct (Dawla 2000; Horne 1999) imposed upon humans.

Men are educated to exert power and control over women, responding to a series of characteristics or masculine stereotypes (Brannon, David 1976). In the first stage of their lives, women obey their father and brothers; in a later stage, they obey their husband, and, subsequently, their sons. This dominance can be of a more or less evident type, but its occurrence cannot be denied. In cases where women do not accept being subordinates, men can use violence understood as a legitimate means to set these deviations – deemed incorrect – straight. This fact has raised our interest to develop a programme aimed to prevent violent behaviour within male prisoners in penitentiaries, since, once they are released from freedom deprivation, these prisoners will return to their homes and to be active members of society.

---

1 We would like to thank the Ministry of Domestic Affairs for their cooperation and permissions, as well as the Secretariat General of Prisons, the Directorate and Deputy Directorate of Treatment in Tenerife 2 Penitentiary. We would also like to thank all prisoners who volunteered to collaborate in our work.

There is a direct connection between patriarchal masculinity and the exertion of violence. Violence in herein understood as a outwards representation of virility as the constitution of a men exerting the power that is – allegedly – given to him by nature, by his biology. At that point, a type of targeted violence based on the patriarchal model rooted in our society may arise: gender-based violence. However, many men use violence as a solution to conflict on a regular basis, not only intended to control women, but also, and equally important, as a way of conducting themselves in their relationships with other men. Within prison, the exertion of violence serves a specific goal: to ensure survival.

We are now faced with an ethical dilemma: Do violent men have the right to be educated? There can be no debate once we conclude that, after servicing sentence, these violent prisoners will be freed, which gives sense to the attempt of transforming their daily use of violence as a way of living into rejection towards it. The main goal is to make them aware of the existing alternatives to violence. Negotiation and anticipation of the consequences of their actions are the axis of their new – or future – life project.

Hitting a woman is a type of violence, as are underestimating them, and insulting them due to their skin colour, creed or sexual orientation, together with many other expressions of violence that go unnoticed in our everyday life. Every day, women considered to be different to what is deemed to be normal suffer from a vast range of loutish acts. These are aimed to subjecting the weakest, the most vulnerable, or anyone – men or woman – that can cause the aggressor to have a sense of power over the others.

The preceding global intervention proposals or the grounds of our interventional programme are based on a work conducted by a research group led by Dr. Barragán, along with various partners in different countries. This line of investigation was based on several educational research and intervention works carried out from 1995 (Arianne and Dapfne projects), implemented during several school years in different secondary education centres within Europe with a variety of social, cultural and economic contexts. But the immediate precedent to our research work is the syllabus guide specifically aimed to work with teenagers: 'Violencia, género y cambios sociales. Un programa que [SÍ] promueve nuevas relaciones de género' (Barragán 2006). This guide resulted from the proyect 'Educación para el presente sin violencia: construir una cultura de paz' (2002–2005).

Planning of an interventional programme

All the aforesaid leads to the necessity of developing an educational programme designed specifically for prisons, aiming to prevent violent behaviours. We divided the activities to be carried out into four blocks: masculinities and gender; sexuality and sexual orientation; the expression of violence in daily life and sexually-related violence; and, lastly, emotional education. Our work was conducted within the Tenerife penitentiary (Tenerife, the Canary Islands, Spain). Two work groups were formed: Group A – 24 prisoners, and Group B – 17 prisoners. The following table shows their type of criminal conduct.

Table 1. Criminal conduct types in Group A

Criminal conduct	Number of prisoners
Physical damages	3
Manslaughter	1
Sexual abuse	1
Threats within the family	1
Violation of the law, theft, threats	1
Theft, attempted sexual assault	1
Threats and violation of the law	3
Ill-treatment, actions against the administration of justice, physical damages	1
Theft and ill-treatment within the family	1
Ill-treatment within the family and violation of the law	1
Non-severe coercions	1
Actions against the rights of foreign nationals, involuntary manslaughter	1
NCO (No Criminal Offence – preventive imprisonment-)	6
OAPH (Offences Against Public Health)	2

Source: own elaboration.

Table 2. Criminal conduct types in Group B

Criminal conduct	Number of prisoners
Ill-treatment within the family	1
Theft and physical damages	2
Violent attempt, physical damages, damages	1
Fire	1
Routinaty expressions of violence within the family	1
Forest fire	1
Theft	4
OAPH (Offences Against Public Health)	5
NCO (No Criminal Offence – preventive imprisonment-)	1

Source: own elaboration.

Methodology

Goals

Raising awareness about the negative consequences of using – and living with – various types of violence among the participants of the programme.

Giving present and future meaning and content to the expression 'quality of life'.

From a critical perspective – suggesting alternative concepts of masculinity.

Analysing and understanding the scope and consequences of using violence in daily life through the development of basic skills that help enhance communication, respect and cooperation – favouring the resolution of conflicts by the means of negotiation.

When conducting our research, we have chosen a qualitative methodology: ethnography. We wished to escape the dogmas on which positivism is based (Atkinson, Hammersley 1994). Ethnography shows a set of conditions that are widely favourable to overcoming the differences existing between researchers and participants, between theory and practice (Woods 1987). We were interested in finding a research methodology that would not only attempt to understand social phenomena, but also that had the ability to have an impact on the subject of investigation, so as to achieve transformation (Alvariño 1992). Our starting point was the paradigm of investigation from the critical theory of education and the intervention model of action research that, as Brock-Utne (1980) remarks, constitutes a type of investigation based on practice, takes place in a context of cooperation with the practices, and is carried out through processes of spiral cycles (Lewin 1946).

We decided upon 'active ethnology', which diagnoses the entire group or community subject to study and subsequently provides it with the results so that they can be used to solve problems that may arise. This is a fieldwork or process that requires the preparation of a monographic study or product at a later stage. For this reason, we decided to position away from a research model based on mere speculations (Angrosino 2012).

The philosophy of the work process endorsed by Ethnology also agrees to that postulated by the Critical Theory of Education and the action research model. All of the above share the same ethic approach in the treatment of the group subjected to study, its main aim being a considerable improvement of the living conditions of the group. This is how the subject group becomes the object of the process. This, and no other, will be the reference of our actions.

We have primarily attempted to conduct a group intervention, as opposed to other interventional programmes within prisons based on a one-on-one intervention, or, more precisely so, an individualistic one. Given that such programmes are ultimately aimed to address a social problem from an incorrect point of view, the results achieved by these are not ideal. Working with groups following the ethnographic approach helps us attain the objectives of our intervention proposal, for it allows us to intervene within a specific context and a specific group of people.

Although the programme on which our educational proposal is based was not originally designed to be implemented with adults, it allows us, after making all the necessary adjustments, to achieve ecological generalization, due to the similarities between the two different contexts. The original programme was implemented in teenage populations in city areas (suburbs of Milan and Copenhagen, amongst others) characterized by the use of violence on a regular basis (juvenile delinquency, use of drugs, etc.) and by a noticeable variety of cultural backgrounds.

We accepted the challenge of adjusting the interventional programme for a different section of the population. Such adjustment to the prisoners' necessities arises from the negotiation processes carried out with them. We saw this as a great opportunity rather than a challenge: an opportunity to put the capacity for ecological generalization of the programme to the test.

Implementation of the programme

The success achieved with our intervention programme is based on various pillars. The first pillar being taking into account the targeted population; rather than describing their pathological conditions, we wanted to make the programme sufficiently flexible, so as to allow the educator to transform its implementation and the actions taken depending on the interests of the participants – this is done through argued debates. This way, activities regarding emotions where included in the programme on the prisoners' request. The second, taking into consideration the unsuitability of the implementation of alleged one-on-one 'therapies' aiming to transform behaviour characteristics. There is a tendency – widely spread amongst certain sectors – to classify prisoners under the 'insane population' group, which is of no use when attempting to implement an intervention that will win the educator the participant's trust[2]. From the very beginning of such treatments, prisoners will show their rejection, and will even put self-defence strategies in use when standard tests are presented. And the third and last pillar, the fact that all they are taught and they put into practice during the sessions of the intervention programme can be used straightaway in their lives makes them more open and trustful of the programme, for they can see immediate effects that help improve their quality of life.

This programme is not about 'keeping prisoners busy', but rather about 'making their time more valuable, thus improving their quality of life'.

---

2 We do not intend to deny the occurrence of certain psychological profiles showing pathologies that would require either psychological or psychiatric interventions. But we do feel it should be made clear that this is a very rare situation, and only very few of the prisoners could be deemed in need for such interventions.

The programme we have implemented requires a full time commitment to its practice, strong negotiation skills to interact with the participants, and ethical and professional self-demandingness to a very high standard, far beyond the minimum official professional requirements. This programme proposes a change in penitentiary system affecting several levels. Prison officers need to give up their role as mere executors of tasks and become aware of and self-critic with their own practices. This would be ideal, but reality is not, and we have no power over decisions taken in relation to penitentiary policies.

Our educational intervention programme has to face reality as it is and yet not abandon the idea of triggering effective changes regardless of the limitations encountered. The fact that we have placed ourselves within the critical theory and the intervention model shown in action research has made us to commit to intervene aiming to create an effective change in the group subject of our actions (Carr 1996). The mere administratively correct implementation of a prescribed syllabus does not suffice, quite on the contrary, it is necessary to reinterpret all areas of the programme that require adjustment to the participant group's needs, pointed out by the group itself. This is possible thanks to the flexibility of our programme, while its main philosophy remains unchanged.

The order in which the proposed activities and blocks under which they are classified take place will be determined by the needs and interests shown by the participants. We are talking about a comprehensive and inclusive syllabus revolving around understandingness. We do not aim to achieve even results in which concepts such as re-education and re-socialization are based-concepts very deeply linked to educational programmes addressing the imprisonment issue from an individualistic perspective. Our programme is not about subjecting the convicted to freedom deprivation to the disastrous exercise of accepting the imposed rules, but rather about pedagogical work and making them reflect about the possibility of creating non-violent ways of life – a liberating perspective. They need to learn how to live in a society that favours violence, a deeply unequal and unfair society in which submitting oneself to the established norms can never lead to accepting the statu quo as a way of democratically healthy lifestyle.

Our intervention programme does not aim to depersonalize or readjust prisoners, for we do not see them as insane population. Our programme is ultimately about accepting diversity within the participant groups, about taking into account their previous concepts and knowledge, as well as social and cultural conditioning aspects and individual idiosyncrasies. We do not mean to justify crime or criminal activities either. We do not aim to standardize behaviour, but alternatively we implement an educational programme that can prepare the prisoners to make an improvement in the quality of their present lives (in prison) and future lives (once they are freed), lives that are not based on the use of violence. This will keep them away from committing further offences. There is no way of ensuring an absolute success of the programme. However, it gains relevance when taking into consideration the fact that, after being freed, a very high proportion of ex-convicts returns to imprisonment.

Results

The results achieved after the implementation of our programme which has been put through both triangulation (Stake, 1998) and cuadrangulation (McKernan 1999) processes- show a significant reduction in violent behaviour and an increase in the level of awareness of violence, which highlights its preventive value. Other accomplishments of the programme include self-regulation (Boekaerts, Maes, Karoly 2005), which refers to the self-control process and the correct management of conflict. Moreover, the group becomes more unite, which is beneficial for a balanced and highly productive working environment. A guided interview was conducted with both groups. During the interview, prisoners described their participation in the educational programme we proposed as very positive. They highlighted various aspects to it. Firstly, becoming aware of certain violent conducts they expressed in their daily lives – insulting others, showing no respect, pushing others, etc. – which in turn generated a new idea of violence; secondly, developping certain skills that help increase their level of self-control; and, thirdly, learning to foresee the consequences of their actions on themselves and on those suffering from their actions – predictability of my actions. The development of the programme also helps unite the group, which results in a balanced and highly productive working environment exceeding the chance of success of individualistic therapies. The results shown in self-assessments on each activity block carried out by all the participants individually point out an improvement from the starting point to the end of the programme.

Conclusions

There is a general objective to this programme that we would like to highlight. It is based on the fact that every action that an individual carries out generates a series of consequences affecting the individual himself, his social and familiar context, and also, the person or persons to which such actions are directed. This way, predicting our actions is a central axis that can help us anticipate the results of such actions. 'I didn't want to do that' and 'I didn't want to cause any harm' are two very common expressions that should be anticipated in previous reflection through the following question: What consequences will the object of my action have on the subjects of my action and on myself? The main objective is to prevent. And this is exactly the goal of our educational programme: to learn how to lead a violence-free life through practising negotiation as a means of solving conflict.

The participation of the prisoners in the programme has help improve it significantly. Through negotiation processes built up with the prisoners, activities related with matters as guilt, emotional autonomy, the need for self-control skills development – in which preceding related programmes have shown little efficiency – or the expression of sexuality in a repressing context are included in the programme. The critical theory and action research model have both been of great help in order to follow this line of work. Ethnography, as a qualitative research model, has allowed us to use the 'boundary breaking' (Goetz, LeCompte 1988), to the extent that it made it possible to intervene correctly in the development of this study. It is important to bear in mind that, whenever a social fact is studied from this perspective, the researcher works within the environment and is influenced by it. But a balance between personal involvement and a certain distance from the object of study is crucial. The ongoing reflection and careful note-taking within the environment has helped us not to get overly involved to the point of becoming full members of the community (Woods 1987).

In the assessment of each activity carried out within each group, prisoners have highlighted the importance of the programme and also that of the pedagogues that have been part of its implementation. They acknowledge having understood the importance of giving up the use of violence in order to achieve an acceptable quality of life. On top of that, they also point out that the programme is not only useful for their future – once they are freed – but also for an improvement of their reality in prison. They strongly value this, for they can see the use and applicability of the intervention from the very beginning. Trying to motivate children and youth in the implementation of educational programmes that have no immediate applicability is quite the challenge, but it is nothing if compared to the difficulties of motivating adult population that carry out their lives in deprivation of freedom.

The interest and relevance of the project are therefore undeniable if we take into consideration the increase – awareness – of violence in our social environment. The potential for future ecological generalization to other social contexts make it a viable tool -once the necessary adjustments to each context are made. The adjustments we carried out based on the original programme (Barragán 2006) support our thesis. We are planning future lines of implementation of the programme in contexts such as: the mining sector, the industrial sector, the agrarian world, etc. We believe this programme has the ability to work out for a variety of qualitatively distinct groups. Without a doubt, the processes herein thoroughly described have had a positive effect in the improvement of the participants' quality of life, which has made it possible for a future ecological generalization to take place among participants of diverse age sectors and cultural backgrounds – its ecological validity is out of the question.

Justyna Kusztal
Jagiellonian University, Poland

Women in prison – basic problems in the context of legal regulations and research on social rehabilitation

Introduction

The issue of women's imprisonment has been present in political and scientific discourse, especially in the area of executive criminal law and rehabilitation pedagogy, for years. In the era of widespread women's emancipation, the statistical and phenomenological picture of girls' and women's crime s undergoing changes as the age of criminal initiation and other deviant forms of behaviour is lowering. It is directly reflected in a slightly increased number of women, especially juvenile, in prison and in the lowering of the age of their first imprisonment. Numerous research studies and the analysis of the current journalistic discourse describe and confirm those facts. Women's crime and their imprisonment are still perceived as breaking a social and moral taboo and that is why their crime is treated as sensational[1]. The analysis of crime and court statistics reveals that a relatively small proportion of women and girls in relation to the whole population is sent to prison, which is connected with the nature of their crimes. Women commit crimes less frequently than men and the types of crimes both sexes commit are similar. The number and the type of crimes committed by both sexes tend to converge, which is linked with women's emancipation and their growing role in various areas of social life, including crime. The scope of rehabilitation, especially prison rehabilitation programmes, reflects certain global, European and Polish, trends and tendencies. Rehabilitation pedagogy has been addressing the issue of rehabilitation of female prisoners for years, it is thus obvious that the conditions for women's rehabilitation

---

1 Cf. the media coverage of the cases when children were killed in the context of trials of women accused of killing their children and studies devoted to new forms of crimes committed by girls and women, for example: Matysiak-Błaszczyk, (2010), Woźniakowska-Fajst (2010).

must differ from conditions for men's rehabilitation (see: Biel 2008, pp. 51–76, Matysiak-Błaszczyk 2010).

The conditions of women's imprisonment

Premises and condition of women's imprisonment are regulated by standards of international law (including peremptory ones which address human rights guarantees and the ones which are not peremptory, but introduce certain standards to be treated as guidelines and recommendations of the international legislative bodies[2]), the Executive Penal Code from 1997 (Journal of Laws, No 90, item 557, as amended) and basic executive subordinate legislation. According to the regulations of the Polish Executive Penal Code from 1997, women are imprisoned in separate places than men – either in different prisons or in women's departments. Art. 87 of the Executive Penal Code reads as follows:

§ 1. Women are housed in prisons separate from men.

§ 2. Women serve their sentences in half-open prisons, unless the level of their depravity or safety considerations justify placing them in other types of prison.

§ 3. A pregnant or breast-feeding woman is provided with specialist care.

§ 4. In order to enable an imprisoned mother to provide constant and direct childcare, selected prisons offer Mother and Child Homes, in which a child can remain, if this is the mother's wish, until the age of three, unless nurturing and health considerations, confirmed by the doctor's or psychologist's opinion, justify the separation of a child from his or her mother or the lengthening or shortening of this period. Such decisions require a decision of the guardianship court [...].

Apart from the above, there are special regulations concerning custody of children under fifteen. Art 87a reads that '[...] in case of convicts with continuous custody of children under fifteen, their needs connected with childcare are taken into account, namely, the need: to initiate, maintain and strengthen their emotional bond with children, to meet their obligations regarding the cost of their upbringing, to provide financial support and to cooperate with Child Care Facilities in which their children are placed' (§ 1 of Art. 87a of the Executive Penal Code, Journal of Laws, No 90, item 557, as amended). Convicts with continuous custody of children who are in Child Care Facilities should be, as far as it is possible, placed in prisons closest to children's whereabouts (§ 2 of Art. 87a of the Executive Penal Code, Journal of Laws, No 90, item 557, as amended).

---

2 The European Prison Rules of 2006 name children, women and prisoners belonging to ethnic minorities as prisoners belonging to special categories, cf. items 34–38, Zalecenia Rec (2006) 2 Komitetu Ministrów do państw członkowskich Rady Europy w sprawie Europejskich Reguł Więziennych, http://www.coe.int/t/DGHL/STANDARDSETTING/PRISONS/EPR/the%20European%20Prison%20Rules_Polish.pdf (Accessed: 03.05.2012).

Statistical data on girls' and women's imprisonment

According to statistical data, in Poland there is a relatively small proportion of female prisoners in relation to the whole population of prisoners. On 31.12.2012 there were 84,156 male prisoners (sentenced to imprisonment, detention or remand in custody) and only 2,695 female prisoners.

Table 1. The number of women in Polish prisons and custody suites

Date	Total	Remand in custody		Sentenced		Punished	
		Juvenile	Adult	Juvenile	Adult	Juvenile	Adult
31.12.2011	2,529	28	336	44	2,094	1	26
31.12.2012	2,695	28	287	29	2,327	0	24

Source: own study on the basis on the statistics provided by the Polish Ministry of Justice available at http://www.bip.ms.gov.pl/pl/dzialalnosc/statystyki_2011 and http://www.bip.ms.gov.pl/pl/dzialalnosc/statystyki_2012 (Accessed: 23.07.2014).

The analysis of judicial statistics reveals that on 31.12.2012 there were 2,380 women convicted and punished in prisons, including 29 juvenile, 1,743 convicted for the first time and 608 recidivists[3].

The Report of European Commission from 2009 contains data on prisoners in 46 European countries. The countries bordering Poland had the following number of prisoners:

---

3 In accordance with the regulations of the Penal Code from 1997 (Journal of Laws, No 88, item 553, as amended) – Art. 115 §10: 'A juvenile offender is a person who committed a forbidden act while still under the age of 21 and was convicted by the Court of First Instance while still under the age of 24'. A recidivist, according to Art. 64 of the Penal Code, is a person who has committed an offence for at least the second time: '§ 1. If the offender convicted of an intentional offence and sentenced to prison commits a similar offence within five years and after serving at least six months in prison, the court can give him/her the highest sentence matching the kind of offence increased by half. § 2.If the offender convicted as described in § 1, who has served at least one year in prison and within five years after serving the whole sentence or its last part commits an intentional offence again, or commits contact crime, rapes, mugs or breaks in and steals, the court can give him/her the sentence that is higher than the lowest sentence matching the kind of offence but not higher than the highest sentence increased by half. § 3. Increasing the highest sentence by half mentioned in § 1 and § 2 does not refer to crimes'. Besides, prison recidivism should be distinguished, it refers to people who serve a prison sentence for at least the second time.

Table 2. The number of imprisoned women in selected European countries

	Total number of prisoners	The number of female prisoners	%
Germany	73,263	3,918	5.3
Czech Republic	22,021	1,189	5.1
Slovakia	9,180	474	5.2
Ukraine	146,394	7,742	5.3
Latvia	8,295	353	4.3
Poland	84,003	2,697	3.2

Source: own study on the basis of Aebi M.F. Delgrande N. (2011).

It is worth noticing that in 46 countries mentioned in the Report the median of the percentage of female prisoners in the total population of prisoners in 2009 amounted to 4.9%[4].

Basic problems faced by female prisoners

Research papers addressing the most important problems connected with imprisonment of women are based on empirical studies and statistical analyses conducted by various national and international institutions. Reports published by the Prison Service and conferences organised by them serve as a source of information not only on female prisoners but also on potential irregularities or deficits in the area of their rehabilitation, as well as on various activities which improve the conditions in prisons[5]. Non-governmental organizations are especially active in this area and they are more than welcome in countries which are not fully democratic.

Women's imprisonment differs from men's imprisonment. Women have a different perception of it and experience different feelings connected with typical prison conditions, such as depersonalization, deprivation of basic needs, standardization, and stigmatization, and have different coping strategies from those of men.

> Women experience imprisonment in a different way than men. [...] they are much more sensitive to the fact that they are in prison, which contributes to their more acute suffering than in case of men. The intensity of their emotions fluctuates, never disappears. The most frequent outcome of intense feelings is deep apathy (Rudnik 1997, as cited in: Matysiak-Błaszczyk 2010, p. 101).

---

4   It is necessary to mention huge differences between them, as e.g. in tiny Andorra women constitute 19% of the whole population of prisoners, while in Liechtenstein, which is also a tiny country, there are no female prisoners at all.

5   Cf. The 4th International Scientific Conference 'In search of an optimal prison model. Rehabilitation of selected categories of prisoners', Uniwersytet Opolski, 21–22.10.2013.

Mothers who do not have any contact with their children undergo gradual atrophy of their maternity needs and report 'anxiety connected with maintaining strong relations with their spouse and ontological safety of their children' (Rudnik 1997, as cited in: Matysiak-Błaszczyk 2010, p. 102). When a mother and her child are separated, the results of their separation will differ and depend on the child's age, the length of the woman's imprisonment, the strength of the bond between the mother and her child before the woman was imprisoned, the woman's ability to maintain the bond with her child while they are separated, the quality of care provided for the child during the period of the mother's absence and the availability of support given to the woman and her child during her imprisonment (Opora 2011, p. 397).

Resisting standardization and depersonalization can be linked with an excessive care about one's physical appearance, as, according to prisoners, physical attractiveness increases one's prestige, the sense of adoration and self-appreciation. They, in turn, are connected with homosexual practices resulting from limited or non-existent contacts with men. Lesbian relations are deeper in term of emotional involvement and last longer than male homosexual relations. According to Robert Opora and Agnieszka Głogowska, the authors of qualitative studies based on in-depth interviews with 39 female prisoners, women (...) aim to fulfil their emotional needs through close contacts with other imprisoned women. This helps them to go through their imprisonment by providing them with a sense of approval and a sense of security (Opora, Głogowska 2012, p. 250). The results obtained by Zbigniew Lew-Starowicz indicate that

> [...] about 40% of prisoners experience sporadic homosexual contacts while they are imprisoned and abandon them when they leave prison. Almost 15% of homosexual practices can be considered consolidated and significant for intimate life outside prison (Lew-Starowicz 1992, p. 161, after Opora, Głogowska 2012, p. 248).

Imprisoned women's rights

The European Prison Rules treat women as a special category of prisoners and impose on authorities an obligation to be guided by their physical, vocational, social and psychological needs, paying particular attention to women who have been physically or sexually abused. Those women should have the priority in obtaining access to special therapeutic and rehabilitation programmes. Additionally, the European Prison Rules emphasise the right of women to give birth outside prison or the right to special treatment, support and comfort if a woman gives birth in prison[6].

---

6 Art. 34.1, 34.2, 34.3, see: Zalecenia Rec (2006)2 Komitetu Ministrów do państw członkowskich Rady Europy w sprawie Europejskich Reguł Więziennych, http://www.coe.int/t/DGHL/STANDARDSETTING/PRISONS/EPR/the%20European%20Prison%20Rules_Polish.pdf (Accessed: 03.05.2012).

The European Committee for the Prevention of Torture and Inhuman or Degrading Treatment or Punishment (CPT) was appointed by the Council of Europe
Convention for the Prevention of Torture and Inhuman or Degrading Treatment
or Punishment in 1989. The activities of the Committee are based on Article 3 of
the European Convention on Human Rights which prohibits torture and inhuman
or degrading treatment or punishment; the Committee does not conduct investigations, focusing instead on preventive actions aimed at the protection of prisoner's
rights against activities of enforcement agencies which are unlawful, degrading, and
disrespect human dignity[7]. The Committee members visit prisons, correctional institutions, police stations etc., in the countries which are parties to the Convention[8].

The CTP Report from 2003, which deals, among other issues, with the execu-
tion of prison sentences with regard to women in the countries the Committee
members have visited, confirms that in all member states of the Council of Europe
women constitute a relatively small percentage of prisoners. As a rule, women are
imprisoned in separate places than men but securing those separate facilities is very
expensive, which results in their small number (sometimes very far from their homes
and children), and the buildings they occupy were designed for and previously in-
habited by men. That is why special care and consideration is necessary to provide
imprisoned women with a safe and neat environment[9]. Employing both men and
women as prison guards is seen as a precaution against maltreatment of prisoners
and can positively influence their perception of care services and give them a sense
of normality. Imprisoned women should be housed in rooms physically separated
from rooms occupied by men in the same prison. Several years ago certain countries
started placing couples together in one prison cell if both of them were imprisoned
and abandoning the rule of single-sex prisons. According to the Committee, it
is permitted, and even desired, on condition that prisoners concerned give their
consent and are selected and supervised with great care[10].

Legal regulations warrant special protection to women who are pregnant or
who have just given birth, with an overriding principle of the best interest of the
child – the quality of childcare before and after a child is born should be the same
in prison and outside the prison. If newborns and infants are in prison, their welfare
should be supervised by specialists qualified in the area of social work and child
development. In practice, prisons are not ideal places for newborns and infants but

---

7 Cf. http://www.hfhr.pl/po-raporcie-cpt-o-sytuacji-zatrzymanych-i-wiezniow-wciaz-te-same-
   zarzuty-wobec-polski/#sthash.dLMAYuGM.dpuf, accessed on 25.11.2013.

8 Cf. The European Committee for the Prevention of Torture, http://www.cpt.coe.int/polish.
   htm, accessed on 25.11.2013.

9 On the basis of: 'Merytoryczne' Fragmenty Sprawozdań Ogólnych Europejskiego Komitetu
   Zapobiegania Torturom – CPT/Inf/E (2002) 1 – Rev. 2003.

10 On the basis of: 'Merytoryczne' Fragmenty Sprawozdań Ogólnych Europejskiego Komitetu
   Zapobiegania Torturom–CPT/Inf/E (2002) 1 – Rev. 2003, cf. also: Fragment Dziesiątego
   Sprawozdania Ogólnego CPT/Inf (2000) 13), p. 70.

obligatory separation of mothers and their children soon after they have been born is highly undesirable (Opora, Głogowska 2012, p. 248).

Legal regulations do not differentiate between the process of rehabilitation of men and women, as, according to Art. 67 § 3 of the Executive Penal Code, Journal of Laws, No 90, item 557, as amended, rehabilitation measures include: work, education, cultural and educational activities, sport, contacts with the world outside prison and therapy. The results of studies described in the literature on the subject indicate that women's psychophysical and social traits determine the way in which they experience isolation, thus creating the need to differentiate rehabilitation methods for both sexes. The results obtained by Ewa Sosnowska and Mark Kalaman in their own study were described and interpreted in relation to the results of other studies within the area of rehabilitation, and the conclusions lead to the suggestion that rehabilitation of women should take into consideration their need to be close to their children, their need to stay in touch with their families, to maintain the bond with their mothers, husbands or partners and the chances of re-adaptation after leaving prison. The authors emphasise that their respondents – rehabilitation specialists working in prisons for women – saw no need for differentiating rehabilitation activities because of the sex.

> While working both with men and women, one should be consistent, committed, ready to help, observe the rules specified by executive regulations, act as role models and adjust methods and measures applied to prisoners' individual capabilities and needs [...], although it would be advisable to take into account each prisoner's individuality and their specific needs, including their emotionality, the need to maintain contacts with family and their closest social environment (Sosnowska, Kalaman 2010, p. 196).

The best way to achieve those aims is, undoubtedly, an individual rehabilitation programme developed together with each prisoner.

Studies devoted to rehabilitation also mention education and training of people who are to rehabilitate female prisoners. According to the international regulations mentioned above, it is essential for prison staff to include both men and women and to ensure that activities infringing on prisoners' intimacy are performed in the presence of same-sex workers. The results of studies subjected to metaanalysis quoted by E. Sosnowska and M. Kalaman indicate that there are arguments

> [...] actually supporting the statement that female prison guards are significantly better at initiating therapeutic contact with prisoners and at providing effective assistance in difficult situations than their male counterparts (Sosnowska, Kalaman 2010, p. 199).

Furthermore, rehabilitation activities conducted by women have a 'calming effect' on prisoners and contribute to treating them in a more humanitarian way' (Sosnowska, Kalaman, 2010, p. 199 and works cited there).

Preparation for leaving prison is conducted mostly through prisoners' participation in various rehabilitation programmes which aim at facilitating social re-adaptation of female ex-prisoners. Those programmes are often oriented towards social and vocational re-adaptation and obtaining specific vocational or educational qualifications. However, there are also more general ones aimed at developing prisoners' social or interpersonal skills or including special therapeutic programmes for victims of violence or addicts. Such programmes are often financed by European funds or Polish public funds and organized by various social and non-governmental organizations. At present, vocational activation programmes aimed at women emphasise flexible employment as an effective tool facilitating their social re-adaptation as well as mechanisms and ways of activating women who embark on a vocational path while far in their middle-age (Gabriel 2011, pp. 43–55, in: Dobrowolska 2011).

Due to the limited space, an exhaustive presentation of all problems and areas connected with women's imprisonment is impossible. The aim of this paper was to address selected basic questions such as: the conditions of imprisonment, statistics regarding this phenomenon, differences between men and women in their emotional perception of imprisonment, legal regulations and problems with their enforcement and directions of social re-adaptation of female former prisoners addressed by various vocational activation programmes. Women's imprisonment is an important research topic in the academic discourse and the need of further empirical research is clear. The practical outcome of such research should be visible in the optimization of the rehabilitation process among female prisoners.

Bibliography

Aebi, M.F., Delgrande N. (2011), *Council of Europe Annual Penal Statistic – Space 1 – Survey 2009*, http://www3.unil.ch/wpmu/space/files/2011/02/SPACE-1_2009_English2.pdf (Accessed: 14.07.2014).

Alvariño, C. (1992), *Criterios de credibilidad de la investigación-acción crítica*, Publicacions de la Universitat Autónoma de Barcelona, Barcelona.

Angrosino, M. (2012), *Etnografía y observación participante en Investigación Cualitativa*, Ediciones Morata S.L., Madrid.

Atkinson, P., Hammersley, M. (1994), *Ethnography and participant observation* [in:] K. Denzin, S. Lincoln (eds.), *Handbook of qualitative research*, Sage, Thousand Oaks, CA.

Badora, S., Karpuszenko, E. (2012), *Tożsamość przestępczyń. Raport z badań* [in:] W. Ambrozik, A. Kieszkowska (eds.), *Tożsamość grupowa dewiantów a ich reintegracja społeczna*, Impuls, Kraków.

Bardwick, J.M., Douvan, E. (1982), *Ambiwalencja: socjalizowanie kobiet* [in:] T. Hołówka (ed.), *Nikt nie rodzi się kobietą*, Czytelnik, Warszawa.

Barlas, A. (2004), *Believing women in islam. Unreading patriarchal interpretation of Qur'aan*, University of Texas Press, Texas.

Barragán, F. (2006), *Violencia, género y cambios sociales*, Aljibe, Archidona.

Barragán, F., De la Cruz, M., Doblas, J.J. (2001), *Violencia de género y currículum*, Aljibe, Archidona.

Barragán, F., Rivadeneira, R., Gómez, J.M., Herrera, P. (2013), *Los chicos de la cárcel*, 'Cuadernos de Pedagogía', 432, 36–38.

Barragán, F., Tomé, A. (1999), *El Proyecto Arianne: Ampliar los horizontes de las masculinidades*, 'Cuadernos de Pedagogía', 284, 44–47.

Bearce, G.D. (1961), *British attitudes towards India 1784–1858*, Oxford University Press, London.

Beaulaurier, R.L. *et al.* (2008), *Barriers to help-seeking for older women who experience intimate partner violence: A descriptive model*, 'Journal of Women & Aging', 20(3/4), 231–247.

Biel, K. (2008), *Przestępczość dziewcząt. Rodzaje i uwarunkowania*, WAM–Wyd. Ignatianum, Kraków.

Biel, K. (2013), *Bariery i możliwości resocjalizacji penitencjarnej kobiet* [in:] I. Mudrecka, M. Snopek (eds.), *Resocjalizacja instytucjonalna – bariery i możliwości*, Wyd. UO, Opole.

Bowker, L.H. (1983), *Beating wife–beating*, DC Heath and Co., Lexington, MA.

Brannon, R., David D.S. (1976), *The male sex role: Our culture's blueprint of manhood and what it's done for use lately* [in:] D.S. David, R. Brannon (eds.), *The forty-nine percent majority. Compilation*, Addison–Wesley, Reading, MA.

Brock-Utne, B. (1980), *What is educational research?* [in:] J. Elliott, D. Whitehead (eds.), *Theory and practice of educational action research*, CARN Bulletin No 4.

Browne, K., Herbert, M. (1999), *Zapobieganie przemocy w rodzinie*, PARPA, Warszawa.

Buekaerts, M., Maes, S., Karoly, D. (2005), *Self-regulation across domains of applied psychology: Is there an emerging consensus?*, 'Applied Psychology: An International Review', 54, 149–154.

Burton, A.M. (1991), *The feminist quest for identity: British imperial suffragism and 'Global Sisterhood' 1900–1915*, 'Journal of Women's History', 3, 2, 46–81.

Burton, A.M. (1992), *The white woman's burden. British feminists and 'the Indian woman' 1865–1919* [in:] N. Chaudhuri, M. Stroebel (eds.), *Western women and imperialism: Complicity and resistance*, Indiana University Press, Bloomington and Indianapolis.

Butler, J. (2008), *Uwikłani w płeć*, Wyd. Krytyki Politycznej, Warszawa.

Carpenter, M. (1868), *Six months in India*, vol. 2, Longmans, Green & Co., London.

Carr, W. (1996), *Una teoría para la educación. Hacia una investigación educativa crítica*, Ediciones Morata y Fundación Paideia, Madrid.

Carr, W., Kemmis, S. (1988), *Teoría crítica de la enseñanza*, Martínez Roca, Barcelona.

Cavalie, A.R. (1899), *In Northern India: A story of mission work in Zenanas, hospitals, schools, and villages*, S.W. Partridge, London.

Centralna Baza Danych Osób Pozbawionych Wolności Noe.NET, *Osoby po 50 roku życia osadzone w jednostkach penitencjarnych wg wieku (w latach ukończonych, stan w dniu 09.04.2013 roku)*, Biuro Informacji i Statystyki, Centralny Zarząd Służby Więziennej (unpublished materials accessed by the author).

Centralna Baza Danych Osób Pozbawionych Wolności Noe.NET, *Aktualnie wykonywane orzeczenia wobec osób powyżej 50 roku życia według rodzajów przestępstw, stan z dnia 09.04.2013*, Biuro Informacji i Statystyki, Centralny Zarząd Służby Więziennej (unpublished materials accessed by the author).

Chapman, P. (1839), *Hindoo female education,* R.B. Seeley and W. Burnside, London.

Dalgaard, L. (1999), *Prevention of sexual violence*, Centre for European Studies and Department for Gender Studies University of Aarhus, Aarhus.

Dawla, A.S. (2000), *Reproductive rights of Egyptian woman: Issues for debate*, 'Reproductive Health Matters', 8, 45–54.

Dąbrowicka, H. (2009), *Przemoc wobec osób starszych*, Instytut Psychologii Zdrowia PTP, Warszawa.

Declaration on the elimination of violence against women (1993), www.un.org/documents/ga/res/48/a48r104.htm (Accessed: 10.07.2014).

Dekret Tymczasowego Naczelnika Państwa Józefa Piłsudskiego z 28 listopada 1918 roku o ordynacji wyborczej do Sejmu Ustawodawczego (Dz. P.P.P. nr 18, poz. 46), Wszechnica Konstytucyjna, http://www.trybunal.gov.pl/wszechnica/akty/dekr_pilsud3.htm (Accessed: 17.07.2014).

Deleuze, G. (2004), *Foucault*, WN DSWE TWP, Wrocław.

Duch-Krzystoszek, D. (2007), *Kto rządzi w rodzinie*, Wyd. IFiS PAN, Warszawa.

Dyson, K.K. (1978), *A various universe: A study of the journals and memoirs of british men and women in the Indian subcontinent 1765–1856,* Oxford University Press, Bombay–Calcutta–Madras.

Europejski Rok Obywateli 2013, europa.eu/citizens-2013/pl/about (Accessed: 11.07.2014).

Forbes, G.H. (1986), *In search of the 'Pure Heathen': Missionary women in nineteenth century India*, 'Economic and Political Weekly', 21, 17, pp. WS2–WS8.

Foucault, M. (1982), *The Subject and Power* [in:] H.L. Dreyfus, P. Rabinow, *Michel Foucault: Beyond structuralism and hermeneutics*, The University of Chicago Press, Chicago.

Foucault, M. (1998), *Nadzorować i karać. Narodziny więzienia*, Fundacja Aletheia, Warszawa.

Foucault, M. (2000), *Techniki siebie* [in:] M. Foucault, *Filozofia – historia – polityka. Wybór pism*, WN PWN, Warszawa–Wrocław.

Foucault, M. (2002), *Porządek dyskursu. Wykład inauguracyjny wygłoszony w Collège de France 2 grudnia 1970*, Słowo/Obraz Terytoria, Gdańsk.

FRA – European Union Agency for Fundamental Rights (2014), *Violence against women: an EU-wide survey. Main results*, http://fra.europa.eu/sites/default/files/fra-2014-vaw-sur--vey-main-results_en.pdf (Accessed on 16.03.2014).

Fuller, M.B. (1900), *The wrongs of Indian womanhood*, Revell, New York.

Gabriel, B. (2011), *Elastyczne formy zatrudnienia jako narzędzia aktywizacji zawodowej kobiet* [in:] M. Dobrowolska (ed.), *Metody wsparcia indywidualnego i środowiskowego na rzecz integracji społeczno-zawodowej grup wykluczonych społecznie z powodu izolacji więziennej*, KMB Press, Katowice.

Garlicki, L. (2003), *Polskie prawo konstytucyjne*, Wyd. K.E. Liber, Warszawa.

Gelles, R.J., Straus, M.A., Steinmetz, S.K. (1988), *Intimate violence. The causes and consequences of abuse in the American family*, Simon & Schuster, New York.

Giddens, A. (2012), *Socjologia*, WN PWN, Warszawa.

Godbey, J.E., Godbey, A.H. (1892), *Light in darkness, or, Missions and missionary heroes: an illustrated history of the missionary work ... taking up principally the work in India, Burmah, Siam, China ... being a history of these countries ... to which is added the adventures of missionaries among the uncivilized races of the world...*, Imperial Pub. Co., St. Louis, MO.

Goetz, J.P., LeCompte M.D. (1988), *Etnografía y diseño cualitativo en investigación educativa*, Morata, Madrid.

Gouges, O. de (2000), *Deklaracja Praw Kobiety i Obywatelki*, 'Biuletyn Ośka', 11, http://www.ekologiasztuka.pl/pdf/fe0021gouges.pdf (Accessed: 10.07.2014).

Haile, J. (2007), *Honour killing, its causes and consequences: suggested strategies for the European Parliament*, European Parliament, Brussels, http://edz.bib.uni-mannheim.de/daten/edz-ma/ep/07/EST18859.pdf (Accessed: 15.07.2014).

Halicka, M., Czykier, K., Sidorczuk, A. (2010), *Środowiskowe uwarunkowania nadużyć i zaniedbań wobec osób starszych* [in:] M. Halicka, J. Halicki, K. Czykier (eds.), *Zagrożenia w starości i na jej przedpolu*, Wyd. UwB, Białystok.

Halicka, M., Halicki, J. (2010), *Przemoc wobec ludzi starych jako przedmiot badań* [in:] M. Halicka, J. Halicki, (ed.), *Przemoc wobec ludzi starych*, Temida, Białystok.

Halicka, M., Halicki, J. (2012), *Podsumowanie i rekomendacje*, 'Praca Socjalna', 5, 176–192.

Halicka, M., Halicki, J., Kramkowska, E., Laskowska, K., Szafranek, A. (2013), *Nigdy nie jest za późno... Informator dla policji i służb społecznych*, Temida 2, Białystok.

Herman, J.L. (1998), *Przemoc. Uraz psychiczny i powrot do równowagi*, GWP, Gdańsk.

Herschelmann, M. (2001), *Prävention sexuller Gewalt mit männlichen Jugendlichen,* Diakonie, Oldenburg.

Home Office, *Prison statistic England and Wales* (2002), http://webarchive.nationalarchives. gov.uk/20131205100653/http://www.archive2.official-documents.co.uk/document/ cm59/5996/5996.pdf (Accessed: 11.07.2014).

Horne, S. (1999), *Domestic violence in Russia*, 'American Psychologist', 54, 50–55.

http://www.bip.ms.gov.pl/pl/dzialalnosc/statystyki_2011 (Accessed: 23.07.2014).

http://www.bip.ms.gov.pl/pl/dzialalnosc/statystyki_2012 (Accessed: 23.07.2014).

http://www.hfhr.pl/po-raporcie-cpt-o-sytuacji-zatrzymanych-i-wiezniow-wciaz-te-same-zarzuty-wobec-polski/#sthash.dLMAYuGM.dpuf (Accessed: 25.11.2013).

Minnesota Advocates for Human Rights (1996), *Summary of the Beijing Declaration and Platform for Action*, http://www.theadvocatesforhumanrights.org/uploads/declaration. pdf (Accessed: 11.07.2014).

Ibáñez, J. (1994), *Cómo se realiza una investigación mediante grupos de discusión* [in:] M. García, J. Ibáñez, F. Alvira (comp.), *El análisis de la realidad social. Métodos y técnicas de investigación*, Alianza, Madrid.

Irfan, H. (2008), *Honour related violence against women in Pakistan*, World Justice Forum, http:// www.lexisnexis.com/documents/pdf/20080924043437_large.pdf (Accessed: 23.07.2014).

Jayawardena, K. (1995), *The white woman's other burden: western women and South Asia during British colonial rule*, Routledge, New York–London.

Juchniewicz, J., Kazimierczuk, M. (2006), *Wolności i prawa polityczne* [in:] M. Chmaj (ed.), *Wolności i prawa człowieka w Konstytucji Rzeczypospolitej Polskiej*, Kantor Wydawniczy Zakamycze, Wolters Kluwer, Kraków.

Kamińska-Jones, D. (2012), *England's affair with India. Bibi in the art of European artists in the second half of the eighteenth century* [in:] B. Łakomska (ed.), *The artistic traditions of non European cultures*, vol. 2, Polish Institute of World Art Studies and Tako Publishing House, Warszawa–Toruń.

Kocik, L. (2002), *Wzory małżeństwa i rodziny, Od tradycyjnej jednorodności do współczesnych skrajności*, Krakowskie Towarzystwo Edukacyjne, Kraków.

Konwencja o zapobieganiu i zwalczaniu przemocy wobec kobiet i przemocy domowej (2011), http://ms.gov.pl/Data/Files/_public/ppwr/akty_prawne/miedzynarodowe/konwencja-re-o-zapobieganiu-i-zwalczaniu-przemocy-wobec-kobiet-i-przemocy-domowej. pdf (Accessed: 15.07.2014).

Kostash, M. (1988), *Literatura to pamięć czasownika pisać*, 'Literatura na świecie', 4, 3–4.

Krakowiak, T. (2008), *Analiza dyskursu – próba nakreślenia pola badawczego* [in:] A. Horolets (ed.), *Analiza dyskursu w socjologii i dla socjologii*, Wyd. Adam Marszałek, Toruń.

Kramkowska, E., Szafranek, A., Żuk, C. (2012), *Przemoc wobec starszych kobiet – sondaż w instytucjach*, 'Praca Socjalna', 5, 32–69.

Kruszka, R. (2008), *Wykluczenie społeczne – rys interpretacyjny i użyteczność badawcza*, 'Kultura i Edukacja', 1.

Kulig, A. (1996), *Prawa i wolności obywatelskie* [in:] M. Bankowicz (ed.), *Słownik polityki*, WP, Warszawa.

Kuźmicz, M. (2007), *Starszy Pan, Starsza Pani...*, 'Świat Problemów', 9, 16–18.

Kvale, S. (2010), *Prowadzenie wywiadów*, WN PWN, Warszawa.

Lagarde, M. (1994), *La regulación social del género: el género como filtro de poder* [in:] C.J. Pérez Fernández (coord.), *Antología de la sexualidad humana*, vol. 1, Miguel Ángel Porrúa, México.

Lewin, K. (1946), *Action research and minority problems*, 'Journal of Social Issues', 2, 34–46.

Lewis Herman, J. (2002), *Przemoc. Uraz psychiczny i powrót do równowagi*, GWP, Gdańsk.

Liggins, J. (1867), *The Oriental picture gallery*, Hurd and Houghton, New York.

Lipowska-Teutsch, A (1995), *Rodzina a przemoc*, PARPA, Warszawa.

Lipowska-Teutsch, A. (1997), *Rodzina a przemoc*, PARPA, Warszawa.

Luoma, M.-L., Koivusilta, M., Lang, G. *et al.* (2011), *Prevalence study of abuse and violence against older women. Results of a multicultural survey in Austria, Belgium, Finland, Lithuania, and Portugal*, European Report of the AVOW Project, http://www.thl.fi/thl-client/pdfs/e9532fd3-9f77-4446-9c12-d05151b50a69 (Accessed 8.12.2013).

Mahler, F. (1993), *Maldevelopment and marginality* [in:] J. Danecki (ed.), *Insights into maldevelopment. Reconsidering the idea of progress*, Wyd. UW, Warszawa.

Majewska, E., Kukowska, M. (2005), *Przemoc wobec kobiet w rodzinie i relacjach intymnych. Podstawowe informacje*, Amnesty International, Sekcja polska, http://amnesty.org.pl/uploads/media/przemoc_wobec_kobiet_w_rodzinie_i_relacjach_intymnych_2006.pdf (Accessed: 17.07.2014).

Malec, D. (2009), *Sejm Ustawodawczy 1919–1922. W 90. rocznicę pierwszego posiedzenia*, 'Przegląd Sejmowy', 1(90), 9–30, http://www.sejm.gov.pl/wydarzenia/przeglad/teksty/ps90.pdf (Accessed: 16.07.2014).

Malinowska, I. (2004), *Prawa człowieka i ich ochrona międzynarodowa*, Elipsa, Warszawa.

Mani Lata (1998), *Contentious tradition. The debate on sati in colonial India*, Oxford University Press, New Delhi.

Marczak, M. (2008), *Przestępczość kobiet w perspektywie drogi życiowej* [in:] M. Konopczyński, B.M. Nowak (eds.), *Resocjalizacja – ciągłość i zmiana*, Pedagogium, Warszawa.

Marczak, M. (2009), *Skuteczność readaptacji społecznej kobiet w Polsce* [in:] F. Kozaczuk (ed.), *Prawne i socjokulturowe uwarunkowania profilaktyki społecznej i resocjalizacji*, Wyd. UR, Rzeszów.

Marczak, M. (2012), *Uwięziona jednostka czy uwięziona rodzina. O funkcjonowaniu rodzin osób przebywających w warunkach izolacji więziennej* [in:] W. Ambrozik, A. Kieszkowska (eds.), *Tożsamość grupowa dewiantów a ich reintegracja społeczna*, Impuls, Kraków.

Mateer, S. (1871), *'The land of charity': a descriptive account of Travancore and its people, with especial reference to missionary labour*, J. Snow and Co., London.

Mateer, S. (1880), *The gospel in South India : The religious life, experience, and character of the Hindu Christians*, Religious Tract Society, London.

Matysiak-Błaszczyk, A. (2010), *Sytuacja życiowa kobiet pozbawionych wolności*, Impuls, Kraków.

Mazur, J. (2002), *Przemoc w rodzinie. Teoria i rzeczywistość*, Żak, Warszawa.

McAlpine, C.H. (2008), *Elder abuse and Neglect*, 'Age and Aging', 37, 132–133, http://ageing.oxfordjournals.org/content/37/2/132.full.pdf (Accessed: 8.12.2013).

McKernan, J. (1999), *Investigación-acción y curriculum. Métodos y recursos para profesionales reflexivos*, Morata, Madrid.

Mill, J. (1826), The history of British India in 6 vols, http://oll.libertyfund.org/titles/840 (Accessed: 15.07.2014)

Millennium Development Goals (2000), http://www.un.org/millenniumgoals/bkgd.shtml (Accessed: 16.07.2014).

Millet, K. (1982), *Teoria polityki płciowej* [in:] T. Hołówka (ed), *Nikt nie rodzi się kobietą*, Czytelnik, Warszawa.

Mishima, Y. (2010), *Música*, Alianza, Madrid.

Mitra, S., Bachchan, K. (2004), *Encyclopedia of women in South Asia*, Mehra Offset Press, New Delhi.

Mumtaz, M. (2012), *Pakistan Penal Code*, Manzoor Law Book House, Lahore.

Noor, J.M. (2004), *Daughter of eye: Violence against women in Pakistan*, Institute of Technology, Massachuttes.

OECD (2013), *How's life? Measuring well-being*, OECD Publishing, http://www.keepeek.com/Digital-Asset-Management/oecd/economics/how-s-life-2013_9789264201392-en#page1 (Accessed: 17.07.2014).

On the basis of: '*Merytoryczne*' *Fragmenty Sprawozdań Ogólnych Europejskiego Komitetu Zapobiegania Torturom* – CPT/Inf/E (2002) 1 – Rev. 2003.

On the basis of: '*Merytoryczne*' *Fragmenty Sprawozdań Ogólnych Europejskiego Komitetu Zapo-biegania Torturom* – CPT/Inf/E (2002) 1 – Rev. 2003.

Ogólnopolskie Pogotowie dla Ofiar Przemocy w Rodzinie 'Niebieska Linia', http://www.niebieskalinia.info (Accessed on 8.12.2013).

Opora, R., Głogowska, A. (2012), *Potrzeby seksualne kobiet w kontekście izolacji więziennej* [in:] W. Ambrozik, A. Kieszkowska A. (eds.), *Tożsamość grupowa dewiantów a ich reintegracja społeczna*, Impuls, Kraków.

Osiatyński, W. (1998), *Szkoła Praw Człowieka. Teksty wykładów*, vol. 1, Helsińska Fundacja Praw Człowieka, Warszawa.

Parkes, F. (1850), *Wandering pilgrims in search of the picturesque*, vol. 1, P. Richardson, London.

Payne, B.J., Gainey, R.R. (2009), *Family violence and criminal justice: A life-course approach*, http://books.google.pl/books?id=m9dZT-ZtICIC&hl=pl&source=gbs_navlinks_s (Accessed on 8.12.2013).

Peggs, J. (1832), *India's cries to British humanity, relative to infanticide, British connection with idolatry, ghaut murders, suttee, slavery, and colonization in India; to which are added, Humane hints for the melioration of the state of society in British India*, Simpkin and Marshall, London.

Pilch, T., Bauman, T. (2010), *Zasady badan pedagogicznych*, Żak, Warszawa.

Pospiszyl, I. (1994), *Przemoc w rodzinie*, WSiP, Warszawa.

Postęp dla wszystkich: równe prawa, równe szanse dla kobiet i mężczyzn (2010), http://www.unic.un.org.pl/dokumenty/ulotka%2002-2010%20internet.pdf (Accessed: 16.07.2014).

Powszechna Deklaracja Praw Człowieka, http://bip.ms.gov.pl/Data/Files/_public/bip/prawa_czlowieka/onz/pdpc.pdf (Accessed: 11.07.2014).

Przemoc w rodzinie – statystyka policyjna (2013), http://statystyka.policja.pl/st/wybrane-statystyki/prze-moc-w-rodzinie/50863,Przemoc-w-rodzinie.html (Accessed: 15.07.2014).

Puleo, A. (2011), *Ecofeminismo. Para otro mundo posible*, Cátedra, Madrid.

Rajska-Kulik, I. (2007), *Przemoc wewnątrzmałżeńska – uwarunkowania pozostawania maltretowanych kobiet w krzywdzącym związku* [in:] E. Mandal (ed.), *Płeć a wybrane problemy społeczne*, Wyd. UŚ, Katowice.

Ramusak, B.N., *Cultural missionaries, maternal imperialists, feminist allies. British women activists in India, 1865–1945* [in:] N. Chaudhuri, M. Stroebel (eds.),*Western women and imperialism: Complicity and resistance*, Indiana University Press, Bloomington and Indianapolis.

Report of the Export Group Meeting 'Rights of Older Persons' (2009), United Nations Department of Economic and Social Affairs Division for Social Policy and Development, Programme on Ageing, Bonn, Germany.

Rezolucja A/54/4 Zgromadzenia Ogólnego Narodów Zjednoczonych – Protokół Fakultatywny do Konwencji w sprawie likwidacji wszelkich form dyskryminacji kobiet z dnia 6 października 1999 roku, http://ms.gov.pl/pl/dzialalnosc/przeciwdzialanie-przemocy-w-rodzinie/akty-prawne-i-inne-dokumenty (Accessed: 16.07.2014).

Richter, J., Moore, S.H. (1908), *A history of missions in India*, Fleming H. Revell Company, New York, Chicago.

Rode, D. (2010), *Psychologiczne uwarunkowania przemocy w rodzinie. Charakterystyka sprawców*, Wyd. UŚ, Katowice.

Roczna informacja statystyczna za rok 2012 (2013), Centralny Zarząd Służby Więziennej, http://sw.gov.pl/Data/Files/001c169lidz/rok-2012.pdf (Accessed on 03.05.2013).

Równe prawa dla kobiet i mężczyzn. Działania ONZ na rzecz kobiet (2003), http://www.unic.un.org.pl/rownouprawnienie/instrumenty_mn.php. (Accessed: 16.07.2014).

Salber, P.R., Taliaferro, E. (1998), *O przemocy domowej. Poradnik dla lekarza pierwszego kontaktu: jak stawiać pytania, by rozpoznać problem i ocalić czyjeś życie*, PARPA, Warszawa.

Saleem, A. (2003), *Honour killing in Pakistan. Oral statement to the UN Commision on Human Rights*, Asian Legal Resource Center.

Santos, M.A. (1990), *Hacer visible lo cotidiano. Teoría y práctica de la evaluación cualitativa de los centros escolares*, Akal, Madrid.

Security Council resolution 1325 on women and peace and security (2000), UNHCR, http://www.refworld.org/docid/3b00f4672e.html (Accessed: 11.07.2014).

Sen, P. (2005), *Crimes of honour, value and meaning*, Zed Books, New York.

Sen, P., Kelly, R. (2007), *Violence Against Women in UK*, http://www2.ohchr.org/english/bodies/cedaw/docs/ngos/UKThematicReportVAW41.pdf (Accessed: 11/07.2014).

Sosnowska, E., Kalaman, M. (2010), *O specyfice resocjalizacji kobiet* [in:] Z. Bartkowicz, A. Węgliński, A. Lewicka (eds.), *Powinności i kompetencje w wychowaniu osób niedostosowanych społecznie*, Wyd. UMCS, Lublin.

Spivak, G.C. (1988), *Can the subaltern speak?* [in:] C. Nelson (ed.), *Marxism and the interpretation of culture*, University of Illinois Press, Champaign, IL.

Spradley, J.P. (1980), *Participant observation*, Holt Rinehart & Winston, New York.

Sprawozdanie Parlamentu Europejskiego zawierające zalecenia dla Komisji Praw Kobiet i Równouprawnienia w sprawie zwalczania przemocy wobec kobiet (2014), http://www.europarl.europa.eu/sides/getDoc.do?pubRef=-//EP//TEXT+REPORT+A7-2014-0075+0+DOC+XML+V0//PL#title1 (Accessed: 17.07.2014).

Stake, R.E. (1998), *Investigación con estudio de casos*, Morata, Madrid.

Stake, R.E. (2009), *Jakościowe studium przypadku* [in:] N.K. Denzin, Y.S. Lincoln (eds.), *Metody badań jakościowych*, vol. 1, WN PWN, Warszawa.

Strobel, M. (1991), *European women and the second British Empire*, Indiana University Press, Bloomington and Indianapolis.

Sulik, M. (2010), *Kobiety w nauce. Podmiotowe i społeczno-kulturowe uwarunkowania*, Wyd. UŚ, Katowice.

Szczepanik, R. (2008), *Struktura i dynamika przestępczości kobiet* [in:] M. Konopczyński, B.M. Nowak (eds.), *Resocjalizacja. Ciągłość i zmiana*, Pedagogium, Warszawa.

Ślęczka, K. (1999), *Feminizm. Ideologie i koncepcje społeczne współczesnego feminizmu*, Książnica, Katowice.

Tazbir, J. (1997), *Polska na zakrętach dziejów*, Sic!, Warszawa.

The European Committee for the Prevention of Torture, http://www.cpt.coe.int/polish.htm (Accessed: 25.11.2013).

The Executive Penal Code (1997), Journal of Laws, June 6, No 90, item 557, as amended.

The Minister of Health Regulation from 22 October 2010 on the format of medical certificates concerning the causes and types of injuries caused by the use of domestic violence, 'Journal of Laws' 2010, 201, entry 1334.

The Penal Code (1997), Journal of Laws, June, No 88, item 553, as amended.

The Universal Declaration of Human Rights (1948), UN, http://www.un.org/en/documents/udhr (Accessed: 15.07.2014).

Tobiasz-Adamczyk, B. (2009), *Przemoc wobec osób starszych*, Wyd. UJ, Kraków.

Tong, R.P. (2002), *Myśl feministyczna. Wprowadzenie*, WN PWN, Warszawa.

Tubert, S. (ed.) (2003), *Del sexo al género. Los equívocos de un concepto*, Cátedra, Madrid.

UNICEF (2000), *Domestic violence against women and girls*, United Nation's Children, Fund, Innocent Research Center, Florence.

Ustawa z 17 marca 1921 roku Konstytucja Rzeczypospolitej Polskiej, Dz. U. Nr 44, poz. 267; Nr 79, poz. 550; Nr 101, poz. 935, http://www.trybunal.gov.pl/wszechnica/akty/konstytucja_marcowa.htm (Accessed: 15.07.2014).

Ustawa z dnia 10 czerwca 2010 roku o zmianie ustawy o przeciwdziałaniu przemocy w rodzinie oraz niektórych innych ustaw, Dz. U. z 2010 r. Nr 125, poz. 842, http://isap.sejm.gov.pl/DetailsServlet?id=WDU20101250842 (Accessed: 15.07.2014).

Vallés, M. (1997), *Técnicas cualitativas de investigación social. Reflexión metodológica y práctica profesional*, Síntesis, Madrid.

Vitoshka, D.Y. (2010), *The modern face of honor killing: Factors, legal issues, and policy recommendations*, 'Undergraduate Journal', 22(2), 1–36.

Walker, L.E. (2009), *The battered woman syndrome*, Springer Publishing Company, New York.

Warraich, A.S. (2005), *Honour killings and the law in Pakistan*, Zed Books, London.

Weiner, G. (2004), *Critical action research and third wave feminism: A meeting of paradigms*, 'Educational Action Research', 12, 4, 631–643.

WHO (2013), *Global and regional estimates of violence against women: prevalence and health effects of intimate partner violence and non-partner sexual violence*, http://apps.who.int/iris/bitstream/10665/85239/1/9789241564625_eng.pdf (Accessed: 16.03.2014).

Williams, L.M. (2003), *Understanding child abuse and violence against women. A life course perspective*, 'Journal of Interpersonal Violence', 18, 441–451.

Women's Suffrage, http://www.ipu.org/wmn-e/suffrage.htm (Accessed: 15.07.2014).

Woods, O. (1987), *La escuela por dentro. La etnografía en la investigación educativa*, Paidós, Barcelona.

Zalecenia Rec (2006)2 Komitetu Ministrów do państw członkowskich Rady Europy w sprawie Europejskich Reguł Więziennych, http://www.coe.int/t/DGHL/STANDARDSETTING/PRISONS/EPR/the%20European%20Prison%20Rules_Polish.pdf (Accessed: 03.05.2012).

Summary

Many examples presented in this paper present courageous and active women that gave rise to world-changing processes. It is worth to draw from those examples. This work presents an image of women in a specific cultural mosaic, an image that at the same time points to issues that require reconsideration – especially in the area of social perception of women, overcoming stereotypes and legislative changes.

Not reflecting upon one's own attitude towards the issue of women, especially when having knowledge of global co-dependencies and conditions, could also be a choice. However, the only way to improve the existing situation is to become aware of cause and effect relationships affecting the lives of contemporary women all over the world and education (global education in particular) is of great significance in this regard.

According to Rachel Mayanja[1]

> [...] the whole world recognizes the fact that empowerment of women is the key to development and elimination of property and helps us overcome the obstacles that are still present (http://www.unic.un.org.pl/kobiety_rozwoj_pokoj/konferencja.php).

Therefore, the editors of this volume hope that future papers devoted to the issue of women will be illustrating achievement of those goals more and more often.

---

[1] Ms. Rachel Mayanja, the Secretary-General's Special Adviser on Gender Issues and Advancement of Women since November 2004, is a long-serving career international civil servant with vast experience in normative, policy and operational work of the United Nations including peace-building, peace-keeping and inter-agency collaboration; see more: http://www.un.org/womenwatch/osaginew/oSpecialAdviser.html) (Accessed: 15.06.2014) – editors' note.

www.ingramcontent.com/pod-product-compliance
Lightning Source LLC
Chambersburg PA
CBHW062159270326
41930CB00009B/1588